CATCH AND RELEASE
IN
MARINE RECREATIONAL FISHERIES

Financial support for the symposium and
the printing of this book provided by

Major Sponsors

National Sea Grant Office
American Fisheries Society
American Sportfishing Association
Atlantic States Marine Fisheries Commission
National Marine Fisheries Service (Office of Intergovernmental and Recreational
Fisheries)
Sea Grant Marine Extension/Advisory Programs (VA, NC, NY, GA, CA)
The Billfish Foundation
Virginia Institute of Marine Science, College of William and Mary
Virginia Marine Resources Commission (Saltwater Recreational Fishing
License Funds)

Co-Sponsors

American Fishing Tackle Company (AFTCO)
Eagle Claw Fishing Tackle
Federation of Fly Fishers
U. S. Fish and Wildlife Service

Cooperating Organizations

American Fly Fishing Trade Association
Chesapeake Bay Foundation
Coastal Conservation Association-Virginia
Massachusetts Division of Marine Fisheries
Texas A & M University, Dept. of Wildlife and Fisheries Science
The Fisherman
TTI True Turn & Daiichi Hooks
Virginia Beach's IGFA Striped Bass World Championship

Catch and Release
in
Marine Recreational Fisheries

Edited by

Jon A. Lucy

Virginia Institute of Marine Science
College of William and Mary

AND

Anne L. Studholme

James J. Howard Marine Sciences Laboratory

American Fisheries Society Symposium 30

Proceedings of the Symposium
National Symposium on Catch and Release in Marine Recreational Fisheries
Held at Virginia Beach, Virginia, USA
5–8 December 1999

American Fisheries Society
Bethesda, Maryland
2002

The American Fisheries Society Symposium series is a registered serial. Suggested citation formats follow:

Entire book

Lucy, J. A., and A. L. Studholme, editors. 2002. Catch and release in marine recreational fisheries. American Fisheries Society, Symposium 30, Bethesda, Maryland.

Chapter within the book

Radonski, G. 2002. History and application of catch-and-release fishing: The *good*, the *bad*, and the *ugly*. Pages 3–10 *in* J. A. Lucy and A. L. Studholme, editors. Catch and release in marine recreational fisheries. American Fisheries Society, Symposium 30, Bethesda, Maryland.

Printed in the United States on acid-free paper

Virginia Institute of Marine Science Publication Number 2459
VSG-02-09

Library of Congress Control Number: 2002106601
ISBN 1-888569-30-1
ISSN 0892-2284

American Fisheries Society
5410 Grosvenor Lane, Suite 110
Bethesda, Maryland 20814-2199
USA

Contents

Angler Attitudes and Behavior

Management Issues

Extended Abstracts

Preface

Held in 1999 at Virginia Beach, Virginia, the National Symposium on Catch and Release in Marine Recreational Fisheries was attended by around 130 persons representing nearly all U.S. coastal states as well as Canada, Norway, Bermuda, and Australia. Four days of information sharing and vigorous debate occurred on the issues of concern. The complexities of angler cultural differences, concerns about effectiveness of release regulations, and a growing database of biological information on effectiveness of catch and release fishing were shared.

This symposium represented the third major symposium to address catch and release as a fisheries management tool. The first two meetings, almost exclusively focusing on freshwater fisheries, were organized in 1977 and 1987 by Humbolt State University's Fisheries Department in Arcata, California. Proceedings were published from each symposium (R. Barnhart and T. Roelofs, editors. Catch-and-Release Fishing as a Management Tool, 1979; and Catch-and-Release Fishing: A Decade of Experience, 1987).

The symposium's steering committee strived to organize a forum in which catch and release issues could be examined and debated from the various perspectives of fisheries scientists, social scientists, extension leaders, educators, fisheries managers, charter-party boat captains, marine fishing media and tackle industry leaders, and angling groups to name a few. Basic funding support critical to launching the symposium, especially a funding commitment toward publishing the proceedings, came from the National Sea Grant Office (Project A/EP-3, Award No. NA56RG0141; J. Lucy, PI).

The National Sea Grant Office (Ron Baird and Ben Sherman) also provided advice and assistance in some of the early planning stages of the symposium as well as helping to promote it to the recreational fishing and fisheries management communities. In a similar manner, numerous individuals in the National Marine Fisheries Service provided constant encouragement and support, in particular Richard Schaefer (just retired), Eric Prince, Bill Price, and Virginia Fay.

The Steering Committee was co-chaired by Jon Lucy (Virginia Sea Grant Marine Advisory Program), Mark Malchoff (at the time, New York Sea Grant Extension Program), and Jim Bahen (North Carolina Sea Grant Marine Advisory Program). The co-chairs could not have worked with a more dedicated committee (see list of committee members). Identifying key speakers, assisting with soliciting speakers and research presentations, identifying and contacting sponsors, and chairing symposium sessions were just a few of the many tasks willingly carried out by committee members to bring the event together. It was the result of everyone's dedication, including that of their agencies and universities regarding individual's time, and often travel support, that the symposium achieved what it did. The editors take this opportunity to specially thank each committee member for all of their individual and collective hard work.

In addition, Mark Malchoff and his office staff made a special contribution to the planning process by providing summary notes of the meetings. Mark also provided much appreciated counsel to the senior editor while handling multiple details too numerous to list. Special thanks also go to Jim Bahen who, working with his North Carolina Sea Grant communicators, produced highly attractive posters highlighting information required for managing the daily activities of the meeting.

Eric Prince (NMFS Southeast Fisheries and Science Center) and Bob Ditton (Department of Wildlife and Fisheries Sciences, Texas A&M University) also warrant special appreciation for the important role each played in helping to organize the symposium. They shared much of the responsibility for developing critical agenda elements, helping to ensure that both biological and human dimension research, respectively, were well represented. The blend of subjects and expertise which resulted was a major contributing factor to the success of the symposium. In addition, Eric Prince and Bill Price, Chief of NMFS Division of Recreational Fisheries, were invaluable in helping the steering committee develop broad sponsor support for the symposium as well as working diligently on details essential to making the proceedings come together. With regard to the latter, especially considering his assistance in helping organize peer-reviews of full papers, Eric Prince served as "assistant editor" for the full biological research papers.

Sponsor support for the symposium, essential for its development and ultimate accomplishments, was graciously provided by a large and diverse group of organizations (see list). All sponsor support was important and critical to getting the job done in a professional manner. The Sea Grant Marine Advisory/Extension programs of New York, North Carolina, Georgia, and California were quick to commit key people to the Steering Committee, requiring devotion of much time and effort to the planning process. The National Marine Fisheries Service (through what was then the Office of Intergovernmental and Recreational Fisheries, Richard Schaefer, Director) and Atlantic States Marine Fisheries Commission came on board quickly with major support, while also contributing key people to the Steering Committee. Similarly, the U.S. Fish and Wildlife Service became a significant supporter as the planning process matured. With the symposium set for Virginia Beach, funds were required for utilizing skills of professional facilitators, both during the planning process and to lead important consensus-building sessions during the event. The Virginia Marine Resources Commission, through its Saltwater Recreational Fishing License Fund, supported a VIMS proposal specifically addressing this need.

The recreational fishing and tackle industry, and fishery research-conservation organizations also strongly supported the project. In particular, The Billfish Foundation, the American Sportfishing Association, and AFTCO Manufacturing Company made significant commitments to the project. Of particular note, the Federation of Fly Fishers volunteered significant funds towards the costs of producing the proceedings. Financial assistance, plus a commitment to participating in key symposium sessions, was also made by Eagle Claw Fishing Tackle (Denver, Colorado), TTI Companies (Wetumpka, Alabama), American Fly Fishing Trade Association (Kelso, Washington), and the Chesapeake Bay Foundation (Annapolis, Maryland).

On the local scene, the Conference Services Office of the College of William and Mary (directed at the time by Mariellyn Mauer along with key staff persons Carol Hankins and Karen Ross) did a phenomenal job setting up and following through on the many details associated with the hotel facilities, registration, poster session, and exhibits. Similarly, the meeting could not have been put together without the support of Dr. Bill DuPaul, Virginia's Sea Grant Marine Advisory Program Leader, and Dr. Bill Rickards, Director of the Virginia Graduate Marine Science Consortium and Virginia Sea Grant College Program.

Crucial help and assistance were provided over a period of months by VIMS Marine Advisory Service program staff, and in particular Cheryl Teagle, Maxine Butler, and Michael Arendt (graduate assistant). During the symposium Mr. Arendt served as technical coordinator for all power point presentations, receiving numerous compliments from the speakers regarding his handling of these essential logistics. Sally Mills, Sea Grant Communicator, designed the layout for the symposium program. She also assisted with symposium sessions, ultimately writing and publishing an overview of symposium highlights in the Virginia Marine Resources Bulletin. Also assisting with the actual meeting were Vicki Clark, Sea Grant Education Specialist, and Susanna Musick, both in VIMS Advisory Services office. From the VIMS Publication Center, Kay Stubblefield designed the symposium logo and, with the Center head Susan Stein, designed attractive and informative symposium brochures, announcements, letterhead paper, posters crediting sponsor support, and numerous other materials required for the meeting.

Critical help with local hospitality, both at the hotel and on the waters of Chesapeake Bay, was coordinated by the Coastal Conservation Association of Virginia (with beyond-the-call-of-duty assistance provided by CCA Executive Director Richard Welton and former CCA president Captain Herb Gordon). Significant support was also provided by Claude Bain, Director of the Virginia Saltwater Fishing Tournament under the Virginia Marine Resources Commission, and Kevin Crum, Director of the Virginia Beach IGFA Striped Bass World Championship.

Regarding the longer, peer-revied papers, special thanks are given to the many reviewers who labored over assisting authors with the fine-tuning of their papers for inclusion in this proceeding. Peer reviewers included: Jim Bohnsack, John Boreman, L.B. Boydstun, Richard Brill, Brad Chase, Sigurd Christensen, Mark Farber, Phil Goodyear, John Graves, John Hoey, David Holts, Andrew

Loftus, Brian Luckhurst, Molly Lutcavage, Pamela Mace, Mark Malchoff, Michael Mohr, Russ Nelson, Eric Prince, Michael Schirripa, Gary Shepherd, Greg Skomal, Mark Terceiro, Doug Vaughn, Alex Wertheimer, Bill White, and James Zweifel. Readers should note that the shorter "extended abstracts" were not peer-reviewed but were edited for clarity and style.

In addition, much gratitude and thanks go to the American Fisheries Society (AFS). The Society worked with us during the planning phase of the symposium to provide counsel and direction regarding what was required to take the symposium to the proceedings stage. The symposium was also strongly supported and promoted in *Fisheries*. In this regard, we want to thank Robert Kendall, Kristin Merriman-Clarke, and Susan Monseur for their much valued advice and direct support.

For advice in the initial stages of starting to plan out proceedings details with AFS, we also wish to thank Eric Wurzbacher and Robert Rand. However, the bulk of the work to pull the proceedings together ultimately fell under the professional and extremely patient tutelage of Laura Schlegel, Book Production Coordinator, to whom we owe the greatest thanks and appreciation. This proceedings could not have been completed without her professional guidance, diligence, care to detail, and above all else, her constant encouragement.

It is hoped that this publication will serve fishery professionals and recreational fishing community leaders as both a reference guide and assessment tool against which to evaluate catch and release as part of continuing efforts to rebuild marine fisheries.

Jon A. Lucy, Co-Editor

Introduction

Jon A. Lucy
Virginia Institute of Marine Science
College of William and Mary
Post Office Box 1346
Gloucester Point, Virginia 23062, USA

As a conservation practice and management tool, catch and release has a long and productive history in freshwater fisheries. In marine recreational fisheries, however, catch and release, which is probably best known for its role in helping rebuild the Atlantic coast striped bass fishery, is relatively new and is still evolving as a marine fisheries management tool. Many in the marine angling community are embracing catch and release as a proactive means for anglers to help conserve the fisheries upon which they depend. Likewise, fishery managers are now increasingly modifying regulations which often result in marine anglers having to release up to 50% or more of their catches to rebuild stocks under heavy pressure from both recreational and commercial fisheries.

As also occurred in freshwater fisheries two to three decades ago, marine fisheries' catch and release research, management, and associated angler issues are becoming more complex and changing at a quickening pace. In 1995, with support from the Atlantic States Marine Fisheries Commission and Sea Grant Marine Extension/Advisory Programs (from New York , New Jersey, and Delaware), VIMS and Virginia Sea Grant convened a conference entitled "Release Mortality in Marine Recreational Fisheries: Current Research & Fishery Management Implications." While progress has been made on some of the conference issues (improved understanding of release mortality factors, mortality rates, etc.), other biological issues (i.e., role of fish stress in release mortality and short-term mortality as a predictor of long-term mortality) require much more focused research effort. Likewise, issues in the management-angler realm are typically not well-defined and are only now beginning to receive serious attention, i.e, the proportion of marine anglers who regularly practice catch and release is poorly known as well as the variations the practice takes under specific fishing situations.

Building from the 1995 conference, The National Symposium on Catch and Release in Marine Recreational Fisheries held in 1999 expanded its focus to include not only rapidly expanding fisheries biological research, but also equally important human dimension aspects of catch and release in marine fisheries. Given the changing marine recreational fisheries scene, the stage was set to bring people together to work on better defining and understanding catch and release fishing in today's complex marine fisheries arena. More and better information is needed: (1) To assess how catch and release is being assimilated into the diverse marine angling community, taking into account new research on anglers' attitudes and behavior, (2) To better understand, and substantiate in the field, critical factors affecting not only short-term, but long-term release mortality, and (3) To assess expanding educational/promotional programs on catch and release (i.e., Are programs working as expected? Might improvements be made to reach a broader marine fishing audience with better quality, science-based information?).

Recognizing the need to address both "biological" as well as "people" issues, symposium planners worked to bring together a broad mix of marine recreational fishery leaders. Therefore, in addition to inviting fishery researchers and managers to share new information on catch and release, special efforts were also made to include representatives of the tackle industry, fishery conservation groups, and the recreational fishing media. Professionally facilitated sessions were included in the program to help participants reach consensus on priority needs for future research and education/outreach efforts.

Impetus for the symposium also developed, in part, from the mixed role catch and release had come to play during the 1990s in major Atlantic coast recreational fisheries, i.e., with striped bass and bluefin tuna. As previously indicated, the striped bass success story represented a major turning point for acceptance of catch and release as a workable management tool in coastal fisheries. In concert with imposing strict commercial fishing quotas on the fishery, managers initiated recreational fishing regulations incorporating seasonal closures and strict size-bag limits during open seasons. These recreational limits represented the first application of coast-wide "regulated catch and release fishing" in a U.S. marine recreational fishery.

Historically the most highly targeted recreational species on the Atlantic coast, the striped bass moved from largely "catch and kill" to "catch and release" under the coordinated management effort (the fishery currently experiences better than a 90% release rate). However, recent concerns have developed over high release mortality rates in the Chesapeake Bay's chumming fishery, which was one of many issues addressed during the symposium.

In contrast to the strong angler support associated with catch and release in the striped bass fishery, tightening bluefin tuna angling regulations requiring anglers to release greater numbers of fish typically met considerable opposition, especially from the charter industry. In the early 1990s the unprecedented North Carolina winter fishery for giant bluefin really "turned up the heat" on management-angler issues.

One of several major bluefin issues quickly coming to the forefront was concern regarding whether the bait "chunking fishery," producing high numbers of gut-hooked fish, was largely releasing 150–300+ pound fish having little chance of surviving their hook wounds. Since angling regulations required that most tuna be released, commercial fishing, charter captains, and angler groups quickly got embroiled with this issue. Fortunately, innovative thinking North Carolina fishing leaders turned this conflict into a positive learning experience for all concerned, by experimenting with, and ultimately leading the fishery to accepting circle hooks and heavy tackle as the fishing gear most favoring high survival rates of released fish. Coupled with researchers examining hooked fish as well as tracking released fish (using telemetry and ultimately satellite pop-up tag technology), this release mortality issue was converted into a productive angler-researcher team effort. Updated research results comparing J-shaped versus circle hook damage in bluefin tuna and billfish were also on the symposium agenda.

More recently the use of circle hooks by anglers has dramatically expanded, especially in fisheries targeting striped bass, red drum, Chinook salmon, bluefin and yellowfin tuna, and billfish. The result has fostered a new fishing conservation partnership between the angling community, fisheries agencies, and the tackle industry. With research increasingly demonstrating that using circle hooks reduces deep hooking in most species, the tackle industry has responded with expanded lines of circle hooks to enhance angler use of the product. Tackle manufacturers are also working with fishing conservation education programs, providing them with complimentary circle hooks and instructional materials.

Research on factors most significantly contributing to low survival rates in marine species targeted by anglers has also steadily advanced. Under fishing conditions in which live or fresh bait is used, injuries associated with deep hooking of fish are being documented as the factor most consistently associated with higher release mortalities. However, the majority of such research focuses on short-term survival (typically three to seven days post release), providing no definitive assurances as to longer-term outcomes.

As one example of such concerns, leaders in the commercial longline fishery are at odds with the recreational fishery regarding whether high release rates of billfish during fishing tournaments in reality translate into comparable long-term survival of the fish. This issue has become a major turning point in a larger debate regarding who exerts the most negative impact on billfish, the longline fishery with its significant billfish bycatch versus billfish tournaments. Research using telemetry and pop-up satellite tags to track billfish released from both fisheries has now been initiated. Similar research is also expanding into other marine recreational fisheries to address the long-term release survival issue.

Incorporating recreational fishery release mortality research results into updated stock assessments has raised another issue of concern between managers and the angling community. Increasingly, more short-term release mortality rate data are being utilized in stock assessment updates, from which changes in fishery regulations often result. The angling community, however, often has difficulty with how the "release mortality variable" appears to affect, or not affect, changing regulations on fish size and bag limits. For fishery managers, there is also the problem of uncertainty as to how consistently anglers carefully release fish alive as required by regulations. Coupled with this concern is to what degree are anglers voluntarily releasing some or all legal fish for conservation purposes.

Such issues add to the difficulties experienced by fishery mangers in assessing the impacts of catch and release on specific recreational fisheries.

Concerning how anglers actually practice catch and release, a great deal of effort goes into promoting catch and release in marine fisheries by people such as fishing conservationists, and proper release methods by angling publications and the fishing video industry. Therefore, managers might assume that the practice is a routine part of marine anglers' fishing activities. However, research on marine anglers' attitudes and behavior regarding how and when they typically incorporate catch and release into their day-to-day fishing indicates the practice means many different things to different people. Catch and release as an acceptable and routine practice for marine anglers is poorly defined and thereby not well understood, particularly across the matrix of diverse cultural strata and different fishing modes.

The complexities of thought and emotion regarding how and when an angler decides, for each fish hooked (especially a trophy fish), whether that fish is going to be kept, or released, was well captured by John A. McPhee (*Coming into the Country*, Macfarlane, Walter, and Ross, Publishers, 1977). Describing in first person the main character's instantaneous thought as he watched his just-subdued, trophy-size Artic Char (the largest fish the angler had ever caught in fresh water), ease out of his hands and swim rapidly away, the author writes, "The best and worst part of catching that fish was deciding to let it go". The human element in recreational fishing fosters patterns of catch and release practices among marine anglers which are hard to define and quantify. Researchers are just beginning to direct much needed attention to these issues. Historically, federal and state marine angler surveys have not done a good job in collecting useful data on how and with what frequency marine anglers practice catch and release.

As previously referenced, an unknown proportion of the marine angling community practices stronger conservation fishing ethics than required by regulations, such as releasing most, or sometimes all, the fish they catch. In contrast, among certain cultures and countries, catch and release is considered inappropriate or even "unethical," especially where subsistence fishing is the norm. In such localities, an angler catching and releasing fish might be perceived to be "playing with fish" which, by local custom, are revered for their food value. Trying to even discuss catch and release fishing issues in such an environment can prove to be difficult. Trying to educate people about the concept, or promoting it, can be insulting to some groups and cultures. This proceeding specifically addresses such issues (see last presentation in the "Overview" section and section on Angler Attitudes and Behavior).

In summary, symposium organizers sought to bring together a broad mix of stakeholder leaders in marine recreational fisheries to take stock of catch and release research and associated fishery management issues. Among organizers' objectives was to better define and improve stakeholders' understanding of catch and release as the practice is now being more broadly applied in managing marine recreational fisheries. Post-symposium feedback from participants indicates the symposium made at least some progress towards meeting its objectives.

However, during consensus-building sessions participants also listed many pressing needs in the areas of "research" and "education/outreach". A brief look at the top- ranked needs indicates the amount of work lying ahead for all claiming sincere interest in the welfare of marine recreational fisheries. Under research, the most important issues to be resolved were: (1) More hook-release research is required over a broader range of species than previously studied, however better coordination and more efficient funding partnerships are essential to distinguishing important differences in hooking injury mortality, stress-induced mortality, and lethal versus sub-lethal effects of catch and release; (2) Research findings must be better incorporated into educational efforts directed at the angling community, the focus being to "tell the science-based truth" regarding how catch and release works, and how it may not work, to enhance specific fisheries (the angling community must know the pros and cons of catch-release fishing in specific fisheries and under variable fishing conditions before it is able to evaluate and embrace the practice); and (3) More research is paramount on long-term effects of catch and release fishing on key species, including impacts on fish growth rates, spawning potential, and overall sustainability of key fish populations.

Top-ranked Education/Outreach needs were no less easy to meet—reinforcing the difficulty of overcoming very complex "people issues". Such issues significantly determine potential accomplishments of any effort to have catch and release more widely accepted and consistently practiced across the marine angling community. Top issues were: (1) To develop an overall (regional or national) media/communication strategy for educating anglers and promoting catch and release (today's approach is too fragmented, too ad hoc, and not well coordinated); (2) To develop more effective outreach/education program partnerships among angler, industry, and government groups to reduce redundancy and improve accuracy of information; and (3) To better define and understand the varied elements associated with marine anglers' practice of catch and release, particularly regarding what "bottom line" aspects of the practice are required for anglers to significantly impact the rebuilding of key recreational fisheries.

Based upon the referenced needs requiring major attention, making concerted headway on catch and release in marine fisheries might seem overwhelmingly difficult. However, hopefully drawing in some way on the symposium's information sharing and synergistic energy, some identified needs are being tackled, both in the U.S. and elsewhere in the world. For example, more comprehensive, science-based information is being provided for the angling community, including: a layman's overview of the symposium's presentations and discussions (Marine Resource Bulletin Volume 32, Number 3) now available through VIMS web site (http://www.vims.edu/GreyLit/SeaGrant.html); a quality, color brochure "Tips for Saltwater Catch & Release" produced and available from the Federation of Fly-Fishers (http://www.fedflyfishers.org); and a recent video titled "North Carolina Red Drum" covering life history, research results on circle hooks, and proven catch and release practices, now available from North Carolina Sea Grant (Jim Bahen, Sea Grant Fisheries Specialist).

Private and government groups are also making progress towards focusing more attention on catch and release, regarding how it benefits fisheries and constitutes an important element in sound fishing ethics. Examples include: NMFS and BOAT/US working in cooperation to promote an Ethical Angling Code among anglers, with special efforts directed toward anglers in marine fishing tournaments during 2002; a new brochure "Catch and Release: A Guide to Ethical Angling" available from North Carolina Sea Grant (bahenj@uncwil.edu), and formation in Florida of the Catch & Release Association which, through its magazine, strives to promote benefits of catch and release as practiced by experienced fishing guides and charter captains in the region (www.thecatchandrelease.com).

On a national scale, and involving several key fisheries leaders attending the symposium, Australia has initiated a national program focused on increasing survivability in released fish caught by anglers. Called the "National Strategy for Survival of Released Line Caught Fish," the program is reviewing release mortality research needs while funding selected research to fill existing gaps. More importantly, it is also working on development of a national communications campaign to promote best practices in releasing fish by the recreational sector. Future work will also target traditional and commercial line fisheries. More information is available from Bill Sawynok (infofish@zbcom.net).

Since the symposium, significant new research results have appeared in various journals addressing survival rates of released fish caught on hook-and line gear. Of particular interest are studies addressing longer-term survival of marine fish (a priority need identified by symposium attendees), work enhanced by use of telemetry tags to monitor individual fish's survival and movement patterns for periods ranging from a week up to months (Fisheries Bulletin, North American Journal of Fisheries Management, Transactions of the American Fisheries Society, Environmental Biology of Fishes, and other journals).

Obviously these are just a small sampling of activities making progress on catch and release issues in marine fisheries throughout the world. However, if catch and release is to achieve its potential in marine recreational fisheries as a truly effective management tool, then researchers, fishery managers, educators, extension leaders, fisheries conservation groups, the recreational fishery media, and anglers must work together to expand and better coordinate efforts like those cited. Given growing pressures on fishery resources, advances in catch and release research, and associated practical applications of the findings, need to move forward at a quicker pace, while having greater utility for a broader mix of marine anglers. It was hoped that the symposium, and now this proceedings, will serve as a catalyst to move catch and release to a more effective level in marine recreational fisheries management.

Steering Committee

National Symposium on Catch and Release in Marine Recreational
Fisheries

Jim Bahen, Fisheries Specialist (Committee Co-Chair)
North Carolina Sea Grant
5001 Masonboro Loop Road
Wilmington, North Carolina 28410
E-mail: bahenj@uncwil.edu

Columbus H. Brown
Special Assistant to the Regional Director
for Councils and Commissions
1875 Century Boulevard, Suite 205
Atlanta, Georgia 30345
E-mail: columbus_brown@fws.gov

Brad Chase, Fisheries Biologist
Massachusetts Division of Marine Fisheries
30 Emerson Avenue
Gloucester, Massachusetts 01930
E-mail: Brad.Chase@state.ma.us

Christopher M. Dewees
Marine Fisheries Specialist
Department of Wildlife, Fish and Conservation Biology
University of California
1 Shields Avenue
Davis, California 95616–8751
E-mail: cmdewees@ucdavis.edu

Robert Ditton, Professor
Department of Wildlife & Fisheries Science
Texas A&M University
College Station, Texas 77840–2258
E-mail: r-ditton@tamu.edu

Virginia Fay
National Fisheries Marine Service
Atlantic Coast Recreational Fisheries Coordinator
Office of Constituent Services
1315 East-West Highway
SSMC3, Room 14752
Silver Spring, Maryland 20910
E-mail: Virginia.Fay@noaa.gov

Jon Lucy, Marine Recreation Specialist (Committee Co-Chair & Event Host)
Virginia Sea Grant Marine Advisory Program
Virginia Institute of Marine Science
College of William and Mary
Post Office Box 1346
Gloucester Point, Virgina 23062
E-mail: lucy@vims.edu

Mark Malchoff*, Extension Specialist (Committee Co-Chair)
New York Sea Grant
Cornell University Research and Extension Center
3059 Sound Avenue
Riverhead, New York 11901–1098

*Current address:
Lake Champlain Sea Grant Project
101 Hudson Hall
Plattsburgh State University
101 Broad Street
Plattsburgh, New York 12901–2681
E-mail: mark.malchoff@plattsburgh.edu

Bill Price, Chief
NMFS Division of Recreational Fisheries
Office of Constituent Service
1315 East West Highway, Room 14752
Silver Spring, Maryland 20910
E-mail: Bill.Price@noaa.gov

Eric D. Prince
NOAA Fisheries
Southeast Fisheries Science Center
75 Virginia Beach Drive
Miami, Florida 33149
E-mail: eric.prince@noaa.gov

Mac Rawson, Director
Georgia Sea Grant Program
University of Georgia
Ecology Building
Athens, Georgia 30602–2206
(706) 542–6009

Anne Studholme*, Officer-in-Charge (retired)
James J. Howard Marine Sciences Laboratory
74 Magruder Road, Sandy Hook
Highlands, New Jersey 07732

*Current address:
4549 Audubon Road
Holland, Michigan 45423
E-mail: alswmbo@wmol.com

Geoff White*
Research and Statistics Department
Atlantic States Marine Fisheries Commission
1444 Eye Street, NW, 6th Floor
Washington, DC 20005
E-mail: gwhite@asmfc.org

*Geoff White ultimately replaced Richard Christian (currently with USF&WS)

Symbols and Abbreviations

The following symbols and abbreviations may be found in this book without definition. Also undefined are standard mathematical and statistical symbols given in most dictionaries.

A	ampere	gal	gallon (3.79 L)
AC	alternating current	Gy	gray
Bq	becquerel	h	hour
C	coulomb	ha	hectare (2.47 acres)
°C	degrees Celsius	hp	horsepower (746 W)
cal	calorie	Hz	hertz
cd	candela	in	inch (2.54 cm)
cm	centimeter	Inc.	Incorporated
Co.	Company	i.e.	(id est) that is
Corp.	Corporation	IU	international unit
cov	covariance	J	joule
DC	direct current; District of Columbia	K	Kelvin (degrees above absolute zero)
D	dextro (as a prefix)	k	kilo (10^3, as a prefix)
d	day	kg	kilogram
d	dextrorotatory	km	kilometer
df	degrees of freedom	l	levorotatory
dL	deciliter	L	levo (as a prefix)
E	east	L	liter (0.264 gal, 1.06 qt)
E	expected value	lb	pound (0.454 kg, 454g)
e	base of natural logarithm (2.71828...)	lm	lumen
e.g.	(exempli gratia) for example	log	logarithm
eq	equivalent	Ltd.	Limited
et al.	(et alii) and others	M	mega (10^6, as a prefix); molar (as a suffix or by itself)
etc.	et cetera		
eV	electron volt	m	meter (as a suffix or by itself); milli (10^{23}, as a prefix)
F	filial generation; Farad		
°F	degrees Fahrenheit	mi	mile (1.61 km)
fc	footcandle (0.0929 lx)	min	minute
ft	foot (30.5 cm)	mol	mole
ft³/s	cubic feet per second (0.0283 m³/s)	N	normal (for chemistry); north (for geography); newton
g	gram		
G	giga (10^9, as a prefix)	N	sample size

NS	not significant	tris	tris(hydroxymethyl)-aminomethane (a buffer)
n	ploidy; nanno (10^{29}, as a prefix)	UK	United Kingdom
o	ortho (as a chemical prefix)	U.S.	United States (adjective)
oz	ounce (28.4 g)	USA	United States of America (noun)
P	probability	V	volt
p	para (as a chemical prefix)	V, Var	variance (population)
p	pico (10^{212}, as a prefix)	var	variance (sample)
Pa	pascal	W	watt (for power); west (for geography)
pH	negative log of hydrogen ion activity	Wb	weber
ppm	parts per million	yd	yard (0.914 m, 91.4 cm)
qt	quart (0.946 L)	α	probability of type I error (false rejection of null hypothesis)
R	multiple correlation or regression coefficient	β	probability of type II error (false acceptance of null hypothesis)
r	simple correlation or regression coefficient	Ω	ohm
rad	radian	μ	micro (10^{26}, as a prefix)
S	siemens (for electrical conductance); south (for geography)	$'$	minute (angular)
		$''$	second (angular)
SD	standard deviation	$\circ$	degree (temperature as a prefix, angular as a suffix)
SE	standard error		
s	second	%	per cent (per hundred)
T	tesla	‰	per mille (per thousand)

Overviews

American Fisheries Society Symposium 30:3–10, 2002

History and Application of Catch-and-Release Fishing:
The *Good*, the *Bad*, and the *Ugly*

G I L B E R T   C .   R A D O N S K I

Introduction

The steering committee of the National Symposium on Catch and Release in Marine Recreational Fisheries requested that I address the "nongovernment" view of how catch and release is working in marine fisheries, both as a conservation ethic and as a fisheries management tool. A second issue I wish to discuss is whether the application of catch and release, as a management concept, is more difficult for marine anglers to buy into than it is for freshwater anglers. To accomplish this assignment, I would like to go through the genesis of catch and release as a conservation ethic and management tool before discussing application to marine recreational fisheries.

In *A History of Angling,* Charles F. Waterman devotes a chapter to the first sport fishermen (Waterman 1981). The chapter goes into detail identifying the classic literature and its authors, as early as A.D. 995. Waterman concludes that, "Anything we know about early sport fishing was written by people who may have been authors first and fishermen second. Thus, our most famous fishermen were not necessarily the best or most informed anglers of their time, but simply the most literarily inclined." The early angler-authors were aristocrats or clergy, who, it seems, had leisure time to fish for pleasure, rather than subsistence, and were literate. References to fishing ethics by early authors included respecting private property, closing gates, and releasing young fish. Waterman also noted, "Through most of the early writings runs a familiar theme of how the fishing waters had been reduced and the number of fishermen had been increased until the good old days seemed to be gone forever. Therefore, 20th century sportsmen feeling put upon by over-pressured water can at least find kindred feelings in the anglers of hundreds of years ago" (Waterman 1981).

Gilbert C. Radonski, Fishery Consultant, 133 Sutton Drive, Cape Carteret, North Carolina 28584. Email: gcrgmr@mail.clis.com

Angling has changed exponentially in the last one hundred years. To look at the development and articulation of the sport fisherman's conservation ethic, I would like to focus on the past one hundred years or so. Mechanical inventions and chemical discoveries have produced high tech and affordable fishing equipment. Leisure time and increasing individual wealth produced the wherewithal to get out and fish, and a seemingly inexhaustible fishery resource provided the attraction. Concomitantly, an army of angler-authors emerged to spread the word of where, when, and how to fish. The angler-authors of today are vastly different from those referenced by Waterman. Many not only can fish better than they write, they access a largely literate population that is hungry for knowledge of new equipment, technique, and places to fish. In the process of providing that information, many of the angler-authors felt compelled to articulate their concept of what constitutes ethical angling. A rich literary history of the evolution of angling ethics exists in the numerous sport fishing periodicals that span species, regions, and gear types, in both fresh and salt water.

There are two angler-authors, in my estimation, who greatly influenced the development of the angling conservation ethic and the raison d'etre for voluntary catch and release. They are Pearl Zane Gray (1875–1939) and Roderick L. Haig-Brown (1908–1976). I selected Gray and Haig-Brown because they were pioneers of modern sport fishing and they wrote with passion about the sport and ethics, tradition, and restraint that define the fisherman-conservationist. Both held dear a respect, bordering on reverence, for the fish they sought, abhorred the idea of fishing just to kill fish, and had a keen understanding and appreciation of the fish's environment.

Haig-Brown was a freshwater trout fisherman, and Gray was predominantly a saltwater, big game fisherman. They shared a common interest in fishing anadromous salmonids of the Pacific Northwest. Both articulated their fishing experiences with vitality and were successful in telling the reader about the total fishing experience. Both were adept at analyzing and describing the stream or ocean, as the case applies, and describing it in exciting detail to the reader. These two authors also described graphically the fragility of the aquatic environment and the fish populations therein. Most importantly, they share with the reader their personal feelings as to when and why they released fish, when fish seemed in great abundance.

Roderick Haig-Brown was born in Lancing, England, in 1908, and came to North America to visit the American West in 1926 (Taylor 1996). He was impressed with what he saw and immigrated in 1926 to Vancouver Island, settling at Campbell River. He made his living by logging, trapping, guiding, and writing. The attraction of the West was the opportunity for abundant fishing and hunting. The first catch-and-release symposium, *Catch-and-Release Fishing as a Management Tool*, held at Arcata, California, in 1977, was dedicated to Roderick Haig-Brown (May 1977).

Pearl Zane Gray was born in 1875 in Zanesville, Ohio. He is best remembered as Zane Gray, the author of western novels. My personal favorite is *30,000 on the Hoof*. In the book *The Undiscovered ZANE GREY Fishing Stories*, George Reiger colorfully describes Gray's fishing exploits (Reiger 1983). He noted that Gray pioneered fly-fishing for steelhead trout *Oncorhynchus mykiss* in the Pacific Northwest, popularized angling for bonefish *Albula vulpes* and permit *Trachinotus falcatus* in the Florida Keys, and bought a three-masted schooner and explored the South Pacific catching world-record fishes.

In his book *Tales of Fishes*, Gray extolled the virtue of matching tackle to the fish (Gray 1919), practicing the ideals of the Tuna Club of Avalon, California and instituting their application at Long Key, Florida. Dr. Charles Fredrick Holder, an author, sportsman, naturalist, and editor of The Los Angles Tribune, formed the Tuna Club of Avalon in 1896. He also founded the *California Illustrated Magazine* and co-founded The Tournament of Roses. The Tuna Club promoted conservation by designing fishing tackle regulations that gave fish a sporting chance. The spirit of these rules was adopted by angling clubs the world over.

In *Tales of Fishes*, Zane Gray, musing on the fisheries of Southern California in1918, wrote, "Let every angler who loves to fish think what it would mean to him to find the fish were gone. The mackerel are gone, the bluefish are going, the menhaden are gone, every year the amberjack and kingfish grow smaller and fewer. We must find ways and means to save our game fish of the sea; and one of the finest and most sportsman-like ways is to use light tackle" (Gray 1919). He spoke to the relationship between the angler and the fish, "...if we are to develop as anglers who believe in conservation and sportsmanship, we must consider the fish—his right to life, and especially, if he must be killed, to do it without brutality," posing the rhetorical question, "Who fishes to kill fish?" (Gray 1919).

The common philosophy that Gray and Haig-Brown expressed in their writings indicated that conservation should be the individual angler's moral imperative. During all of Gray's and the early part of Haig-Brown's writing years, there were skeletal fisheries enforcement programs, not the expansive governmental fishery agencies that we know today staffed with fishery scientists whose tendency is to impose conservation through regulation of harvest. Gray did not directly discuss the issue of government regulation but frequently spoke to the individual fisherman's responsibility to conserve. Haig-Brown wrote, "I have two hopes for the future. The first and lesser one is that game commissions will one day have the sense enough to set limits that measurably reflect the sport safely available. The second and deeply urgent one is that we shall grow a race of sportsmen no one of whom will ever consider it a matter for pride to have killed a limit." (Haig-Brown 1975). The expressed philosophy of these two forward thinkers, that conservation and ethics were an individual responsibility, was planted among sport fishermen in the midst of abundant fishing opportunities. As present day fishery mangers pursue building support for government-imposed conservation, they will visit the fishery literature and learn from these two great teachers.

With the passage of time, the angler's elective moral imperative began to emerge as government-imposed regulation. In the period from 1940 to 1950, fishery management as a government responsibility was practiced by a small, but growing, cadre of fishery scientist/culturists; fledgling state and federal fishery agencies were in the fish culture and regulation business. Fishery management as a science was just emerging, and regulations were largely intuitive, taking the form of size and bag limits and seasons; fish stocking was the principle management tool.

The first science-based, fishery management scheme that involved catch and release was instituted in Michigan in 1952 (Eschmeyer and Ficher 1959). The scheme was applied to high-quality trout streams with naturally-reproducing populations, requiring the release of all trout caught, and anglers were restricted to the use of flies and artificial baits. It was concluded that natural or live baits induced a post-release mortality that was too high. An important element of the scheme was that fishing mortality was to be measured, since it was assumed previously, through subjective observation, that fish that were properly handled would survive. There was a need to quantify objectively the mortality of released fish. The intent of the program was to eliminate the need for very expensive stocking. The popular name of the scheme was "Fishing-For-Fun" and was the product of fishery scientist, Albert S. Hazzard (Hazzard 1952). The program was emulated by many states under the name of the "Hazzard Plan." (Stroud 1961)

Not everyone was enthusiastic about the program. Richard H. Stroud said of the Hazzard Plan, "In our considered view, some of the recent attempts by a few of the more emotionally-involved folk and special-interest user groups to synonymize *Catch-and-Release* trout fishing (so-called "Fishing-For-Fun") *exclusively* with fly-fishing-only—worse, *exclusively* with sportsmanship or fun in fishing—are principally self-serving. We believe they have not been in the long-range best interests of 'the contemplative sport.' Correlated efforts to attempt justification of the program on the basis of alleged long-term biological stockpiling are clearly at variance with published research findings." (Stroud 1964). Stroud further identified concerns with catch-and-release fishing, "In this case, the anglers elect to increase the catching and give up the *take-home* of any proof of their angling prowess. We suspect, however, that the latter will remain as an important aspect of the fishing trip for the vast majority, and that it constitutes one of the intrinsic charms of fishing. The opportunity to eat the catch is also an intrinsic part of the total outdoor experience." (Stroud 1964)

The Hazzard Plan soon became a very popular trout management scheme. It created the term *Fishing-For-Fun* that Stroud insisted should be *Catch-and-Release* (Stroud 1975). Over the years, catch-and-release fishing spread to other freshwater species such as muskellunge *Esox masquinongy*, largemouth bass *Micropterus salmoides* and smallmouth bass. The fishing pressure exerted by a rapidly-expanding number of anglers that doubled in the period from 1955 (20.8 million) to 1975 (41.3 million) (U.S. Department of the Interior 1988) made anglers and fishery managers aware that catch-and-release fishing (mandatory or voluntary) is an essential fishery management tool for the development and maintenance of high-quality recreational fisheries.

Albert S. Hazzard independently formulated a management scheme that put into practice basic conservation concepts similar to those articulated by Gray and Haig-Brown. The Hazzard Plan was designed to reduce waste, recycle fish (to be caught more than once), require fishing gear that gave the fish a fighting chance, and promised a quality fishing experience in a quality environment. It was done essentially in a closed system and the impact on fish stocks monitored. And, it also was cost effective; it eliminated costly stocking. All of that, originally Fishing-for-Fun, was dubbed Catch and Release by Stroud in 1964, and it stuck.

Catch and release as a personal moral imperative originated in marine big game fisheries and found its footing as a fishery management program in freshwater to enhance the fishing experience. Freshwater anglers largely embraced the concept with modification. Critics of catch and release were concerned that anglers should not be forced into a guilt trip when desiring to take home some portion of their catch for the table. Catch and release was modified to the concept of not taking more than you need and releasing the rest. The gist of freshwater catch and release was that unless a captured fish was to be consumed, fish should be released to grow, reproduce, or provide sport for some one else; this is the defining element of a conservation-minded angler. Freshwater fishermen realize that, in most circumstances, they alone control the destiny of their sport, since this resource was shared only infrequently with commercial fishermen.

Consequently, in its early days (1960s), freshwater Catch and Release was a program, a noun. Although the scheme has been modified to fit the species, it has remained a noun in freshwater application. However, for the most part, the principle exception being big game fisheries, it is a verb applied to marine fisheries as a management tool, an action, not a program.

The magnitude of voluntary catch and release in marine recreational fisheries is difficult to determine, due to management-imposed regulations. That notwithstanding, the number of fish being released is at a very high level. A majority of fish, 60% over the past ten years, caught by marine recreational anglers along the Atlantic Coast, are released alive according to the National Marine Fishery Services's (NMFS) Marine Recreational Fishing Statistical Survey (MRFSS; Table 1). Atlantic coastal marine recreational fishermen, in proportion to the total number of U. S. marine recreational fishermen, account for a majority of trips taken and fish caught. Of the nine species listed in Table 1, eight have been rigorously managed for part or all of the ten years. The only largely-unregulated species, the dolphin, reflects a very low level of voluntary release.

It is safe to say that marine recreational fishermen are highly regulated under a variety of fishery management plans, and the high level of regulation-mandated release will be with us for a long time. Stock rebuilding, an integral part of most management plans, will result in more young fish available that are likely to be released.

Earlier, it was stated that freshwater fishermen realized that they alone largely controlled the destiny of their sport; the resource was shared with infrequently commercial fishermen. Marine recreational fishermen, on the other hand, in almost all circumstances, share the resource with commercial fishermen. The success of mandatory government-instituted catch and release, and the growth of voluntary catch and release, will depend on recreational and commercial fishermen fairly sharing the burden imposed by fishery management measures.

Similar to the recreational fishermen, commercial fishermen have been practicing catch and release. In the past, the release was accomplished with a shovel over the side. That ugly side of catch and release is rapidly ending. Success in reducing the commercial bycatch in the Atlantic croaker *Micropogonias undulatus* and weakfish *Cynoscion regalis* fisheries with fish excluder devices (FED) and net-size requirement in the summer flounder *Paralichthys dentatus* fishery are positive examples of shared fishery resource management. The indiscriminate nature of mixed-trawl and longline fisheries and the bycatch they produce is a continuing problem that must be dealt with. Continued effort to work toward resolution of the bycatch problems that divide commercial and recreational fishermen is crucial to the successful application of catch and release, both as a noun and a verb, as a management tool in marine recreational fisheries.

It is very difficult to quantify that portion of catch and release, which is voluntary. Even in the highly-migratory species, that is, big game fisheries, there are increasing levels of size restrictions, closed seasons, and areas. Nevertheless, the legacy of catch-and-release pioneers such as Zane Gray, Charles

Table 1. The top nine species caught and released by recreational fishermen in the Atlantic Coastal Region from 1989 to 1998, according to the National Marine Fisheries Service, Marine Recreational Fishing Statistical Survey.

Species (common name)	Number of fish × 1,000		Percent
	Caught	Released	
Micropogonias undulates (Atlantic croaker)	161369.7	86775.7	54
Paralichthys dentatus (Summer flounder)	158385.3	103635.5	65
Morone saxatilis (Striped bass)	81895.8	74801.4	91
Pomatomus saltatrix (Bluefish)	65185.6	29867	46
Cynoscion regalis (Weakfish)	40268.7	22830.1	57
Coryphaena hippurus (Dolphin)	15278.9	1172.6	8
Scomberomorus maculatus (Spanish mackerel)	13684.3	3441.1	25
Sciaenops ocellatus (Red drum)	12420.0	8838.4	71
Scomberomorus cavalla (King mackerel)	6006.9	565.4	9
Total all species	554495.2	331927.2	60

Fredrick Holder, and Roderick Haig-Brown has prevailed, and retention of "legal" fish by big game fisherman is the exception to the rule; only a very small percentage of legal fish are retained. Even "hang-them-on the-hook" big-game fish tournaments are becoming outdated. Currently, most marine fish tournaments have included an element of catch and release as a result of public resentment towards "kill" tournaments.

This is the fourth catch-and-release symposium in twenty-two years, reflecting the importance of this practice in marine recreational fishing. Hitherto, the question addressed was "will catch-and-release work in marine recreational fisheries as compared with the 'program' concept in freshwater fisheries" remains a persistent issue. The billfish fishery is an example. The recreational billfish fishery practices catch and release as a program; they want to reduce waste, recycle fish, and use gear that give the fish a sporting chance. The corollary commercial catch-and-release program of the longline fishery is wanton and wasteful. Until such issues are resolved, it will be difficult, if not impossible, to significantly increase catch and release as a voluntary measure in marine recreational fisheries. Marine fishery resources are a shared resource, and conservation measures must apply across the board.

Catch-and-release, as a verb, in marine recreational fisheries is going to be with us for a long time and is probably the most important marine recreational fishery management measure that can be used to rebuild stocks. However, its impacts must be monitored and measured, and corollary measures imposed on the commercial fisheries. It will take such efforts to retain the high level of catch and release currently practiced. An integral part of accomplishing continued participation is to communicate to anglers and commercial fishermen, through structured outreach programs, their responsibilities in the management and conservation of the shared marine fishery resource.

References

Eschmeyer, R. W., and G. S. Ficher. 1959. Good fishing. Harper & Brothers, New York.

Gray, Z. 1919. Tales of fishes. Harper & Brothers, New York.

Haig-Brown, R. L. 1975. Fisherman's winter. Nick Lyons Books, New York.

Hazzard, A. S. 1952. Better trout fishing and how. Sports Afield 128(2):17–19.

May, R. H. 1977. A tribute to Roderick L. Haig-Brown. Pages 3–6 in R. A. Barnhart and T. D. Roelofs, editors. A national symposium on catch-and-release fishing. Proc. Sym. 7–8 March 1977. California Cooperative Fishery Research Unit, Humboldt State University, Arcata, California.

Reiger, G. 1983. The undiscovered Zane Grey fishing stories. New Century Publishers, Inc., Piscataway, New Jersey.

Stroud, R. S. 1961. Trout fishing-for-fun. Sport Fishing Institute Bulletin 115:4.

Stroud, R. S. 1964. Most fishing is for fun - what else? Sport Fishing Institute Bulletin 150:1.

Stroud, R S. 1975. Specialized use of recreational fisheries resources. Sport Fishing Institute Bulletin 268:1.

Taylor, C. J. 1996. The Canadian encyclopedia plus. McClelland & Steward, Inc. Toronto, Ontario, Canada.

U.S. Department of the Interior, and the Fish and Wildlife Service. 1988. 1985 National Survey of Fishing, Hunting, and Wildlife Associated Recreation. Page 150, Table B.3.

Waterman, C. F. 1981. A history of angling. Winchester Press, Tulsa, Oklahoma.

American Fisheries Society Symposium 30:11–14, 2002

Catch and Release:
A Management Tool for Florida

RUSSELL S. NELSON

Introduction

The expansion of the population of the United States demographic trends, which have moved increasingly higher proportions of that population towards the southeastern coastal states, losses of critical habitat, years of unregulated fishing on saltwater finfish, and, of late, an expanding economy and increasing disposable income are factors that have combined to create a much larger population of anglers focused on decreasing our stable numbers of saltwater fish stocks. Florida is perhaps the prime example of this shifting of fishing effort on overfished stocks, primarily from commercial harvesting operations to recreational angling (Marston and Nelson 1994).

Prior to 1984, Florida had no agency with the authority to manage saltwater fisheries resources. Occasional regulation through the legislative process was undertaken reluctantly and often with mixed results. The Florida Marine Fisheries Commission (FMFC) began functioning in 1984 and was quickly faced with the reality that almost all recreationally popular fish species available in the coastal waters of Florida were in an overfished condition (Marston and Nelson 1994). Snook *Centropomus undecimalis*, red drum *Sciaenops ocellatus*, Spanish mackerel *Scomberomorus maculatus*, king mackerel *S. cavalla*, spotted seatrout *Cynoscion nebulosus*, black drum *Pogonias cromis*, and striped mullet *Mugil cephalus* stocks were subject to extensive regulation and rebuilding programs in the decade that followed (Marston and Nelson 1994). The use of extensive seasonal closures and low daily bag limits forced the issue of catch-and-release practices early on in this process.

Russell S. Nelson, Nelson Consulting, 115 Hoffman Drive, Tallahassee, Florida 32312, USA. Email: drrsnnc@aol.com; Phone: (850)544-4616.

The Evolution of Catch-and-Release Practices

The FMFC was challenged by an increasingly conservation-minded angling public to utilize strict regulations necessary to rebuild these stocks, and also to encourage the use of release practices. In 1988, the commission, supported by the Florida Conservation Association and most organized fishing guides in the state, introduced legislation that created a US$50 tarpon tag. This tag was required to be placed on any tarpon *Megalops atlanticus* that an angler retained. The intent of this regulation was to reduce the number of tarpon killed in order to increase angling opportunities. Over the first five years of this program, the number of tags purchased annually declined from just in excess of 1,000 to less than 300. In 1998, only 50 tags were used to keep and land a tarpon. The public response to this shift in management focus was mostly positive. The few tarpon tournaments that had required the landing and weighing of entered fish soon shifted to a release format, and today, tournaments in the Boca Grande area utilize an innovative floating sling that can weigh a tarpon at boat side before release.

Today, tarpon, permit *Trachinotus falcatus*, bonefish *Albula vulpes,* and sailfish *Istiophorus platypterus* fisheries in Florida have evolved into de facto catch-and-release fisheries. No tournaments exist that require dead animals to be weighed, though there exist numerous tournaments that include or target these species. The angling public has by-and-large self-regulated the recreational fisheries for these species.

Accounting for All Sources of Mortality

Catch-and-release fishing is not assumed to be a panacea for recreational fisheries. Florida stock assessments for snook, spotted seatrout, red drum, black drum, Spanish mackerel, and king mackerel use estimates of postrelease mortality in conjunction with National Marine Fisheries Service Marine Recreational Fisheries Statistics data on numbers of fish caught and released, to include this source of mortality along with direct fishing and natural mortality. Studies conducted by the Florida Marine Research Institute and Mote Marine laboratory have used a variety of methods to estimate post-release mortality (Jolley and Irby 1979; Edwards 1992; Haymans et al. 1993; Murphy et al. 1995; Edwards, Mote Marine Laboratory, personal communication). These estimates have ranged from as high as 15–20% for coastal pelagic (mackerel) species to as low as 0–3% for snook. Research techniques have included using a variety of volunteer anglers using any angling method, and retained fish have been observed in holding pens for up to one month. The inclusion of postrelease mortality in stock assessments assures a more accurate look at stock status and provides a realistic test of the utility of catch-and-release practices in management plans.

Population Growth and the Future of Inshore Angling

As the Florida angling public continues to increase, expectations for high quality saltwater angling opportunities will remain high and will become increasingly harder to meet. Today, Florida snook are protected by an array of closed seasons, slot size limits, and a two-fish bag limit. The management goal of maintaining at least a 40% spawning potential ratio had been reached in 1996 after stocks were rebuilt from the 5% level. However, recent assessments indicate that this goal is no longer being met (Muller et al. 2001). As this stock recovered, the number of anglers targeting snook has increased dramatically. The large number of snook taken and released by anglers, because they are either under or oversize or because of conservation ethics, combined with an estimated 3% postrelease mortality, now account for more than one-third of all fishing mortality on the species in Florida. Clearly, catch-and-release fishing has helped to generate a recovery of a severely overfished resource, but the success of this recovery has brought more anglers releasing more and more fish into the fishery. The increase in angling effort has now reached the point where it is pushing the stock back towards an overfished condition. In the future, it is likely that the issue of snook angling during closed seasons will need to be addressed. Further limits on angler participation in the fishery during open seasons may well be considered.

Responsible Use of Catch-and-Release Management

Experience in Florida indicates that catch-and-release practices can be an effective management tool, provided the following elements are included in the management scenario: high levels of compliance can be achieved if the angling population exhibits a high level of support for the idea; release mortality must be estimated accurately and included as a portion of total mortality in stock assessments; effective outreach programs are included to communicate the advantages of proper angling and release practices to maximize survival of released fish; and the impacts of this management strategy on fish stocks are critically monitored and reviewed periodically.

References

Edwards R. 1992. Tarpon release mortality assessment using acoustic tracking. Final project report. Grant Agreement 6634. Florida Department of Natural Resources, Marine Research Institute, Saint Petersburg, Florida.

Haymans, D. E., J. A. Whittington, K. S. Howard, and R. G. Taylor. 1993. Hooking mortality of common snook associated with "catch-and-release" fishing. Snook symposium. Mote Marine Laboratory. Sarasota, Florida.

Jolley, J. W., and E. W. Irby. 1979. Survival of tagged and released Atlantic sailfish (*Istioophorus platypterus*: Istiophoridae) determined with acoustical telemetry. Bulletin of Marine Science 29(2):155–169.

Marston, R. Q., and R. S. Nelson. 1994. New directions in the management of Florida's marine fisheries: a report to the Florida Marine Fisheries Commission following passage of article X, section 16 of the Constitution of the State of Florida. Florida Marine Fisheries Commission 94-1, Tallahassee, Florida.

Muller, R. G. M. D. Murphy, and F. S. Kennedy. 2001. The 2001 stock assessment update of common snook, *Centropomus undecimalis*. Fish and Wildlife Conservation Commission. Florida Marine Research Institute. St. Petersburg, Florida.

Murphy, M. D., R. F. Heagey, V. N. Neugebrauer, M. D. Gordon, and J. L. Hinz. 1995. Mortality of spotted seatrout released from gill-net or hook-and-line gear in Florida. North American Journal of Fishery Management 15:748–753.

American Fisheries Society Symposium 30:15–18, 2002

Why Does Marine Fisheries Management Now Require Releasing Caught Fish?

GARY C. MATLOCK

Introduction

Until about 20 years ago, the commonly held view was that the ocean and its resources were so vast and bountiful that it was virtually impossible for man, more precisely fishing, to affect them in any significant way. That view, however, was replaced in 1996 with a federal regulatory environment which requires the reversing of the overfished condition of many marine fish stocks by accounting for and managing all sources of fishing mortality. The effects of catching, not just harvesting, fish by all fishers, including recreational, were formally recognized and now these effects must be minimized. Catch and release is indeed becoming an integral part of U.S. marine fisheries. Atlantic billfish now support the first formally designated federal recreational catch and release program, and there are now 25 other species (not including Pacific salmonids listed under the Endangered Species Act) for which their retention when caught in federal waters is prohibited. Unfortunately, the application of catch and release is far outpacing our ability to predict its success.

Now, the above introduction to the issue of catch and release in recreational fishing is undoubtedly a bit overstated. However, it does not miss the mark by much. As we began to Americanize marine fisheries off our coasts in 1976, Congress expressed the view that marine fish were being overfished by foreign vessels and set about to correct that situation by eliminating foreign fishing, to the benefit of United States citizens. The Fishery Conservation and Management Act (FCMA) of 1976 was passed and created regional fishery management councils to assist in correcting the problems created by excessive foreign fishing. But, simultaneously, the U.S. government initiated a fisheries research and development policy that encouraged our citizens to fill the void left by the absence of foreigners. And, fill the void we did, with almost no constraints or controls, until the reality of the rhetoric on which the FCMA was founded became all

Gary C. Matlock, National Centers for Coastal Ocean Science, National Ocean Service, 1305 East West Highway, Silver Spring, Maryland 20910, USA. Phone: (301)713-3020, Fax: (301)713-4353, Email: gary.c.matlock@noaa.gov.

too evident. Overfishing by U.S. vessels has occurred, and the painful process of regulating our citizens to reduce fishing mortality is now firmly a part of our landscape. Regulations that reduce the catch of many species, reconfigure the retained catch, or even completely prohibit the retention of some species are now common burdens imposed on both commercial and recreational U.S. fishermen. Put simply, we are reducing fishing mortality because it is generally too high.

As recently as 1994, fishing mortality was commonly perceived as pertaining only to the harvested (retained) portion of the catch, with mortality resulting from nonharvest fishing regarded as inconsequential (Muoneke and Childress 1994). We recognized that many fish are unintentionally caught because there is no perfectly selective fishing gear that can catch only the kind, size, or sex of fish sought. However, this unintended fishing mortality was generally ignored in our scientific stock assessments and in fishery conservation and management measures. Indeed, many regulations even increase fishing mortality by increasing the discard of dead fish that are unavoidably caught and killed or by requiring the release of fish below minimum size limits, or that exceed quotas or bag and trip limits. The approach usually taken is to affect retention instead of prohibiting fishing because commercial fishing requires, by definition, dead fish for its survival and because recreational fishing's success has generally been measured by the number of fish in the cooler or hanging from a scaffold. But, the regulatory environment was dramatically changed in 1996 when the Sustainable Fisheries Act amended the FCMA (now the Magnuson-Stevens Fishery Conservation and Management Act, or Magnuson-Stevens Act, for short) to require accounting for all sources of fishing mortality. The effects of catching, not just harvesting, fish were formally recognized and must now be minimized. Fish that are caught, but not retained, were defined in the act as bycatch. A requirement was added to minimize bycatch to the maximum extent practicable, and to the extent that bycatch cannot be avoided, mortality is to be minimized. Recreational fishing was not exempt from these requirements. But, unique attributes of recreational catch-and-release fishing were recognized by excluding this activity from the bycatch definition. The regional fishery management councils are specifically required to assess the type and amount of fish caught and released alive under catch-and-release fishery management programs and to minimize mortality resulting from these programs.

There is currently only one recreational catch-and-release program, as defined in the Magnuson-Stevens Act, in place in the United States. That program is for the Atlantic billfish fishery in which the vast majority of recreationally caught billfish are released. Billfish in the Atlantic are overfished, and fishing mortality must be reduced. Recreational fishermen are attempting to accomplish a reduction by releasing most of what they catch, rather than reducing their attempts to catch the fish. This approach capitalizes upon the fishermen's preference for the recreational experience over the desire to return to dock with the catch in hand. The premise on which this program is founded is that there are insufficient numbers of fish currently available to warrant reaping short-term gains provided by dead fish on the dock and foregoing the future benefits afforded by releasing these fish. The fundamental assumption required to realize future expectations is that the released fish survive capture and contribute to the population as if they had never been caught. But, it is unlikely that every released fish survives. Therefore, the benefits of catch and release are seldom fully maximized. To the extent that this assumption is violated, the utility of catch and release is reduced. Unfortunately, our estimates of the survival of released billfish are not well quantified. We know that at least some fish not only survive capture, but also being tagged before release. So, the conclusion at this point is that the program is beneficial. It is worth noting that the effectiveness of the recreational billfish program also depends on the fishing mortality caused by other fisheries (e.g., the commercial longline fishery).

While Atlantic billfish support the only formally designated recreational catch-and-release program, there are 25 other species for which their retention in federal waters is prohibited. This list does not include any of the Pacific salmonids listed under the Endangered Species Act. In every case, the prohibition has been the result of dramatic declines in the species. The result of these prohibitions has been generally positive in terms of population increases, again indicating the importance of the impacts of fishing. The "poster child" of fish, used to demonstrate the success of catch and release in the marine environment, has been striped bass *Morone saxatilis*. This species has recovered from severe overfishing in a relatively short time after retention was essentially prohibited on the Atlantic coast. Fish were still caught, but most were released. Hooking-mortality studies have demonstrated that the survival of these fish is generally very high. So, fish that would have otherwise died from having been caught were allowed to grow, reproduce, and even get caught by fishermen more than once. However, Atlantic salmon and Atlantic sharks have not yet responded favorably for a variety of reasons.

Catch and release is indeed becoming an integral part of U.S. marine fisheries. Unfortunately, its application is far outpacing our ability to predict its success. We simply do not understand and have not quantified the factors affecting postrelease survival for very many species in the diversity of habitats from which fishermen remove them. Studies done to date indicate that individual fish that do not survive being caught depends upon the kind of fish they are, their size, the type of gear used, where on the body they are hooked, how they are handled, and the environments to which they are exposed. Much work is needed, and it must be done much faster. The National Marine Fisheries Service conducts and financially supports many scientific research projects in this area, including some of the results you will hear this week. We are very interested in your results and look forward to their application in the management of our extremely important and valuable recreational fisheries.

References

Muoneke, M. I., and W. M. Childress. 1994. Hooking mortality: a review for recreational fisheries. Reviews in Fishery Science 2(2):123–156.

American Fisheries Society Symposium 30:19–28, 2002

A Human Dimensions Perspective on Catch-and-Release Fishing

ROBERT B. DITTON

Introduction

There are several as yet unanswered questions that deserve our attention, namely, the who, what, where, and why of catch-and-release fishing in marine waters of the United States. First, we have no reliable estimates of the number of marine anglers in the United States that practice catch-and-release fishing. Second, whereas anecdotal evidence would seem to indicate the number of people who practice catch-and-release fishing is on the increase, we cannot be sure, since there are so many different definitions of catch and release. Accordingly, generic survey questions that inquire about anglers' "catch-and-release" behavior do not yield useful information. Third, we know little about which variables would predict why some people practice catch and release and others do not. And lastly, there is no agreement as to the best approaches for promoting the adoption and diffusion of this practice to other anglers. Ad hoc approaches seem to be the order of the day. These are fundamental questions that need to be answered, if we expect to see meaningful "changes" in fishing behavior soon.

So Many Ways to Define Catch and Release

Information deficits exist because there is little agreement on a definition of the term "catch and release." It can and does mean many different things to many different people. Some of the inherent complexity of the catch-and-release concept is demonstrated in the following statements made by anglers: "I release all of the fish I catch" (a conservation statement on their part); "I release all of the fish caught on this trip/in the past 12 months/recently/in my lifetime"; "I release all blue marlin caught but don't always release other species caught"; "I release all blue marlin caught except for trophies and tournament winners"; "I tag and

Robert B. Ditton, Department of Wildlife and Fisheries Sciences, Texas A&M University, College Station, Texas 77843-2258, USA. Email: r-ditton@neo.tamu.edu.

release all (or some) of the fish caught in support of science"; "I sometimes release all of the fish caught"; "I always release some of the fish caught"; "I release all fish caught not of legal size"; "I sometimes release fish caught that are not of legal size but are too small/not good eating/don't want to bother with the catch"; "I release all fish caught after bag limit is reached" (with or without culling); "I release some fish when I catch fish, but I don't catch much though"; "I don't catch any fish to release"; and "I release all fish at designated catch-and-release areas." And you have surely heard other statements made by anglers that help make the point that there is little shared understanding of the catch-and-release concept out there in the diverse marine recreational fishing social world. Voluntary and required actions alike are all considered "catch and release" by anglers.

If catch and release can mean so many different things to anglers, just how are they to react to the term when it is undefined by fisheries managers and outdoor writers? Also, angler survey questions will need to be more explicit if they are to produce reliable and valid data in support of management. The specific context of catch and release must be clear when questioning anglers; for example, is the concern only with catch-and-release behavior that is voluntary, or does catch and release mandated by management regulations count as well? Questions need to be well framed, so that the context of catch and release is clear to anglers. Once specified clearly, there must also be some attention to the extent to which anglers practice catch and release: always, never, and sometimes. Most of our attention will probably be devoted to understanding the range of "sometimes." And finally, questioning needs to be as species-specific as possible, since angler meanings and understandings likely vary by species.

Without careful attention to the aforementioned matters, the typical catch-and-release question used previously (i.e., "Do you practice catch-and-release fishing?") is not likely to yield the information sought. From personal experience, it will elicit one of the following three answers: Sure, It depends, and Sometimes.

Asking Better Questions to Get Meaningful Data

Then, there is the problem of "two-headed questions." The following three questions used by various state agencies (R. Baur, Illinois Department of Natural Resources, personal communication) fall into this category: "How often do you catch and keep a 'limit" of fish?"; "How important to you is catching and releasing fish?"; and "How important to you is catching and keeping a 'limit' of fish?" The questions do not establish any sort of voluntary/mandatory, size, and species context to assist the angler in responding, and they also treat "catching and keeping" and "catching and releasing" as singular concepts. Whereas anglers are expected to respond to the concept of catching and releasing, they may respond more to the catching part of the question than the releasing part, or vice versa. In the final analysis, it may not be clear to what anglers are responding. Such questions pose reliability and validity problems for angler data-collection efforts.

Other questions reported by Baur (Illinois Department of Natural Resources, personal communication) ask anglers for answers without any timeframe established, and therefore, "recall bias" is a potential problem. For example, "What percentage of the time on average do you release the legal size (insert species name here) you catch?" (10% intervals from 0% to 100%), or "Do you usually keep the legal (insert species name here) you catch or release them?" (Keep, Release, Not Applicable). Such questions do not make it clear what the period of observation entails, and anglers are left to make the "calculation" over an unspecified timeframe. Much more reliable data could probably be collected using a creel intercept methodology instead of an angler population survey. In this way, anglers could be asked about catch and disposition in detail for their trip that day.

Other questions used previously appear more interested in "snagging" answers than in collecting reliable and valid data. For example, the question "How important is it that you bring fish home after a day of fishing" focuses on none of the contextual matters raised previously and includes only one means of disposition of fish caught, bringing the fish home. What about anglers who retain their catch but dispose of it in other socially-acceptable ways? Also, it would seem that the question is directed toward anglers who have the ability to catch fish and who catch fish; responses might vary for those anglers who are not in the custom of having to make a retention decision. One of my least favorite questions among those reported by Baur (Illinois Department of Natural Resources, personal communication) is as follows: "What is your attitude towards releasing legal size (insert species name here)? Instead of providing a scale, whereby anglers could report how "they feel" about catch and release, they were instead asked to characterize their behavior (always release, almost always release, release half the time, regularly release, etc.)

Poor Questions Yield Poor Data

Without careful attention to how angler survey questions are drafted and potential reliability and validity problems, catch-and-release results are of limited value. Accordingly, the following results presented by Baur (Illinois Department of Natural Resources, personal communication) are either meaningless or confusing:

• More than 33% of anglers indicated that catching and releasing was a very important outcome for them.

• 84% of anglers practice some form of catch-and-release fishing in state waters that do not have designated catch-and-release regulations.

Even the results presented in the 1996 National Survey of Fishing, Hunting, and Wildlife-Related Recreation (U.S. Fish and Wildlife Service and U.S. Bureau of the Census 1997) are suspect. This study asked the question "Did you participate in catch-and-release fishing in the U.S. from January 1, 1996 to 31 December 31, 1996." No effort was made to define catch-and-release fishing for respondents; they were left to define it in their own terms. Accordingly, the result that 58% of all anglers participated in catch-and-release programs in 1996 lacks meaning. Further, the question asked in the 1996 national survey varied from the one contained in the 1991 national survey, so a trend perspective is not possible either.

NMFS is on the Right Track

The Marine Recreational Fisheries Statistics Survey (MRFSS), conducted by the National Marine Fisheries Service (NMFS) since 1979, appears to be "well along" in understanding disposition of recreationally-caught fish. Their disposition categories are as follows:

• Type A: fish caught, landed whole, verifiable;
• Type B: fish caught, either not kept or verifiable;
• Type B1: fish caught and filleted, released dead, given away, or disposed of in some other way besides Types A or B2;
• Type B2: fish caught and released alive.

Accordingly, the 1998 private boat catch (A + B1 + B2) for King mackerel *Scomberomorus cavalla* for the South Atlantic region equals 215,915 fish. Of this, B2 catch (released alive) constituted 56,217 fish. But, since fisheries management is more about managing anglers than fish, why is it that we know more about the number of fish caught than the number of anglers who practice various patterns of disposition behavior on each trip where King mackerel were caught? It would be helpful to estimate the distribution of anglers who release all, some, or none of their catch, if for no other reason than to identify various King mackerel angler "market types" for follow-up study. It is my understanding, from subsequent discussions with NMFS personnel, that these understandings can in fact be gleaned from the MRFSS data sets but is not seen as pertinent to allocation decision making. Hence, these types of analyses are possible but remain to be done using their data sets.

What Do Our Questions Look Like?

Mindful of some of the problems and criticisms made earlier, our work in this area has sought to avoid some of the pitfalls identified. We have also had the good fortune to work within a single species framework of rare event fisheries featuring memorable catches (i.e., billfish and bluefin tuna *Thunnus thynnus*). In our 1989–1990 Survey of U.S. Atlantic billfish tournament anglers, we asked anglers the following two questions in the context of their "most recent fishing tournament in which you attempted to catch a billfish"(Ditton and Fisher 1990; Fisher and Ditton 1992):

1. During the tournament, *how many* of each of the following species did *your boat* hook and bring to the boat? –Blue marlin, white marlin, sailfish, swordfish, etc.

2. During the tournament, how many of each of the following species did your boat retain and not release back into the water? –Blue marlin, white marlin, sailfish, swordfish, etc.

In Costa Rica, we followed up with a sample of charter boat billfish anglers within 12 months following their fishing trip there (Ditton and Grimes 1996). We asked them to recall their billfish fishing trips over the past 12 months, where they caught or attempted to catch billfish. We asked them to report the number of billfish caught and released in Costa Rica with catch and release referring to "fish brought to the boat and released intentionally." Just prior to this question, we asked anglers to report the number of billfish brought back to the dock or kept in Costa Rica. We then inquired about their most recent billfish trip to Costa Rica (including the date of when it occurred) and asked the two questions shown above but in the context of that trip.

These types of trip, event, and species-specific questions can be modified to fit with a creel intercept methodology to collect data from anglers in other situations. Accordingly, detailed data on catch-and-release behavior can be collected from anglers targeting particular fishery resources.

Predictors of Participation in Catch and Release

There has been little previous work completed to understand the best predictors of catch-and-release behavior in salt water. Using data from the National Survey of Fishing, Hunting, and Wildlife-Associated Outdoor Recreation, Grambsch and Fisher (1991) provide rates of participation in catch and release (sometimes or all the time) for various subgroups of freshwater anglers, to identify likely predictors of catch-and-release behavior. They concluded that rates of catch and release were highest for anglers who were: male; 18–24 years of age; rural residents; resided in the mid-Atlantic states; had household incomes of US\$ 30,000–\$49,999; had four or more years of college; fished 30 days or more in the previous year; and caught 26 or more fish in the previous year.

Building on this work, Graefe and Ditton (1997) sought to identify the best predictors of catch-and-release behavior among billfish anglers in the U.S. Atlantic. The dependent variable of catch-and-release behavior was operationalized through direct questioning, whereby mail survey respondents were asked how many billfish they had brought to the dock during the past 12 months. Responses ranged from 0 to 25, with 62% reporting none. The analysis focused on discriminating between the 62% who kept no billfish and the remaining 38% who reported keeping one or more. They found that the best predictors of releasing all billfish caught were the number of trips targeting billfish and the number of tournaments entered (the more trips and tournaments, the more likely an angler was to keep one billfish), geography (anglers in tournaments in Puerto Rico were more likely to keep billfish than those anglers from the mainland United States), and income (the greater the income, the less likely to keep billfish). It was noteworthy that level of formal education showed no relationship with either keeping or releasing billfish. Membership in fishing clubs and organizations, on the other hand, contributed to releasing behavior, as those who belonged to membership organizations were significantly more likely to release all billfish caught.

The implications for educational efforts and fisheries management should be apparent. Catch-and-release messages in the billfish angler community are particularly salient to older, wealthier anglers and those who belong to fishing clubs and organizations. Continued use of these messages by membership organizations, as well as expanded efforts to include more such anglers in their membership, would appear to be major agenda items. Additional catch-and-release messages that highlight catch and release in different terms are likely salient to other angler groups; we need a predictive understanding of the role that independent variables play in the practice/non-practice of various catch-and-release behaviors.

Graefe and Ditton (1997) identified several directions for additional research in this important research area. First, they called for greater specificity in terms of how questions are asked, instead of just asking whether they released the fish they catch or, in their case, whether they released the *billfish* they catch; their example was that anglers may be more likely to release a sailfish than a blue marlin. Second, they called for greater use of creel intercept results that provide data on the number of particular fish species caught and released and also include the requisite demographic descriptors to better understand the role that various independent variables play in catch-and-release behavior. And third, they called for the use of species-specific scenarios, whereby anglers are told how many fish of various lengths they have caught and asked to identify which ones (if any) they would release. This would allow for further investigations of various catch-and-release configurations as defined by the researcher. Instead of the potential for recall bias with a 12-month recall period used by many researchers, responses would be hypothetical, like the contingent valuation willingness-to-pay questions used by nonmarket, natural resources economists.

Bumper Stickers Won't Get the Job Done!

Unlike the billfish fishery, where catch and release is fast approaching the norm, there are other marine fisheries where the innovation or technology of catch and release is still seen as something new. It doesn't matter that the idea has been around for some time if anglers have not yet developed a favorable or unfavorable attitude toward it. In these situations, anglers may have little basic understanding of catch-and-release practice and its benefits, have not been sufficiently persuaded, or have not made the decision to adopt yet. We see those who adopt the catch-and-release innovation early; they are referred to as innovators and early adopters. Outdoor writers and other communicators devote much of their time to getting the message to those who are already converts. These first two groups are followed by what Rogers (1995) calls the early and late majority groups and, finally, the laggards. These three groups of individuals are in need of basic knowledge of the practice, how it works, what they need to do and why, and how it benefits them. What are the basic advantages and disadvantages of catch and release? Because of how they define recreational fishing and what they seek from their fishing experiences, they may choose to adopt catch and release as their preferred type of fishing in certain circumstances, or they may reject the idea entirely, or in part. We need to find ways to communicate with anglers in these latter groups. Most efforts to date, to promote catch-and-release fisheries, have focused almost exclusively on the fishing social world of "insiders"; we also need appropriate messages that resonate with the entire cross section of anglers, including what Unruh (1979) refers to as "strangers, tourists, and regulars" (Ditton et al. 1992).

Much more detailed information needs to be communicated to the marine angler population if catch and release is to be more universally adopted. Typically, those innovations that are viewed as having greater relative advantage, that are compatible with the person's values and norms, that are easy to understand and use, that are easy to use on a trial basis, and that yield observable results will be adopted more rapidly than other innovations (Rogers 1995). This provides outdoor writers and other communicators with some better idea of what they need to include in their persuasive messages.

Whereas numerous ad hoc efforts seek to promote the catch-and-release philosophy today, there is no overall strategy in place, currently, for promoting the widespread adoption of catch-and-release behaviors by marine anglers. If the goal is to promote adoption of catch-and-release fishing in marine waters, more attention needs to be devoted to the innovation-decision process, as developed extensively in the social science literature. The innovation-decision process is the process through which individuals pass, from when they gain first-hand knowledge of the innovation, to forming an attitude toward the idea to a decision to adopt or reject the new idea, to implementing it, and finally to confirmation of this decision. The process by which innovations are diffused and adopted is well known; it has been shown to be effective in other situations. It was the basis by which the Agricultural Extension Service, for example, originally promoted the adoption of new technologies and practices within the farm and ranch community. They are considered the world's most successful change agency today (Rogers 1995: 357–364). We can learn from their experience and that of others, as efforts are made to promote more widespread adoption of catch and release. There is no reason to "make it up as we go along" just because many of us feel more comfortable dealing with fish than people. There are fundamental social science understandings of the innovation-process available that need to be the cornerstone of our communication and outreach efforts.

Each person has an important role to play in diffusing the catch-and-release idea. The biologists who have seen the benefits and costs of using various fishing practices and gears have to get their research results to the communicators. Individual anglers will not be persuaded to convert to catch and release if the persuasive messages they receive are not knowledge-based: thus, the earlier reference to bumper stickers that do not provide anglers with the awareness they need to be persuaded to adopt new fishing practices and technologies. For increased adoption to occur, we will need increased attention to persuasive efforts by "change agents." Change agents are those who seek to influence innovation-decisions in the desirable direction by sharing information and include leaders of nongovernmental recreational fishing organizations (NGOs), state agency aquatic education personnel, and Sea Grant extension agents, among others. Efforts to persuade others to adopt new fishing practices and technologies are likely to be more successful if these change agents work through "near-peer" opinion leaders, including outdoor writers using various media, local fishing icons and celebrities, tournament winners, well-regarded local anglers, and the like. Opinion leaders are people who have their own following of anglers. The enlistment of opinion leaders by change agents can help magnify the change agent's efforts to promote adoption of the desired innovation.

Looking Ahead

In conclusion, we all need to be a lot more precise about how we use the term "catch and release." It can and does mean lots of things to many people. There is no need for a single definition, in my view, but the various definitions need to be clarified. Second, we need to develop survey questions that ascertain the extent of angler participation according to these various definitions to achieve valid and reliable understandings of the number of anglers practicing catch-and-release variations. More angler survey designs that build on creel intercepts that feature a trip-specific and species-specific focus are encouraged. Only with credible baseline data on catch-and-release participation will we be able to ascertain whether diffusion efforts have been successful. Third, the establishment of agreed-upon definitions and measures will assist ongoing research efforts to understand predictors of catch-and-release participation. And finally, a national strategy is needed for promoting greater adoption of catch-and-release behaviors among all marine anglers. This communications strategy should build upon "state of the art" diffusion and innovation-decision processes widely-used today by business and industry for the effective dissemination of new ideas and technologies. The ultimate goal of a national strategy is to make sure state and local communication efforts are conceptually well grounded and likely to yield measurable results.

References

Ditton, R. B., and M. R. Fisher. 1990. Characteristics, behavior, attitudes, expenditures, harvest, and management preferences of billfish tournament anglers (with technical appendix volume). Report prepared for the Billfish Foundation, Miami, Florida.

Ditton, R. B., and S. R. Grimes. 1996. A social and economic study of the Costa Rica recreational billfish fishery. Report prepared for the International Billfish Research and Conservation Foundation, Fort Lauderdale, Florida.

Ditton, R. B., D. K. Loomis, and S. Choi. 1992. Recreation specialization: re-conceptualization from a social world's perspective. Journal of Leisure Research 24:33–51.

Fisher, M. R., and R. B. Ditton. 1992. Characteristics of U.S. billfish anglers in the Atlantic Ocean. Marine Fisheries Review 54(1):1–6.

Graefe, A. R., and R. B. Ditton. 1997. Understanding catch and release behavior among billfish anglers. Pages 430–455 in Proceedings of the 49th Gulf and Caribbean Fisheries Institute.

Grambsch, A. E., and W. L. Fisher. 1991. 1985 catch-and-release statistics for U.S. bass and trout anglers. Pages 390–396 in D. Guthrie, J. M. Hoenig, M. Holliday, C. M. Jones, M. J. Mills, S. A. Moberly, K. H. Pollock, and D. R. Talhelm, editors. Creel and angler surveys in fisheries management. American Fisheries Society, Symposium 12, Bethesda, Maryland.

Rogers, E. M. 1995. Diffusion of innovations. 4th edition. The Free Press, New York.

Unruh, D. R. 1979. Characteristics and types of participation in social worlds. Symbolic Interaction 2:115–130.

U.S. Fish and Wildlife Service and U.S. Bureau of the Census. 1997. 1996 National Survey of Fishing, Hunting, and Wildlife-Associated Recreation. U.S. Government Printing Office, Washington, D.C.

American Fisheries Society Symposium 30:29–36, 2002
© Copyright by the American Fisheries Society 2002

Cultural Values and Change:
Catch and Release in Alaska's Sport Fisheries

J O N L Y M A N

Introduction

Catch and release is a culturally inspired ethical response justified by anglers to preserve wild fish populations. In order to understand the reaction of some Alaska Natives to releasing fish we should consider some of the influences on anglers as they developed catch and release. In this paper I will contrast Alaska Native cultural traditions and three elements of the American sporting tradition. I will also discuss the potential for respectful negotiation and offer some avenues for change.

I believe that three elements of western culture led to an acceptance and even reverence for catch and release among fly anglers today. The development of the catch and release ethic in sport fishing required the anthropocentrism of stewardship as a system of behavior toward other living things, a belief in the individual's right to choose his own ethical course, and a separation from the tradition of the taking of trophies (trophyism) in contests of skill.

Contrasting these cultural influences, Alaska Native cultures see humans as part of the cycle of nature, not superior to it; mistreatment of living things can lead to misfortune for the human community; and, while individualism is valued, the individual boasts at his or her own peril.

The Evolution of Catch and Release

Catch and release is rooted in the Christian dogma of man's dominion over the beast of the air and the fish of the seas. "Be fertile and multiply, fill the earth and subdue it. Have dominion over the fish of the sea," –Genesis 1:28

The biblical steward evolves into the river keeper on the streams of England. Stewardship becomes the manipulation of nature to the benefit of man, pre-

Jon Lyman, Alaska Department of Fish and Game, Division of Sport Fish, Post Office Box 25526, Juneau, Alaska 99802, USA. Email: Jon_lyman@fishgame.state.ak.us

supposing an understanding of how nature works. It is still often the underlying justification for manipulation of fish or wildlife population by managers. Stewardship as a foundation for development of an environmental ethic, however, has been questioned by Dr. Stephen Kellert, Associate Professor of the School of Forestry, Yale University. Speaking at a recent workshop on environmental ethics, Dr. Kellert said,

"I am personally doubtful, however, that a management and stewardship approach is a sufficient basis for attaining a personally meaningful and powerful environmental ethic. I believe the case could be made that a management and stewardship perspective has a tendency to perpetuate a view of homo-sapiens as 'outside' if not 'above and superior' to nature." (Kellert 1987)

American outdoor/angling ethics are founded on the importance of the individual. Sport fishing workshops discuss activities to help the individual develop his/her angling ethics. It seems universally accepted that one's ethics are a moving target, changing as the individual grows in his/her understanding of the out of doors.

"Our contemporary individualism gives us only un-firm ground to base our enacted ethics: often the right thing to do is simply what makes us feel right doing it" (Machlis 1987).

"Your ethics are a gift to yourself," is a statement I use to introduce the concept of angling ethics to my 4-H club members. I am asserting, as have so many before me, the primacy of the self in relation to the wilderness. With catch and release this gift of ethics is turned inward, not focused on the prize as a trophy, rather on the skill and understanding that is required to both capture and release the prize unscathed.

Medieval treatises offer a defense of hunting for sport as a means for the nobility to practice the arts of war. Essential to this tradition was the taking of the trophy; the word derived from the Greek *tropaion* referring to the monument of an enemy's defeat, a cache of arms or prizes (or heads) taken from a defeated enemy. In the Middle Ages tale "Sir Gawain and the Green Knight" a hunting scene ends with the head of the great boar impaled on a spear and "borne before the lord himself, who had slain the beast in the ford by the skill and strength of his hands." (McDonald 1963)

The fly fishing tradition, however, is at odds with this display of trophies. The first known text on fly fishing is attributed to Dame Juliana Bernes, a nearly mythical figure whose heraldic name gives authority to the rules she dictates for fly fishing. Published in1496, the Dame's "Treatise of Fishing with an Angle" asserts that fishing is the best of sports and the art of fishing itself is of more value than the fish harvested. (McDonald 1963) Today, a saying among fly fishers is that catching fish is the least important part of fly fishing.

The genteel English tradition of fly fishing was lost in America in the 19th century during the westward expansion. Along with the necessity of surviving on the frontier came a utilitarian attitude toward fishing (Schullery 1987). In the late twentieth/early twenty-first century, competitive, heroic, trophy-mad America has sport fishing trophies adorning bars and dens. Most states offer a trophy certificate for catching and killing a large fish. Today, catch and release has its own version of honoring, or recognition of, trophy catches, through photographs and taxidermists' production of fiberglass wall mounts of released fish (as opposed to skin mounts of killed fish), and a growing number of state catch and release certificate programs.

Alaska Native Cultural Traditions

Alaska has over 250 individual Native tribes, each with distinct cultural traditions. It is impossible to characterize all Alaska Native traditions just as it is impossible to group all anglers and their ethical beliefs. Even so, Native cultures share a respect for nature which, while the particulars vary from tribe to tribe, can be contrasted to the sporting tradition common to many sportsmen.

Western Alaska Natives have very strict cultural taboos about fish. When discussing the actions of catch and release anglers, Yup'ik elders say, "You do not play with your food." The words they use in Yup'ik are quite specific: play is the same word used to describe children's activities and fish is the same word as food. When fish are mishandled, when they are damaged, not taken and respected as food, it is thought they simply go away. It is implied that where they go is a concurrent domain where they receive better treatment and are not available to human beings. (Wolfe 1988)

In 1970, Robert Zuboff, a Tlingit master storyteller and chief of the Beaver clan in Angoon, told me a story of a boy who was taken by the salmon people because he was disrespectful of them. The boy scoffed at the old dry fish that his mother gave him just prior to the return of the salmon of the New Year. The salmon people took him into the water to teach him respect. The boy lived with the salmon people for a year, returning to his tribe as a salmon the next summer.

In 1988, on a horse-packing trip in the Pelly River country, in Canada along the Yukon River, my Native guide was struck speechless when I returned from fishing for Arctic grayling with no fish. From high on a nearby ridge he had seen me catch several grayling, but I carried no fish with me. It was beyond his comprehension that I would release the fish. He insisted I return to the river and catch the same fish again. They would surely give themselves to me once more so that they could be removed from the river.

Northwest Alaska Native cultures believe in a cycle of life and death which must be followed if wildlife is to give itself to humans. The role of human beings is to harvest the fish people. Humans must follow strict cultural patterns of behavior to assure that the spirit of those self-same salmon people will return as additional fish next year. To these Natives, consumption of the fish that give themselves to humans is an essential element in the preservation and restoration of fish resources, year after year.

Many Alaska Natives believe that proper behavior of the individual is a prerequisite to wildlife giving itself to them for use as food. In Yup'ik traditions, people are cautioned not to overly boast about fish and game harvested, but to be grateful to have the good fortune to harvest them. Of course there are Yup'iks who boast. And there are stories about misfortunes that sometimes follow. (Robert Wolfe, Alaska Department of Fish and Game, personal communication)

Changing Values

The outlook for reconciling the apparently very different cultural points of view surrounding catch and release has been, and in some areas remains, bleak. In some areas, however, the expansion of the cash economy in villages, the decline in prices paid for commercially caught fish, severe declines in the numbers of fish available for harvest, and increased job opportunities in sport fisheries for Natives have led individuals into the sport fish industry.

Native sport fishing guides now operate from Quinhagak, the village that, a few years ago, was at the center of opposition to sport fishing in Western Alaska. Today, Native corporation lands are sometimes leased to guides for camps and lodge locations (often over the objection of local residents). I was asked recently to help start a fly fishing club in Craig, a village on Prince of Wales Island. When I asked why Native persons would be interested in such a club, I was told "commercial fishing is dying, logging is dead; the only people making money here are the sport fishing guides." (Native cab driver, Klawock, personal communication)

As part of my job I sponsor education programs in outdoor skills in rural Alaska. Many villagers want to understand the values of anglers and sportsmen. This willingness to consider alternative points-of-view I attribute to the efforts of individuals from urban areas that have forged long-term relationships within the village.

Alaska Communications Service (ACS) is the electronics service provider throughout much of rural Southeast Alaska. Their linemen are on-call at all hours to resurrect phone service, re-establish navigation signals, and, when time allows, install telephones and internet service in the village schools. Ken Coate, an ACS lineman, is also a volunteer 4-H shotgun and hunter safety instructor. His commitment goes far beyond his job, helping to start shooting education programs in the villages he serves. This level of involvement is an essential element in establishing a dialogue between cultures.

In Yakutat in the spring of 1999, we taught fly fishing and firearms safety two weeks after the Columbine High School tragedy. Ken led the firearms safety course. Jimmy Chesbro, a dedicated Federation of Fly Fishers member and an ardent catch and release angler, taught angling ethics and catch and release. It was an amazing week, the highlight of which occurred for me when I looked in on a discussion of angling ethics in the library. Students in grades 9–12 were leaning forward, eagerly involved with Jimmy discussing ethics and catch and release. Last spring, Yakutat tribal elders asked our area biologist for all the catch and release materials available, in order to design a display for the airport which would reflect best practices for catch and release and cultural differences.

In 1999, the night before the students were to take their hunter education exam, a few of the fifteen volunteers who taught the course expressed concern that there were no tangible incentives for students to do well on the test. The students did not need the hunter safety card to go hunting locally and we offered no prizes. I told the volunteers that I believed that the students wanted to do well because the volunteers had made the effort to communicate with them, as individuals, about things that mattered greatly to both groups.

Ninety-eight students took the firearm safety exam and all but one passed. I was told that the next week, at the school's graduation ceremony, the principal showed Robert Redford's "A River Runs Through It" to resounding applause.

This is not to say that catch and release has been accepted widely in rural Alaska. The angler can anticipate different receptions in different communities, from acceptance of the practice to outright hostility toward it.

Toward a Unified Tradition of Respect

Management programs and research into the effectiveness of catch and release in supporting angler opportunity largely postdate Lee Wulff's 1939 admonition that "Game fish are too valuable to be caught only once." (Seldon 1994; Radonski, this volume) The rise of interest in catch and release, especially among fly fishers, may be seen as a return to an earlier tradition of the application of the angler's craft being more important than the harvesting of fish.

The return to this tradition of noncompetitiveness and the practice of the fly fisher's craft may appeal to Native guides. Both Native and fly fishing traditions are of great antiquity and rely upon an intimate knowledge of nature and an understanding of fish behavior for success. Both require respect for the resource and discount the taking of trophies. Both traditions are steeped in the artist's mysteries and a conscientious devotion to one's craft. "The traditional nature of fly fishing and the difficulty of the fly angler's craft may have significance in easing cultural changes in Alaska." (Thomas Thornton, University of Alaska, personal communication)

The Politics of Change

The federal government now has responsibility for management of subsistence fisheries on federal lands in Alaska. Native persons have already called for significant changes in the management of sport fisheries. Some regional advisory committee members are seeking ways to deny anglers access to public waters in parts of rural Alaska. It would require pure speculation on my part to forecast what the management of sport fishing will look like in rural Alaska ten years hence. "The practice of potentially controversial behaviors, such as catch and release, in communities with multiple value systems must be "negotiated" in order to be publicly acceptable….In some Alaska Native communities the negotiation has been relatively smooth and in others it has been very stormy." (Robert Wolfe, ADF&G, personal communication)

Influence of the Media in Rural Alaska

When the State of Alaska created a bush television network, legislators ignored the evidence of the Canadian Broadcast Network and failed to allow for local television production. Instead, rural residents, many of whom never travel to urban areas, have gained a distorted world-view of America from our pop-culture and violence-riddled commercial television. Rural residents also watch a lot of nature programming. (Isett 1995)

In Chulathbaluk, on the Kuskokwim River, in 1999 I met an eleven-year-old boy named Michael. Michael appeared at a fly tying clinic I had been asked to teach by the mayor. His sneakers were breaking out at the sole. He wore the same tattered tee-shirt each day. He knew the names and uses of every plant and bush on our afternoon fishing excursions. Michael was not an advocate of catch and release. He and his grandmother truly subsisted off the land. He spoke constantly, wanting to share what he knew about his country. He also rattled on about the lives of elephants and whales. His world was that of the Kuskokwim River valley and nature programming available on the Rural Alaska Television Network.

With the spread of satellite television receivers, popular sport fishing shows may also be influencing public opinion about catch and release in rural Alaska. According to Dan Dunaway, ADF&G area biologist in Dillingham, Native viewers are offended by behavior of many sport anglers on sport fishing television programming. Playing fish to exhaustion, removing fish from the water for extended periods, and releasing distressed fish are behaviors at which many anglers and Alaska Natives take offense.

For rural Alaskans, even the best sport fishing programming still suffers from a fatal flaw: it is not real, they cannot interact with it. As mentioned above, the most effective means of communicating and affecting change in any society is through one on one discussion and negotiation.

Selective Harvest

In all of my Alaska education programs, I advocate selective harvest as a compromise. It is often acceptable to both catch and release anglers and Natives. When done properly, selective harvest involves using catch and release techniques to assure released fish the best chance to survive while assuring the meat angler the best possible fish for food. Selective harvest implies that we understand our role in the environment as both conservator and predator and attempt to minimize waste.

Those who would proselytize for the release of fish must remember that Alaskans eat fish. Alaska Natives believe in "catch and keep" because they eat wild foods. In parts of rural Alaska the average resident annually eats 610 pounds of wild resources. The average person living in the western United States purchases approximately 222 pounds of meat, fish, or poultry annually. (Wolfe 1989)

A few years ago, I was asked by the U.S. Forest Service to host a 'Pathways to Fishing' clinic in Hoonah, a Tlingit village just south of Glacier Bay. Native elders met my plane, saying that I could not teach catch and release. I showed them materials on selective harvest and explained how I would discuss catch and release as part of taking fish for consumption. They immediately gave permission for the course to proceed. Cultural values are constantly being negotiated by all of us. The acceptance of catch and release as a means of assuring additional angling opportunity on limited stocks of fish depends upon the world view of the community in which the fishery occurs. Roderick Haig-Brown once wrote that he could not fully appreciate travel to different countries unless he understood the culture of the people who live there. (Haig-Brown 1996) As with the creation of the catch and release ethic, it is left to the individual angler to promote his/her beliefs when encountering new cultures. The extent to which he/she succeeds depends, I believe, upon the degree to which anglers take Haig-Brown's admonition to heart.

If proponents of catch and release expect to have their values understood, they must make the effort to understand those of the Native peoples among whom they would practice their craft. Acceptance of catch and release or selective harvest in additional areas of rural Alaska depends upon interaction between individuals who value cultural differences and share a respect for the common resource.

References

Haig-Brown, V. 1996. To Know A River. Lyons and Burford, New York.

Isett, R. A. 1995. Publicly Funded Satellite Television in Alaska: Lost in Space. Doctoral dissertation, Michigan State University, East Lansing, Michigan.

Kellert, S. J. 1987. Social and Psychological Dimensions of an Environmental Ethic. Proceedings of the International Conference on Environmental Ethics. Sponsored by the Izaak Walton League of America.

Machlis, G. 1987. Outdoor Ethics in America. Proceedings of the International Conference on Environmental Ethics. Sponsored by the Izaak Walton League of America.

McDonald, J. 1963. The Origins of Angling. Lyons and Burford, New York.

Schullery, P. 1987. American Fly Fishing. Lyons and Burford, New York.

Seldon, M. M. 1994. Catch-and Release Notes and Bibliography, Federation of Fly Fishers, Bozeman.

Wolfe, R. J. 1988. "The Fish Are Not to be Played With": Yup'ik Views of Sport Fishing and Subsistence-Recreation Conflicts along the Togiak River. Paper presented at the Alaska Anthropological Association, Anchorage, Alaska.

Wolfe, R. J. 1989. "Alaskans' Per Capita Harvests of Wild Food" Alaska Fish and Game. November-December issue: 14-15.

Comparative Hooking
Effects and Mortality

American Fisheries Society Symposium 30:39–56, 2002

Hook-and-Release Mortality of Chinook Salmon from Drift Mooching with Circle Hooks: Management Implications for California's Ocean Sport Fishery

ALLEN M. GROVER[1]

California Department of Fish and Game
Ocean Salmon Project
475 Aviation Boulevard, Suite 130
Santa Rosa, California 95403, USA

MICHAEL S. MOHR

National Marine Fisheries Service
Southwest Fisheries Science Center, Santa Cruz Laboratory
110 Shaffer Road
Santa Cruz, California 95060, USA

MELODIE L. PALMER-ZWAHLEN

California Department of Fish and Game
Ocean Salmon Project
475 Aviation Boulevard, Suite 130
Santa Rosa, California 95403, USA

Abstract.—A total of 276 chinook salmon *Oncorhynchus tshawytscha*, less than 660-mm total length, were drift mooch-caught using barbless circle hooks and held for four days in 8,700 L, onboard holding tanks for wound location-specific, mortality rate evaluation. Only gut-hooked fish died in the first 24 hours of holding, and only lower-jaw hooked and gut-hooked fish died within the first 48 hours of holding. Gut-hooked fish that survived the four day holding period but whose internal organs were severely damaged were considered mortalities. The four day mortality rate attributable to the effects of handling and holding alone was estimated to be 0.048, based on a surrogate control group consisting of tank-held fish having no wounds or superficial wounds. The control-adjusted, four day mortality rates depended strongly on hook wound location. The distribution of wound locations in the California recreational drift mooch salmon fishery was estimated based on a sample of 522 fish, less than 660-mm total length; the relative frequency of gut-hooked fish (0.406) was twice that of any other location. The fishery overall hook-and-release mortality rate was estimated to be 0.422 (95% confidence interval of 0.342–0.502), obtained by weighting the wound location-specific, four day mortality rates by the relative frequency of those wound locations in the fishery. The distribution of wound locations was found to depend on both hook size and fish-size class, but the effects of these factors were not additive on the log-odds scale. Blood plasma cortisol concentration, a measure of stress, was significantly higher in fish held for four days than in ocean-caught (presumably stress-free) fish, but there was considerable variation among individuals and the results were not useful in evaluating the effects of wound-induced stress. The requirement that (only) barbless circle hooks be used in the California drift mooch fishery substantially reduced the hook-and-release mortality rate in this fishery; however, the rate is still high. Hook-and-release mortality might be reduced further by educating anglers on the use of drift mooch methods that lessen the probability of gut hooking. If such education is effective in changing the fishery's wound location profile, our estimate of the hook-and-release mortality rate can be easily updated using the methods described in this paper.

Introduction

Hook-and-release (*H/R*) mortality has become an increasingly significant source of mortality in West Coast ocean salmon fisheries, given the depressed status of many Pacific salmon *Oncorhynchus* spp. stocks. Several stocks of chinook salmon *O.*

[1]Corresponding author: agrover@dfga.ca.gov

tshawytscha and coho salmon *O. kisutch* found in California's nearshore waters are currently listed under the U.S. Endangered Species Act (ESA; PFMC 2001). Yet, there are other chinook salmon stocks found in these waters that are not at-risk and are capable of sustaining significant harvest.

The Pacific Fishery Management Council (PFMC) manages these mixed-stock West Coast fisheries under its Salmon Framework Management Plan (PFMC 1984), taking into account jeopardy standards established in ESA recovery plans and biological opinions (PFMC 2001). Fishery regulations are designed by the PFMC to maximize fishing opportunity subject to meeting all existing stock-specific conservation criteria (spawner escapement goals, maximum permissible exploitation rates, etc.). Whether a proposed set of regulations can be expected to satisfy these conservation criteria requires forecasts of all fishery-related impacts on stocks under management, including *H/R* mortality.

Regulations used by the PFMC that result in the *selective* retention of fish, and thus *H/R* mortality, include species-specific, mark-specific, and size-specific restrictions. For example, the retention of coho salmon is prohibited off California (PFMC 2000), and in some instances, only marked (hatchery) salmon may be retained off Washington and Oregon (PFMC 2000). In certain areas off California, the minimum size limit for chinook salmon has been increased to reduce the fishery mortality on the endangered Sacramento River winter chinook salmon (PFMC 2000), which tends to be smaller at age than other stocks found off California (OSP 1989; Meyers et al. 1998; Yoshiyama et al. 1998). To forecast the impacts associated with these and other selective-retention fisheries, the PFMC's Salmon Technical Team (STT) uses mathematical models that require reliable estimates of the fishery-specific *H/R* mortality rates (STT 2000).

In the early 1990s, a new fishing technique now known as "California-style drift mooching" rapidly gained popularity among recreational anglers in the San Francisco and Monterey areas off California. Developed to catch salmon on light tackle gear, the drift mooching technique consists of drifting whole bait through schools of salmon, most commonly with the bait threaded on the hook in the "head down" direction (Figure 1). The technique differs from "motor mooching," where the bait is rigged on

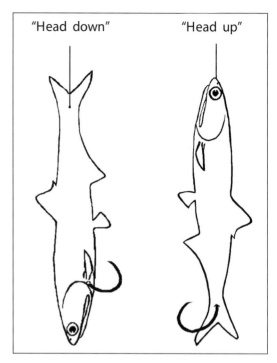

Figure 1. Bait orientation and hook threading methods used in California's recreational ocean salmon fisheries. The "Head down" orientation is currently the most common method used by anglers when drift mooching.

one or two J-hooks in the "head up" direction, and the head of the bait is sliced off at an angle ("plug cut") to produce a spinning motion in currents, or when slowly trolled. In drift mooching, when the bait is taken by a salmon, the angler strips out line to encourage the salmon to swallow the hook before the angler sets it by quickly retrieving (jerking) the bait. Drift mooching thus increases the probability that a fish will be gut hooked.

The PFMC initially assumed an *H/R* mortality rate, for this fishery, of 0.08, the same rate used for the recreational troll fishery (STT 1994). Grover (1992, 1995a) sought to improve upon this estimate by weighting hook wound location-specific *H/R* rates (specific to the gut, lower jaw, maxillary, etc.) by the relative frequency of those hook wound locations in the drift mooch fishery. For conciseness and specificity, we hereafter abbreviate "hook wound location" as H_ℓ, and "hook wound location-specific *H/R*" as H_ℓ/R. The *H/R* mortality rate estimate obtained using this method was as high as 0.63 for chinook salmon less than 660 mm total length (Grover 1995b), substantially higher than the recreational troll rate of 0.08, primarily due to the higher incidence of gut hooking in the drift mooch fishery (Grover 1995b). However, troll-caught chinook salmon H_ℓ/R mortality rates (Wertheimer et al. 1989), along with a "best guess" for the H_{Gut}/R mortality rate, were used to derive this estimate.

A pilot holding study was then initiated by California Department of Fish and Game (CDFG) Ocean Salmon Project (OSP) personnel to estimate the short-term (24–34 h) H_{Gut}/R mortality of chinook salmon drift mooch caught on light tackle using barbless 2/0 J-hooks (Grover 1995c). More than 51% of these gut-hooked fish died during holding. Necropsies revealed that most of these fish died due to severe injuries to the heart, liver, and stomach. In addition, Grover (1995c) reported that 98% of the gut-hooked fish that survived the short-term holding period would eventually die, due to the severity of observed internal damage.

In 1996, OSP staff investigated the use of barbless circle hooks and other terminal gear to lower the incidence of gut-hooked fish when drift mooching and, thereby, reduce the H/R mortality rate on released salmon (Grover and Palmer-Zwahlen 1996; Palmer-Zwahlen and Grover 1997). The study found that the use of circle hooks substantially reduced the frequency of gut-hooking, and beginning in September of 1997, the PFMC required the California drift mooch fishery to use (only) barbless circle hooks (PFMC 1997). However, the actual magnitude of the underlying H/R mortality rate was unclear, given that: (1) Orsi et al. (1993) surmised the H/R mortality rate for circle hook caught fish could be different than for J-hook caught fish; (2) the Wertheimer et al. (1989) H_ℓ/R mortality rates were based on troll-caught fish taken with heavy tackle and hooked on large, commercial-type, barbed J-hooks; and (3) the OSP pilot-study H_{Gut}/R mortality rate was a preliminary result based on a short-term holding study of fish caught on small J-hooks.

This paper presents the results of research specifically designed to estimate the overall H/R mortality rate for the California drift mooch fishery. The H_ℓ/R mortality rates are derived from an onboard holding study and applied to the fishery H_ℓ relative frequency (profile) to obtain an estimate of the fishery H/R mortality rate. The statistical uncertainty of this estimate is quantified using a variance estimator developed expressly for this purpose. The effects of circle hook

size and fish size on the H_ℓ profile are examined. We also report on the potential use of blood cortisol concentration, which has been used to indicate the severity of certain types of stressors in salmon (Fagerlund et al. 1995), as a measure of stress in tank-held fish mortality studies. Finally, we discuss the management challenges arising from the practice of California-style, drift mooch salmon fishing.

Methods

H_ℓ/R Mortality Rates

The study was conducted onboard the CDFG's 26-m research vessel *R/V Mako* for 21 days in June and July 1996 and 12 days during July 1997. Fishing occurred in nearshore waters between Salmon Creek and Pigeon Point (Figure 2). Ten 2.6-m, medium-weight, mooching rods with 6.8 kg leaders and 9 kg test lines were fished. Terminal gear used were Eagle Claw 3/0, 4/0, and 5/0 barbless "Circle Bait Seaguard" L-197 series hooks and Gamakatsu 5/0 and 6/0 barbless "Texas Bend Circle Hooks" (Figure 3). Whole northern anchovies *Engraulis mordax* were used as bait and were generally threaded on the hook in the "head down" direction (Figure 1). Anglers

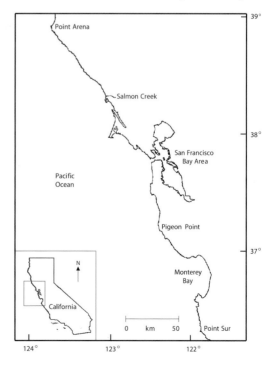

Figure 2. Map of study area.

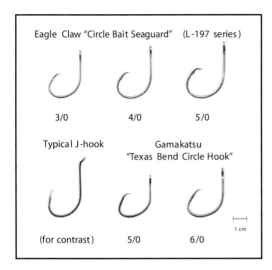

Figure 3. Circle hooks used when drift mooch fishing aboard the *R/V Mako*. Note that Gamakatsu 5/0 and 6/0 hooks are comparable in size to Eagle Claw 4/0 and 5/0 hooks, respectively. A typical J-hook is shown for contrast.

fished at depths of 5–20 m and were instructed to follow the hook manufacturer's (Eagle Claw) package directions—"On the take, do NOT set hook; just reel fish in"—rather than using the California-style, mooching method of feeding out line on the first bite to encourage the fish to swallow the bait and then setting the hook abruptly.

All salmon caught were landed with a soft, small-mesh, knotless net and placed immediately into a large plastic bag to reduce scaling and slime removal, as well as to increase the ease of restraining the fish while handling. Each "bagged" fish was then placed in a fish cradle to obtain an approximate total length (TL) and to allow a quick examination of hook wounds. Hooks were removed from all fish, except for gut-hooked fish, where the leader was cut as short as possible. All salmon were externally tagged just below the dorsal fin with a numbered Floy T-bar anchor tag (model FD-68B). Salmon less than 660-mm TL were placed in one of two 8,700-L, below-deck, live tanks for four days holding or released, depending on H_ℓ and tank densities at the time. Processing of the fish that were held generally took less than two minutes, from the time of initial hook-up to release into the tank.

Fresh seawater taken from 3 m below the ocean surface was pumped continuously into the bottom of each holding tank and overflowed at the top of

each tank into the ocean. The pumping rate was sufficient to replace the volume of each tank in 17 minutes. Fish were not fed. Tank stocking densities were maintained at less than 45 salmon per tank at all times. Fish were checked twice daily, at approximately 0600 and 1800 hours, by pumping the water out from the bottom of the tank to a level where all salmon could be seen from the top of the tank. The resulting water depth in each tank depended on both water clarity and tank stocking density but was never less than 1 m. Dead fish and those surviving four days were removed for further evaluation. Each fish, identified by tag number, was measured to the nearest mm TL and survival time recorded. Each hook wound was closely examined and its location (H_ℓ) classified as in Wertheimer (1988): eye, snout, maxillary, lower jaw, corner of mouth, cheek, isthmus, tongue, and gill. We also included three additional locations that occur when mooching: gut, palate, and fin (Figure 4). The "gut" location included all postpharyngeal wound locations, principally superficial epithelial tissues, the stomach, the liver, and the heart. Necropsies were performed on all fish to determine whether there was significant damage to

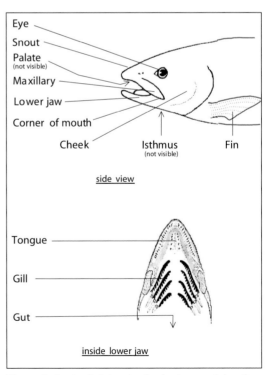

Figure 4. Anatomical key to the hook wound locations reported in this paper.

the internal organs.

Survival times were aggregated into 24 hour periods, from the date and time that individual fish were first captured and held. Mortalities were tabulated by day (1, 2, 3, 4) of occurrence and H_ℓ. Fish that were hooked in the gut and survived four days but whose internal organs were mortally damaged were designated as "day 4+" mortalities. Cumulative H_ℓ mortality rates by day were calculated by accumulating the observed mortalities across days and dividing by the initial number held. Locations with similar mortality rates were combined, yielding the following H_ℓ categories: (1) "Low," included "no wound," palate, snout, cheek, fin, isthmus, and tongue; (2) "Eye/gill," included eye and gill locations; (3) "Maxillary"; (4) "Corner of mouth"; (5) "Lower jaw"; and (6) "Gut." Fish with "no wound" were fish that were caught and retrieved but had dropped off the line at the time of netting and suffered no apparent hook wound.

Because the "Low" category consisted of no wound or superficial wound locations, it was treated as a surrogate control group, and its day 4+ cumulative mortality rate used as an estimate of the mortality rate due to the effects of handling and holding alone. The rates of the remaining categories were then adjusted to eliminate these effects, assuming (1) the handling/holding instantaneous mortality rate was the same for all categories, and (2) wound and handling/holding effects acted as two competing risks of death. In this case, results from the standard two risk (natural and fishery) mortality model (Ricker 1975, equation 1.14) apply, where the conditional fishing (wound) mortality rate may be solved for given the total (wound and handling/holding) mortality rate and the conditional natural (handling/holding) mortality rate. Specifically, denoting by $\ell = 1, 2, 3, 4, 5, 6$ the H_ℓ categories as numbered in the preceding paragraph (with $H_1 = H_{\text{Low}}$), and by $\hat{r}_\ell$ the day 4+ cumulative mortality rate estimates, the adjusted day 4+ rates $\hat{q}_\ell$ were calculated as:

$$\hat{q}_\ell = \frac{\hat{r}_\ell - \hat{r}_{\text{Low}}}{1 - \hat{r}_{\text{Low}}}. \qquad (1)$$

This formula is valid "regardless of whether the two causes of death operate concurrently, or consecutively, or in any intermediate fashion" (Ricker 1975, page 11). In particular, equation (1) is valid for the gut-hooked group as well, even though the

day 4+ mortalities do not include the effects of handling and holding. The competing risks adjustment acts to increase the rate over that otherwise obtained by simply subtracting off the control-group rate; with the risks of handling and holding removed, additional fish may die from the hook wound itself. The resulting $\{\hat{q}_\ell\}$ served as estimates of the H_ℓ/R mortality rates in this paper.

Fishery H/R Mortality Rate

The overall *H/R* mortality rate for the drift mooch ocean salmon sport fishery in California additionally depends on the fishery's H_ℓ profile. From September 1997 to October 2000, OSP staff directly observed circle hook H_ℓ frequencies on salmon less than 660-mm TL aboard commercial passenger fishing vessels (CPFVs) fishing out of the San Francisco and Monterey port areas in nearshore waters between Point Arena and Point Sur (Figure 2). For the July–August 1998, and August 1999 periods, these observations were made while "first-two fish" regulations were in place. These regulations required anglers to keep the first two chinook salmon caught, regardless of size, and this allowed observers to make an accurate assessment of the H_ℓ and TL of all salmon, including those normally considered sublegal size. In the remaining periods, when a minimum size limit was in effect, sublegal size fish were retained momentarily next to the boat by CPFV deckhands, to allow our observers to assess the H_ℓ and to estimate TL to the nearest inch prior to releasing the fish. Legal size fish were brought aboard and accurately assessed. The fishery H_ℓ frequencies from all periods were combined and classified into the $\ell = 1, 2, 3, 4, 5, 6$ categories given above, and the relative frequencies $\{\hat{w}_\ell\}$ (profile) calculated.

The fishery *H/R* mortality rate, p, was then estimated as a weighted average of the H_ℓ/R mortality rates:

$$\hat{p} = \sum_{\ell=1}^{6} \hat{w}_\ell \hat{q}_\ell. \qquad (2)$$

For purposes of contrast only, we also estimated the *H/R* mortality rate for the non-gut-hooked class of fish by renormalizing the $\{\hat{w}_\ell\}$ profile over the nongut H_ℓ and applying equation (2) over this restricted set. The sampling variance of the estimator, $V(\hat{p})$, depends on the variances and covariances of $\{\hat{w}_\ell\}$ and $\{\hat{q}_\ell\}$. An estimator $\hat{V}(\hat{p})$ for $V(\hat{p})$ is derived in the appendix (equation A15) under assumption that the fishery H_ℓ frequencies are multinomially distributed and the day 4+ unadjusted cumulative mortalities are independent binomial variables. A confidence interval for p was constructed as $\hat{p} \pm 2SE$, where $SE = \sqrt{\hat{V}(\hat{p})}$.

To further evaluate the statistical properties of $\hat{p}$ and $\hat{V}(\hat{p})$ as estimators of p and $V(\hat{p})$, the sampling distributions of $\hat{p}$ and $\hat{V}(\hat{p})$ were constructed empirically, conditional on the study design. Denote by $\{\hat{r}_\ell^{obs}\}$ the observed day 4+ mortality rates, based on observed sample sizes $\{m_\ell^{obs}\}$, and denote by $\{\hat{w}_\ell^{obs}\}$ the observed fishery H_ℓ relative frequencies, based on the observed sample size n^{obs}. We used these realized values as parameters to stochastically generate 50,000 artificial data sets, assuming *multinomial* $(n^{obs}; \{\hat{w}_\ell^{obs}\})$ H_ℓ frequencies and $\{binomial\ (m_\ell^{obs}; \hat{r}_\ell^{obs})$, $\ell = 1, 2, 3, 4, 5, 6\}$ cumulative day 4+ holding tank mortalities. For each simulated data set, we calculated estimates $\{\hat{w}_\ell\}$, $\{\hat{r}_\ell\}$, and $\{\hat{q}_\ell\}$, and from them calculated $\hat{p}$, $\hat{V}(\hat{p})$, and the interval $\hat{p} \pm 2SE$. The mean value of $\hat{p}$ over the 50,000 data sets was then compared with the "true" value $\hat{p}^{obs}$ for an empirical assessment of the $\hat{p}$ estimator sampling bias. Similarly, the mean value of $\hat{V}(\hat{p})$ over the 50,000 data sets was compared with the observed variance of $\hat{p}$ over the 50,000 data sets ($\approx V(\hat{p})$) for an empirical assessment of the $\hat{V}(\hat{p})$ estimator sampling bias. Finally, the fraction of intervals containing the "true" value $\hat{p}^{obs}$ over the 50,000 data sets provided an empirical assessment of the coverage probability associated with a $\hat{p} \pm 2SE$ interval, interpreted to represent a 95% confidence interval. These empirical assessments are conditional on the assumed model structure and parameter values.

H_ℓ Dependence on Hook Size, Fish Length

To evaluate the dependence of the H_ℓ profile on size of circle hook and fish length, all fish less than 660-mm TL that were caught aboard the *R/V Mako* with the bait threaded on the hook in the "head down" direction were cross-classified according to Eagle Claw circle hook size (3/0, 4/0, 5/0) and fish length class (TL < 508 mm, 508 mm ≤ TL < 660 mm). The Gamakatsu Texas Bend 5/0 and 6/0 hooks are comparable in size to Eagle Claw 4/0 and 5/0 hooks, respectively (Figure 3), and were treated as such in the analysis. The length-class boundaries used correspond to the two minimum size limits (508 mm, 660 mm) most commonly used in regulating California ocean salmon fisheries.

The H_ℓ frequencies for the hook × length combinations were regarded as independent multinomial outcomes, and a generalized logit model (Agresti 1990) appropriate for such data was used to examine the influence of hook size (*Hook*) and fish length class (*Length*) on the H_ℓ profile $\{w_\ell\}$. The model assumes that the log-odds of each location (ℓ) relative to the *gut* location is an anova-like function of the *Hook* and *Length* effects:

$$\log(w_\ell / w_{\text{Gut}}) = \alpha_\ell + \beta_{h\ell}^{Hook} + \beta_{i\ell}^{Length}, \quad (3)$$

where h indexes hook size, i indexes fish length class, and all α and β parameters are location-specific (ℓ). We employed the SAS computer program CATMOD (SAS Institute Inc., Cary, North Carolina, USA) to fit the model using maximum likelihood and to compute the associated likelihood-ratio goodness-of-fit statistic, G^2. The G^2 statistic is distributed as a chi-square variable, assuming the model provides a satisfactory representation of the data (Agresti 1990).

Cortisol Levels

To investigate the potential use of blood cortisol level as an indicator of stress in fish mortality holding studies, we collected blood from a sample of fish taken directly from the ocean and from a sample of tank-held fish that survived for four days. The ocean-caught fish were taken aboard the *R/V Mako* during the holding study, landed within one minute, immediately sacrificed, and 5 mL of blood drawn to determine baseline cortisol levels. The elapsed time (t) between initial hook-up and sacrifice was recorded. The tank-held fish were netted and immediately sacrificed as the holding tanks were pumped down to a level of 1 m. It then required up to 1.5 hours of continual "net-chasing" to retrieve all of the remaining fish, and it was hypothesized that the cortisol concentration in these fish would be an increasing function of the time under pursuit. Once netted from the tank, fish were immediately sacrificed and their blood drawn, as above. The elapsed time (t) between initiating tank pumpdown and sacrifice was recorded. In all cases, each blood sample was spun down for 10 minutes, the plasma collected in two 1.5-mL aliquots, frozen, and given to C. B. Schreck (Oregon Cooperative Fish and Wildlife Research Unit), who determined the cortisol concentration using the assay method of Redding et al. (1984b).

For juvenile coho salmon, Sumpter et al. (1986) and Fagerlund et al. (1995) found a four to eight minute lag time in cortisol level response to a stress stimulus, and Fagerlund (1967) suggested similar cortisol levels are to be expected for resting adult and juvenile salmon. Thus, to provide a measure of the holding-related and wound-related stress experienced by the tank-held fish, we compared the mean cortisol level of ocean-caught fish to that of tank-held fish netted within four minutes of initiating tank pumpdown. In addition, we compared the cortisol levels of gut-hooked and nongut-hooked fish and, for the tank-held fish, examined the time-trend in cortisol level, starting with initiation of tank pumpdown. For the two-sample mean comparisons, we used the Satterthwaite-version of the t-test (Snedecor and Cochran 1989), which is appropriate when the two underlying population variances are unequal.

Results

During the *R/V Mako* study, 354 chinook salmon less than 660 mm TL were caught drift mooching with the bait threaded on the hook in the "head down" direction, using 3/0, 4/0, and 5/0 barbless circle hooks. A total of 276 fish were held for four days H_ℓ mortality evaluation, and an additional 27 fish were used to establish baseline cortisol levels.

H_ℓ/R Mortality Rates

No mortalities occurred within the first 24 hours (day 1) of holding, except for gut-hooked fish (Table 1). The increase in the cumulative mortality rates across the holding period lessened on day 4 in all categories (Table 2; Figure 5).

The surrogate control group ("Low") consisted of 21 salmon hooked in locations we considered to be nonlethal, including 11 for which no wound was apparent. Most of these 11 fish were never hooked; they simply held on to the bait until they were netted. Only one mortality occurred in the "Low" group during the four day holding period (on day 3) and

Table 1. Number of chinook salmon (< 660 mm TL) held and subsequent mortality by hook wound location (H_ℓ) during the four day *R/V Mako* holding study. Mortalities grouped by day (1, 2, 3, 4) of occurance. "Low" is a combination of non-wounded or superficially-wounded fish. Additional mortalities expected beyond day 4 (see text for explanation) are listed under "4+".

H_ℓ	Number held	Number of mortalities by day				
		1	2	3	4	4+
Low						
No wound	11	0	0	1	0	.
Pallet	5	0	0	0	0	.
Snout	3	0	0	0	0	.
Cheek	1	0	0	0	0	.
Fin	1	0	0	0	0	.
Isthmus	0	.	.	.	.	.
Tongue	0	.	.	.	.	.
	21	0	0	1	0	.
Maxillary	58	0	0	3	2	.
Corner of mouth	36	0	0	4	2	.
Lower jaw	67	0	3	8	4	.
Eye / gill						
Eye	39	0	0	12	6	.
Gill	2	0	0	0	1	.
	41	0	0	12	7	.
Gut	53	13	6	6	5	15
Total	276	13	9	34	20	15

Table 2. Hook wound location (H_ℓ) cumulative mortality rates for chinook salmon over the four day holding period, and final adjusted rates. The rates by day were calculated by accumulating the observed mortalitites (Table 1) across days and dividing by the initial number held, m_ℓ. The $\hat{r}_\ell$ rate includes the day 4+ mortalities, and the $\hat{q}_\ell$ rate is the $\hat{r}_\ell$ rate adjusted for the effects of handling and holding (Equation (1)). The $\{\hat{q}_\ell\}$ serve as estimates of the H_ℓ/R mortality rates in this paper.

	Number held	*Cumulative mortality rate by day*					
H_ℓ	m_ℓ	*1*	*2*	*3*	*4*	$\hat{r}_\ell$	$\hat{q}_\ell$
Low (control group)	21	0	0	0.048	0.048	0.048	0
Maxillary	58	0	0	0.052	0.086	0.086	0.041
Corner of mouth	36	0	0	0.111	0.167	0.167	0.125
Lower jaw	67	0	0.045	0.164	0.224	0.224	0.185
Eye / gill	41	0	0	0.293	0.463	0.463	0.437
Gut	53	0.245	0.358	0.472	0.566	0.849	0.842

was attributed to the effects of handling and holding, since this fish suffered no apparent hook wound (Table 1). The four day cumulative mortality rate for this group was 0.048 (Table 2).

For the "Maxillary," "Corner of mouth," "Lower jaw," and "Eye/gill" locations, the sample size was 58, 36, 67, and 41 fish, respectively. No mortalities occurred until the third day of holding for these locations, except for the "Lower jaw" group, in which 3 of 67 fish died on day two (Table 1). The four day cumulative mortality rate for the "Eye/gill" location was very high (0.463) relative to these other locations, where the four day rates ranged from 0.086 to 0.224 (Table 2).

Mortalities occurred in the gut-hooked group

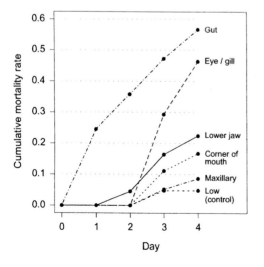

Figure 5. Cumulative mortality rate trends over the four day holding period by hook wound location category.

throughout the holding period (Table 1). Of the 53 fish initially held, 24.5% died within the first 24 hours, and the cumulative mortality rate climbed steadily thereafter, resulting in a four day rate of 0.566 (Table 2; Figure 5). The steady death toll for the gut-hooked fish over the four day holding period strongly suggested that, were the experiment to be continued beyond four days, additional mortalities would have been observed. Following the four day holding period, necropsies were performed on the 23 surviving gut-hooked fish, and 15 of them were found to have suffered major internal damage to the stomach, heart, or liver (Figure 6). We believe the severity and nature of these wounds indicated that near-term death was highly probable for these 15 fish. We designated this postholding, inferred mortality as "day 4+" mortality in Table 1. Including these 15 fish as mortalities yielded a "day 4+" cumulative mortality rate for the gut-hooked group of $\hat{r}_{Gut}$ = 0.849, an increase of 0.283 over the four day rate of 0.566 (Table 2). No adjustment was made for the other groups; for these, their "day 4+" cumulative mortality rate, $\hat{r}_\ell$, was identical to their four day rate.

The $\{\hat{r}_\ell\}$ were then adjusted to eliminate mortality caused by handling and holding (as estimated by $\hat{r}_{Low}$ = 0.048), using equation (1). The lower the $\hat{r}_\ell$ value, the greater the adjustment, both in absolute and relative terms. The adjusted rates, $\{\hat{q}_\ell\}$, are this study's H_ℓ/R mortality rate estimates (Table 2).

Fishery H/R Mortality Rate

A total of 522 H_ℓ observations were made aboard CPFVs, of which 223 (43%) were made during "first- two fish" fisheries. The relative frequency of gut-hooked fish was 0.406 (Table 3), with most of

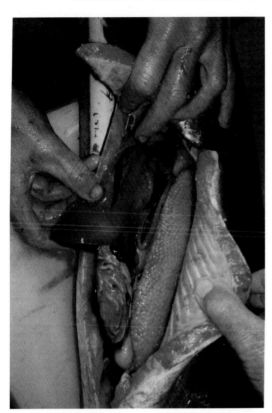

Figure 6. Illustration of the severity of internal wounds (here a hook-torn liver and stomach) and amount of bleeding that often results when a salmon has been gut-hooked using the California-style drift mooch fishing technique.

Table 3. Hook wound location (H_ℓ) profile estimate for California's recreational drift mooch circle hook chinook salmon fishery, and resulting H/R mortality rate estimate. Sample frequencies $\{f_\ell\}$ and relative frequencies $\{\hat{w}_\ell\}$ collected aboard CPFVs, 1997–2000; all fish < 660 mm TL. The $\{\hat{q}_\ell\}$ are the H_ℓ/R mortality rate estimates from Table 2. The sum of the $\{\hat{w}_\ell\hat{q}_\ell\}$ is the fishery H/R mortality rate estimate, $\hat{p}$.

H_ℓ	Fishery profile f_ℓ	$\hat{w}_\ell$	$\hat{q}_\ell$	$\hat{w}_\ell\hat{q}_\ell$
Low	33	0.063	0	0
Maxillary	82	0.157	0.041	0.006
Corner of mouth	97	0.186	0.125	0.023
Lower jaw	66	0.126	0.185	0.023
Eye / gill	32	0.061	0.437	0.027
Gut	212	0.406	0.842	0.342
Total	$n = 522$			$\hat{p} = 0.422$

slightly skewed from normal to the left (Figure 7), but $\hat{p}$ and $\hat{V}(\hat{p})$ are essentially unbiased, their empirical expectations found to be within 1% and 4% of the respective targets p and $V(\hat{p})$. The target p was contained in 94.7% of the simulated intervals, confirming the interpretation of $\hat{p} \pm 2SE$ as a 95% confidence interval.

H_ℓ Dependence on Hook Size, Fish Length

R/V Mako drift mooch H_ℓ frequencies cross-classified by hook size and fish-length class indicated that for every hook × length combination, the proportion of fish that were gut hooked was at least 0.20, except in the case of small fish (TL < 508 mm) caught on a 5/0 hook where gut-hooking was a rare event (0.04; Table 4). While the two length classes have very sim-

the remaining frequency distributed fairly evenly into the "Maxillary" (0.157), "Corner of mouth" (0.186), and "Lower jaw" (0.126) locations. A smaller fraction was caught in each of the "Eye/gill" (0.061) and "Low" (0.063) locations.

Weighting the H_ℓ/R mortality rates $\{\hat{q}_\ell\}$ by the H_ℓ profile $\{\hat{w}_\ell\}$ yielded a fishery H/R mortality rate estimate of $\hat{p} = 0.422$ (Table 3). The "Gut" location dominates this calculation, with more than 40% of the fish being gut hooked, and more than 84% of these expected to die, if released. The estimated sampling variance of $\hat{p}$ was $\hat{V}(\hat{p}) = 0.0016$, giving a confidence interval for p of

$$\hat{p} \pm 2SE = 0.422 \pm 0.08. \qquad (4)$$

For the nongut-hooked class of fish, the estimated H/R mortality rate was considerably less: 0.134 ± 0.094.

The sampling distribution for $\hat{p}$ was found to be

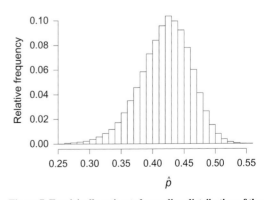

Figure 7. Empirically estimated sampling distribution of the H/R mortality rate estimator $\hat{p}$, conditional on this paper's study design (see text for explanation). Note that the distribution is slightly skewed from normal to the left.

ilar marginal frequencies, there are considerable differences among the within-hook H_ℓ profiles and among the within-length H_ℓ profiles.

Hook size and fish length, taken alone or as additive effects in the generalized logit model, did not provide a satisfactory fit of these data (Table 5). The low *P*-values indicate that there is a significant amount of interaction between the two factors; the effect of hook size on the H_ℓ profile depends on fish length (Table 5). This interaction is due in part to variation in the gut-hooking pattern (Table 4). For the smaller fish, the proportion gut-hooked declined steadily from 0.40 (most likely location) to 0.04 (least likely location), as hook size was increased from 3/0 to 4/0 to 5/0. For the larger fish caught on 4/0 and 5/0 hooks, the odds of gut-hooking was greater than for smaller fish, and the rate of gut-

hooking again declined as hook size was increased from 4/0 to 5/0. But these trends were interrupted by larger fish caught on 3/0 hooks, where the odds of being gut-hooked was half that for the smaller fish and nearly half that for those caught on 4/0 hooks. For these larger fish caught on 3/0 hooks, there was a corresponding rise in the proportion maxillary-hooked (0.42), which was double that for the smaller fish and for those caught on 4/0 hooks.

Cortisol Levels

A total of 27 ocean-caught fish and 84 tank-held fish that survived the four days holding period were sacrificed to determine the concentration of cortisol in their blood. Of the 84 tank-held fish, 16 were sampled within four minutes of initiating tank pump-down ($t \leq 4$ minutes; Table 6). The within-group

Table 4: Drift mooch hook wound location (H_ℓ) profile data by circle hook size and fish-length class. Sample frequencies $\{f_\ell\}$ and relative frequencies $\{\hat{w}_\ell\}$ collected aboard the *R/V Mako*, 1996–1997, with the bait threaded on the hook in the "Head down" direction. Circle hook size refers to Eagle Claw L-197 series scale (Figure 3). Gamakatsu 5/0 and 6/0 hooks were considered equivalent in size to Eagle Claw 4/0 and 5/0 hooks, respectively.

| | Circle hook size | | | | | | | |
| | 3/0 | | 4/0 | | 5/0 | | Total | |
H_ℓ	f_ℓ	$\hat{w}_\ell$	f_ℓ	$\hat{w}_\ell$	f_ℓ	$\hat{w}_\ell$	f_ℓ	$\hat{w}_\ell$
			TL < 508 mm					
Low	3	0.07	11	0.11	5	0.20	19	0.11
Maxillary	10	0.23	12	0.12	5	0.20	27	0.16
Corner of mouth	5	0.12	15	0.15	2	0.08	22	0.13
Lower jaw	6	0.14	23	0.22	8	0.32	37	0.22
Eye / gill	2	0.05	15	0.15	4	0.16	21	0.12
Gut	17	0.40	27	0.26	1	0.04	45	0.26
Total	43		103		25		171	
			508 mm ≤ TL < 660 mm					
Low	7	0.13	0	0.00	5	0.09	12	0.07
Maxillary	23	0.42	16	0.22	9	0.16	48	0.26
Corner of mouth	5	0.09	6	0.08	15	0.27	26	0.14
Lower jaw	5	0.09	10	0.14	12	0.21	27	0.15
Eye / gill	4	0.07	14	0.19	4	0.07	22	0.12
Gut	11	0.20	26	0.36	11	0.20	48	0.26
Total	55		72		56		183	

Table 5. Summary of generalized logit model (Equation (3)) fits to the *R/V Mako* H_ℓ profile data (Table 4). G^2 is the likelihood ratio statistic, *df* is the degrees of freedom, and *P* is the tail probability of the corresponding chi-square distribution. The low *P*-values indicate a significant lack of fit due to the presence of interaction.

Model	G^2	df	P
Hook size	37.90	15	0.001
Length class	61.83	20	< 0.001
Hook + length	26.91	10	0.003

Table 6. Blood cortisol concentration summary statistics for ocean-caught and tank-held chinook salmon in the *R/V Mako* study. For the ocean-caught group, "elapsed time" refers to minutes between initial hook-up and sacrifice. For the tank-held fish, "elapsed time" refers to minutes between the initiation of tank pumpdown and sacrifice. *N* denotes sample size, and "SD" denotes standard deviation.

Elapsed time (t)	N	Cortisol (mg/mL)			
		Minimum	Mean	Maximum	SD
		ocean-caught			
t ≤ 4 min	27	2.3	60.7	201.5	51.6
		tank-held			
t ≤ 4 min	16	30.8	211.4	403.3	117.4
t > 4 min	68	38.9	186.6	571.4	86.0
tank, all t	84	30.8	191.3	571.4	92.5

concentration was highly variable, particularly among the tank-held fish. However, this variation did not obscure the large difference in the mean levels of the ocean-caught (60.7 ng/mL) and "tank-held, t less than or equal to four minutes" (211.4 ng/mL) groups ($P < 0.0001$); on average, fish that survived four day holding had higher levels of cortisol than did fish just taken from the ocean (Table 6). For the two tank-held groups, t less than or equal to four minutes and t greater than four minutes, the mean levels were similar and not significantly different ($P = 0.78$), indicating that the protracted period of tank pumpdown and "net-chasing" did not act to further elevate the average cortisol level.

The 111 individual cortisol concentrations plotted against elapsed time show the considerable variation present in these data (Figure 8). The maximum observed value of 571.4 ng/mL is 250 times that of the minimum value 2.3 ng/mL. Two tank-held fish had unusually high concentrations of 419.6 ng/mL at $t = 46$ minutes, and 571.4 ng/mL at $t = 79$ minutes; both were gut hooked (Figure 8). In general, however, the variation in cortisol among tank-held fish actually diminished with increasing t, while the average remained unaffected. There was no evidence to suggest (except perhaps for the two outliers) that either ocean-caught or tank-held, gut-hooked fish had higher cortisol levels than their counterparts (Figure 8).

Discussion

Ocean salmon *H/R* studies have employed a variety of means to process, transfer, and hold fish. For example, Wertheimer (1988) and Wertheimer et al. (1989) stunned individual fish with an electrically-charged basket for processing and then held them in onboard 175-L tanks prior to placing them in large, deep net-pens; total transfer time (from capture/netting to final holding environment) was less than one hour. Other investigators (NRC 1991, 1994) used MS-222 or physical restraint to process fish and held fish in 375-L tanks and 113-L ice chests prior to placing them in net-pens; total transfer time was less than six hours. Cox-Rogers (1998) initially placed fish in individual flow-through bags tethered to the stern of the fishing vessel, transferred the fish to a 300-L tank aboard a transport vessel, and then transferred them a second time to a live-hold vessel where physical restraint was used to process the fish prior to their release into 1230-L onboard tanks; total transfer time was not reported. All of these studies reported mortalities within the first 24 hours of holding, in non-gut-hooked fish, and several reported that most of the observed mortalities occurred during this initial 24 hour period.

In this study, fish were netted at the side of the boat, within 30 seconds to 5 minutes of being hooked, and immediately placed in a plastic bag for processing. Fish were then released into 8,700-L (3 m deep), onboard, holding tanks, where they remained for the four day holding period. Total elapsed time, from initial netting to release into the holding tanks, ranged from 30 seconds to 2 minutes and was usually less than 1 minute. Once in the holding tank, fish were observed to swim slowly around the tank from top to bottom in an elliptical pattern. Using these handling techniques and holding environment, we observed no mortalities in the first 24 hours of holding, except in the case of gut-hooked fish.

Most holding-based *H/R* mortality studies have

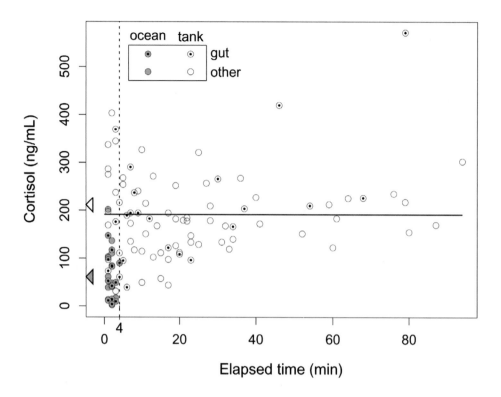

Figure 8. Blood cortisol concentration (ng/mL) versus elapsed time for ocean-caught and tank-held chinook salmon in the ***R/V Mako*** **study. For the ocean-caught fish, "elasped time" refers to minutes between initial hook-up and sacrifice. For the tank-held fish, "elapsed time" refers to minutes between the initiation of tank pumpdown and sacrifice. Shaded circles represent ocean-caught ("ocean") fish; unshaded circles represent tank-held ("tank") fish. Gut-hooked fish are marked by a center-dot within the circle. Vertical dashed line delineates four minute mark. Shaded triangle at left axis indicates mean concentration for ocean-caught fish; unshaded triangle indicates mean concentration for tank-held fish with elapsed time less than or equal to four minutes; horizontal line indicates mean concentration for all tank-held fish.**

been unable to catch and hold a "control group" of fish, a prerequisite for estimating the portion of observed mortality due to the experimental handling and holding of wild salmon. The fishing technique examined in this study (drift mooching using circle hooks) was fortuitous in this regard, in that fish were occasionally brought to the boat and netted without the hook having been set. These individuals, together with fish having only superficial hook wounds, formed a surrogate control group from which we were able to estimate the experimental mortality attributable to handling and holding, alone (1 out of 21, over 4 days), and to adjust our observed mortality rates accordingly.

The large difference between the 24 hour mortality rate reported in this paper and other values that have been reported in the literature leads us to believe that the 24 hour mortalities observed in other stud-

ies are largely attributable to the added stresses of small-tank confinement, multiple transfers, or prolonged processing and preholding periods. Wertheimer (1988) found a significant, but weak, positive relationship between live tank-holding time and mortality. Strange and Schreck (1978, 1980) and Strange et al. (1979) demonstrated an elevation of cortisol and increased mortality in juvenile chinook salmon following transfer and confinement, and Sumpter et al. (1986) demonstrated an increase in stress (as measured by changes in plasma ACTH and cortisol) in juvenile coho salmon subjected to handling and confinement. In the previously described *H/R* mortality studies, fish that died within 24 hours of confinement due to handling and holding stress alone may have subsequently died from their hook wounds at a later date, absent this stress, but there is no way to disentangle the effects of these two sources of mortality without a control group.

We attempted, in this study, to directly measure stress experienced by tank-held fish and its repercussions, but our results were decidedly mixed. We were able to introduce to the literature "baseline" blood cortisol levels for free-ranging ocean chinook salmon; stress hormone work on salmonids, by and large, has been conducted in freshwater (Redding et al. 1984a; Strange and Schreck 1978; Schreck and Lorz 1978). We were also able to provide an estimate of the maximum cortisol response to stress in chinook salmon taken from the ocean. Based on their blood cortisol concentration, we determined that the four day, tank-held, surviving fish were indeed more stressed on average than those fish just taken from the ocean, despite the considerable response variation among individuals. However, we were unable to explain this result in terms of either the physiological expression of stress or the manner in which fish were sampled from the tank at the end of the four day holding period. Our results are in general agreement with Fagerlund et al. (1995), who reported that cortisol concentrations in Pacific salmon under presumably stress-free conditions vary widely, and we would add that this is also true for salmon exposed to chronic stress. We were also unable to make any inferences regarding the likelihood of delayed mortality in tank-held, four day survivors based on their blood cortisol concentration; on average, fish with gut wounds appeared to be no more stressed than other survivors. Finally, we observed no difference in the mean cortisol concentration among tank-held, four day survivors that were immediately sacrificed versus those that experienced tank pumpdown and net chasing. Perhaps this resulted from an increased cortisol clearance rate in the maximally stressed fish, as has been demonstrated in yearling coho salmon (Redding et al. 1984a), and/or perhaps the chronic stress of confinement experienced by all of these fish over the four day period inhibited further increases in the cortisol response, due to a suppression of the cortisol secretion rate (Redding et al. 1984a). In either case, it appears that, on average, the surviving fish were maximally stressed at the end of the holding period.

The mortality rate of gut-hooked chinook salmon caught in the ocean on barbless circle hooks, provided in this paper, is the first such estimate to appear in the literature. This wound/hook type is infrequent in ocean salmon fisheries, outside of the recently developed drift mooch fishery off California (Grover 1995a, 1995b). Only gut-hooked fish died in the first 24 hours, while the cumulative mortality rate for these fish increased at a steady rate over the four day holding period. Because gut hooking often results in severe internal injuries, we necropsied the four day survivors and found that near-term death ("delayed mortality") was highly probable in 15 of the remaining 23 fish. Obtaining an estimate of delayed mortality, particularly when it is this high, is essential, if the mortality rates derived from holding-based studies are to be applied meaningfully in a harvest management setting.

Among the other hook-wound locations, the highest H_ℓ/R mortality rate obtained was 0.437 for the "Eye/gill" category (all but two of the fish in this category were eye-wounded fish). Extracting a circle hook from an eye-hooked salmon is difficult because the point exits the eye orbit from the inside, and the shank limits the rotation of the hook to a circular direction, which results in the point cutting or tearing its way out of the tissue, causing additional damage to the eye tissue. Consequently, this may have contributed to the high mortality rate observed for this H_ℓ. Our rate of 0.437 for this H_ℓ is higher than the eye-specific rates of 0.261 and 0.219, obtained by Wertheimer (1988) and Wertheimer et al. (1989), respectively. However, Wertheimer (1988) noted that many of the eye-hooked fish encountered in that study had their eye destroyed or torn out, and that, as a consequence, additional mortality would be expected to occur beyond that observed during that study's holding period. We note that, even though the "Eye/gill" mortality rate is high, the relative frequency of this H_ℓ in the drift mooch fishery is low (0.061), and thus, the fishery H/R mortality rate estimate is insensitive to its value.

The H_ℓ/R mortality rates obtained for the "Lower jaw" and "Maxillary" locations, 0.185 and 0.041, respectively, were comparable to those reported by: Wertheimer et al. (1989), 0.176 and 0.040, respectively; and Wertheimer (1988), 0.234 and 0.059, respectively. For the "Corner of mouth" location, we estimated an H_ℓ/R mortality rate of 0.125, about twice the rates of 0.054 and 0.076 obtained by Wertheimer et al. (1989) and Wertheimer (1988), respectively. Given the substantial underlying differences between these studies and ours, in terms of gear, methods, and holding environment, the general level of between-study agreement among these nongut H_ℓ/R mortality rates is somewhat remarkable.

The effect of hook size on the *R/V Mako* H_ℓ profile was dependent on fish size, and this interaction was due in part to variation in the gut-hooking pattern between the two size-classes of fish. Fish less than 508-mm TL, caught on smaller (3/0) hooks were mostly gut hooked, but those caught on larger (5/0) hooks were rarely gut hooked. This trend in the gut-hooking rate for fish less than 508-mm TL was also observed by Grover and Palmer-Zwahlen (1996), who found that the gut-hooking rate could be further reduced if 5/0 hooks were used with the bait threaded on the hook in the "head up" direction. Grover and Palmer-Zwahlen (1996) speculated further that the contact rate, itself, on fish less than 508-mm TL is also reduced with the use of large circle hooks.

We did not include the *R/V Mako* H_ℓ profile with the fishery H_ℓ profile in estimating the fishery H/R mortality rate, for the following reasons. First, on the *R/V Mako*, we controlled for hook size and targeted on small fish, and we have shown that both of these factors affect the H_ℓ profile. Second, when catching fish aboard the *R/V Mako*, we did not feed line on the bite and "jerk-set" the hook on the take (both standard techniques used by California anglers), and this altered the percentage of gut-hooked fish. "Line-feeding and jerk-setting," along with the fact that both anglers and tackle retailers often increase the offset of the hook, are at least partially responsible for the fishery's elevated gut-hooking rate.

In 1999, the PFMC's STT reviewed the salmon recreational H/R mortality literature, along with recent unpublished studies, and recommended that a single value be used in assessing all PFMC recreational fisheries, except California-style drift mooching (STT 2000). For this value, the STT first took the median (0.10) of the 24 hour rates from all studies with sample sizes of at least 50 fish, then scaled this value by 1.25 to estimate the corresponding four day rate [scalar based on NRC (1994, 1999) data], and further scaled this value by 1.13 to account for delayed mortality based on a recommendation of the Pacific Salmon Commission's Chinook Technical Committee (PSC 1997). The resulting value of 0.14 was adopted by the PFMC for use in its chinook and coho recreational-harvest

models, except in the case of the California drift mooch fishery. For this fishery's H/R mortality rate, the PFMC deferred to the CDFG, and we have presented in this paper the derivation of that rate: 0.422 ± 0.08. It is interesting to note, however, that for the nongut-hooked class of fish, our point estimate of the H/R mortality rate was 0.134. While remarkably close to the STT estimate of 0.14, it is perhaps not that surprising, given the extremely low frequency of gut-hooking in recreational troll fisheries (Grover 1995a, 1995b).

Hook-and-release mortality is a significant component of nonretention mortality in species-selective, mark-selective, or size-selective fisheries (Lawson and Sampson 1996). By requiring the use of (only) barbless circle hooks in the California drift mooch fishery, the H/R mortality rate has been reduced from an estimated 0.59 for J-hooks (Grover and Palmer-Zwahlen 1996) to an estimated 0.422. Because a number of additional factors can influence the gut-hooking rate, such as hook size, bait orientation, line feeding, and potentially the degree of hook offset, additional regulations could be crafted to further lower the H/R mortality in this fishery. Alternatively, H/R mortality could be reduced, by altogether banning drift mooching or simply prohibiting H/R fishing and reducing the angler bag limit. However, the effectiveness of such measures would depend on angler compliance. Regulation enforcement officials have pointed out the inherent difficulties of enforcing the circle hook requirement, and of enforcing the occasional prohibition on H/R fishing while simultaneously enforcing the ESA requirement of coho salmon nonretention off California. It would be even more difficult to enforce hook size, degree of hook offset, bait orientation, and line feeding (behavioral) requirements. Drift mooching in California has become important to the economics of the local fishing industry, and banning it altogether would cause economic hardship to local communities. However, a sincere effort to educate anglers on the use of methods that reduce the probability of gut hooking may prove successful. Perhaps the industry is not fully aware that the high H/R mortality rate associated with drift mooching leads to a shorter fishing season than would otherwise be available. If this fact were made clear, the industry might voluntarily choose to use fishing gear and methods that reduce the gut-hooking rate. Because the estimator for the fishery H/R mortality rate is formulated as a weighted average of the H_ℓ/R rates, this estimate can be easily updated in the future, should there be a shift in this fishery's H_ℓ profile.

Acknowledgments

We thank all of the OSP staff and CDFG volunteers who participated in this study; Roger Thomas and Harry Garabedian of the Golden Gate Fishermen's Association, and Jonah Li of Hi's Tackle Shop, for their expert advise and technical support; Bob Schroth of Gamakatsu and Linda Martin of McGill and Wright Co/Eagle Claw for supplying the various hooks used; Carl Schreck and Elizabeth Siddens of Oregon State University for assisting in the design of the cortisol study and processing the blood plasma samples; William Cox, CDFG Senior Fish Pathologist, for training OSP staff in proper blood extraction and plasma collection procedures; Gene Fowler of Pomona College and Michael Lacy of CDFG Listed Salmonids for their review of our cortisol findings; and the three anonymous referees of this manuscript for their constructive criticism. Our sincere thanks to Rod McGinnis and Dan Viele of NMFS Southwest Region for securing funding and participating in the study development; and to Matt Erickson and Scott Barrow of OSP for assisting with the preparation of the manuscript figures. Finally, we extend a special thanks to LB Boydstun, CDFG Intergovernmental Affairs, for his continuing encouragement, advice, and support throughout our studies.

References

Agresti, A. 1990. Categorical data analysis. Wiley, New York.

Cochran, W. G. 1977. Sampling techniques, 3rd edition. Wiley, New York.

Cox-Rogers, S. 1998. Catch and release mortality rates for coho salmon captured on motor mooched cut-plug herring near Work Channel, British Columbia. Unpublished report. Fisheries and Oceans Canada, Science Branch, Pacific Region, 417 2nd Avenue West, Prince Rupert, British Columbia, Canada.

Fagerlund, U. H. M. 1967. Plasma cortisol concentration in relation to stress in adult sockeye salmon during the freshwater stage of their life cycle. General and Comparative Endocrinology 8:197–207.

Fagerlund, U. H. M., J. R. McBride, and I. V. Williams. 1995. Stress and tolerance. Pages 461–503 in C. Groot, L. Margolis, and W. C. Clarke, editors. Physiological ecology of Pacific salmon. University of British Columbia Press, Vancover, British Columbia, Canada.

Goodman, L. A. 1960. On the exact variance of products. Journal of the American Statistical Association 55:708–713.

Gray, G. 1999. Covariances in multiplicative estimates. Transactions of the American Fisheries Society 128:475–482.

Grover, A. 1992. Proposal for a study of the uses of mooching in sport and commercial fisheries and the effect of mooching on shaker mortality. Unpublished report. California Department of Fish and Game, Ocean Salmon Project, 475 Aviation Boulevard, Suite 130, Santa Rosa, California.

Grover, A. 1995a. The evaluation of hook mortality in the California ocean salmon fisheries (1992 and 1993). Report to Pacific Fishery Management Council. Available from the California Department of Fish and Game, Ocean Salmon Project, 475 Aviation Boulevard, Suite 130, Santa Rosa, California.

Grover, A. 1995b. Evaluation of hook mortality in the California ocean salmon fisheries, 1994 and 1995. Report to Pacific Fishery Management Council. Available from the California Department of Fish and Game, Ocean Salmon Project, 475 Aviation Boulevard, Suite 130, Santa Rosa, California.

Grover, A. 1995c. Cruise Report 95-M-8. California Department of Fish and Game, Ocean Salmon Project, 475 Aviation Boulevard, Suite 130, Santa Rosa, California.

Grover, A., and M. L. Palmer-Zwahlen. 1996. Hooking mortality of sublegal chinook salmon caught by drift mooching with various terminal gear. Report to Pacific Fishery Management Council. Available from the California Department of Fish and Game, Ocean Salmon Project, 475 Aviation Boulevard, Suite 130, Santa Rosa, California.

Lawson, P. W., and D. B. Sampson. 1996. Gear-related mortality in selective fisheries for ocean salmon. North American Journal of Fisheries Management 16:512–520.

Meyers, J. M., and ten coauthors. 1998. Status review of chinook salmon from Washington, Idaho, Oregon, and California. NOAA (National Oceanic and Atmospheric Administration) Technical Memorandum NMFS-NWFSC-35.

NRC (Natural Resources Consultants). 1991. Hooking mortality study final project report. A report on a study to determine rates and causes of mortality in coho and chinook salmon caught and released with sport fishing tackle. Report to National Marine Fisheries Service in fulfillment of Saltonstall-Kennedy Cooperative Agreement No. NA89AB-H-00012. Available from Natural Resources Consultants, Inc., 1900 W. Nickerson Street, Suite 207, Seattle, Washington.

NRC (Natural Resources Consultants). 1994. 1992–1993 hooking mortality study final project report. A report on an expanded study to determine rates and causes of mortality in coho and chinook salmon caught and released with sport fishing tackle. Report to National Marine Fisheries Service in fulfillment of Saltonstall-Kennedy Cooperative Agreement No. NA26FD0138-01. Available from Natural Resources Consultants, Inc., 1900 W. Nickerson Street, Suite 207, Seattle, Washington.

NRC (Natural Resources Consultants). 1999. Review of recent hooking mortality studies. Report to Pacific States Marine Fisheries Commission. Available from Natural Resources Consultants, Inc., 1900 W. Nickerson Street, Suite 207, Seattle, Washington.

Orsi, J. A., A. C. Wertheimer, and H. W. Jaenicke. 1993. Influence of selected hook and lure types on catch, size, and mortality of commercially troll-caught chinook salmon. North American Journal of Fisheries Management 13:709–722.

OSP (Ocean Salmon Project). 1989. Description of winter chinook ocean harvest model. Unpublished report prepared in consultation with the National Marine Fisheries Service and the U.S. Fish and Wildlife Service. Available from the California Department of Fish and Game, Ocean Salmon Project, 475 Aviation Boulevard, Suite 130, Santa Rosa, California.

Palmer-Zwahlen, M. L., and A. Grover. 1997. Cruise Report 96-M-2. California Department of Fish and Game, Ocean Salmon Project, 475 Aviation Boulevard, Suite 130, Santa Rosa, California.

PFMC (Pacific Fishery Management Council). 1984. Final framework for managing the ocean salmon fisheries off the coasts of Washington, Oregon, and California commencing in 1985. Pacific Fishery Management Council, 7700 NE Ambassador Place, Suite 200, Portland, Oregon.

PFMC (Pacific Fishery Management Council). 1997. Preseason Report III. Analysis of council adopted management measures for 1997 ocean salmon fisheries. Prepared by Salmon Technical Team and Staff Economist. Pacific Fishery Management Council, 7700 NE Ambassador Place, Suite 200, Portland, Oregon.

PFMC (Pacific Fishery Management Council). 2000. Preseason Report III. Analysis of council adopted management measures for 2000 ocean salmon fisheries. Prepared by Salmon Technical Team and Staff Economist. Pacific Fishery Management Council, 7700 NE Ambassador Place, Suite 200, Portland, Oregon.

PFMC (Pacific Fishery Management Council). 2001. Preseason Report II. Analysis of proposed regulatory options for 2001 ocean salmon fisheries. Prepared by Salmon Technical Team and Staff Economist. Pacific Fishery Management Council, 7700 NE Ambassador Place, Suite 200, Portland, Oregon.

PSC (Pacific Salmon Commission). 1997. Incidental fishing mortality of chinook salmon: mortality rates applicable to Pacific Salmon Commission fisheries. Joint Chinook Technical Committee Report TCChinook (97)-1. Pacific Salmon Commission, 600–1155 Robson Street, Vancouver, British Columbia, Canada.

Redding, J. M., R. Patiño, and C. B. Shreck. 1984a. Clearance of corticosteroids in yearling coho salmon, *Oncorhynchus kisutch*, in fresh water and seawater after stress. General and Comparative Endocrinology 54:433–443.

Redding, J. M., C. B. Shreck, E. K. Birks, and R. D. Ewing. 1984b.

Cortisol and its effects on plasma thyroid hormone and electrolyte concentrations in fresh water and during seawater acclimation in yearling coho salmon, *Oncorhynchus kisutch*. General and Comparative Endocrinology 56:146–155.

Ricker, W. E. 1975. Computation and interpretation of biological statistics of fish populations. Fisheries Research Board of Canada Bulletin 191.

Schreck, C. B., and H. W. Lorz. 1978. Stress response of coho salmon (*Oncorhynchus kisutch*) elicited by cadium and copper and potential use of cortisol as an indicator of stress. Journal of the Fisheries Research Board of Canada 35:1124–1129.

Seber, G. A. F. 1982. The estimation of animal abundance and related parameters, 2nd edition. Charles Griffin & Company, London, England.

Snedecor, G. W., and W. G. Cochran. 1989. Statistical methods, 8th edition. Iowa State University Press, Ames, Iowa.

Strange, R. J., and C. B. Schreck. 1978. Anesthetic and handling stress on survival and cortisol concentration in yearling chinook salmon (*Oncorhynchus tshawytscha*). Journal of the Fisheries Research Board of Canada 35:345–349.

Strange, R. J., and C. B. Schreck. 1980. Seawater and confinement alters survival and cortisol concentration in juvenile chinook salmon. Copeia 1980(2):351–353.

Strange, R. J., C. B. Schreck, and R. D. Ewing. 1979. Cortisol concentrations in confined juvenile chinook salmon. Transactions of the American Fisheries Society 107:812–819.

STT (Salmon Technical Team). 1994. Nonlanded mortality of chinook and coho salmon in Pacific Fishery Management Council ocean recreational and commercial salmon fisheries. Report to Pacific Fishery Management Council, 7700 NE Ambassador Place, Suite 200, Portland, Oregon.

STT (Salmon Technical Team). 2000. STT recommendations for hooking mortality rates in 2000 recreational ocean chinook and coho fisheries. March supplemental report B2. Pacific Fishery Management Council, 7700 NE Ambassador Place, Suite 200, Portland, Oregon.

Stuart, A., and J. K. Ord. 1994. Kendall's advanced theory of statistics, volume 1: distribution theory, 6th edition. Halsted Press, New York.

Sumpter, J. P., H. M. Dye, and T. J. Benfey. 1986. The effects of stress on plasma ACTH, α-MSH, and cortisol levels in salmonid fishes. General and Comparative Endocrinology 62:377–385.

Wertheimer, A. 1988. Hooking mortality of chinook salmon released by commercial trollers. North American Journal of Fisheries Management 8:346–355.

Appendix: Derivation of $V(\hat{p})$ Estimator

In this Appendix we develop an estimator for the sample variance of the fishery H/R mortality rate estimate

$$\hat{p} = \sum_{\ell=1}^{6} \hat{w}_{\ell} \hat{q}_{\ell} \tag{A1}$$

with $\ell = 1$ denoting the H_{Low} category (surrogate control group). We assume that the fishery H_{ℓ} frequencies are *multinomial* $(n, \{w_1, \ldots, w_6\})$ data, and the day 4+ cumulative mortality data are an independent set of *binomial* (m_{ℓ}, r_{ℓ}), $\ell = 1, \ldots, 6$ outcomes, with the $\{\hat{q}_{\ell}\}$ being a function of the $\{\hat{r}_{\ell}\}$:

$$\hat{q}_{\ell} = \frac{\hat{r}_{\ell} - \hat{r}_1}{1 - \hat{r}_1}, \quad \ell = 1, 2, \ldots, 6. \tag{A2}$$

The variance of $\hat{p}$, a sum of random variables, is given by (Stuart and Ord 1994)

$$V(\hat{p}) = \sum_{\ell=1}^{6} V(\hat{w}_{\ell} \hat{q}_{\ell}) + 2 \sum_{\ell=1}^{5} \sum_{k=\ell+1}^{6} COV(\hat{w}_{\ell} \hat{q}_{\ell}, \hat{w}_k \hat{q}_k). \tag{A3}$$

Since $V(\hat{p})$ is a linear function, an unbiased estimator for it may be obtained by substituting into Equation (A3) unbiased estimators of the $V(\cdot)$ and $COV(\cdot, \cdot)$ components. Because the two sets of estimates $\{\hat{w}_{\ell}\}$ and $\{\hat{q}_{\ell}\}$ are derived from separate data sets, they are pairwise independent ($\hat{w}_{\ell}$ is independent of $\hat{q}_k$ for all ℓ, k), and thus an unbiased estimator for $V(\hat{w}_{\ell} \hat{q}_{\ell})$ is (Goodman 1960)

$$\hat{V}(\hat{w}_{\ell} \hat{q}_{\ell}) = \hat{w}_{\ell}^2 \hat{V}(\hat{q}_{\ell}) + \hat{q}_{\ell}^2 \hat{V}(\hat{w}_{\ell}) - \hat{V}(\hat{w}_{\ell}) \hat{V}(\hat{q}_{\ell}); \tag{A4}$$

assuming $\hat{w}_{\ell}$, $\hat{q}_{\ell}$, and $\hat{V}(\hat{w}_{\ell})$, $\hat{V}(\hat{q}_{\ell})$ are themselves unbiased estimators. The pairwise independence between $\{\hat{w}_{\ell}\}$ and $\{\hat{q}_{\ell}\}$ also provides that an unbiased estimator for $COV(\hat{w}_{\ell} \hat{q}_{\ell}, \hat{w}_k \hat{q}_k)$ is (Gray 1999)

$$\widehat{COV}(\hat{w}_{\ell} \hat{q}_{\ell}, \hat{w}_k \hat{q}_k) = \hat{w}_{\ell} \hat{w}_k \widehat{COV}(\hat{q}_{\ell}, \hat{q}_k) + \hat{q}_{\ell} \hat{q}_k \widehat{COV}(\hat{w}_{\ell}, \hat{w}_k) - \widehat{COV}(\hat{w}_{\ell}, \hat{w}_k) \widehat{COV}(\hat{q}_{\ell}, \hat{q}_k); \tag{A5}$$

assuming $\widehat{COV}(\hat{q}_{\ell}, \hat{q}_k)$ and $\widehat{COV}(\hat{w}_{\ell}, \hat{w}_k)$ are themselves unbiased. Therefore, what remains is to find unbiased estimators $\hat{w}_{\ell}$, $\hat{V}(\hat{w}_{\ell})$, $\widehat{COV}(\hat{w}_{\ell}, \hat{w}_k)$, and $\hat{q}_{\ell}$, $\hat{V}(\hat{q}_{\ell})$, $\widehat{COV}(\hat{q}_{\ell}, \hat{q}_k)$.

Given the H_{ℓ} frequency data are *multinomial* $(n, \{w_{\ell}\})$, the sample relative frequency $\hat{w}_{\ell}$ is an unbiased estimator of w_{ℓ}, and

$$\hat{V}(\hat{w}_{\ell}) = \hat{w}_{\ell}(1 - \hat{w}_{\ell}) / (n - 1) \tag{A6}$$

and

$$\widehat{COV}(\hat{w}_{\ell}, \hat{w}_k) = -\hat{w}_{\ell} \hat{w}_k / (n - 1), \quad \ell \neq k \tag{A7}$$

are unbiased for $V(\hat{w}_{\ell})$ and $COV(\hat{w}_{\ell}, \hat{w}_k)$, respectively (Cochran 1977).

Approximately unbiased estimators $\hat{V}(\hat{q}_{\ell})$ and $\widehat{COV}(\hat{q}_{\ell}, \hat{q}_k)$ may be obtained based on the relationship between $\hat{q}_{\ell}$ and the $\{\hat{r}_{\ell}\}$ (equation (A2)), and the uncertainty of the $\{\hat{r}_{\ell}\}$. Given the cumulative day 4+ mortality data are independent *binomial* (m_{ℓ}, r_{ℓ}), $\ell = 1, 2, \ldots, 6$ outcomes, the sample proportion $\hat{r}_{\ell}$ is an unbiased estimator of r_{ℓ}, and

$$\hat{V}(\hat{r}_{\ell}) = \frac{\hat{r}_{\ell}(1 - \hat{r}_{\ell})}{m_{\ell} - 1} \tag{A8}$$

is unbiased for $V(\hat{r}_\ell)$ (Cochran 1977). Independence of outcomes implies $COV(\hat{r}_\ell, \hat{r}_k) \equiv 0$, $\ell \neq k$.

We now use these results to obtain estimators $\hat{V}(\hat{q}_\ell)$ and $\widehat{COV}(\hat{q}_\ell, \hat{q}_k)$. Denote by $s_\ell = 1 - r_\ell$ and $\hat{s}_\ell = 1 - \hat{r}_\ell$ the true and observed day 4+ cumulative survival rates, and note that $V(\hat{s}_\ell) = V(\hat{r}_\ell)$ and $\hat{V}(\hat{s}_\ell) = \hat{V}(\hat{r}_\ell)$. Equation (A2) may be re-expressed in terms of the $\{\hat{s}_\ell\}$ as

$$\hat{q}_\ell = 1 - \frac{\hat{s}_\ell}{\hat{s}_1}; \tag{A9}$$

a simpler form to work with. We first consider its expectation (Cochran 1977, page 162)

$$E(\hat{q}_\ell) = q_\ell + \frac{1}{s_1} COV\left(\frac{\hat{s}_\ell}{\hat{s}_1}, \hat{s}_1\right). \tag{A10}$$

For our holding experiments, $s_1 = 1 - r_1$ is in the neighborhood of 1, and $\hat{s}_\ell$ and $\hat{s}_1$ are independent, so that the covariance term in Equation (A10) is near 0, and as a result $\hat{q}_\ell$ is approximately unbiased for q_ℓ. An unbiased estimator of $V(\hat{q}_\ell) = V(\hat{s}_\ell \hat{s}_1^{-1})$ is (Goodman 1960)

$$\hat{V}(\hat{q}_\ell) = \begin{cases} 0, & \ell = 1 \\ \hat{s}_\ell^2 \hat{V}(\hat{s}_1^{-1}) + \left[\hat{E}(\hat{s}_1^{-1})\right]^2 \hat{V}(\hat{s}_\ell) - \hat{V}(\hat{s}_\ell)\hat{V}(\hat{s}_1^{-1}), & \ell = 2,3,...,6; \end{cases} \tag{A11}$$

assuming $\hat{E}(\hat{s}_1^{-1})$ and $V(\hat{s}_1^{-1})$ are unbiased, in which case

$$\widehat{COV}(\hat{q}_\ell, \hat{q}_k) = \begin{cases} 0, & \ell \neq k; \ \ell = 1 \text{ or } k = 1 \\ \hat{s}_\ell \hat{s}_k \hat{V}(\hat{s}_1^{-1}), & \ell \neq k; \ \ell, k = 2,3,...,6 \end{cases} \tag{A12}$$

is also unbiased since the $\{\hat{s}_\ell\}$ are an independent set (Gray 1999). The delta method (Seber 1982) provides $V(\hat{s}_1^{-1}) \approx V(\hat{s}_1)/s_1^4$, so that $\hat{V}(\hat{s}_1^{-1}) = \hat{V}(\hat{s}_1)/\hat{s}_1^4$ is approximately unbiased, as is $\hat{E}(\hat{s}_1^{-1}) = \hat{s}_1^{-1}$. Making these substitutions into Equations (A11) and (A12), and setting $\hat{s}_\ell = 1 - \hat{r}_\ell$ and $\hat{V}(\hat{s}_\ell) = \hat{V}(\hat{r}_\ell)$, yields approximately unbiased estimators

$$\hat{V}(\hat{q}_\ell) = \begin{cases} 0, & \ell = 1 \\ \dfrac{1}{(1-\hat{r}_1)^2}\left[\hat{V}(\hat{r}_\ell) + (1-\hat{q}_\ell)^2 \hat{V}(\hat{r}_1) - \dfrac{\hat{V}(\hat{r}_\ell)\hat{V}(\hat{r}_1)}{(1-\hat{r}_1)^2}\right], & \ell = 2,3,...,6, \end{cases} \tag{A13}$$

and

$$\widehat{COV}(\hat{q}_\ell, \hat{q}_k) = \begin{cases} 0, & \ell \neq k; \ \ell = 1 \text{ or } k = 1 \\ \dfrac{(1-\hat{q}_\ell)(1-\hat{q}_k)}{(1-\hat{r}_1)^2}\hat{V}(\hat{r}_1), & \ell \neq k; \ \ell, k = 2,3,...,6. \end{cases} \tag{A14}$$

Finally, for the $V(\hat{p})$ estimator, we substitute: Equations (A6) and (A13) into (A4); Equations (A7) and (A14) into (A5); Equations (A4) and (A5) into (A3); collect terms; and obtain the approximately unbiased estimator

$$\hat{V}(\hat{p}) = \frac{1}{n-1}\left\{ \frac{m_1(1-\hat{r}_1)-1}{(m_1-1)(1-\hat{r}_1)^3}\sum_{\ell=2}^{6}\hat{w}_\ell(n\hat{w}_\ell-1)\frac{\hat{r}_\ell(1-\hat{r}_\ell)}{m_\ell-1} - \frac{\hat{r}_\ell}{(m_1-1)(1-\hat{r}_1)}\sum_{\ell=2}^{6}\hat{w}_\ell(1-\hat{q}_\ell)^2 + \sum_{\ell=2}^{6}\hat{w}_\ell\hat{q}_\ell^2 \right.$$

$$\left. + \frac{\hat{r}_1 n}{(m_1-1)(1-\hat{r}_1)}\sum_{\ell=2}^{6}\sum_{k=2}^{6}\hat{w}_\ell\hat{w}_k(1-\hat{q}_\ell)(1-\hat{q}_k) - \sum_{\ell=2}^{6}\sum_{k=2}^{6}\hat{w}_\ell\hat{w}_k\hat{q}_\ell\hat{q}_k \right\}. \tag{A15}$$

American Fisheries Society Symposium 30:57–65, 2002

A Comparison of Circle Hook and Straight Hook Performance in Recreational Fisheries for Juvenile Atlantic Bluefin Tuna

GREGORY B. SKOMAL

Massachusetts Division of Marine Fisheries
Martha's Vineyard Research Station
Post Office Box 68
Vineyard Haven, Massachusetts 02568, USA

BRADFORD C. CHASE

Massachusetts Division of Marine Fisheries
Annisquam River Marine Fisheries Station
30 Emerson Avenue
Gloucester, Massachusetts 01930, USA

ERIC D. PRINCE

U.S. Department of Commerce
National Oceanic and Atmospheric Administration
National Marine Fisheries Service
Southeast Fisheries Science Center
Miami Laboratory
75 Virginia Beach Drive, Miami, Florida 33149, USA

Abstract.—Catch quotas, bag limits, and minimum sizes have been the primary management tools to limit mortality in U.S. Atlantic bluefin tuna *Thunnus thynnus* fisheries. As a result of these regulations, increasing numbers of bluefin tuna are released annually by recreational and commercial fishermen. Post-release survival is highly dependent on the degree of physiological stress and physical trauma experienced by the fish. The type of terminal fishing tackle strongly influences hook location in the fish, as well as the degree of hook damage. This study compared the performance of circle hooks to straight hooks, relative to hooking location, damage, and catching success in natural bait fisheries for bluefin tuna that are practiced on the U.S. Atlantic coast. During the summers of 1997–1999, fishing trips were made offshore of Virginia and Massachusetts to catch juvenile bluefin tuna with comparable size circle hooks (sizes 10/0–12/0) and straight hooks (sizes 5/0–8/0), while drifting with natural bait. A total of 101 bluefin tuna was caught and dissected to quantify hooking location and to assess the extent of hooking damage. There was a significant association between hook type and hook location ($p < 0.05$). Ninety-four percent of the bluefin tuna caught on circle hooks were hooked in the jaw, and four percent were hooked in the pharynx or esophagus. Fifty-two percent of the bluefin tuna caught on straight hooks were hooked in the jaw, and thirty-four percent were hooked in the pharynx or esophagus. Based on the observed hook damage, we estimated that release mortality would have occurred in four percent of the bluefin tuna caught on circle hooks and twenty-eight percent caught on straight hooks. The ability of each hook type to hook and hold tuna was significantly different; however, overall catching success was similar. This comparison indicates that circle hooks cause less physical damage than straight hooks, while catching juvenile bluefin tuna, using natural baits and can be a valuable conservation tool in these recreational fisheries.

Introduction

The North Atlantic bluefin tuna *Thunnus thynnus*, the largest of the scombrid species, is widely distributed in the Atlantic Ocean. Bluefin tuna migrate to the U.S. continental shelf to feed during the warm months and attract popular and economically important fisheries at many locations (Mather et al. 1995). Commercial and recreational fisheries in the U.S. have targeted Atlantic bluefin tuna since the late 19th century, using purse seine, trap net, harpoon, and hook-and-line gear. The predominant gear has been hook and line during the last two decades. A traditional component of these fisheries has been recreational fishing for juvenile or school (< 150 cm curved fork length [CFL]) bluefin tuna with rod and reel.

The spawning stock biomass of western North Atlantic bluefin tuna is estimated to be well below the level that would allow maximum sustainable yield, and the western stock has been designated as overfished (National Marine Fisheries Service 1999). Numerous regulatory measures have been in effect over the last decade to reduce fishing mortality and to manage the U.S. Atlantic quota. Under the current management system, a relatively small quota (< 300 mt) of juvenile bluefin tuna must be divided among more than 10,000 permitted boats in the U.S. recreational fishery. To reduce the catch of juvenile bluefin tuna, bag limits and minimum sizes for both commercial sale and recreational landings have been established. These restrictions have greatly limited the retention of this species in U.S. fisheries and, along with a growing conservation ethic, have resulted in a dramatic increase in the catch and release of bluefin tuna in recent years.

Post-release survivorship is highly dependent on the degree of physiological stress and physical trauma experienced during fishing (see Muoneke and Childress 1994, for review). It is generally accepted that jaw-hooked fish experience less physical trauma and have a higher probability of survival than fish hooked in the pharynx or gut (deep-hooked). The type of terminal fishing tackle used can have a strong influence on hooking location. Circle hooks have gained popularity in several recreational fisheries because of their propensity to lodge in the hinge of the jaw, resulting in less physical damage to the fish (Grover et al; Prince et al; both this volume).

Concern over the survival of bluefin tuna caught and released in recreational fisheries grew in response to the development of a winter fishery for bluefin tuna off Cape Hatteras, North Carolina in the early 1990s (Skomal and Chase 1996). Very high catch rates were achieved in this rod and reel fishery, which used baited hooks in conjunction with chumming methods. Federal fishery restrictions mandated that a large number of these bluefin tuna

be released. Consequently, North Carolina fishing captains in this catch-and-release fishery adopted the circle hook, after seeing very low numbers of deep-hooked fish while using this hook type. Observations of the successful use of circle hooks in the Cape Hatteras fishery inspired us to conduct a comparative study on hooking location, tissue damage, and catching success of circle hooks and traditional straight hooks used in natural bait fisheries for juvenile bluefin tuna.

Methods

Bluefin tuna were collected during the summers of 1997–1999 on sampling trips conducted primarily 30–50 km southwest of Martha's Vineyard, Massachusetts (Figure 1, Area A), as well as on Stellwagen Bank in the Gulf of Maine (Figure 1, Area B) and offshore of Chincoteague, Virginia (Figure 1, Area C). These areas support active fisheries for juvenile bluefin tuna on the continental shelf off the eastern United States. All trips were made on chartered sportfishing boats or research vessels of the Massachusetts Division of Marine Fisheries. Bluefin tuna were caught using the standard sportfishing technique of drifting baited lines while chumming. Two paired treatments of terminal tackle were offered to feeding bluefin: one with Mustad[1] circle hooks (sizes 10/0, 11/0, and 12/0) and the other with Mustad[1] #9174 straight hooks (sizes 5/0, 6/0, 7/0, and 8/0; Figure 2). Straight hooks are also commonly called "J hooks." Although manufacturers use different units to size circle hooks and straight hooks, the sizes selected for the two hook types were comparable (Figure 2). Other than hook types, the gear and handling methods used were the same for both treatments. Hooks were baited with chunks of butterfish *Peprilus triacanthus* or silver hake *Merluccius bilinearis*, and chunks of bait were routinely chummed around the lines to attract bluefin tuna. Rods were placed in rod holders, and line was stripped from the reel to present the baited hook to fish at desired depths. Upon detecting a bite on the baited line, the angler would increase the reel drag to set the hook. Anglers were instructed not to actively set the hook, but to allow the rod to react to the bite in the rod holder or in the angler's hands.

Information on hook type, hook size, line test, and fight time was recorded for each fish. The "hooking

---

1. Use of brand names does not imply government endorsement.

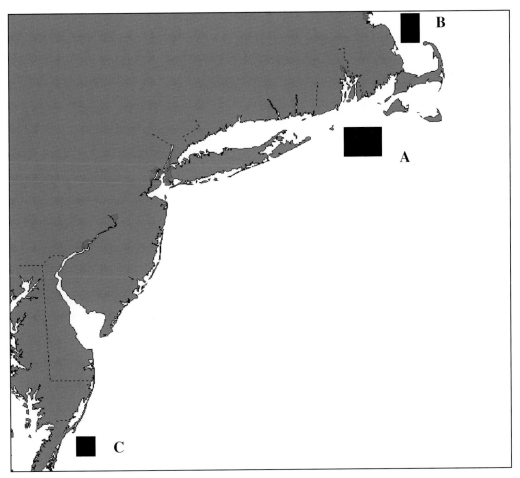

Figure 1. Study areas where juvenile Atlantic bluefin tuna *Thunnus thynnus* **were sampled with circle and straight hooks: (A) 30–50 km southwest of Martha's Vineyard, Massachusetts, (B) Stellwagen Bank in the Gulf of Maine, and (C) offshore of Chincoteague, Virginia.**

outcome" of each feeding attempt by bluefin tuna on a baited hook was recorded by three categories: biting the bait but not hooking, hooked fish that were not captured or "lost" during angling, and landed fish. The hooking outcome categories reflect on the catching success (landed fish/bites) of each hook type. Hooking outcome data were only recorded when it was certain the observation involved bluefin tuna. Hooked bluefin tuna were brought quickly to the boat, landed, and sacrificed to conduct a detailed dissection of hooking location and associated hook damage and potential mortality. The mouth, pharynx, esophagus, and abdominal cavity of each fish were inspected for hook location and tissue damage. All bluefin tuna were measured (CFL), and ages were assigned based on Mather and Schuck (1960) length-age classification.

Chi-square analysis was conducted on hook location data to test the null hypothesis that hooking location was independent of hook type. The two treatments (hook types) were offered evenly, and it was assumed that the selection of hook type was random. A two-by-two contingency table (Category 1) was constructed, and a correction was made for continuity (Zar 1984)). Chi-square analysis was also conducted to test the hypothesis that unsuccessful hooking outcome was independent of hook type.

Results

Hook Location

From 1997 to 1999, a total of 142 bluefin tuna bites were recorded: 69 with circle hooks of which 51 (74%) were landed, and 73 with straight hooks of

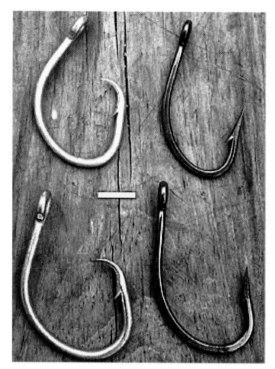

Figure 2. Two hook types used to catch bluefin tuna: Mustad circle hooks (left) sizes 11/0 (top) and 12/0 (bottom) and Mustad #9174 straight hooks (right) sizes 6/0 (top) and 7/0 (bottom). A one-centimeter scale is provided in the center of the figure.

Table 1. Hooking locations for circle hooks ($N = 51$) and straight hooks ($N = 50$) used to catch juvenile bluefin tuna during 1997–1999 on the Continental Shelf off the U.S. Atlantic Coast.

Hooking location	Circle hook (no.)	Straight hook (no.)
Jaw hinge[a]	43	24
Jaw (other)[a]	5	2
Palate[a]	0	5
Pharynx[b]	1	1
Esophagus[b]	1	16
External (body)[a]	1	2

a. nonlethal locations
b. potentially lethal locations

sidered to be potentially lethal. Bluefin tuna samples outside these two categories were excluded from the chi-square analysis (five palate and three body-hooked specimens). This comparison resulted in 93 samples composed of 50 fish caught on circle hooks and 43 caught on straight hooks, with hook location significantly dependent on hook type ($p < 0.001$; Table 2).

Hook Damage

Hook wounds were considered potentially lethal when trauma occurred to highly vascularized tissue or viscera. This condition was found with hooks that lodged in the pharynx or esophagus. Hook wounds to the jaw, palate, and body produced minor bleeding and were considered unlikely to threaten survival upon release. Bluefin tuna possess a wide gape that provides easy passage of food from the oral cavity past the pharynx and into the esophagus. The transition from the posterior pharynx to the esophagus and to the anterior lumen of the stomach is continuous and contains little variation in the dense muscle tissue that is heavily striated anterior to the pylorus. The esophagus passes through the transverse septum, a thin membrane that separates the pericardial cavity from the peritoneal (abdominal) cavity. Of the 101 bluefin tuna sampled, 19 were hooked in locations that were considered potentially lethal (Table 1); 17 of these hook locations were a few centimeters anterior or posterior of the transverse septum.

Only two (4%) of the fifty-one bluefin tuna caught on circle hooks were deep-hooked. One age-4 fish had a circle hook protruding through the lumen of the anterior stomach (Figure 4). The exposed hook point ripped tissue that supports viscera in the

which 50 (68%) were landed (Table 1). All of the 101 bluefin tuna that were landed and dissected were classified as ages one to four (63–131 cm CFL, with about 50% age-1, 25% age-2, and 25% age-4). Almost all bluefin tuna caught on circle hooks were hooked in the jaw (94%) with most hooked in the jaw hinge (84%) (Table 1; Figure 3). Only two (4%) of the circle hook caught fish were hooked in the esophagus or pharynx, areas considered potentially lethal (Table 1). Greater variability in the hooking location was observed for bluefin tuna caught on straight hooks: 52% in the jaw, 32% in the esophagus, 10% in the oral cavity or palate, and 6% at other locations (Table 1).

To simplify the comparison and avoid sparsity rule violations for chi-square analysis, the contingency table was arranged for the two hook types and the two major hooking locations (Table 2). Hooks found in the jaw hinge and any other part of the jaw were classified as "jaw" and not considered to be life threatening. Hooks found in the pharynx or in the esophagus were classified as "deep" and con-

Figure 3. Typical hooking location in the "hinge" of the jaw of 88-cm CFL bluefin tuna caught on circle hook.

abdominal cavity and caused internal bleeding. An age-1 fish had a circle hook that lodged between two gill arches in the pharynx and caused extensive bleeding from gill filament damage. Seventeen (34%) of the fifty bluefin tuna caught on straight hooks were deep-hooked. Only one of these was lodged in the gill arches of the pharynx and caused gill filament damage. The rest were in close proximity to the transverse septum and caused a variety of traumatic wounds.

Two important factors influenced the extent of

Table 2. Chi-square analysis of hooking location dependence on circle hooks ($N = 50$) and straight hooks ($N = 43$). The null hypothesis (H_0: hooking location is independent of hook type) is rejected ($X^2 = 15.84$; $P < 0.001$).

Hooking location	Circle hook (no.)	Straight hook (no.)
Jaw	48	26
Deep (esophagus or pharynx)	2	17

internal wounds: the exposure of the hook point and barb and the location of exposed hook in the abdominal cavity. Three of the deep-hooked fish had hooks embedded in the thick muscle tissue of the esophagus or posterior pharynx. These hook wounds resulted in much less tissue damage and bleeding than wounds where the hook was exposed and free to lacerate other tissues. In most instances where hooks penetrated the abdominal cavity, tissues and blood vessels supporting viscera were damaged. Hooks positioned close to the transverse septum with the point facing anteriorly would often tear the septum and sever the hepatic veins leading to the sinus venosus (Figure 5). Hooks positioned closer to the pylorus were observed to damage the anterior liver lobe. No observations were made of hook damage to vascular retes or the pericardium, although it is expected such wounds could occur with the specific placement of a large hook.

In addition to the potentially lethal internal hook

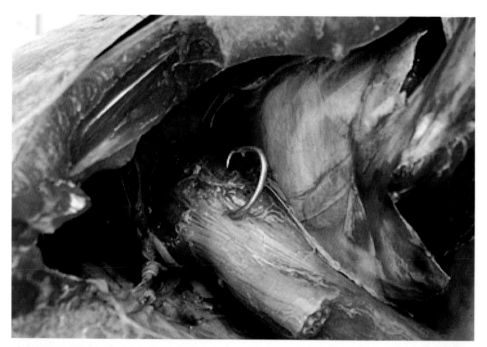

Figure 4. A 106-cm CFL bluefin tuna with a circle hook protruding through the lumen of the anterior stomach, between the esophagus and pylorus (severed in foreground).

wounds, we observed external hook damage that may not be lethal but would have a metabolic cost to repair tissues. For example, large hooks embedded in the jaws of age-1 fish could result in scraping of facial tissue. This occurred primarily in age-1 bluefin tuna hooked in the jaw with size 11/0 circle hooks and appeared to be related to the angle of the circle hook point (90°). Nine of the 25 fish caught in the jaw with circle hooks larger than 10/0 had external damage caused by the hook point and barb. In two of these cases, the hook point caused severe damage to the eye socket. Extensive hook point damage to facial tissue was not observed in age-4 bluefin tuna and occurred only once with straight hooks (eye socket damage to an age-1 bluefin from a 6/0 straight hook).

Hooking Outcome

In addition to the 101 landed bluefin tuna, 41 observations were made of "lost" bluefin, 18 with circle hooks and 23 with straight hooks (Table 3). Hooking outcome for bluefin that were lost during angling was significantly dependent on hook type ($p = 0.041$; Table 3). The data collected coupled with field observations indicate that this result is influenced by the propensity of straight hooks to hook

the fish more readily when bit and for circle hooks not to pull out once the fish is hooked. Despite this difference in the way bluefin were lost, overall catching success was similar for the two hook types. Sixty-eight percent of recorded straight hook bites and seventy-four percent of circle hooks bites resulted in landed tuna.

Other Species

Four other species were caught incidentally while fishing for bluefin tuna. No species was taken in high enough numbers to conduct a statistical analysis of hook location data. Less than ten were caught of each of the following species: six spiny dogfish

Table 3. Chi-square analysis of hooking outcome dependence on hook type: circle hooks ($n = 18$) and straight hooks ($n = 23$). Occurrences when bluefin tuna interacted with the baited hook but were not landed were classified according to whether they were hooked and lost or were not hooked during the initial bite. The null hypothesis of hooking outcome is independent of hook type was rejected ($X^2 = 4.266, P = 0.041$).

Hooking outcome	Circle hook (no.)	Straight hook (no.)
Bite-not hooked	13	8
Hooked and lost	5	15

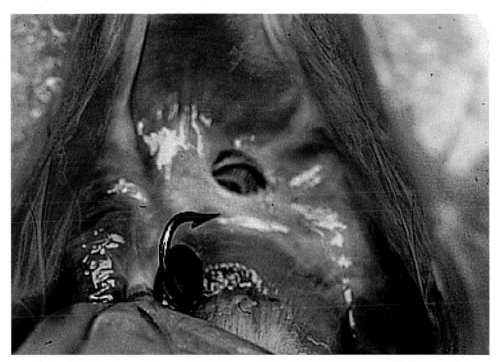

Figure 5. An 88-cm CFL bluefin tuna deep-hooked with a straight hook. This hook was embedded close to the transverse septum with the point facing forward. A liver lobe is present in the foreground, and the heart can be seen through the transverse septum in the background.

Squalus acanthias; five blue sharks *Prionace glauca*; and nine bluefish *Pomatomus saltatrix*, and for each catch on circle hooks, the hook location was the jaw hinge. Observations were recorded for 22 Atlantic bonito *Sarda sarda*, of which 9 were caught on straight hooks and 13 were caught on circle hooks in the jaw hinge. For the straight-hooked bonito, three hooks were in each of the following locations: jaw, palate, and deep-hooked. It was observed that these relatively smaller tuna (2–5 kg) did not easily swallow the larger hooks, but could still experience extensive damage anterior to the gut (gill filaments and eye socket).

Discussion

The results of this study are comparable to the authors' observations that circle hooks used in the catch-and-release fisheries for larger bluefin tuna (primarily 50–150 kg) off North Carolina supported live release. Our current study shows that nearly 95% of juvenile bluefin tuna caught on circle hooks were consistently hooked in the jaw as opposed to straight hooks that were hooked in the jaw for about half the cases. Greater variation was observed in the

location where straight hooks embedded, with nearly a third lodged in the esophagus.

In addition to hook location data, this study documents the damage that hooks can cause in the pharynx and abdominal cavity. Wounds to the pharynx were not common, occurring in 2% of the landed bluefin tuna; in both cases however, the hooks lodged between the gill arches and severely damaged gill filaments. The hard surface area of the buccal cavity and the gill arches are adapted to receive sharp or abrasive objects during feeding, and this protection appears to minimize hooking in the pharynx and buccal cavity regions. The region that experienced the most traumatic injuries was between the pylorus of the stomach and the transverse septum. Hooks that penetrated the muscle of the esophagus in this region could encounter the transverse septum as well as a variety of support tissues for the viscera. The orientation of the hook point once exposed in the abdominal cavity was critical to the resulting damage. An exposed hook close to the transverse septum could tear this sensitive membrane and sever the hepatic veins running from the liver to the sinus venosus. An exposed hook closer to the pylorus could tear connective tissues for the viscera (observed), the liver (observed), or visceral retes (not observed). Severe internal bleeding accompanied most wounds when the hook penetrated the esophagus, but was not detected in the three cases where the hook point remained buried in the muscle of the esophagus.

In the absence of published studies on bluefin tuna, the documentation of hook wounds presents an opportunity to discuss the potential for release mortality. Overall, only wounds occurring in the pharynx and esophagus appeared to cause enough physical trauma to threaten immediate survival upon release. Of the wounds in these deep-hooked locations, only those that lacerated sensitive tissues and/or caused internal bleeding were considered potentially lethal. Under this assumption, about 4% of circle hook wounds and 28% of straight hook wounds were considered potentially lethal. These estimates do not take into account the potential for delayed mortality associated with less traumatic internal and external wounds.

Patterns of tissue damage external to the mouth appeared to be influenced by hook size and the orientation of the circle hook point. Larger circle hooks (11/0 and 12/0) caused extensive scraping of facial tissue between the jaw hinge and eye socket in more than a third of age-1 bluefin tuna caught with these hook sizes. This occurred only once with the straight hook and not at all in any age-4 bluefin. This damage is probably not lethal and can be avoided by selecting a smaller hook size for catching age-1 or age-2 bluefin tuna. However, eye socket damage found in three of the bluefin sampled (two circle, one straight), could cause blindness, thereby impacting feeding and potentially causing mortality (Prince et al.,[2] this volume).

A comparison of the relative catching success of the two hook types is essential to convince anglers to adopt the potentially less damaging circle hook. We found that catching success outcome was similar with the two hook types; however, there was a significant dependence in the way that fish were lost on hook type, which probably reflects the physical attributes of each hook. The small sample size in the analysis limits the strength of this finding, but several trends are apparent from the data and field observations. The circular shape and bent point of the circle hook reduces the probability of a lodged hook coming loose once hooked. Moreover, the tendency

2. Prince, E. D., M. Ortiz, and A. Venizelos

for this hook to embed in the corner of the mouth may result in fewer fish lost after hooking. The greater gap of the straight hook provides more chance for the hook to rip loose if not firmly embedded. The difference in gap width may diminish the effectiveness of circle hooks under certain conditions. When bluefin tuna are feeding cautiously, the bent point and narrow gap of the circle hook may have a reduced probability of hooking when the bait is picked up. When surface waters were calm with high water visibility, there was a tendency to hook more successfully with a straight hook during the initial bite. Under most conditions of active feeding, the circle hook was as effective as the straight hook at hooking upon initial bite.

In summary, this comparison of circle hooks and straight hooks should help convince recreational anglers to adopt circle hooks, which under most conditions caused less physical damage, had a greater tendency to hold tuna once hooked, and had similar overall catching success as straight hooks. Therefore, circle hooks can be an effective and important conservation tool in bait fisheries for juvenile Atlantic bluefin tuna.

Acknowledgments

This study received funding from the Highly Migratory Species Division of the National Marine Fisheries Service. The study was conducted by the Massachusetts Division of Marine Fisheries with financial support from the Sportfish Restoration Act. We owe much appreciation to the experiences related by the fishing community of Cape Hatteras, North Carolina, and to Captain Bob Eakes for inspiring the use of circle hooks for bluefin tuna. The following charter captains were essential to the success of this study, and we very much appreciate their diligent efforts to improve our sample size: Al Anderson, Dave Preble, Charlie Johnson, Perry Romig, and Andy D' Angelo. We are also grateful to the following eager corps of anglers who labored to bring samples to the boat: Rob Goodwin, Jeff Plouff, Luke Gurney, and Paul Skomal. This is Massachusetts Division of Marine Fisheries Contribution No. 4.

References

Mather III, F. J., J. M. Mason, Jr., and C. A. Jones. 1995. Historical document: life history and fisheries of Atlantic bluefin tuna. National Oceanic and Atmospheric Administration Technical Memorandum 370.

Mather, F. J., and H. Schuck. 1960. Growth of the bluefin tuna of the western North Atlantic. Fishery Bulletin 179:39–52.

Muoneke, M. I., and W. M. Childress. 1994. Hooking mortality: a review for recreational fisheries. Reviews in Fisheries Science 2:123–156.

National Marine Fisheries Service. 1999. Final fishery management plan for Atlantic tunas, swordfish, and sharks. Volume 1. National Marine Fisheries Service, Silver Spring, Maryland.

Skomal, G. S., and B. C. Chase. 1996. Preliminary results on the physiological effects of catch and release on bluefin tuna (*Thunnus thynnus*) caught off Cape Hatteras, North Carolina. International Commission for the Conservation of Atlantic Tunas, Standing Committee on Research and Statistics, Madrid, Spain, SCRS/96/126.

Zar, J. H. 1984. Biostatistical analysis. 2nd edition. Prentice-Hall, Inc., Englewood, California.

American Fisheries Society Symposium 30:66–79, 2002

A Comparison of Circle Hook and "J" Hook Performance in Recreational Catch-and-Release Fisheries for Billfish

ERIC D. PRINCE,[1] MAURICIO ORTIZ, *and* ARIETTA VENIZELOS

U.S. Department of Commerce
National Oceanic and Atmospheric Administration
National Marine Fisheries Service
Southeast Fisheries Science Center
75 Virginia Beach Drive
Miami, Florida 33149, USA
[1]*Email: eric.prince@noaa.gov*

Abstract.—This study evaluates the performance of circle and comparable-size "J" hooks on Atlantic and Pacific sailfish *Istiophorus platypterus* and, to a lesser extent, on Pacific blue marlin *Makaira nigricans*. Terminal gear performances were assessed in terms of fishing success, hook location, and bleeding associated with physical hook damage and trauma. Evaluations of trolling with dead bait took place off Iztapa, Guatemala, during the spring and summer of 1999, and assessment of drifting/kite fishing with live bait took place off South Florida during the summer of 1999.

Three hundred and sixty Pacific sailfish were caught in Iztapa, Guatemala, to assess terminal gear performance; 235 sailfish were on circle hooks, and 125 were on "J" hooks. Circle hooks used on sailfish had hooking percentages (i.e., fish hooked/fish bite) that were 1.83 times higher compared with "J" hooks. Once the fish were hooked, no difference in catch percentage (i.e., fish caught/fish hooked) between hook types was detected. Significantly more sailfish were hooked in the corner of the mouth using circle hooks (85%), as compared with "J" hooks (27%). In contrast, significantly more sailfish were deep hooked in the throat and stomach with "J" hooks (46%), as compared with circle hooks (2%). Only one sailfish (1%) was foul hooked using circle hooks, while 11 (9%) sailfish caught on "J" hooks were foul hooked. Sailfish caught on "J" hooks are 21 times more likely to suffer hook-related bleeding than those caught on circle hooks.

Seventy-five Atlantic sailfish were caught using circle hooks in the South Florida live bait recreational fishery to assess possible differences in hook performance between circle hooks with and without an offset point. No difference in catch percentage or bleeding was found between circle hooks with no offset, minor offset (about 4 degrees), or severe offset points (about 15 degrees). However, the percentage of deep hooking in the throat and stomach for circle hooks with a severe offset (44%) was comparable to the deep hooking percentage for "J" hooks (46%) used in the Guatemala study. A comparison of circle and "J" hook catch rates of Pacific sailfish and blue marlin, using logbook catch statistics from recreational fishing off Iztapa, Guatemala, was also conducted. In general, use of circle hooks resulted in measures of fishing success that were comparable to or higher than "J" hooks. Circle hooks also minimized deep hooking, foul hooking, and bleeding. Thus, the use of circle hooks has con-

Introduction

Stocks of Atlantic sailfish *Istiophorus platypterus*, blue marlin *Makaira nigricans*, and white marlin *Tetrapturus albidus* have been identified as overexploited or fully exploited by the International Commission for the Conservation of Atlantic Tunas (ICCAT) for more than two decades (ICCAT 1998). The most current summaries of stock status for Atlantic sailfish and marlin note the high rates of fishing mortality observed in recent years (ICCAT 2000). Under the current harvest rates, the stock status and

biomass for these species are expected to continue to decline. In response to the need to reduce mortality, particularly for the marlins, ICCAT mandated a 25% reduction in landings from 1996 levels, to be implemented by 1999. Given the current prohibition on retention of billfish in the U.S. commercial longline fishery and the increasingly restrictive management measures imposed on the U.S. recreational billfish fishery (SAFMC 1988), alternative approaches for reducing mortality are warranted.

Recent reports indicate that circle hooks used in rod and reel recreational fisheries for striped bass

Morone saxatilis, chinook salmon *Oncorhynchus tshawytscha*, and Atlantic bluefin tuna *Thunnus thynnus* have been shown to reduce deep hooking significantly, and thus promote the live release of these species (Grover et al; Lukacovic and Uphoff Jr; Skomal et al, all this volume). Circle hooks have been used for many years in both commercial pelagic and demersal longline fisheries, but rod and reel recreational fisheries for sailfish and marlin have not traditionally used circle hooks as the primary terminal gear. Although nonconsumptive fishing practices (i.e., catch-and-release fishing) among U.S. recreational billfishermen in the Atlantic started in the late 1960s, and have increased dramatically in recent years to about 90% release (Farber et al. 1997), it was only recently that advances in circle hook rigging techniques using natural bait allowed increased use of circle hooks for trolling/pitch baiting or live bait drifting for sailfish and marlin.[1, 2] This study was initiated in response to requests for more information on the use of circle hooks for catching billfish, in order to promote the live release of these important resources (USDOC 1999). Specific objectives were: to compare hooking and catch percentages between terminal gear (circle and "J" hooks) used in the trolling/pitch bait recreational fisheries for billfish; to assess the hook location and degree of hook-associated physical damage and bleeding between terminal gears; and to evaluate the different levels of offset points in circle hooks relative to catch percentages, hook location, and bleeding in the live bait recreational fishery for sailfish.

Materials

Terminal Gear Comparisons Using Dead Natural Bait

We defined circle hooks as hooks having a point that is perpendicular to the main hook shaft, whereas "J" hooks are defined as hooks having a point parallel to the main hook shaft (Figure 1). Iztapa, Guatemala, was chosen as the primary research site because of high seasonal catch rates for sailfish and local coop-

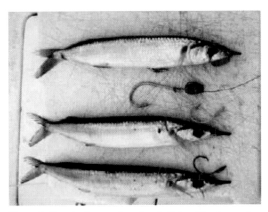

Figure 1. Terminal gears rigged on ballyhoo *Hemirammphus brasiliensis*, used in the troll/pitch bait recreational fishery for billfish in Iztapa, Guatemala. Top, long shank "J" hook (Mustad model 3407, size 8/0), used prior to 1998; middle, short shank "J" hook (Mustad model 9175, size 6/0); and bottom, circle hook (Eagle Claw model L2004, size 7/0), used in this study.

eration of the fishing fleet, insuring that sufficiently high sample size targets could be obtained in a minimum amount of time for a species that is commonly known as a rare event species (Prince and Brown 1991). The fishing fleet in Iztapa, Guatemala, consisted of five modern recreational vessels 30–40 feet in length, all of which participated in the study; the F/V *Captain Hook*, the F/V *Magic*, the F/V *Intensity*, the F/V *Pelagian*, and the F/V *Classic*.

In order to promote valid comparisons of terminal gears, both hook types were rigged in the same manner on the forehead of ballyhoo *Hemirammphus brasiliensis* (Figure 1). Ballyhoo are the bait of choice for trolling/pitch baiting Pacific sailfish off Iztapa, Guatemala, and were used in this study. Our choices of hooks were the Mustad[3] short shank "J" hook (size 6/0, model 9175) and the Eagle Claw[3] circle hook (size 7/0, model L2004), which has a minor offset point of less than four degrees. An offset is a deviation of the hook point relative to the main axis of the hook shaft. The Mustad "J" hook has no offset point and a silver finish, while the circle hook has a pearl gray finish. The difference in hook color between hook types helped facilitate identification of hooks embedded in live sailfish at boatside, where hook location and hook-related

---

1. Fogt, J. 1999. Circle of life. Marlin Magazine 18(3):44–50.

2. Rizzuto, J. 1998. Get to the point. Marlin Magazine 17(3):46–50.

3. The mention of commercial products or entities does not imply endorsement by the National Marine Fisheries Service or the authors.

damage assessment were conducted. Circle hook styles and sizes are not consistent between models, nor do they correspond to hook size for traditional "J" hooks[1,2]. Although the commercially-listed sizes of the two hooks used in this study were different ("J" hook was 6/0 and circle hook was 7/0), the actual sizes of the hook types were almost identical (Figure 1). Traditional hook setting techniques of jerking the fishing rod vertically were used for sailfish caught on "J" hooks. These techniques were modified for circle hooks[1,2] to a more passive approach, by simply reeling the line tight as the fish swam away from the vessel.

Catch/Hooking Performance and Hooking Injury: A fish bite was considered to be a strike that resulted in the line being pulled out of the outrigger pin while trolling, or a bite witnessed visually during pitch bait fishing. Visual confirmations of species identification were made to ensure sailfish catch-and-hooking percentages were only for sailfish. Hooking percentage was defined as the number of fish hooked divided by the number of fish bites. A fish was considered hooked when it took drag and continued to remain on the line for at least 10 seconds. Catch percentage was defined as the number of sailfish brought close enough to boatside for the crew to touch the leader (i.e., a catch), divided by the number of sailfish hooked.

Fish injuries associated with hooking were characterized by evaluating hook location, as well as incidence and amount of bleeding. When possible, fish were pulled out of the water by the crew using the upper bill, and the head of the fish was lifted onto the gunnel of the vessel, the mouth opened, and the hook location and amount and source of bleeding were noted (Figures 2, 3, 4, and 5). Since the recreational fishery of Iztapa, Guatemala, is almost exclusively catch and release, more detailed evaluations of hook damage using autopsy examinations of dead fish were not made. If hook location and amount and location of bleeding were unclear prior to release, these data were not recorded. Hook location categories included: corner of mouth or jaw hinge (Figure 2); lower or upper jaw; deep hooked, including hooks lodged inside the mouth, throat or deeper, the upper/lower palate, pharynx, esophagus, gill arch, or stomach (Figures 3 and 5); and foul hooked (i.e., hooks lodged outside of the mouth; Figure 4). Some typical foul-hooked locations included the upper

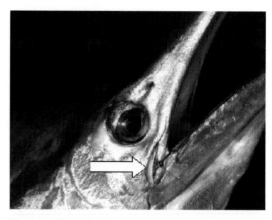

Figure 2. Eighty-five percent of sailfish caught on circle hooks had them lodged in the hinge of the jaw. Arrow indicates hook location.

Figure 3. Forty-six percent of sailfish caught on "J" hooks had them lodged inside the mouth, throat, gill arch, esophagus, pharynx, or stomach(i.e., deep hooked). Arrow indicates hook location.

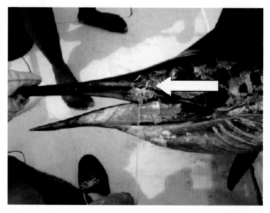

Figure 4. Nine percent of sailfish caught on "J" hooks were foul hooked, such as this hook, which lodged on the outside of the upper bill. See text for definition of foul hooking.

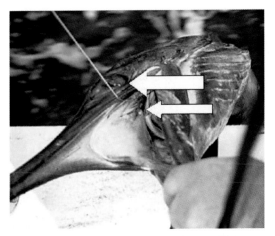

Figure 5. Upper palate wounds incurred by sailfish were exclusively "J" hook-related injuries. The depth and location of this upper palate laceration (lower arrow) also resulted in hemorrhaging in the eye (upper arrow).

bill, operculum, dorsal musculature, and eyeball.

The amount of bleeding was subjectively categorized into three general levels based on the volume of blood observed: severe bleeding; moderate bleeding; and minor bleeding. The general location of bleeding was noted whenever possible, but data on source of bleeding could not be taken consistently because not every fish could be examined out of the water.

Gear Specific Fishing Success in Guatemala: A comparison of catch rates reported by the Iztapa recreational fleet was conducted to evaluate the fishing success for Pacific sailfish and blue marlin. Captains in the fleet have kept detailed logbook records of the number of fish bites and fish caught since 1993. The analysis used the catch data information from the fishing year June 1996 through June 1997, when the fleet used "J" hooks exclusively, and from the fishing year June 1998 through June 1999, when the fleet had switched entirely to circle hooks. Because there was no overlap in periods between the use of the two hook types in time, it was not possible to distinguish catch rate effects due to the fishing gear used and changes in stock abundance between years. This limitation would apply to any statistical analysis using these data. Thus, we assumed that the stocks were equally available in number and spatio-temporal distribution between the two consecutive years. Standardized catch rates were computed using a generalized linear mixed model (GLMM) that discriminated between effects

on catch rates due to seasonality, boat-captain characteristics, and hook type. Catch rates were defined as the number of fish caught per day (CPUE).

Evaluation of Circle Hooks in the South Florida Sailfish Live Bait Fishery

Three types of Eagle Claw circle hooks with different degrees of an offset point were used to assess hook performance in the live bait fishery for sailfish off south Florida. Eagle Claw[3] model 197 L has an offset point of 15 degrees (severe), model L2004 has an offset point of about 4 degrees (minor), and model L2004 EL has no offset point (all hooks were size 7/0). These differences allowed us to compare catch percentages and potential hook damage among circle hooks with different degrees of offset. Two live bait-fishing techniques were involved: drifting with flat lines with and without weights, and live bait fishing with kites. The primary live baits of choice were Atlantic thread herring *Opisthonema oglinum*, blue runner *Caranx crysos*, and bigeye scad *Selar crumenophthalmus*. Occasionally, smaller baits were used, including round scad *Decapterus punctatus* and scaled sardine *Harengula jaguana* (pilchards). Three south Florida charter boat captains, who specialize in live bait fishing for sailfish, participated in this study during the summer of 1999.

Statistical Analyses

The chi-square goodness-of-fit procedure (Steel and Torrie 1960) was used to examine the null hypothesis that there were no differences in catch percentages, hooking percentages, hook location, or associated bleeding between terminal gears in the sailfish fishery off Guatemala. In cases where the number of observations per cell was lower than the number of degrees of freedom, Fisher's exact test or Odds ratio test was used instead (Shoukri and Pause 1999). For comparisons of data with more than two levels per factor, a Cochran-Mantel-Haenszel (CMH) test was used. This test evaluates the association between X and Y (row levels) in any of the strata (Shoukri and Pause 1999). Chi-square and CMH tests evaluated whether or not there is independence between two factors. If the null hypothesis was rejected (i.e., nonindependence between factors), a correspondence analysis test was carried out to show the degree of association among levels, based on a weighted principal components evaluation (Manly 1994). Similar procedures were also used to evaluate differences associated with the degree of offset in circle hooks used in the live bait fishery for sailfish off South Florida. Catch rates (CPUE) for blue marlin and sailfish, based on captains' logbooks of the recreational fishing fleet in Guatemala, were evaluated for differences associated with hook type by using a Generalized Linear Mixed model (GLMM) approach (SAS 1997).

Results

Terminal Gear Comparisons Using Dead Natural Bait

From March through May 1999, a total of 590 sailfish bites were recorded off Iztapa, Guatemala (Table 1). Of these, 461 sailfish were hooked, and 360 were caught, examined at boatside, and released. The number of sailfish hooked and caught on each terminal gear are as follows: 300 were hooked on circle hooks and 235 of these were caught, while 161 were hooked on "J" hooks and 125 of these were caught (Table 1). Circle hooks showed significantly higher ($p < 0.002$) hooking percentages compared with "J" hooks (Table 2). Odds ratio tests indicated

that, on average, circle hooks were 1.83 times more likely to hook a sailfish than a "J" hook (Table 2). In contrast, once a fish was hooked, the catch percentage (78%) was virtually identical for each type of terminal gear. Chi-square and CMH tests indicated that the percentage of hook location also differed significantly ($p < 0.001$) between circle and "J" hooks (Table 2). The Correspondence analysis was then used to determine particular associations between hook type and hook location levels. This test showed that circle hooks were closely associated with hooking in the corner of the mouth, while "J" hooks were closely associated with deep hooking and foul hooking (Table 2; Figure 6).

Seventy-one of the 125 sailfish caught on "J" hooks were observed bleeding, as compared with 14 of 235 sailfish caught on circle hooks (Table 1). This difference was highly significant ($p \leq 0.001$), and the Odds Ratio test indicated that a sailfish caught on a "J" hook was 20.75 times more likely to bleed compared with one caught on a circle hook (Table 2). Analysis of the degree of bleeding associated with the two types of terminal gear indicated a significant difference ($p < 0.001$; Table 2). Correspondence analysis showed that "J" hooks were highly associated with minor/moderate/severe bleeding,

Table 1. Circle and "J" hook comparisons for Pacific sailfish caught in the recreational dead bait fishery off Iztapa, Guatemala, from March through May, 1999. See text for descriptions of terminal gear and definitions of catch and hooking percentages, hook locations, and degree of bleeding.

	"J" Hooks		Circle Hooks[a]	
	number	%	number	%
Fishing success				
bites	225		365	
fish hooked	161	72	300	82
fish caught	125	78	235	78
Hook location				
hooked in corner of mouth	34	27	200	85
hooked in lower or upper jaw	21	17	30	13
deep hooked	58	46	4	2
foul hooked	11	9	1	0.4
unknown hook location	1	1	0	0
Bleeding				
severe bleeding	32	26	6	3
moderate bleeding	23	18	4	2
minor bleeding	16	13	4	2
no bleeding	54	43	221	94
Bleeding source				
gills	13		3	
gut	8		1	
eyes	1		0	

a. offset 4°

Table 2. Statistical comparison of circle hook and "J" hook caught sailfish from the recreational fishery off Iztapa, Guatemala, March through May, 1999, See text for descriptions of terminal gear and definitions of hook/catch percentage, hook location, bleeding, and degree of bleeding.

Comparison	Circle hook	"J" hook	Test	Statistic value	p	Odds ratio		95% confidence bounds	
Hook percentage = fish hook/ number of fish bites	82% (300/365)	72% (161/225)	Chi-square	9.217	0.002	Circle / J hook	1.831	1.236	2.723
Catch percentage = fish caught / number of fish hooked	78%(235/300)	78% (125/161)	Chi-square	0.029	0.864	Circle / J hook	1.041	0.656	1.652
Hook location									
Corner of mouth	200	34	Chi-square Contingency table	155.235	0.001	N/A			
Deep	4	58							
Foul	1	11	Cochron-Mantel-Haenszel Non-zero correlation	39.318	0.001	N/A			
Upper/lower Jaw	30	21							
Bleeding									
Yes/No	14 / 235	71 / 125	Chi-square	116.945	0.001	J hook / Circle	20.755	10.89	39.59
Degree of bleeding									
Severe	6	32	Chi-square Contingency table	116.582	0.001	N/A			
Moderate	4	23							
Minor	4	16	Cochran-Mantel-Haenszel Non-zero correlation	5.127	0.024	N/A			
None	220	54							

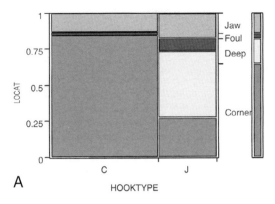

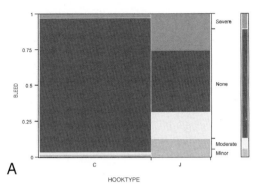

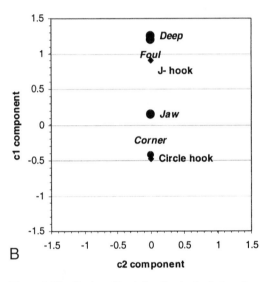

Correspondence Analysis Plot

Correspondence Analysis Plot

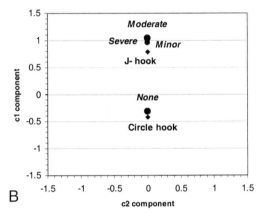

Figure 7. Distribution of degree of bleeding by hook type (circle and "J" hooks) for Pacific sailfish (A, bar width is proportional to sample size). Bleeding was characterized as none, minor, moderate, or severe. See text for definitions of bleeding categories. Correspondence analysis plot (B).

Figure 6. Distribution of hook location by hook type from Pacific sailfish caught off Iztapa, Guatemala (A, bar width is proportional to sample size). Hook locations were characterized as corner of mouth, upper/lower jaw, deep, and foul hooked. See text for definitions of hook locations. Correspondence analysis plot (B).

while circle hooks were associated with no bleeding (Figure 7, Tables 1 and 2).

Bleeding from the gills was found in 10% of the sailfish caught on "J" hooks and 1% of the sailfish caught on circle hooks. However, circle hooks were not found embedded in gill arches or filaments, whereas numerous "J" hooks were found lodged in these structures. After closer observation, it was determined that monofilament frequently became caught behind the gill plates during the fight, regardless of the type of terminal gear. Monofilament coming into contact with the gill structure appeared to

irritate the gill filaments and resulted in mostly moderate or minor bleeding. This was the only injury we documented during the study that could not be directly attributed to hook damage, and monofilament irritation of the gills was observed in sailfish caught on both terminal gears. However, in cases of severe bleeding from the gills, most of these instances were due to hook damage and not monofilament irritation.

Gear-Specific Fishing Success in Guatemala

Catch data derived from captain's logbooks included species, number of fish caught, bites, and number of fish raised, number of fishing days per month, and vessel name from 1996 through 1999 (Table 3; Figure 8). Sample sizes for sailfish and blue marlin during both fishing years (1996/1997 sailfish $N = 5,778$,

Table 3. Summary of catch statistics for Pacific sailfish and blue marlin from captains' logbooks of the recreational fishing fleet in Iztapa, Guatemala, by hook type and species. "J" hooks were used during the fishing year, June 1996–June 1997, and circle hooks were used during the fishing year June 1998–June 1999.

	"J" Hooks(1996/1997)		Circle Hooks(1998/1999)	
	Sailfish(n)	Blue marlin(n)	Sailfish(n)	Blue marlin(n)
Fishing days	776	776	517	517
Billfish raises	13,344	134	15,198	102
Billfish bites	10,297	106	11,610	85
Billfish caught	5,778	60	6,639	46
Catch percentage[a] (%)	56	57	57	54
Nominal CPUE (std mean)[b]	7.443 (0.489)	0.2011 (0.0669)	12.015 (0.884)	0.2617 (0.0533)

a. Catch % = number caught/number bites
b. CPUE = number caught/number fishing days per month.

blue marlin N = 60; 1998/1999 sailfish N = 6,639, blue marlin N = 46) were high (Table 3). As mentioned earlier, if we assumed that availability and stock density was similar between the 1996/1997 and 1998/1999 fishing years, differences in catch rates could be attributed to the terminal gear used. Thus, analysis of catch rates (catch per unit effort [CPUE] = number of fish/fishing day) was performed for sailfish and blue marlin using a GLMM model assuming a lognormal error distribution with autoregressive covariance structure (Littell et al. 1996). This covariance model accounts for large correlations for nearby time observations within each boat compared with distant observations. The factors included in the GLMM were quarter grouping

of monthly CPUEs, hook type ("J" hook and circle hook), and boat. The boat effect was considered a random factor. First-level interactions of main factors were also evaluated. The CPUE model can be expressed as

$$\log CPUE = \beta_0 + \sum_{i=1} \beta_i X_i + d_{ij} + e_{ijk} \qquad (1)$$

where X_i is the vector of fixed factors of hook type and quarter, d_{ij} is the random block factor boat, and e is the normally distributed error. The mean CPUE for each hook type was estimated from the least square means (LSMeans), and this variable was used as a test for significance between hook types. The Akaike's Information Criterion (AIC) and Schwarz's

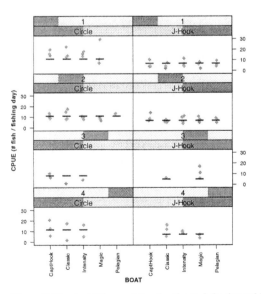 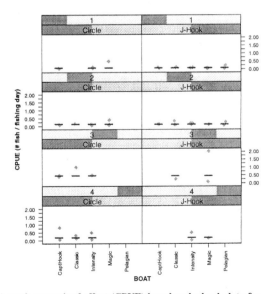

Figure 8. Nominal (diamonds) and estimated (horizontal line) catch per unit of effort (CPUE) based on logbook data for Pacific sailfish and blue marlin by quarter (1, 2, 3, and 4), hook type (Circle and J-type hooks), and boat from the recreational fleet off Iztapa, Guatemala.

Bayesian Criterion (SBC) showed that the autoregressive covariance model explained the overall variability (Table 4) better than the compound symmetric and unstructured covariance models (Littell et al. 1996). For sailfish, the model results showed that the hook-type factor was significant, and the mean estimated CPUEs were 10.25 sailfish per fishing day for circle hooks and 6.34 sailfish per fishing day for "J" hooks (Table 4; Figure 9). In contrast, for blue marlin, model results showed that hook type was not a significant factor, and mean estimated CPUEs were 0.174 blue marlin per fishing day and 0.167 blue

marlin per fishing day for circle hooks and "J" hooks, respectively (Table 4; Figure 9). Only, in the case of blue marlin, the quarter was a significant factor, reflecting the seasonal character of the blue marlin fishery off Iztapa, Guatemala.

Use of Circle Hooks in the South Florida Sailfish Live Bait Fishery

Seventy-five sailfish were caught on circle hooks using live bait in the recreational fishery off South Florida (Table 5). Analysis of catch percentages (fish caught/fish bites) using the CMH test showed no dif-

Table 4. Generalized linear mixed model (GLMM) analyses for Pacific sailfish and blue marlin catch rates from logbook reports of the recreational fisheries off Iztapa, Guatemala for two separate fishing years, June 1996/June 1997 and June 1998/June1999.

		Sailfish			Blue marlin	
		Covariance structure models				
Description		*Unstructured matrix*	*Compound symmetric*	*Autoregressive (1)*	*Unstructured matrix*	*Autoregressive (1)*
Observations		88	88	88	53	53
Residual log likelihood		-74.376	-76.778	-76.954	-61.689	-60.278
Akaike's Information criterion		-76.376	-78.778	-78.954	-63.867	-62.278
Schwarz's Bayesian criterion		-78.795	-81.197	-81.373	-65.738	-64.150

Model Summary						
Class	*Level*	*Values*				
Hook type	2	Circle	J-type			
Quarter	4	Jan-Mar	Apr-Jun	Jul-Sep	Oct-Dec	
Boat	5	CaptHook	Classic	Intensity	Magic	Pelagian

Blue marlin		*Test for fixed Effects*						
Source	*NDF*	*DDF*	*Type III F*	*p > F*				
Hook type	1	44	0.04	0.834				
Quarter	3	44	11.17	0.0001				

		Least Square Means		*Difference of LS Means for Hook type*			
Hook type	*LSMean*	*Std error*	*df*	*Difference*	*Std err Diff*	*t*	*p > |t|*
Circle	-1.7573	0.1375	44	0.0384	0.18202	0.210	0.8339
J-Type	-1.7957	0.1328	44				

Sailfish		*Test for fixed Effects*						
Source	*NDF*	*DDF*	*Type III F*	*p > F*				
Hook type	1	79	10.85	0.0015				
Quarter	3	79	0.72	0.5403				

	Least Square Means			*Difference of LS Means for Hook type*			
Hook type	*LSMean*	*Std error*	*df*	*Difference*	*Std errDiff*	*t*	*p > |t|*
Circle	2.3210	0.1122	79	0.4797	0.1456	3.29	0.015
J-Type	1.8413	0.1102	79				

A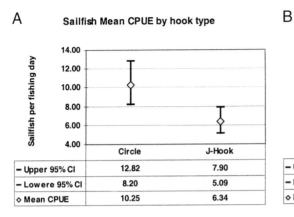

B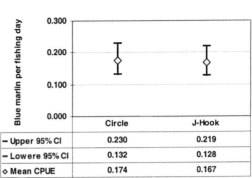

Figure 9. Estimated mean (LSMean) CPUE by hook type and 95% confidence intervals for Pacific sailfish (A) and blue marlin (B) based on logbook data from the recreational fleet off Iztapa, Guatemala. Long shank "J" hooks were used during the fishing year 1996/1997, and circle hooks were used during the fishing year 1998/1999.

ferences associated with the three categories of offset circle hooks (Table 6). Similar results were obtained using Fisher's exact test if the samples from minor offset and no offset were combined and compared with the severe offset category. However, the analysis of hook location indicated that the level of circle hook offset and hook location were not independent (Table 6). Correspondence analysis revealed that severe offset circle hooks were highly associ-ated with deep hooking, while minor and no offset circle hooks were associated with jaw and corner of mouth hook locations (Table 6; Figure 10). Bleeding was analyzed by grouping minor and no offset observations and this category was compared with severe offset circle hooks using the Fisher's exact test. Results indicated no statistically significant differences in bleeding between the offset categories (Table 6).

Table 5. Atlantic sailfish caught using live bait and circle hooks with different offset points off south Florida. Severe and minor offset hooks had 15° and 4° offsets, respectively. See text for definition of offset point, catch percentage, hook location, and degree of bleeding. The model of Eagle Claw circle hooks used in this study is given in parentheses.

	Offset Circle Hooks							
	Severe[a]		Minor[b]		None[c]		Minor & None combined	
	number	%	number	%	number	%	number	%
Fishing Success								
Fish hooked	18		22		47		69	
Fish caught	16	89	18	82	41	87	59	86
Hook location								
Corner	2	11	7	32	12	26	19	28
Jaw	3	17	4	18	7	15	11	16
Deep	8	44	3	14	3	6	6	9
Foul	0	0	0	0	0	0	0	0
Unknown	3	17	4	18	19	40	23	34
Bleeding								
Severe	1		0		0		0	
Moderate	0		0		2		2	
Minor	0		0		1		1	
None	15		18		38		56	

a. Eagle Claw model number L197 with 15° offset
b. Eagle Claw model number L2004 with 4° offset
c. Eagle Claw model number L2004EL

Table 6. Atlantic sailfish caught on circle hooks with three different offset points in the live bait recreational fishery off south Florida. Samples for no offset and minor offset were combined into a single category for the analysis of bleeding.

Comparison	No offset	Minor offset	Severe offset	Test	Statistic value	p	Odds ratio	95% confidence bounds
Catch percentage =				Chi-square				
fish caught/ fish bites	87%	82%	89%	Contingency table	0.507	0.776	N/A	
				Cochran-Mantel-				
	(41/47)	(18/22)	(16/18)	Haenszel	0.501	0.778	N/A	
Hook location								
Corner of mouth	12	7	2	Chi-square	17.205	0.009		
				Contingency table				
Deep	3	3	8					
Upper/lower Jaw	7	4	3	Likelihood Ratio	15.859	0.015		
				Chi-square				
Unknown	19	4	3	Fisher's Exact test		0.014		
Bleeding							Severe /Minor	
Yes/No		3 / 59	1 / 15	Fisher's Exact test		0.626	0.804	0.077 8.387

Discussion

Fishing Success

One of the first concerns in attempting to change the terminal gear in any recreational fishery is that such a change will negatively impact fishing success[1,2,4]. This study showed that catch percentages were unaffected by a change in hook type using the different terminal gears during dead bait trolling/pitch baiting for sailfish in Iztapa, Guatemala. Catch percentages for sailfish and blue marlin obtained from captain's logbooks in previous years were also consistent with these results. Analysis of standardized catch rates from captain's logbooks indicated that for Pacific sailfish, the number of fish caught per fishing day was higher during 1998–1999 year, when the fleet used circle hooks. However, this analysis could not differentiate between increases in fish availability and hook type catchability. Sailfish catch percentages were also high for circle hooks fished

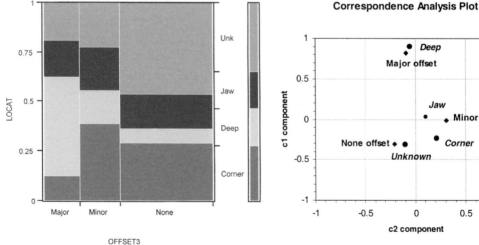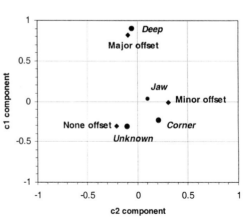

Figure 10. Distribution of hook location by degree of offset in circle hooks from Atlantic sailfish caught off South Florida (bar width is proportional to sample size) and correspondence analysis plot.

4. Jordan, J. 1999. Going full circle. Big Game Fishing Journal 12(3):52–62.

with live bait off Florida. However, it should be noted that catch percentages and catch rates for circle hooks depended on the novel forehead hook placement used to rig the baits, as well as a certain amount of training to implement a more passive approach to setting circle hooks. Our findings on fishing success were similar to those reported by Skomal et al. (this volume), who found no statistical differences in recreational catch rates between circle hooks and "J" hooks in the dead chunk bait fishery for juvenile Atlantic bluefin tuna.

Circle hooks fished in the manner described in this study were found to have a higher hooking percentage for sailfish compared with "J" hooks, and this result was corroborated with field observations. For example, it was observed that "J" hooks often dehooked during the fight when sailfish jumped out of water, and this was less likely to occur with a circle hook. The curved point of the circle hook appeared to reduce dehooking under these circumstances. Recreational anglers have noticed similar advantages of using circle hooks while targeting tarpon *Megalops atlanticus* in South Florida. In many Florida locations, circle hooks are now the terminal gear of choice for tarpon fishers because of their ability to hold in place, despite the fact that this species is known for dramatic leaps out of the water[4]. Skomal et al. (this volume) reported that once Atlantic bluefin tuna were hooked, there were three times as many instances of dehooking using "J" hooks, as compared with circle hooks. Overall, catch percentages (sailfish, blue marlin), hooking percentages (sailfish), and catch rates (sailfish) reported in this study generally were comparable with or were higher for circle hooks than for "J" hooks. These results are likely to encourage recreational billfishing constituents, who might not otherwise be receptive to changes in their fishing tackle, to consider the use of circle hooks as a terminal gear alternative to "J" hooks.

Physical Injuries Due to Hooking

It was beyond the scope of this study to measure release mortality directly, due in part to the difficulty of holding billfish in captivity (Post et al. 1997; de Sylva et al. 2000) and the prohibitively high cost of using pop-up satellite tags to monitor postrelease survival (Graves et al., unpublished data). However, hook location, physical hooking injuries, and amount of bleeding between hook types were evaluated in this study, and these data provide insight into survival potential. Hooks found in the jaw hinge or mouth, or fish bleeding from these locations, were not considered life threatening. Conversely, hooks found in the upper palate, throat, pharynx, esophagus, or stomach, and fish showing lacerations or bleeding from these areas, were considered potentially lethal. The lack of autopsies to examine hook-related injuries closely prevented estimates of potential release mortality in this study. Skomal et al. (this volume) were able to conduct detailed autopsies on Atlantic bluefin tuna in their hook-damage study and produced estimates of 2% potential release mortality for bluefin tuna caught on circle hooks and 28% potential mortality for tuna caught on "J" hooks. Nevertheless, difficulties in holding tuna and billfish in captivity or making direct in situ measurements continue to hinder release mortality studies of these species.

The results of this study clearly indicate that the use of circle hooks can minimize deep hooking and foul hooking in the recreational trolling/pitch bait fisheries for sailfish. Numerous other studies have found similar results for a wide variety of species, including striped bass (Lukacovic and Uphoff, this volume), Atlantic bluefin tuna (Skomal et al., this volume), and chinook salmon (Grover et al., this volume).

Although deep hooking was considered to be potentially lethal, sailfish and marlin are very large species that may not necessarily die if deep hooked in the throat, pharynx, esophagus, or stomach. For example, on numerous occasions, rusty hooks have been found in the stomachs of large billfish that appeared to be healthy otherwise (E. Prince, author's personal observation). In addition, it is common for all billfish to evert their stomachs outside their mouth once hooked (Harvey 1989; Figure 3). This appears to be a protective mechanism used by billfishes to dislodge bones and other indigestible materials that they routinely consume (Rivas 1975; ICCAT 1999). Therefore, having a bone or hook penetrate the stomach of a billfish may not necessarily result in mortality, unless it also injured a vital organ and/or initiated a lethal infection.

Only one sailfish mortality was documented during this study. This individual was caught on a "J" hook, which appeared to have cut one of the major gill arches. The assumption was that this fish bled to death. Conversely, some of the injuries that were not associated with deep hooking could also be potentially lethal. For example, several instances were documented where "J" hooks were foul hooked in the eye. If eye injuries result in blindness, then this injury could potentially affect survival because Istiophorids are highly dependent on daytime sight feeding in the upper portions of the water column (Rivas 1975; Block at al. 1992). Blindness in one eye would negatively impact peripheral vision and could seriously inhibit the ability of these species to feed. Numerous instances were also documented where "J" hook injuries that were not foul hooked could have caused eye damage. For example, in some cases, "J" hooks caused deep lacerations to the upper palate (Figure 5), which, on occasion, affected the occipital orbit and resulted in hemorrhaging in the eye. These types of injuries can be deceptive and are particularly difficult to observe in fish at boat-side because, in most cases, the lack of tissue in the upper palate results in the hook dehooking from its initial location and rehooking in another area. Although these fish would appear lively alongside the boat, upper palate injuries could be potentially lethal, due to eye damage. Upper palate injuries can also affect the integrity of the cranial cavity by making this area susceptible to infection. Belle (1997) reported that numerous juvenile Atlantic bluefin tuna caught on trolled cider plugs with "J" hooks suffered upper palate injuries. However, these injuries were not immediately evident upon capture and were only detected after conducting autopsies on mortalities observed in the tuna held in a sea pen for up to two weeks. Belle (1997) hypothesized that upper palate injuries suffered during capture resulted in cranium related infections, and these infections likely caused delayed mortality in bluefin tuna.

Perhaps the most significant finding in this study was the evaluation of bleeding, which indicated that sailfish caught on "J" hooks were more than 20 times more likely to bleed compared with those caught on circle hooks. This result was supported by corre-spondence analysis of the degree of bleeding, in which sailfish caught on "J" hooks were associated with severe, moderate, or minor bleeding, while sail-fish caught on circle hooks were associated with no bleeding. The reduced bleeding of circle hook caught sailfish has been cited as the primary reason why recreational anglers are voluntarily promoting the use of circle hooks over "J" hooks for dead bait trolling/pitch bait fishing for these species[1, 2, 4].

Although small sample sizes for the main treat-ments in the live bait study precluded more rigorous statistical analysis of fishing success, hook location, and amount of bleeding (Table 5), several trends in these data are noteworthy. For example, the severe offset deep hooking percentage (44%) was two to three times higher than minor or no offset deep hook-ing percentages. This result was a bit surprising because, prior to this finding, we had consistently experienced much lower overall deep hooking per-centages (< 10%) using circle hooks. Lukacovic and Uphoff (personal communication) also found a high deep hooking percentage (46%) on striped bass, using the same model severe offset circle hook as used in this study. Malchoff et al. (this volume) examined the use of circle hooks on summer flounder *Paralichthys dentatus* and speculated that the severe offset in the circle hook used may have resulted in higher deep hooking percentages than expected. The association of severe offset circle hooks and high rates of deep hooking have management implications because any conservation benefits of minimizing deep hooking rates realized when using circle hooks can be cir-cumvented by bending the circle hooks with pliers to increase the degree of offset.

Conclusions

The current high rate of fishing mortality and depressed stock status of most Atlantic Istiophori-dae justify development of alternative approaches for reducing hook-induced mortality for these species. One such approach would be the modification of ter-minal gear in order to reduce hook-related injuries and trauma experienced during catch-and-release fishing (Muoneke and Childress 1994). This study compared circle hook and similar-sized "J" hook performance, while trolling/pitching dead bait or drifting live bait for billfish, methods commonly used by anglers targeting these species. Rates of fishing success and hooking percentage were com-parable or higher for circle hooks compared with "J" hooks. In addition, use of circle hooks resulted in lower rates of deep hooking, foul hooking, and bleeding compared with "J" hooks. During live bait experiments, severe offset circle hooks were asso-ciated with increased deep-hooking percentages that were similar to percentages observed for "J" hooks using dead bait (46%). Given the multiple benefits of minimized hook-related injury, along with comparable or improved fishing success and hooking percentages using circle hooks in dead or live bait recreational fisheries for billfish, this terminal gear appears to have potential as a means to promote the live release of these species.

Acknowledgments

The investigators would like to thank the captains, crews, and fisherman from Fins and Feathers fleet (including vessels F/V *Captain Hook*, F/V *Magic*, F/V *Intensity*, F/V *Pelagian*, and F/V *Classic*) in Iztapa, Guatemala, for their cooperation and enthusiastic support in providing their logbooks, experience, and boats to carry out this study. In particular, we thank Captain Ron Hamlin of F/V *Captain Hook* for his innovative bait rigging and initial use of circle hooks in the sailfish fishery off Guatemala. The authors are grateful to South Florida Captains Nick Smith, Angelo Durante, and Bouncer Smith, for their willingness to participate in the live bait portion of the study. This research was partially funded by a grant from Tim Choate of ARTMARINA in Miami, Florida, and owner of the Fins and Feathers Resort in Iztapa, Guatemala. Without Choate's active participation and enthusiasm, this project would not have been possible. Circle hooks used in this study were provided by George Large and Mike Praznovsky of Eagle Claw Fishing Tackle, Wright & McGill Company.

References

Belle, S. 1997. Bluefin tuna project. Final report for National Oceanic and Atmospheric Administration Award NA37FL0285. New England Aquarium, Edgerton Research Laboratory, Central Wharf, Boston, Massachusetts.

Block, B. A., D. T. Booth, and F. G. Carey. 1992. Depth and temperature of the blue marlin, *Makaira nigricans*, observed by acoustic telemetry. Marine Biology 114:175–183.

de Sylva, D. P., W. J. Richards, T. R. Capo, and J. E. Serafy. 2000. Potential effects of human activities on billfishes (Istiophoridae and Xiphiidae) in the western Atlantic Ocean. Bulletin of Marine Science 66:187–198.

Farber, M. I., C. D. Jones, D. S. Rosenthal, M. T. Judge, A. M. Avrigan, E. D. Prince, T. L. Jackson, D. W. Lee, and C. J. Brown. 1997. 1994/1995 report of the Southeast Fisheries Science Center Billfish Program. National Oceanic and Atmospheric Administration Technical Memorandum NMFS-SEFSC-398.

Graves, J. E., B. E. Luckhurst, and E. D. Prince. Unpublished data. An evaluation of pop-up satellite tag technology to estimate post-release survival of Atlantic blue marlin *Makaira nigricans*. Abstract. Presented at the National Symposium on Catch and Release in Marine Recreational Fisheries, held December 5–8, 1999, Virginia Beach, Virginia.

Harvey, G. C. 1989. An historical review of recreational and artisanal fisheries for billfish in Jamaica, 1976–1988. Collected Volume of Scientific Papers. International Commission for the Conservation of Atlantic Tunas (ICCAT), Madrid, Spain 30(2)440–450.

ICCAT (International Commission for the Conservation of Atlantic Tunas). 1998. Report for biennial period, 1997–98. ICCAT, Spain. Part 1 (1997), volume 2.

ICCAT (International Commission for the Conservation of Atlantic Tunas). 1999. Executive Summary Report for Blue Marlin (1999). Report for biennial period, 1998–99. ICCAT, Madrid, Spain. Part 1 (1998), volume 2.

ICCAT (International Commission for the Conservation of Atlantic Tunas). 2000. Report of the standing committee on research and statistics (SCRS). ICCAT, Madrid, Spain.

Littell, R. C., G. A. Milliken, W. W. Stroup, and R. D. Wolfinger. 1996. SAS Systems for mixed model. SAS Institute, Cary, North Carolina.

Manly, Brian F. J. 1994. Multivariate statistical methods. A primer, 2nd edition. Chapman and Hall, CRC.

Muoneke, M. I., and W. M. Childress. 1994. Hooking mortality: a review for recreational fisheries. Review Fishery Science 2:123–156.

Post, J. T., J. E. Serafy, J. S. Ault, T. R. Capo, and D. P. de Sylva. 1997. Field and laboratory observations on larval Atlantic sailfish (*Istiophorus platypterus*) and swordfish (*Xiphias gladius*). Bulletin of Marine Science 60:1026–1034.

Prince, E. D., B. B. Brown. 1991. Coordination of the ICCAT enhanced research program for billfish. Pages 13–18 *in* D. Guthrie, J. M. Hoenig, M. Holliday, C. M. Jones, M. J. Mills, S. A. Moberly, K. H. Pollock, and D. R. Talhelm, editors. Creel and angler surveys in fisheries management. American Fisheries Society, Symposium 12, Bethesda, Maryland.

Rivas, L. R. 1975. Synopsis of biological data on blue marlin, *Makaira nigricans*, Lacepede, 1802. In R. S. Shomura and F. Williams, editors. Proceedings of the International Billfish Symposium Kailua-Kona, Hawaii, 9–12 August 1972. Part 3. Species synopses. National Oceanic and Atmospheric Administration Technical Report NMFS SSRF-675.

SAFMC (South Atlantic Fishery Management Council). 1988. Fishery management plan, final environmental impact statement, regulatory impact review, and initial regulatory flexibility analysis for the Atlantic billfishes.

SAS Institute Inc. 1997. SAS/STAT Software: changes and enhancements through Release 6.12. SAS Institute Inc., Cary, North Carolina.

Shoukri, M. M., and C. A. Pause. 1999. Statistical methods for health sciences. 2nd edition. CRC Press LLC.

Steel, G. D., and J. H. Torrie. 1960. Principles and procedures of statistics. McGraw-Hill Book Company, Inc., New York.

USDOC (U.S. Department of Commerce) 1999. Amendment 1 to the Atlantic billfish fishery management plan. Highly Migratory Species Management Division, National Oceanic and Atmospheric Administration, Silver Spring, Maryland.

American Fisheries Society Symposium 30:80–87, 2002

A Preliminary Comparison of the Relative Mortality and Hooking Efficiency of Circle and Straight Shank ("J") Hooks Used in the Pelagic Longline Industry

BRETT FALTERMAN *and* JOHN E. GRAVES[1]

School of Marine Science
Virginia Institute of Marine Science
College of William and Mary
Post Office Box 1346
Gloucester Point, Virginia 23062, USA

Abstract.—The fishing characteristics of circle hooks and straight shank or "J" hooks were investigated in the pelagic longline fishery during two successive trips. In one trip, circle hooks and J-hooks of comparable size were alternated along the length of the longline on six sets of approximately 400 live-baited hooks each, allowing a preliminary comparison of catch per unit effort (CPUE), hooking location, and mortality between the two hook types. On a previous trip, records of hooking location and mortality were obtained for J-hooks on nine additional longline sets. Yellowfin tuna *Thunnus albacares* accounted for 60% of the catch; the remainder was composed of 15 other species, none of which was represented by more than eight individuals. There was higher CPUE for all species combined, using circle hooks (5.05 fish/100 hooks) as compared with using "J" hooks (2.28 fish/100 hooks). Similar results were observed with the catch of the target species (yellowfin tuna), for which CPUE was approximately 2.5 times higher with circle hooks (3.33 tuna/100 hooks) as compared with J-hooks. Circle hooks also resulted in a lower mortality for all species (31% versus 42%) and for the target species (21% versus 39%). For all species, 95% of the fish taken on circle hooks were hooked in the jaw. Hooking location varied by species, but for all species combined, circle hooks consistently had a higher frequency of jaw hooking and a lower frequency of gut hooking than J-hooks. These preliminary results suggest that use of circle hooks in the pelagic longline fishery targeting yellowfin tuna may not only increase CPUE and survival of this species but also improve the survival of incidental catch and bycatch.

Introduction

The pelagic longline is the major gear type used to catch swordfish *Xiphias gladius* and adult tunas *Thunnus* spp. in the Atlantic Ocean. A single pelagic longline set is typically composed of several hundred to several thousand baited hooks attached by gangions to a mainline that may extend 60 km or more. Baited hooks are available to virtually all large, piscivorous predators that feed in epipelagic waters. Longline catches usually include not only target species, but also incidental catch species (nontarget fishes retained for sale or personal consumption) and bycatch species (animals taken on the gear that are discarded).

Stocks of many of the species that interact with longline gear in the Atlantic Ocean, either as target catch, incidental catch, or bycatch, are considered to be either fully fished or overfished (ICCAT 2000).

The International Commission for the Conservation of Atlantic Tunas (ICCAT) and the U.S. National Marine Fisheries Service (NMFS) have listed stocks of North Atlantic swordfish and Atlantic bigeye tuna *Thunnus obesus* as overfished and Atlantic yellowfin tuna *T. albacares* as fully fished. These represent the major target species for U.S. pelagic longliners. North Atlantic albacore tuna *T. alalunga*, an incidental catch, is considered overfished (ICCAT 2000). Many bycatch species, including Atlantic blue marlin *Makaira nigricans*, Atlantic white marlin *Tetrapturus albidus*, and western Atlantic sailfish *Istiophorus platypterus*, are overfished (ICCAT 2000), while other bycatch species, including some marine mammals and turtles, are listed as threatened or endangered.

National Standard 9 of the Magnuson-Stevens Fishery Conservation and Management Act requires that fishery management plans approved by the Sec-

[1]Corresponding author. Email: graves@vims.edu.

retary of Commerce minimize bycatch to the extent practicable and minimize the mortality of bycatch that cannot be avoided. Methods of minimizing bycatch in the pelagic longline fishery include time/area closures and/or gear modifications that increase gear selectivity. While such measures may reduce bycatch in the fishery, the spatial and temporal co-occurrence of target and bycatch species in epipelagic waters suggests that bycatch will not be completely eliminated. Therefore, means of minimizing bycatch mortality must be considered.

Circle hooks have been suggested as one means of gear modification that may reduce mortality of fishes in recreational and commercial fisheries. Relative to straight shank or "J" hooks in "catch-and-release" recreational fisheries, circle hooks are reported to result in fewer deep hookings and increased survival (observed or inferred) for bluefin tuna *Thunnus thynnus* (Skomal et al., this volume), sailfish and blue marlin (Prince et al., this volume), striped bass *Morone saxatilis* (Lukacovic and Uphoff, this volume), and chinook salmon *Oncorhynchus tshawytscha* (Grover et al., this volume). Although not as extensively investigated, similar trends are evident in commercial fisheries. In a study of the Gulf of Mexico pelagic longline fishery, Berkeley and Edwards (1997) noted higher immediate mortality for billfish caught on straight shank J-hooks than on circle hooks. Although their sample size was small, a significant fraction of billfish was alive at the time of pelagic longline haulback, some even after being hooked for 12 hours.

Any measure that significantly reduces bycatch mortality will have little acceptance by the fishing community if it also significantly decreases catch per unit effort (CPUE) of the target species. For example, incorporation of turtle exclusion devices (TEDs) and bycatch reduction devices (BRDs) in the southeastern United States and Gulf of Mexico shrimp fishery was not thoroughly embraced because fishermen believed the gear modifications allowed much of their target catch to escape. In contrast, preliminary results for the use of circle hooks suggest that they may actually increase fishing power (CPUE) for target species such as Pacific halibut *Hippoglossus stenolepis* (Sullivan et al. 1999). In the Gulf of Mexico pelagic longline fishery, Hoey (1996) reported an increased CPUE for circle hooks relative to J-hooks, based on observer data. However, comparisons of hook types were not made on the same longline sets. In this paper, we present the results of a study in which we alternated circle hooks and J-hooks on gangions of similar length on a pelagic longline to determine if the different hook types resulted in differential CPUE, hooking location, and mortality of target, incidental, and bycatch species.

Methods

Two successive trips, Trips 1 and 2, were made during June and July 1999 aboard the F/V *Triple Chass*, a commercial longline vessel that fishes the Caribbean Sea and adjacent waters out of Port de la Cruz, Venezuela. Fifteen sets of approximately 400 live-baited hooks each were deployed during the two trips. The design of this study was to alternate circle hooks and J-hooks along the length of the mainline, providing both hook types an equal probability of catching a given fish. Because this particular vessel fished exclusively with 7/0 Mustad J-hooks (#7698), we initially selected 14/0 Mustad circle hooks (#39960) for comparison. These hooks were chosen because of the similarity in size and reports of success of these hooks in previous experimental fishing operations from recreational boats targeting sailfish (Dr. Eric Prince, Southeast Fisheries Science Center, NMFS, personal communication).

Circle hooks were offset manually as required by the captain. Providing a slight offset to circle hooks is a common practice among both recreational and commercial fishermen and is thought to increase hooking efficiency (Prince et al., this volume) and facilitate manual baiting. At the beginning of Trip 1, the captain was hesitant to fish the 14/0 circle hooks because he suspected the hooks would be straightened by large yellowfin tuna, the primary target species. Therefore, these hooks were only alternated along one quarter of the mainline for the first two sets. During these sets, many 14/0 circle hooks were bent, each resulting in the loss of a potential "money" fish. After candid discussions with the captain and crew, it was decided to remove all 14/0 circle hooks from the mainline for the remainder of that trip. As a result, data were recorded from the nine sets of Trip 1 for J-hook mortality and hooking location only (Table 1).

During Trip 2, 16/0 Mustad circle hooks (#39960) were alternated along the entire mainline for all six

Table 1. Study design. The number of sets, bait types, hook types, and data collected are presented for Trips 1 and 2.

	Trip 1	Trip 2	
Sets	9 sets	3 sets	3 sets
Bait	live bait	live bait	live and dead baits
Hooks	"J" hooks	"J" and circle hooks	"J" and circle hooks
Data collected	hooking mortality	hooking mortality	hooking mortality
	hooking location	hooking location	hooking location
		CPUE	

sets. In most cases, hooks were baited with live bigeye scad *Decapturus* spp; however, dead bait was used on sections of the line during three of the six sets. Previous research suggested there may be significant differences in pelagic longline fishing CPUE between live and dead baits (Hoey and Moore 1999); therefore, hooking location and mortality were recorded for all fish taken on all baits, but CPUE was recorded only for the sections of the line that contained live bait (Table 1).

Hook location was reported for total catch and by species for all sets. Locations were designated by the following terminology: corner of the mouth (corner); medial hinge of the lower jaw (mid-lower); anterior mouth roof (roof); lateral surface of mouth anterior to esophagus and posterior to jaw hinge (inside); esophageal area, which could be seen through the mouth (throat); lower esophagus or stomach, which could not be seen through the mouth (gut); anywhere on the exterior of the body (foul); entanglement in gangion without hook-set (bill). Hook location was designated as "not specified" if fish were de-hooked or released before hook location could be noted.

Relative mortality was reported by hook type and hook location based on all sets. For the purpose of this study, fish that did not actively move in the water or on deck were considered dead. Fishing power or CPUE (the number of fish caught per 100 hooks) was determined for live-baited hooks (Trip 2) for all fishes combined and by species.

Differences in CPUE between circle hooks and J-hooks for all catch and for yellowfin tuna were tested with t-tests using Microsoft Excel. Because these data were not normally distributed, they were adjusted using the $\log(X + 1)$ transformation, so the assumption of normality for Student's t-test would not be violated (Zar 1996). The t-test was also used to compare mean yellowfin tuna length between

hook types for Trip 2 to determine if there was any size selective factor accompanying hook type. Analysis of variance (ANOVA) was used to test for differences in relative mortality, based on hook type, hook location, and species, using Quattro Pro. These analyses were based on relative mortalities expressed as proportions. An arcsine transformation allowed the data to conform to the assumption of normality for ANOVA (Zar 1996).

Results

Location, time, and surface temperatures for all sets are recorded in Appendix 1. A total of 5,480 hooks deployed on 15 longline sets caught 163 fishes representing 16 species. Yellowfin tuna, the target species, comprised 61% of the total catch. Bigeye tuna, albacore, wahoo *Acanthocybium solandri*, sailfish, oilfish *Ruvettus* sp., gempylids *Alepisaurus* spp., and other fishes made up the remainder of the catch (Table 2).

Estimates of CPUE were based on 77 fishes caught across 2,105 live-baited hooks from the six sets of Trip 2. CPUE for all fishes caught with circle hooks (Figure 1) ranged from 2.5 to 8.8 fish per 100 hooks ($x = 5.05$), while for J-hooks CPUE ranged from 0.6 to 5.9 fish per 100 hooks ($x = 2.3$). Yellowfin tuna CPUE ranged from 1.2 to 6.6 tuna per 100 circle hooks ($x = 3.3$), while CPUE ranged from 0.5 to 3.7 tuna per 100 J-hooks ($x = 1.3$; Figure 2). Differences in overall CPUE for all fishes and for yellowfin tuna were statistically significant between circle hooks and J-hooks ($p = 0.033$ and $p = 0.026$, respectively). Circle hook CPUE was higher for most other species as well. No difference was detected between mean yellowfin tuna length and hook type (Figure 3).

Mortality differed between hook types, among species (Table 2), and among hooking locations (Table 3). Overall, 31% of the fishes caught on cir-

Table 2. Catch composition and mortality by hook type of 163 fishes collected from 15 pelagic longline sets, nine using J-hooks and six alternating circle hooks and J-hooks.

Species	Percent composition (n)	Percent mortality	
		Circle hook	J-hook
Yellowfin tuna *Thunnus albacares*	60.7 (99)	21.0	39.3
Albacore *Thunnus alalunga*	4.9 (8)	33.3	40.0
Wahoo *Acanthocybium solandri*	4.9 (8)	100.0	100.0
Bigeye tuna *Thunnus obesus*	4.3 (7)	0	0
Gempylid *Alepisaurus* spp.	4.3 (7)	100.0	100.0
Oilfish *Ruvettus* spp.	3.7 (6)	0	25.0
Sailfish *Istiophorus platypterus*	3.7 (6)	100.0	80.0
Dolphin fish *Coryphaena hippurus*	2.5 (4)	—	0
Longbill spearfish *Tetrapturus pfluegeri*	2.5 (4)	—	50.0

Other species included swordfish *Xiphius gladius* (3), great barracuda *Sphyraena barracuda* (3), pelagic stingray *Dasyatis violacea* (3), pelagic puffer *Lagocephalus* spp. (2), horse-eye jack *Caranx lugubris* (1), skipjack tuna *Katsuwonis pelamis* (1), and blue shark *Prionace glauca* (1).

cle hooks were dead, compared with 42% dead on J-hooks. The difference in mortality by hook type was more pronounced for yellowfin tuna, where observed mortality was 21% for circle hooks and 39% for J-hooks. When each set was treated as an independent observation and subjected to the *t*-test, these differences were not statistically significant, due to low sample size and high variance.

Mortality differed greatly among species. Some fishes, such as gempylids and wahoo, experienced 100% mortality, regardless of hook type. For albacore, yellowfin tuna, and oilfish, all of which experienced intermediate rates of on-line mortality, lower relative mortalities were observed on circle hooks

than on J-hooks (Table 2). No mortality was observed for bigeye tuna ($N = 7$) or dolphin fish *Coryphaena hippurus* ($N = 4$). Neither longbill spearfish *Tetrapturus pfluegeri* nor dolphin were caught on circle hooks. A two-way ANOVA of relative mortality using hook type and species as factors indicted that relative mortality was significantly different among species ($p = 0.023$) but not between hook types.

Of the 163 fishes caught, 62 were taken on circle hooks (Trip 2) and 101 on J-hooks (Trips 1 and 2). Hook locations for both hook types are presented in Table 3. The vast majority (95%) of fishes caught on circle hooks were hooked in the jaw; of these,

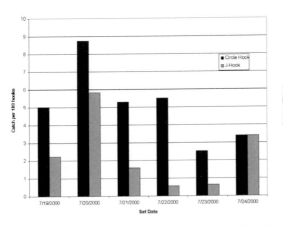
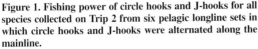

Figure 1. Fishing power of circle hooks and J-hooks for all species collected on Trip 2 from six pelagic longline sets in which circle hooks and J-hooks were alternated along the mainline.

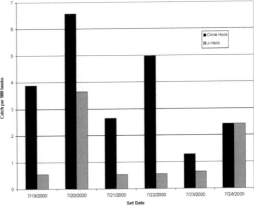

Figure 2. Fishing power of circle hooks and J-hooks for yellowfin tuna collected on Trip 2 from six pelagic longline sets in which circle hooks and J-hooks were alternated along the mainline on each set.

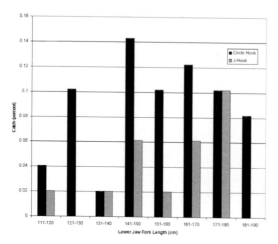

Figure 3. Distribution of yellowfin tuna taken on circle hooks and J-hooks by size on Trip 2. Fish were taken on six pelagic longline sets in which circle hooks and J-hooks were alternated along the mainline.

Table 3. Hooking location (number and percent frequency) of circle hooks (N = 62) and J-hooks (N = 101) for all species. Percent mortality for all species with hook types combined is presented for each hooking location.

Hooking location	Circle hook %(n)	J-hook % (n)	Mortality %
Corner	82.3 (51)	57.4 (58)	25.0
Mid-lower jaw	12.9(8)	3.0(3)	72.7
Roof	0	5.0(5)	80.0
Inside	0	0	—
Throat	3.3(2)	4.0(4)	83.3
Gut	0	5.0(5)	80.0
Foul	0	10.9 (11)	70.0
Bill-wrap	1.6(1)	0	0
Not specified	0	14.9 (15)	—

82% were hooked in the corner of the jaw and 13% in the hinge of the lower jaw (Table 3). Greater variation in hooking location was observed in fish caught with J-hooks, with the majority (57%) hooked in the lower corner of the mouth and 11% foul hooked (Table 3). Several fish taken on J-hooks were hooked deeply, with 5% hooked in the gut and 4% hooked in the throat. Hook locations in the lower jaw were uncommon, and no fish were taken with a hook interior to the lateral jaw hinge. Hook location was unspecified for 15% of the fish caught on J-hooks (Table 3).

Hook location varied among species. All yellowfin tuna caught on circle hooks were hooked in the corner of the mouth (N = 38), while only 61% of yellowfin tuna caught on J-hooks were hooked in the corner of the mouth (37 of 61). Six of seven gempylids were hooked in the mid-lower jaw, summed over the two hook types.

A total of only 13 billfishes were caught on the two trips. Ten were taken on Trip 1, when only J-hooks were fished. Of these, five were either deep or foul hooked, two were hooked in the anterior roof of the mouth, and three were hooked in the jaw. Of the three billfishes caught on circle hooks, two were swordfish. One was a large fish that was bill-wrapped in the gangion, and the other was a small fish that was hooked in the jaw. The only sailfish caught on a circle hook was hooked in the throat.

Of 109 fish hooked in the corner of the mouth,

only 27 (25%) were dead at the time of haul back (Table 3). In comparison, higher mortalities (70–83%) were recorded for fish that were foul-hooked or hooked in the gut, roof of the mouth, throat or mid-lower jaw. When hook location and hook type were used as factors in a two-way ANOVA, neither factor was found to be significant. Interaction factors could not be calculated for the ANOVA because collection of replicate data was not possible.

Entanglement in the gangion, a factor that may contribute to mortality of longline-caught fishes, was observed for eight fish. Four yellowfin tuna, one albacore, one sailfish, and one spearfish had the gangion wrapped around the tail and/or body and were dead at the time of haulback. One swordfish had the gangion entangled on its bill (bill-wrapped) and was alive when the gear was retrieved.

Discussion

Circle hooks appear to have different fishing characteristics than J-hooks when deployed in an alternating fashion on pelagic longline gear. These differences were evident in target species CPUE, mortality, and hooking location. We found an increased CPUE for circle hooks relative to J-hooks for all species (5.05 fish/100 circle hooks versus 2.28 fish/100 J-hooks) and for yellowfin tuna, the target species (3.33 yellowfin tuna/100 circle hooks versus 1.33 yellowfin tuna/100 J-hooks). These results are consistent with those of Hoey (1996) who reported an increased catch rate for circle hooks relative to J-hooks on observed pelagic longline sets from the Gulf of Mexico. In that study, J-hooks caught an average of 25.5 fish per set, and circle hooks caught 32.9 fish per set. Similarly increased fishing power for circle hooks has been reported in the Pacific halibut fishery (Sullivan et al. 1999). At 174 fixed survey stations that were fished twice, once with circle hooks and once with J-hooks, circle hooks caught 2.3 times as much legal halibut (by weight) as J-hooks.

There were pronounced differences in hooking location between circle hooks and J-hooks. The vast majority (95%) of fishes caught on circle hooks were hooked in the corner or lower hinge of the jaw. In contrast, of the fishes caught on J-hooks for which hooking location was specified, only 71% were hooked in the corner or lower hinge of the jaw. The difference in hooking location between hook types was also evident in the target species. All yellowfin tuna taken on circle hooks in this study were hooked in the corner of the jaw, compared with 61% of those taken on J-hooks. Similar results demonstrating a very high frequency of hooking location in the corner of the jaw have been noted for recreational species taken on circle hooks, including billfishes (Prince et al., this volume), striped bass (Luckacovic and Uphoff, this volume), and chinook salmon (Grover et al., this volume).

The mortality of fishes taken on pelagic longline gear differed between the two hook types. In this study, fishes taken on circle hooks had a mortality of 31%, compared with 42% on J-hooks. While not significant, these values display the same trend as those reported by Hoey (1996) for fishes taken on pelagic longline gear in the Gulf of Mexico. He noted a mortality of 49% for fishes captured on circle hooks and a mortality of 62% for those taken on J-hooks. Differences in absolute levels between the two studies may be the result of sample sizes and/or bait types (live versus dead).

The mortality levels in the present study were influenced by the composition of the species taken by the two hook types and are more pronounced if one does not consider the gempylids. Seven gempylids were taken in this study, five on circle hooks and two on J-hooks. Each fish was hooked in the hinge of the lower jaw, a probable result of their method of feeding and elongate mouth. Unlike other species in this study that were hooked in the lower jaw hinge, all seven gempylids were recorded as dead at the time of haulback. However, none was recovered whole. Gempylids are soft-bodied fish, and as a result of the speed of the haulback, all were mutilated in the process of gear retrieval. We were unable to discern if these mortalities were the result of hook damage or the haulback process itself. If the fish were alive before mutilation, survival values for both hook types would increase, but much more for circle hooks than J-hooks.

The mortality of the target species, yellowfin tuna, like the overall catch, differed between hook types. Although not statistically significant due to sample size, the observed mortality for circle hooks (21%) was almost half of that for J-hooks (39%). These results suggest that use of circle hooks could increase the survival of target, incidental catch, and bycatch species. While the benefits for bycatch species is obvious, the value of target and incidental catch species is greater for fish that are alive at the time of haulback, due to increased product quality.

There was clearly a relationship between hooking location and survival for all species and for the target species. Fish hooked in the jaw exhibited higher rates of survival than those that were hooked deeply. This is consistent with reports from studies of recreational fisheries (Grover et al.; Luckacovic and Uphoff; Prince et al.; Skomal et al., all this volume). Fishes that became entangled in the gangion experienced high mortalities independent of hooking location. This was likely due to restriction of body movement leading to suffocation, especially for the tunas, which are dependent on ram ventilation.

The inferences that can be drawn from this study are limited by sample sizes. The numbers of target, incidental catch, and bycatch species captured on the pelagic longline gear were not large enough to provide considerable power to the statistical analyses. Further analyses will be required to evaluate the use of circle hooks as a means of reducing bycatch in the pelagic longline fishery. This is especially true for billfishes, which represented a minor component of the catch in this study. Nevertheless, the results of this preliminary analysis indicate that the use of circle hooks may decrease on-line mortality of target, incidental catch, and bycatch species and increase overall CPUE. While only trends for the most part, the increased fishing power for yellowfin tuna alone convinced the captain of our vessel to switch completely to circle hooks. Further analyses into differences in relative mortality between bait types, set depth, and soak time will help to isolate practical management schemes to decrease bycatch and bycatch mortality in the pelagic longline fishery.

Acknowledgments

We would like to thank Captain January Bragg and the crew of the F/V *Triple Chass* for the opportunity to conduct this study on their vessel. Eric Prince and Freddy Arocha provided invaluable logistical support throughout the study. Funding was provided by the Highly Migratory Species Management Division, NMFS (contract # 40AANF900331) and the ICCAT Enhanced Billfish Program. The manuscript benefited from the comments of John Hoey, Eric Prince, and an anonymous reviewer. VIMS contribution # 2363.

References

Berkeley, S. A., and R. E. Edwards. 1997. Factors affecting capture and survival in longline fisheries: potential application for reducing bycatch mortality. Standing Committee for Statistics and Research 97/63, International Commission for the Conservation of Atlantic Tunas, Madrid, Spain.

Hoey, J. J. 1996. Bycatch in Western Atlantic pelagic longline fisheries. Pages 193–203 *in* Solving bycatch: considerations for today and tomorrow. Alaska Sea Grant College Program Report No. 96-03.

Hoey, J. J., and N. Moore. 1999. Captain's report: multi-species catch characteristics for the U.S. Atlantic pelagic longline fishery. National Fisheries Institute, Arlington, Virginia.

ICCAT (International Commission for the Conservation of Atlantic Tunas). 2000. Report of the Standing Committee for Research and Statistics. Report for biennial period. 1998–1999. Part II, volume 2, Madrid, Spain.

Sullivan, P.J, A. M. Parma, and W. G. Clark. 1999. Pacific halibut stock assessment of 1997. International Pacific Halibut Commission, Scientific Report No. 79. Seattle, Washington.

Zar, J. H. 1996. Biostatistical Analysis, 3rd Edition. Prentice Hall, New Jersey.

Appendix 1. Set location, time, and surface temperature for all sets.

Date	Time	Temp	Latitude (N)	Longitude (W)	Date	Time	Temp	Latitude (N)	Longitude (W)
		Trip 1			7/6/1999				
6/30/1999					Set	1150	81.8	12 20.0	66 08.8
Set	1308	80.4	11 38.9	64 48.2		1518	82.9	12 32.2	66 21.3
	1641	81.2	11 47.5	65 05.3	Haul	1830	82.8	12 31.9	66 22.2
Haul	2002	80.7	11 47.7	65 06.0		2345	81.8	12 25.2	66 08.5
	120	79.5	11 46.9	64 49.5	7/9/1999				
7/1/1999					Set	1236	81	11 29.9	65 30.4
Set	1100	80.7	11 57.9	65 19.8		1523	81.4	11 45.9	65 37.8
	1408	81.9	12 08.8	65 25.8	Haul	1900	81.3	11 46.1	65 37.8
Haul	1915	81.6	12 10.2	65 16.0		2251	81.2	11 33.1	65 25.2
	2349	80.5	12 07.1	65 27.7	7/10/1999				
7/2/1999					Set	1456	82.1	11 40.0	65 07.4
Set	1310	82.7	12 28.5	66 09.6		1740	81.8	11 29.2	65 00.5
	1617	82.6	12 30.3	66 25.5	Haul	2000	80.8	11 41.8	65 10.3
Haul	1930	82.5	12 29.0	66 25.1		2321	80.8	11 34.7	65 04.0
	2400	82.6	12 29.2	66 09.8					
7/3/1999							Trip 2		
Set	1425	82.7	12 05.6	65 54.6	7/19/1999				
	1715	82.9	12 07.8	66 08.0	Set	1135	82.4	11 26.8	67 26.6
Haul	2125	82.8	12 07.1	66 07.6		1515	83	11 19.7	67 45.4
	104	82.3	12 05.3	65 52.5	Haul	1945	82.7	11 20.6	67 44.6
7/4/1999						128	82.6	11 22.6	67 27.4
Set	500	81.9	12 11.5	65 51.7	7/20/1999				
	818	82.2	12 11.6	66 06.6	Set	1316	82.8	11 22.6	67 35.3
Haul	1700	84.4	12 05.5	66 07.0		1639	83.1	11 13.4	67 52.1
	2026	82.6	12 05.6	65 58.2	Haul	1830	82.9	11 13.4	67 51.0
7/5/1999							82.6	11 21.0	67 34.0
Set	905	81.4	12 14.0	66 04.9	7/21/1999				
	1320	83.1	12 30.5	66 10.8	Set	128	82.8	11 21.8	67 32.3
Haul	1845	82.8	12 31.9	66 08.9		1705	82.9	11 25.0	67 52.9
	302	82.4	12 14.3	66 10.3	Haul	2110	82.7	11 24.8	67 53.3

Date	Time	Temp	Latitude (N)	Longitude (W)	Date	Time	Temp	Latitude (N)	Longitude (W)
	359	82.7	11 23.3	67 32.9		1557	83.3	11 12.1	67 45.6
7/22/1999					Haul	2030	83.1	11 12.4	67 45.2
Set	1455	83.1	11 19.9	67 30.6		0:52	82.9	11 16.2	67 30.4
	1800	82.9	11 16.3	67 47.9	7/24/1999				
Haul	2115	82.7	11 16.0	67 47.1	Set	1410	83.6	11 20.9	67 51.5
	230	82.7	11 18.3	67 31.0		1722	83.5	11 26.7	67 30.4
7/23/1999					Haul	1921	83.5	11 26.5	67 34.1
Set	1300	83.1	11 17.2	67 30.1		100	83.1	11 20.9	67 51.3

American Fisheries Society Symposium 30:88–96, 2002

A Review of the Methods Used to Estimate, Reduce, and Manage Bycatch Mortality of Pacific Halibut in the Commercial Longline Groundfish Fisheries of the Northeast Pacific

Robert J. Trumble[1]

MRAG Americas
110 South Hoover Blvd
Tampa, Florida 33609-3437, USA

Stephen M. Kaimmer[2] *and* Gregg H. Williams[3]

International Pacific Halibut Commission
Post Office Box 95009
Seattle, Washington 98145-2009, USA

Abstract.—Management of the hook-and-line-only fishery for Pacific halibut *Hippoglossus stenolepis* in waters off the United States and Canada requires discard to the sea of Pacific halibut bycatch (out of season, undersized, or by fishermen without individual quotas or licenses). Depending on hook type and release methods, survival from longline discards can vary from nearly 100% to none. Conversion in the early 1980s from J-hooks, used by foreign fleets and the domestic halibut fleet, to circle hooks, now used by most domestic longline fishermen, increased survival potential through less damaging hooking locations. Bycatch mortality caused by a fishery was estimated by applying a discard mortality rate to the total halibut discarded. On-board observers collected viability data used to calculate annual fishery-specific Pacific halibut discard mortality rates and collected fishery-specific bycatch rate data used to estimate total bycatch. Limits on bycatch mortality, which closed fisheries when exceeded, provided an incentive for the longline fleet to practice careful release. Estimated halibut bycatch mortality dropped following careful release regulations. Results of tagging studies on halibut released using careful release demonstrated that the distribution of hook injuries shifted to minor and moderate injuries compared with moderate and severe injuries when careful release did not occur. Tag return rates used to quantify survival by injury type led to criteria describing the injuries.

Introduction

The International Pacific Halibut Commission (IPHC) manages the Pacific halibut *Hippoglossus stenolepis* resource for the United States and Canada, under a 1923 treaty between the two countries (Bell 1981; Trumble et al. 1993). In 1944, the IPHC established a hook-and-line-only commercial harvesting regulation for Pacific halibut. Since then, all halibut caught out of season, with other gear, or in excess of individual fishing quota or individual vessel quota limits must be released with a minimum of damage. Commercial fishermen must also release Pacific halibut smaller than the legal size (81.3 cm [32 in]). Recreational fishermen must release Pacific halibut in excess of bag limits, and a minimum size for

Pacific halibut occurs only off Oregon, but many practice catch and release in other areas to extend fishing trips or to seek out trophy fish. The minimum size limit and bycatch discard regulations work effectively because Pacific halibut have a high survival potential (Kaimmer and Trumble 1998; Trumble et al. 2000).

The North Pacific Fishery Management Council (NPFMC) set fishery-specific limits on allowable Pacific halibut bycatch mortality caused by commercial fisheries for other species (Wilson and Weeks 1996). Fisheries shut down when their estimated bycatch reaches the applicable bycatch mortality limits. The estimated bycatch mortality consists of the estimated total bycatch (in weight) multiplied by a discard mortality rate (DMR). At-

[1]Email: bobtrumble@msn.com
[2]Email: steve@iphc.washington.edu
[3]Email: gregg@iphc.washington.edu

sea observers provide data for estimating bycatch and DMR. The estimation of DMRs occurred by year/region/gear/fishery strata, calculated from viability data collected by observers from approximately 100,000–300,000 Pacific halibut per year (trawl, longline, and pot fisheries combined).

Vessel operators can reduce bycatch mortality by reducing encounters (bycatch) or by reducing DMR. The estimated bycatch mortality enters directly into Pacific halibut management, through incorporation into the IPHC stock assessment calculations as age-specific removals, and leads to reduction by the IPHC of directed Pacific halibut harvest to account for this mortality (Sullivan et al. 1999). The proper estimation of DMR is critical to effective management of Pacific halibut.

Commercial fisheries around the world release large amounts of catch (Alverson et al. 1994; Alverson 1997), either driven by economic decisions or required by regulation. Not all of the fish released die, but few estimates of DMR exist. Boggs (1992) used hook timers to assess hooking time and duration on the hooks for billfish and tuna caught in pelagic longline fisheries off Hawaii. He demonstrated a relationship between hooking time and mortality for several species, with survival at the time of release up to 50% for bigeye tuna *Thunnus obesus* at hooking times up to nine hours. Hoey (1996) reviewed the pelagic longline fisheries of the U.S. Atlantic and Gulf of Mexico waters and generally found that 20–30% of the longline catch was alive at the time of discard. Neither Boggs nor Hoey addressed postrelease mortality or the possibility that apparently dead fish did not actually die. Neilson et al. (1989) monitored survival of Atlantic halibut *Hippoglossus hippoglossus* caught by longlines as part of a study to evaluate minimum size. For fish smaller than 81 cm (the proposed minimum commercial size), 77% survived more than 48 hours in onboard tanks. Fish continued to die after 48 hours, but some lived more than 10 months in captivity.

The IPHC conducted a series of tagging experiments (Kaimmer 1994; Kaimmer and Trumble 1998) to assess the mortality of Pacific halibut released as bycatch from the groundfish fisheries or as sublegal releases from the Pacific halibut fishery. From these and earlier experiments, estimates of mortality by condition category or injury type resulted. Observers onboard groundfish vessels collected condition category data from randomly-

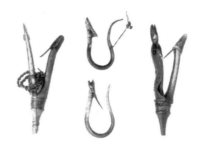

Figure 1. Examples of hooks used in the traditional Indian fishery for Pacific halibut. From IPHC 1998.

selected individual Pacific halibut, which formed the basis for calculating DMR for gear types or specific fisheries within gears. This paper reviews the development of discard mortality estimates for Pacific halibut released as bycatch from commercial longline fisheries or as undersized fish from the commercial Pacific halibut fishery, the effects of hook type and size on discard mortality, and application of discard mortality reduction techniques in management of the longline groundfish fisheries.

Characteristics of Hooks

Pacific coast Native Americans developed highly effective Pacific halibut hooks that out-fished the gear used by early explorers and settlers (Stewart 1977). Native Americans made the hooks of steamed-and-bent wood or of two pieces of carved wood lashed together with a bone or stone barb (Figure 1; IPHC 1998). Pacific halibut sucked in the bait that covered the barb, could not swallow the hook, and were impaled by the barb as they tried to expel the hook.

The early non-Indian commercial fishery for Pacific halibut, which began in 1888 as a longline fishery, used flattened, offset J-hooks (Figure 2A; IPHC 1998), seized with ganging twine to branch lines called gangions, for over 60 years (IPHC 1998). The eyed offset J-hook (Figure 2B) replaced the flattened hook in the 1960s. During 1982–1983, the entire commercial Pacific halibut fleet converted to the circle hook (Figure 2C). The commercial fishery sets consisted of tied-together lengths of groundline, each typically 457–549 m (1,500–1,800 ft) long, with size 16/0 (about 20-mm [0.8-in] gap) circle hooks attached to gangions, usually spaced 1–5.5 m (3.3–18.0 ft) apart (IPHC 1998). A set may contain 5–15 sections of gear, or 2.5–7.5 km (1.4–4.5 mi) total. Soak times range from several hours to 24

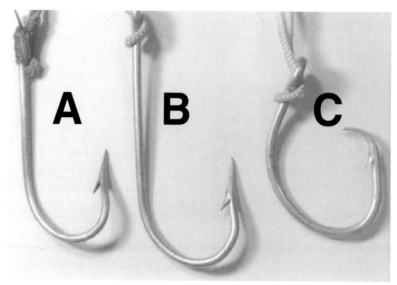

Figure 2. Hooks used over the years in the Pacific halibut fishery: (a) flattened offset hook, (b) eyed hook, and (c) circle hook. From IPHC 1998.

hours in duration. Commercial longline fisheries that target other species typically use spacing in the 1–2 m (3.3–6.6 ft) range and circle hooks in sizes of 13/0 (about 13-mm [0.5-in] gap) or 14/0 (about 15-mm [0.6-in] gap) or similar-sized semicircle autoline hooks used with machines that set and retrieve the gear and automatically bait the hooks.

Following the conversion from J-hooks to circle hooks and anecdotal reports of higher catch rates, the IPHC staff surveyed the central Gulf of Alaska and waters off British Columbia, fishing with both hook types. In the aggregate, the circle hooks caught 2.2 times as much in weight as the J-hooks. Circle hooks caught more than J-hooks, at all fish sizes observed and in both areas surveyed, and caught proportionately higher numbers of fish at sizes near the legal size limit (81.3 cm [32 in]) than at smaller and larger sizes (Sullivan et al. 1999).

The IPHC staff recorded injuries from more than 54,000 Pacific halibut observed on setline research fishing experiments that used J-hooks, large and small circle hooks, and autoline hooks (Kaimmer and Trumble 1997). Typically, circle and semicircle autoline hooks encircled the jaw in more than 95% of the observations, while J-hooks caught the jaw about 80% of the time. Pacific halibut swallowed J-hooks about 20% of the time. All hook types occasionally caught Pacific halibut in the eye.

Johannes (1981) described the mechanics of the circle hook that lead to the high proportion of fish caught in the corner of the jaw. As a fish takes a baited circle hook and moves away, the hook pulls to the side of the mouth. The point catches on flesh at the jaw and pivots as pressure increases. As tension increases, the hook pulls over the jaw and rotates as the fish moves. The hook will not back out on its own and holds the fish even under slack line conditions.

The hooking characteristics of the circle hook make the survival potential of released Pacific halibut very high. If a fisherman backs a circle hook out of the mouth, little injury occurs except for a small hole in the cheek. However, use of automatic hook strippers that hold a fish stationary while hydraulic power continues to haul the line will pull the hook through the jaw (Kaimmer 1994), in some cases ripping off the side of the face. Automatic hook stripping is illegal for release of Pacific halibut bycatch or sublegal fish, but probably still occurs in some areas, especially on vessels that do not carry observers.

While the commercial fishery for Pacific halibut has moved exclusively to circle hooks, the recreational fishery uses both J-hooks and circle hooks. Conversations with Pacific halibut charter operators show that fishing skill and technique affect the choice of hook. For areas where recreational fishermen know or readily learn to let Pacific halibut run with the baited hook, the circle hook is the hook of choice. In areas where fishermen quickly and forcefully set the hook at the first bite, J-hooks are the choice. A quick setting will pull a circle hook from the mouth without a hook up, while the J-hook more often results in a hook up. If fishermen plan on catch and release, properly removed circle hooks typically do less damage.

Development of Viability Criteria for DMR

Large-scale Pacific halibut bycatch discards in groundfish fisheries did not occur until the late 1950s and early 1960s when foreign fleets, primarily trawlers, moved into the northeast Pacific waters adjacent to the United States and Canada. As a result of bilateral and multilateral negotiations with the foreign fishing countries, the United States and Canada placed observers on foreign vessels to obtain data on catch and bycatch, including subjective information on the viability of Pacific halibut discarded from Japanese trawlers (Hoag 1975). The subjective assessments of viability were not used to calculate survival because some live fish probably died post-release.

Hoag (1975) released more than 2,000, tagged Pacific halibut from domestic groundfish trawlers off Canada and assigned a condition category ("Excellent," "Good," "Fair," "Poor," "Dead") using criteria based on body and opercular movements. Tag return rates were used to estimate the relative survival of legal and sublegal-sized fish in these five condition categories, and scaled to absolute values using data from other studies. Subsequent analysis led to compressing the five categories into three and combining legal and sublegal fish (Clark et al. 1993). An aggregate DMR was then calculated from the proportion of fish in each category and the survival rate estimated for each category (Williams and Wilderbuer 1995). From the mid-1960s to the mid-1970s, the foreign trawl fisheries harvested from one to two million mt of groundfish annually and caused an annual Pacific halibut bycatch mortality of 6,000–9,000 mt, as estimated using Hoag's (1975) methods (Williams et al. 1989).

No direct studies to estimate survival for foreign longline gear occurred. The relatively low annual longline groundfish harvest (10,000–20,000 mt) and survival rates of about 50% assumed from other studies (Williams et al. 1989) kept estimated annual Pacific halibut bycatch mortality from hook-and-line fisheries below about 100 mt through the 1970s. In the early 1980s, U.S. observers began collecting viability data for Pacific halibut discarded from foreign longline vessels. However, the IPHC did not quantify the DMR of the foreign longline fleet directly from the trawl viability data because longline-caught Pacific halibut did not experience the same type of injuries as trawl-caught fish. Rather, the IPHC subjectively applied results of survival studies conducted for other purposes to set an overall rate, initially at 50% and later at 25%, for the total Pacific halibut setline bycatch (Trumble et al. 2000). Increased foreign longline harvesting of groundfish resulted in a maximum mortality of approximately 600 mt in 1983, and both bycatch and harvest declined subsequently as foreign longline operations were phased out through the late 1980s. As domestic longline fisheries expanded during the early 1990s, the annual estimate of Pacific halibut bycatch mortality from longlining increased to a peak of 3,300 mt in 1992 before tapering back to about 1,000 mt by the end of the decade (Williams 2000).

Since 1990, only domestic fishing and processing occurred in the Alaskan groundfish fishery. An effort to estimate and control the halibut bycatch mortality in the groundfish longline fishery required estimation of DMR. The IPHC developed viability criteria for the longline fishery, based on fish condition using Hoag's (1975) work as a model (Williams and Wilderbuer 1995). Previous work had estimated that longline-caught Pacific halibut in Excellent condition held in pens suffered only a 2–5% mortality (Peltonen 1969) and that halibut tagged in Poor condition survived at about half the rate of tagged Excellent fish (Myhre 1974). All fish categorized as Dead were assumed to die. Thus, the IPHC set mortality by viability condition category at 3.5% for Excellent, 52% for Poor, and 100% for Dead (Williams and Wilderbuer 1995). The IPHC estimated DMRs specific to each fishery using proportions of discarded fish in each condition category and mortality rates for each category by year, region, gear, and fishery strata.

Careful Release

Regulations that made Pacific halibut a prohibited species, except when authorized by the IPHC, also required returning discarded halibut to the sea with minimal injury. Bycatch mortality calculations in 1991 by the IPHC, from 1990 observer data, indicated that the Bering Sea Pacific cod *Gadus macrocephalus* fishery, which used small hook gear, inflicted a DMR of approximately 20% (Figure 3). Such a rate could occur only if fishermen violated the minimum injury requirement by causing more poor and dead category fish than would occur with reasonable care. Reduction of Pacific halibut bycatch mortality, resulting in an opportunity for increased groundfish harvest, could occur if longline fishermen used less damaging release techniques. The IPHC met with industry representatives in 1991 to discuss a regulation to require specific careful release methods.

The initial careful release proposals to the NPFMC specified two techniques: traditional shaking (rolling the hook out with the gaff) and cutting the gangion (preferably close to the hook). A proposal later added hook straightening (placing the gaff in the bend of the hook, then holding the gaff against the rollers that guide the line until the hook straightens out around the gaff) as a third approved technique. To estimate the effects of careful release, the IPHC assumed a DMR of 12.5%, the average of the DMR at the time, and a potential rate estimated from viability conditions during an IPHC tagging survey (NPFMC 1992). The National Marine Fisheries Service (NMFS) put the careful release regulation into effect in May 1993.

When NMFS observer data for 1993 became available in mid-1994, estimated DMR for the Bering Sea Pacific cod fishery following the implementation of the careful release requirement remained near 18%. Later in 1994, as the NPFMC developed management plans for 1995, the careful release requirement came under close scrutiny. The longline industry acknowledged that support of the program by industry leaders had not transferred to the fishing deck where halibut releases occurred, but made a compelling case that a self-monitoring program would result in lower 1994 rates (data for which would become available in 1995), and even lower rates for 1995 (Smith 1996). Management of the 1995 fishery proceeded with the lower DMR. About two-thirds of the Bering Sea Pacific cod fleet in 1994 and 1995 agreed to report observer data to a consultant who calculated DMR for individual vessels on a weekly basis and reported results back to the vessels. Vessels with high DMR would know to increase emphasis on proper release techniques. Observers from the Bering Sea Pacific cod fishery also reported 1995 Pacific halibut bycatch data to

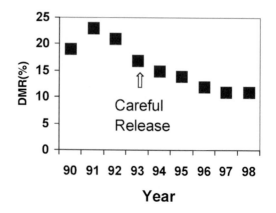

Figure 3. Discard mortality rates (DMR) for Pacific halibut from 1990 to 1998 for the Bering Sea Pacific cod longline fleet.

the IPHC for in-season data entry. Nearly all vessels had rates for winter and spring of 1995 lower than the 1993 rates, and the average rate of 11.5% was lower than the assumed rate (Trumble 1996). While the Bering Sea Pacific cod fleet did not maintain the 11.5% rate for the rest of the year, the results showed potential for the careful release program. The fleet continued gradual improvements in DMR, and reached an average rate near 11% in 1997 and 1998 (Figure 3; Williams and Hare 2000).

Other Alaskan longline fisheries in the Bering Sea or the Gulf of Alaska did not perform as well as the Bering Sea Pacific cod fishery. The Bering Sea fishery for Greenland turbot *Reinhardtius hippoglossoides* and the Gulf of Alaska Pacific cod fishery experienced estimated average 1997–1998 DMRs of 20% and 17%, respectively (Williams and Hare 2000). However, each of these fisheries harvests less than 10% of the groundfish harvested by the Bering Sea Pacific cod fishery. So far, the careful release program has focused on the fishery with the greatest Pacific halibut bycatch mortality and, therefore, the greatest potential for bycatch mortality reduction.

Tagging to Determine DMR

The IPHC conducted two tagging experiments to evaluate the effects of different release techniques on survival of halibut discarded from longline gear. The first ("hook strippers"), in 1986, compared traditional shaking with automatic removal using a hook stripper (Kaimmer 1994) for the large-hook

Table 1. Discard survival of Pacific halibut by injury type estimated from tagging results for cod-style (small) hooks and halibut-style (large) hooks (from Kaimmer 1994; Kaimmer and Trumble 1998). The tag return ratio for cod-style hooks is the average of the ratios from the 1993 and 1994 returns.

| Injury type | Cod-style hooks | | Halibut-style hooks | |
	Tag return ratio[a]	Discard survival	Tag return ratio[a]	Discard survival
Minor	1	96.5	1	96.5
Moderate	0.75	73	0.57	55
Severe	0.46	44	0.24	23
Fleas, bleeding	0.00	0	No data	No data

a. Return rate for an injury type divided by return rate for minor injury.

gear typical of the Pacific halibut fishery. For this hook stripper study, the injury of each Pacific halibut released was recorded, but no data were collected on viability condition categories. The second effort ("careful release"), in 1993 and 1994, compared the traditional shaking, gangion cutting, and hook straightening methods approved by the North Pacific Council and automatic hook stripping from small-hook gear typical of the groundfish fisheries for sablefish *Anoplopoma fimbria* and Pacific cod (Kaimmer and Trumble 1998). The careful release experiment collected data on injury and condition category from cruises in both years. The careful release methods resulted in predominantly minor injuries, while hook stripping caused more severe injuries. Minor, moderate, and severe injury categories observed during the careful release study generally corresponded to Excellent, Poor, and Dead categories. Some fish with minor injuries would have been categorized Poor or Dead, and some with moderate injuries would have been categorized Dead under the old procedures because of predation by amphipods (sand fleas) or bleeding caused by hook removal.

The relative survival of Pacific halibut by injury or condition code was determined by comparing the ratio of tag return rates among the groups. Absolute survival was estimated from the ratio of the Excellent condition fish to the other groups, and scaling with the 96.5% survival (equivalent to the 3.5% mortality set by IPHC, as discussed earlier) assumed for Excellent fish. Tag return rates and calculated survivals for the hook stripper (halibut-style large hooks) experiment and for the careful release (cod-style small hooks) experiment (Table 1) varied by hook size for the same injury type, even though the distribution of injuries was similar (Trumble et al. 2000). Survival for moderate and severe injuries was

approximately 1.5–2.0 times higher for small hooks than for large hooks. Trumble et al. (2000) added a fourth injury category, sand fleas and bleeding, with assigned survival of zero because no tag returns occurred for any of these injuries.

During review of the injury criteria, we received a suggestion to convert the criteria to a dichotomous key, which would standardize the observer application. We concurred and constructed the key with the most important and obvious elements first, so that an observer must put a fish into a category or move to the next step (Table 2). The dichotomous key for the longline fisheries (and for trawl and pot fisheries) went into effect for the year 2000 fishing year.

Summary and Conclusions

Management of the groundfish fisheries in the northeast Pacific requires closures of specific fisheries or individual vessels (Canadian trawl vessels have individual quotas for halibut bycatch mortality) when they reach bycatch mortality limits set for Pacific halibut. This management requirement provides an incentive for individual fishermen to find ways to reduce the Pacific halibut bycatch mortality. Mortality reductions occur by reducing bycatch or reducing mortality of the bycatch. The wholesale conversion from J-hooks to circle hooks by the commercial longline fisheries—to increase catch rates—also turned out to offer an opportunity to reduce discard mortality. Circle hooks cause less hooking damage than J-hooks because circle hooks predominantly catch in the jaw, while J-hooks catch more in the throat and gills. Removing the circle hooks by rotating them out of the jaw leaves little damage other than a puncture wound in the cheek.

Research and monitoring activities designed to estimate discard mortality enhanced the success of a careful release program. Results from experiments

Table 2. Dichotomous key for Pacific halibut discarded from setline vessels, developed from the injury-based criteria.

1a. Fish is alive . . . . Go to 2a
1b. Fish is dead when brought to the surface on the gear . . . . Code DEAD
     Fish is in rigor and lifeless, even if no apparent injuries. Gills appear completely devoid of blood (light pink or
     white in color).
2a. No penetration of the body or head by sand fleas . . . . Go to 3a
     Membranes surrounding eyes and anus are intact, without any holes from sand fleas. A few sand fleas may be
     seen on body and can be wiped off with your hand. Typically, no penetration has occurred when only a few
     (e.g., < 10) sand fleas are found on the body.
2b. Sand fleas have penetrated the body via the eyes, fins, or anus. . . . . Code DEAD
     Membrane surrounding eye may be partially or completely missing. Dorsal and/or anal fin membranes may be
     eaten away, leaving fin rays exposed. Skin on the body is separated from tissue where sand fleas have eaten.
3a. No wounds of any kind to abdominal organs. Abdominal wall not punctured . . . . Go to 4a
3b. Abdominal organs are damaged, possibly by a gaff . . . . Code DEAD
     Abdominal cavity wall is punctured or torn. Viscera are visible and exposed, and may be protruding.
4a. Fish is not bleeding from gills (but may be bleeding from elsewhere) . . . . Go to 5a
4b. Fish is bleeding from gills . . . . Code DEAD
     Bleeding is occurring from a torn or severed gill arch.
5a. Fish is not bleeding at all, or bleeding is minor to moderate (not from gills) . . . . Go to 6a
     Blood may be seen around mouth and/or jaw. Blood may be oozing continuously, or bleeding may be continu-
     ing very slowly a few drops at a time, or bleeding may have stopped.
5b. Bleeding is severe . . . . Code DEAD
     Blood from any source is flowing freely and continuously in large quantity.
6a. Injuries to head and/or jaw are minor to moderate, but no structures are missing . . . . Go to 7a
6b. Major injuries to head and jaw, resulting in missing pieces . . . . Code SEVERE
     Side of the head, possibly including the jaw, has been torn loose and missing from the fish, and/or lower jaw
     has been torn away and is missing.
7a. Bleeding, if any, is stopped or few drops . . . . Go To 8a
7b. Bleeding is not flowing profusely but is oozing continuously. . . . . Code MODERATE
8a. Wounds to the head (forward of preopercle and above cheek and jaw) are only surface scratches on the skin. . . . Go to 9a
8b. Skin on head (forward of preopercle) is ripped and torn deeply . . . . Code SEVERE
     Internal organs are likely exposed.
9a. Eye or eye socket is not punctured . . . . Go to 10a
9b. Eye or eye socket is punctured . . . . Code MODERATE
10a. No wounds to the body are evident . . . . Go to 11a
10b. Wounds in body consist of puncture holes in skin, with possibly a flesh tear . . . . Code MODERATE
11a. Lower jaw is significantly damaged. . . . . Code MODERATE
     Lower jaw may be broken into 2 pieces at the snout, but each is still attached at the base of the jaw. Jaw may
     be torn on one side or the other, possibly extending through the cheek.
11b. Damage to lower jaw, if any, is slight . . . . Code MINOR
     Injuries include the hook entrance/exit hole around the jaw or in the cheek, or a tear in the cheek. A piece of
     the lip may be torn and hanging from the jaw. If gangion was cut, the hook and some length of residual gan-
     gion may be hanging from the mouth.

on fishing power of circle and J-hooks, on variation in hooking locations and injuries with different hooks under different release techniques, and on relative survival of return ratios of tagged and released fish provided the information needed to formulate a procedure for estimating and managing bycatch mortality in the longline fisheries. Observers, mandatory on most groundfish vessels, collected data to estimate survival of Pacific halibut released from commercial longline vessels. Improvements in the criteria used by observers to collect viability data enhanced the reliability and accuracy of the estimates.

Commercial longline fishermen supported a concept of careful release of Pacific halibut to reduce the discard mortality rate, as a means of maintaining harvest levels in the face of bycatch mortality limits. Industry leaders worked with IPHC, NPFMC, and NMFS staff to design and implement a careful release program. As observer data came in from the careful release fisheries, however, we soon realized that the support of industry leaders was not sufficient to make the program a success. The fishermen at the roller, perhaps inexperienced or tired from long fishing days, continued the use of automatic hook strippers or other methods that caused severe damage to released Pacific halibut. Estimated DMRs remained high in spite of the regulations. As the industry faced harvest reductions of nearly 50%, to stay within the bycatch mortality limits at the high DMRs calculated from observer data, industry leaders and agency staff realized that the regulations would not work without the support of the fishermen on the deck.

In-season programs for the Bering Sea Pacific cod fleet consisting of self-monitoring by participating vessels and re-estimation of DMRs by IPHC staff brought feedback to the fleet on their compliance with the careful release requirements. The DMRs fell annually as the consequences of bycatch mortality closures moved from owners through the wheelhouse to the deck. The program worked only when the fishermen on deck participated and accepted the intent of careful release. Fisheries with less groundfish harvest and concomitantly less Pacific halibut bycatch currently perform poorly in compliance with careful release. The DMRs for these fisheries remain at high levels, reached by disregarding the regulations. Management must focus on these fisheries, using lessons learned from the Bering Sea Pacific cod fishery, to bring them into compliance with the careful release regulations.

References

Alverson, D. L. 1997. Global assessment of fisheries bycatch and discards: a summary overview. Pages 115–125 in E. L. Pikitch, D. D. Huppert, and M. P. Sissenwine, editors. Global trends: fisheries management. American Fisheries Society, Symposium 20, Bethesda, Maryland.

Alverson, D.L, M. H. Freeberg, S. A. Murawski, and J. G. Pope. 1994. A global assessment of fisheries bycatch and discards. Food and Agriculture Organization of the United Nations Fisheries Technical Paper 339, Rome, Italy.

Bell, F. H. 1981. The Pacific halibut, the resource and the fishery. Alaska Northwest Publishing Co., Anchorage, Alaska.

Boggs, C. H. 1992. Depth, capture time, and hooked longevity of longline-caught pelagic fish: timing bites of fish with chips. Fishery Bulletin 90:642–658.

Clark, W. G., S. H. Hoag, R. J. Trumble, and G. H. Williams. 1993. Re-estimation of survival for trawl caught halibut released in different condition factors. Pages 197–203 in International Pacific Halibut Commission Report of Assessment and Research Activities, 1992, Seattle, Washington.

Hoag, S. H. 1975. Survival of halibut released after capture by trawls. International Pacific Halibut Commission Scientific Report 57, Seattle, Washington.

Hoey, J. J. 1996. Bycatch in western Atlantic pelagic longline fisheries. Pages 193–203 in Solving bycatch: considerations for today and tomorrow. Alaska Sea Grant Report 96–03, Fairbanks, Alaska.

IPHC (International Pacific Halibut Commission). 1998. The Pacific halibut: biology, fishery, and management. IPHC Technical Report 40, Seattle, Washington.

Johannes, R. E. 1981. Words of the lagoon: fishing and marine lore in the Palau District of Micronesia. University of California Press, Los Angeles, California.

Kaimmer, S. M. 1994. Halibut injury and mortality associated with manual and automated removal from setline hooks. Fisheries Research 20:165–179.

Kaimmer, S. M., and R. J. Trumble. 1997. Survival of Pacific halibut released from longlines: hooking location and release methods. Pages 101–105 in Proceedings of fisheries bycatch: consequences and management. Alaska Sea Grant Report 97–02, Fairbanks, Alaska.

Kaimmer, S. M., and R. J. Trumble. 1998. Injury, condition, and mortality of Pacific halibut bycatch following careful release by Pacific cod and sablefish long-liners. Fisheries Research 38:131–144.

Myhre, R. J. 1974. Minimum size and optimum age at entry for Pacific halibut. International Pacific Halibut Commission Scientific Report 55, Seattle, Washington.

Neilson. J. D., K. G. Waiwood, and S. J. Smith. 1989. Survival of Atlantic halibut (Hippoglossus hippoglossus) caught by longline and otter trawl gear. Canadian Journal of Fisheries and Aquatic Sciences 46:887–897.

NPFMC (North Pacific Fishery Management Council). 1992. Environmental assessment/Regulatory impact review/Initial regulatory flexibility analysis for the proposed careful release of Pacific halibut caught on hook and line in the Gulf of Alaska and Bering Sea Aleutian Islands. NPFMC. Anchorage, Alaska.

Peltonen, G. J. 1969. Viability of tagged Pacific halibut. International Pacific Halibut Commission Report 55, Seattle, Washington.

Smith, W. T. 1996. Reduction of halibut bycatch and associated mortality in the Bering Sea cod fishery. Pages 205–209 in Solving bycatch: considerations for today and tomorrow. Alaska Sea Grant Report 96–03, Fairbanks, Alaska.

Stewart, H. 1977. Indian fishing. Early methods on the Northwest Coast. University of Washington Press, Seattle, Washington.

Sullivan, P. J., A. M. Parma, and W. G. Clark. 1999. The Pacific halibut stock assessment of 1997. International Pacific Halibut Commission Scientific Report 79, Seattle, Washington.

Trumble, R. J. 1996. Management of Alaskan longline fisheries to reduce halibut bycatch mortality. Pages 183–192 in Solving bycatch: considerations for today and tomorrow. Alaska Sea Grant Report 96–03. Fairbanks, Alaska.

Trumble, R. J., S. H. Kaimmer, and G. H. Williams. 2000. Estimation of discard mortality rates for Pacific halibut bycatch in groundfish longline fisheries. North American Journal of Fisheries Management 20:931–939.

Trumble, R. J., J. D. Neilson, W. R. Bowering, and D. A. McCaughran. 1993. Atlantic halibut (Hippoglossus hip-

poglossus) and Pacific halibut (*H. stenolepis*) and their North American fisheries. Canadian Bulletin of Fisheries and Aquatic Sciences 227.

Williams, G. H. 2000. Incidental catch, and mortality of Pacific halibut, 1962–1999. Pages 161–171 *in* International Pacific Halibut Commission Report of Assessment and Research Activities, 1999, Seattle, Washington.

Williams, G. H., and S. R. Hare. 2000. Pacific halibut discard mortality rates (DMRs) for the 1990–1998 Alaska groundfish fisheries, with recommendations for monitoring in 2000. Pages 193–223 *in* International Pacific Halibut Commission Report of Assessment and Research Activities, 1999, Seattle, Washington.

Williams, G. H., C. C. Schmitt, S. H. Hoag, and J. D. Berger. 1989. Incidental catch and mortality of Pacific halibut, 1962–1986. International Pacific Halibut Commission Technical Report 23, Seattle, Washington.

Williams, G. H., and T. K. Wilderbuer. 1995. Discard mortality rates of Pacific halibut bycatch: Fishery differences and trends during 1990–1993. Pages 611–622 *in* Proceedings of the International Symposium on North Pacific flatfish. Alaska Sea Grant Report 95–04. Fairbanks, Alaska.

Wilson, W. J., and H. J. Weeks. 1996. Policy and regulatory measures to control incidental mortality of Pacific halibut in groundfish fisheries of the North Pacific Ocean. Pages 219–239 *in* R. M. Meyer, C. Zhang, M. L. Windsor, B. J. McCay, L. J. Hushak, and R. M. Muth, editors. Fisheries resource utilization and policy, proceedings of the World Fisheries Congress, Theme 2. Oxford and IBH Publishing, New Delhi, India.

American Fisheries Society Symposium 30:97–100, 2002
© Copyright by the American Fisheries Society 2002

Hook Location, Fish Size, and Season as Factors Influencing Catch-and-Release Mortality of Striped Bass Caught with Bait in Chesapeake Bay

RUDOLPH LUKACOVIC *and* JAMES H. UPHOFF

Striped bass *Morone saxatilis* catch-and-release mortality is influenced by hook location, bait and hook type, angler experience, and season (Diodoti and Richards 1996). Anatomical location of hook wounds is the most important factor in hooking mortality (Muoneke and Childress 1994). In comparison with artificial lures, natural baits generally cause higher mortalities because they tend to be swallowed more often (Muoneke and Childress 1994). Temperature, salinity, and fish size were cited as risk factors when Maryland's striped bass catch-and-release policy was formulated.

We conducted two catch-and-release mortality experiments on striped bass using natural bait, one each during October 1996 and June 1997, to measure mortality associated with fish size, hook location, and season. We also appraised the potential of nonoffset circle hooks to reduce deep hooking of released fish.

To assess mortality associated with catch-and-release angling, striped bass were caught by volunteer anglers aboard contracted charter boats in Maryland's Chesapeake Bay. Standard 3/0 offset J-style bait hooks were used in October; 6/0 offset J-style bait or 11/0 nonoffset circle hooks were used in June (the latter two hooks were similarly sized). Ground Atlantic menhaden *Brevoortia tyrannus* were used as chum. If a fish was shallow hooked (lip, mouth or gills), a hole was punched in the lower lobe of the caudal fin and the hook was removed. If a fish was deep hooked (hooked past the gills), the hook was left in place, the line cut, and a hole was punched in the dorsal lobe of the caudal fin. Fish were

Rudolph Lukacovic, Maryland Department of Natural Resources, Fisheries Service, Matapeake Work Center, 301 Marine Academy Drive, Stevensville, Maryland 21666, USA. Email: mata-fish-2@dnr.state.md.us

James H. Uphoff, Maryland Department of Natural Resources, Fisheries Service, Tawes State Office Building, 580 Taylor Avenue, Annapolis, Maryland 21401, USA. Email: juphoff@dnr.state.md.us

taken to 4.6 m × 4.6 m × 3.7 m (15 ft × 15 ft × 12 ft) holding pens. Pens were checked every day for five days and dead fish removed and measured. All dead, deep-hooked fish were necropsied.

Overlap of 95% confidence intervals (CI) was used to determine whether October or June percent mortality or deep-hooking percentages were significantly different from zero and from each other (Ott 1977). Confidence intervals for October or June were estimated from the normal distribution approximation of the binomial distribution (proportions converted to percentages). We considered fish size (legal or sublegal), season (October or June), and hook location (deep or shallow) explanatory factors and coded them as binary (0 or 1) variables. A three-way, log-linear model tested mortality as a combination of season, hook location, and fish size using the Statistical Analysis System's (SAS) Proc Catmod (SAS 1988).

Finally, to examine the potential of nonoffset circle hooks to offset deep hooking we compared the 95% CI of the percentage of deeply-hooked striped bass caught on standard chumming hooks or on nonoffset circle hooks during trials conducted on 23 and 24 June 1997. On these dates, our anglers also fished with circle hooks, and we recorded the number of deeply and shallow-hooked striped bass.

Seasonal differences were documented in both deep-hooking rates and overall mortality. During October, eleven of ninety striped bass died (12.2%, SD = 3.5). Seventeen fish (18.8%, SD = 4.1) were deeply hooked, and seven of these died. Approximately 69% of striped bass were above the fall season's legal size of 457 mm (18 in). During June 1997, 47 of 131 striped bass died (35.9%, SD = 4.2). Based on 95% CI overlap, striped bass hooking mortality was greater in June than in October. Seventy-one striped bass (54.2%, SD = 4.4) were deeply hooked. Twenty-five fish (19%) were above the spring season's minimum size of 660 mm (26 in).

Size, season, and hook location were not independent influences on hook-and-release mortality; main effects and their three-way interaction were significant ($P < 0.05$) in the saturated log-linear model and were kept in the reduced model (Table 1). Two-way interactions were not significant and were dropped.

Deeply-hooked, legal-sized striped bass were predicted to be most likely to die after release (50–60%), regardless of season. In June, more than 30% of shallow-hooked, legal-sized striped bass died. High mortality of shallow-hooked, large striped bass in June suggests a broader catch-and-release problem not confined to chumming. Low mortality (7–9% dead) was predicted after release for shallow-hooked legal or sublegal fish in October or shallow-hooked sublegal fish in June. High release mortality (> 50%) was predicted when fish were deeply

Table 1. Explanatory factor, binary codes of main effects, and Chi-square values of the reduced log-linear mortality model. All explanatory factors were significant at $P < 0.05$.

	Binary code		
Explanatory factor	0	1	χ^2
Size	Sublegal	Legal	19.76
Season	October	June	29.72
Hook location	Shallow	Deep	65.13
Size × season × location			22.76

hooked and legal or sublegal size in June or deeply hooked and legal size in October (Table 2).

Fewer fish were deeply hooked on circle hooks, 10.6% (SD = 2.9%, $N = 113$), than on standard hooks, 45.6% (SD = 5.6%, $N = 79$). Mean lengths were not significantly different (Wilcoxson Rank Sum test, $P = 0.62$) between fish caught on circle hooks (542 mm, $N = 63$) and standard hooks (561 mm, $N = 40$).

Deeply-hooked fish of any species generally suffer higher mortality than shallow-hooked fish (Muoneke and Childress 1994), and the differential mortality that we observed appears typical. Deep-hooking percentage decreased approximately four-fold in June when circle hooks were used instead of standard chumming hooks.

Circle hooks provide anglers with an option that lowers deep hooking, and their use should be promoted. Lowering the size limit in June 1998 to that of October 1996 (457 mm) allowed quicker filling of the creel. If a 457-mm size limit were substituted for the 660-mm minimum length in our June experiment, potentially harvestable fish would have increased from 19% to 88%.

Table 2. Observed (O) and predicted (P) hooking mortalities of striped bass released after being caught by chumming from the reduced log-linear model of size, season, and hook location. N = number of fish in category and SE = standard error of predicted mortality.

Combination	N	O (%)	P (%)	SE
Sublegal, October, shallow	23	4.3	7.8	1.5
Sublegal, October, deep	5	20.0	14.0	2.6
Sublegal, June, shallow	53	7.5	8.6	1.6
Sublegal, June, deep	55	58.2	59.6	6.3
Legal, October, shallow	50	6.0	7.4	1.4
Legal, October, deep	12	50.0	51.1	5.9
Legal, June, shallow	8	37.5	31.5	4.6
Legal, June, deep	15	53.3	56.8	6.2

References

Diodoti, P. J., and R. A. Richards. 1996. Mortality of striped bass hooked and released in salt water. Transactions of the American Fisheries Society 125:300–307.

Muoneke, M. I., and M. W. Childress. 1994. Hooking mortality: a review for recreational fisheries. Reviews in Fisheries Science 2:123–156.

Ott, L. 1977. An introduction to statistical methods and data analysis. Duxbury Press, North Scituate, Massachusetts.

SAS Institute. 1988. SAS/Stat users guide, release 6.03 edition. Cary, North Carolina.

American Fisheries Society Symposium 30:101–105, 2002

EXTENDED ABSTRACT

The Influence of Hook Type, Hook Wound Location, and Other Variables Associated with Post Catch-and-Release Mortality in the U.S. Summer Flounder Recreational Fishery

MARK H. MALCHOFF[1], JEFF GEARHART,
JON LUCY, *and* PATRICK J. SULLIVAN

Major recreational and commercial fisheries in the mid-Atlantic region of the United States are dependent upon summer flounder or fluke *Paralichthys dentatus*, currently managed under the Summer Flounder Fishery Management Plan (MAFMC 1995). The number of flounder caught by recreational anglers and subsequently released alive has grown from less than 6 million fish in 1990 to over 16 million fish in 2000, and now regularly exceeds 60% of the total recreational catch (National Marine Fisheries Service, Fisheries Statistics and Economics Division, personal communication). Only limited data, however, exist on post release mortality rates in the fishery and the most important factors which contribute to this mortality (Lucy and Holton 1998).

In 1997, a field study on flounder release mortality was begun in New York (NY), with similar work planned in 1998 for Virginia (VA) and North Carolina (NC) where researchers coordinated data collection during that year. From July 1997 to December 1998, using conventional angling gear, researchers and volunteer anglers conducted 17 fishing trials catching 623 summer flounder (200–650 mm total length).

Mark H. Malchoff, Lake Champlain Sea Grant Program, 101 Hudson Hall, Plattsburgh State University, 101 Broad Street, Plattsburgh, New York 12901–2681, USA
[1]*Corresponding Author: Phone (518)564-3037, Fax (518)564-3152, Email: mark.malchoff@plattsburgh.edu.*

Jeff Gearhart, North Carolina Department of Environment & Natural Resources, Division of Marine Fisheries, Post Office Box 769, Morehead City, North Carolina 28557, USA

Jon Lucy, Virginia Sea Grant Marine Advisory Program, Virginia Institute of Marine Science, College of William and Mary, Post Office Box 1346, Gloucester Point, Virginia 23062–1346, USA

Patrick J. Sullivan, 214 Fernow Hall, Cornell University, Ithaca, New York 14853, USA

In the New York trials, fish were primarily caught aboard party/charter vessels (Great South Bay area) with small open research vessels used in Virginia's lower Chesapeake Bay, and along beaches and sounds in the Cape Lookout, North Carolina area. Fish were typically caught by drifting or slow trolling using medium action spinning and bait casting rods (5.5–7.7 kg test line) and natural baits (live and dead). Barbed sproat (J-shaped hook, used only in New York), wide gap, and offset circle hooks (sizes #1–4/0) were used without spinners or skirts on conventional bottom rigs.

Capture event data included hook type and size, hook wound location (anterior to pharynx; posterior to pharynx), presence-absence of severe bleeding, and fish length. In the Virginia and North Carolina trials, fish hooked posterior to the pharynx (i.e., deep or "gut-hooked") had the leaders cut, leaving hooks in the fish. In New York, party boat mates removed all hooks regardless of hook wound location as per local custom in the Captree fleet.

Following capture, individual fish were tagged with T-Bar anchor tags (Floy and Hallprint) then placed in onboard tanks/live-wells. Aerator pumps (New York) and water exchanges maintained adequate oxygen levels. Onboard fish holding densities were less than or equal to 48 g/L, and holding times ranged from one to four hours. In Virginia and North Carolina fish were transferred to holding cages directly from sampling boats. In New York, logistical constraints necessitated the additional transport (< 3.2 km) of live fish via aerated tank equipped trucks.

Cages were constructed of 13–25 mm bar plastic mesh (NY), plastic-coated wire (NC), and galvanized wire (VA), and placed either under piers (NY), on the bottom (NC, about 3 m depth), or moored from docks using flotation collars (VA). Mesh size was sufficient to enable prey to enter, though the extent of such prey entry during the trials is unknown. Cage shape was rectangular (NY and VA) or cylindrical (NC); cage volumes were 3.5 m^3 (NY) and 0.4 m^3 (VA/NC). In Virginia and North Carolina, cage bottoms were covered with material to reduce fish chaffing and in Virginia alone the floating cages were shaded on top. Maximum fish densities were 9, 10, and 20 fish/m^2 (NY, VA, and NC, respectively). Fish were held for 72 hours without food (Malchoff and Heins 1997). All fish were recovered, dead fish identified by tag number, and surviving fish either released (NY, VA) or some kept for aging (NC). Water temperature and salinity were 17–28°C and 17–26 ppt at holding sites. During trials, mean water temperatures were: NY (21°C in 1997; 17°C in 1998), VA (25°C, September–October 1998), NC (18°C, October–December 1998).

Post release mortality rates for the 72 hour holding period were determined for New York trials, and Virginia/North Carolina trials combined, since fish in New York were subject to different hook recovery methods. Bootstrapping

(1000 samples, $N = 247$ for NY, and 376 for NC and VA) was used to calculate mean mortality and 95% confidence interval from a cumulative binomial distribution. Calculated P values were ordered (lowest to highest), enabling selection of those corresponding to P less than or equal to 0.25 and P greater than or equal to 0.975 (SYSTAT 1997)[1]. Fitted logistic regression models were compared using likelihood ratio tests to develop a parsimonious model from which to identify significant predictors of mortality and interaction relationships among variables (S-Plus 1998)[2].

Mean mortality estimates, 14.6% (7.9–21.2% CI) for New York trials compared to 6.1% (3.2–9.5% CI) for Virginia/North Carolina trials, were not significantly different (Table 1). Overall mean mortality for all trials combined was 9.5% (7.4–11.9% CI)

Working through the logistic regression model, hook type-size variables were reduced from nine to three (sproat, wide gap, and offset circle). While "state" was available as a predictor variable, "leader status," which varied by state, better represented the physical differences between treatments. Furthermore, "state" provided no additional statistically significant information (at the alpha = 0.05 level) after "leader status" had been included in the model. Therefore selected model variables were: leader status, hook type, hook wound location, and bleeding (discrete), along with temperature and fish length (continuous). Regressions were conducted and F-tests were used to examine significance of inclusion of interaction terms. While main factors of hook type and length appeared to be not statistically significant with main effects alone, a more complex model that included these terms as interactions with bleeding, significantly improved the fit ($p < 0.0001$). All factors but hook type and fish length were significant predictors of release mortality (Table 2).

Our interest was the elucidation of those factors (some controllable by anglers) most closely associated with hooking mortality. Significant predictors of mortality included leader status, wound location, bleeding, and water temperature. These results largely support similar research on striped bass *Morone saxatilis* where deep hooking and higher water temperatures were found to contribute significantly to release mortality (Diodati and Richards 1996; Lukacovic and Uphoff, this volume). Hook type (as a main effect) was not a significant predictor of mortality. These results are in general agreement with an earlier analysis on part of these data where hook type was not a significant predictor of deep hooking (Gearhart 2000). However, these results remain unexpected

[1]SYSTAT 7.0 for Windows": New Statistics. Copyright " 1997. by SPSS Inc., 444 North Michigan Ave. Chicago, Ilinois 60611
[2]S-PLUS 6.0 Copyright. 1988–2000 Insightful Corporation. 1700 Westlake Avenue N, Suite 500, Seattle, Washington 98109–3044.

Table 1. Mean release mortality rates and 95% confidence intervals (CI) calculated from cumulative binomial distribution. (bootstrapping = 1,000 iterations; ranked *P* values lowest to highest, selecting those for *P* ≤ 0.25 and *P* ≥ 0.975); rates not significantly different for VA/NC and NY (overlapping CI's).

State	Trials	N	Mean mortality (%)	95% C. I.
NC and VA combined	8	376	6.1	3.2 – 9.5
NY	9	247	14.6	7.9 – 21.2
Overall (total)	17	623	9.5	7.4 – 11.9

Table 2. Significance of each component in the model after adjusting for the other components listed. The main effects are included for consistency. Leader status had two levels: leaders cut and hooks left in (VA/NC fish with hook wound posterior to pharynx); all leaders and hooks removed (VA/NC fish with hook wound anterior to pharynx, and all NY fish, regardless of hook wound location).

Parameter	Probability
Leader status	< 0.0001
Hook type	> 0.05
Wound location	< 0.0001
Bleeding	< 0.0001
Temperature in degrees Celsius	< 0.05
Length (mm)	> 0.82
Bleeding × hook type (interaction)	< 0.0001
Bleeding × length (interaction)	< 0.01

given the popular thinking about circle hooks and their demonstrated utility in the striped bass and billfish fisheries (Lukacovic and Uphoff, this volume; Prince et al., this volume). We speculate that the degree of offset (15° in the Eagle Claw 197 hooks used here) may have negated the normal "jaw hooking only" pattern normally seen with circle hooks. This is corroborated in the sailfish fishery where highly offset circle hooks were associated with significantly more deep hooking than were minor offset (4°) and nonoffset hooks (Prince et al., this volume). As importantly, these hooks were found to be particularly difficult to extract by mates in the New York flounder samples. This probably explains the strong interaction between bleeding and hook type, and the importance of "leader status" in deeply hooked fish (Table 2). Taken together these observations underscore the importance of proper techniques when preparing to release fish alive. Also noted is the strong interaction between bleeding and fish length, despite the fact that length alone was not a significant predictor of mortality. Additional research on summer flounder post release mortality is warranted regarding nonoffset circle hooks across a larger fish length range as well as quantifying catch rates using circle and noncircle hooks.

Acknowledgments

This work was greatly assisted by the efforts of numerous individuals associated with: New York Fishing Tackle Trades Association, Captree Boatmen's Association, USCG Stations Fire Island Inlet, Fort Macon, and Ocracoke Island, Town of Cape Charles, Virginia, Kiptopeke State Park, Virginia, and NCDMF staff. Project support included Virginia Saltwater Recreational Fishing Development Funds and ACFCMA funds via NYSDEC.

References

Diodati, P. J., and R. A. Richards. 1996. Mortality of striped bass hooked and released in salt water. Transactions of the American Fisheries Society 25 (2):300–307.

Gearhart, J. 2000. Short-term hooking mortality of summer flounder in North Carolina. Interstate Fisheries Management Program Implementation for North Carolina. Completion Report for Cooperative Agreement No. NA57FG0171/1-3. Documentation, and Reduction of Bycatch in North Carolina Fisheries, Job 3.

Lucy, J. A., and T. D. Holton. 1998. Release mortality in Virginia's recreational fishery for summer flounder, *Paralichthys dentatus*. Virginia Institute of Marine Science, College of William and Mary, Virginia Marine Resource Report No. 97-8, VSG-97-09.

MAFMC (Mid-Atlantic Fishery Management Council). 1995. Amendment 7 to the fishery management plan for summer flounder. Dover, Delaware.

Malchoff, M. H., and S. W. Heins. 1997. Short-term hooking mortality of weakfish caught on single-barb hooks. North American Journal of Fisheries Management 17:477–481.

American Fisheries Society Symposium 30:106–109, 2002

EXTENDED ABSTRACT

Evaluation of the Effectiveness of Circle Hooks in New Jersey's Recreational Summer Flounder Fishery

STEVEN R. ZIMMERMAN *and*

ELEANOR A. BOCHENEK

Summer flounder *Paralichthys dentatus* support an important commercial and recreational fishery in the Mid-Atlantic Bight and are currently under a rebuilding plan. As a result, size and bag limits have been imposed upon recreational anglers to reduce fishing mortality. An important factor that affects the success of implemented minimum size limits is the survival of undersized fish. Minimum size limits have little success if there is high mortality occurring in released undersized fish (Waters and Huntsman 1986). Therefore, information on recreational catch-and-release mortality is crucial for effective management of summer flounder (Diodati 1996).

Many studies have examined the effects of hook-and-release mortality on recreational fishes (Bugley and Shepherd 1991; Malchoff 1995, 1997; Williams 1995; Diodati 1996; Bettoli and Osborne 1998; Lucy and Holton 1998), but few have studied the effectiveness of hook types and how these particular gear relate to hook sets. Lucy and Holton (1998) found the average hook-and-release mortality of summer flounder to be 11%, with 95% of the mortality the result of being hooked in the esophagus (76%), gills (16%), and tongue area (8%). Other studies (Bugley and Shepherd 1991; Diodati 1996) have also found that hooking fish in the esophagus/gill area contributed to high release mortality. The use of gear that will reduce the number of cases in which summer flounder are hooked in the esophagus, gill, and tongue area could greatly reduce hook-and-release mortality, in turn making management practices such as the implementation of minimum size limits more effective at conserving the resource (Waters and Huntsman 1986).

Steven R. Zimmerman, NYU School of Medicine, Skirball Institute of Biomolecular Medicine 540 1st Avenue, New York, New York 10016, USA. Email: zimmerman@saturn.med.nyu.edu.

Eleanor A. Bochenek, Haskin Shellfish Research Laboratory, Institute of Marine and Coastal Sciences, Rutgers University, 1636 Delaware Avenue, Cape May, New Jersey 08204, USA. Email: bochenek@hsrl.rutgers.edu.

Some managers believe that the use of circle hooks will reduce the amount of hook sets occurring in the esophagus, gills, and tongue area and keep hook sets confined to the jaw of the fish. The objectives of this study were to determine the location of circle hook sets on recreationally-caught summer flounder and to compare circle hook sets with standard hook sets.

A survey form was developed to collect information on hook type used, hook size, rig type, length of time that the rig was fished, number of fish caught and released on each rig, hook set location, unhooked condition, fish length, and difficulty unhooking fish in New Jersey's recreational summer flounder fishery. Survey forms were distributed to summer flounder anglers with various levels of experience (anglers in their first year of fishing to those with more than 20 years of fishing experience) at the beginning of each season (May 1998, 1999) and collected at the end of each season. Eagle Claw circle hooks, sizes 4/0 (#L197BM) and 5/0 (#L197Fs), were also given to these anglers. Fishing was conducted from shore and party and private boats. Summer flounder rigs were either drifted from a boat or fished stationary from shore. Data were analyzed using a Mann–Whitney rank sum test to test the null hypothesis that the results of the two hook types (circle and standard) were not different. "Standard" hook types were long shank J hook, short shank J hook, and English bend flounder hooks.

Seventeen anglers participated in the study and hooked 160 summer flounder (circle hooks $N = 64$, standard hooks $N = 96$). Anglers used hook sizes ranging from 2/0 to 5/0. The majority (69%) of anglers using circle hooks fished with size 4/0. Anglers fishing with standard hooks fished with hook sizes of 4/0 (55%) and 5/0 (36%).

Most (> 80%) of the hook sets on circle hooks occurred in the upper and lower jaws (Figure 1A), and the summer flounder were easily unhooked with no damage. Only 1.6% of summer flounder experienced gill damage, 4.7% experienced gut damage, and 12.5% experienced bleeding as a result of the hook set.

In the standard hook treatment, hook set location was observed to be primarily in the upper and lower jaws with some sets located in the tongue, throat, and gut (Figure 1B). Release condition of summer flounder caught with standard hooks was 77.1% easily unhooked with no damage, 2.1% gill damaged, 11.5% gut damaged, and 9.4% exhibited bleeding as a result of being hooked.

There was no statistical difference between circle hook and standard hook sets for both hook set location and release condition ($p = 0.05$). This study found that in the recreational summer flounder fishery, circle hooks were not more effective than standard hooks at keeping hook sets confined to the jaw area.

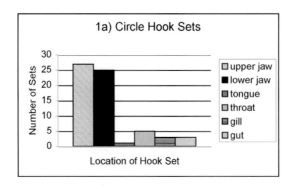

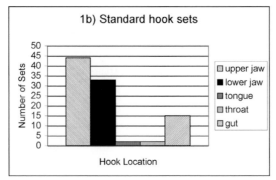

Figure 1. Number of hook sets located in the upper jaw, lower jaw, tongue, throat, gill*, and gut of recreationally-caught summer flounder using A) circle hooks (*N* = 64 fish) and B) standard hooks (*N* = 96 fish).
*No hook sets occurred in the gills of summer flounder in the 1B standard hook treatment.

However, the instances of gut hooked summer flounder were lower (4.7%) in fish caught with circle hooks than in fish caught with standard hooks (15.6%).

Angler comments concerning deep-hooked fish indicated that summer flounder were more prone to experience deep hooking from circle hooks when the rig was slowly drifted. Angler experience, particularly the ability to detect a strike, may have had an effect on the amount of time the fish was allowed to manipulate and ingest the hook.

In this study, hook size did not seem to affect hook set location. Further studies should be conducted to look more closely at the effects of hook size on circle hook set location or how drift speed affects the location of circle hook sets. In addition, recreational release mortality could be reduced once future studies are conducted to determine the best terminal tackle to use in reducing hook sets in the gills, esophagus, and tongue area of summer flounder.

References

Bettoli, P. W., and R. S. Osborne. 1998. Hooking mortality and behavior of striped bass following catch and release angling. North American Journal of Fisheries Management 28:609–615.

Bugley, K., and G. Shepherd. 1991. Effects of catch and release angling on the survival of black sea bass. North American Journal of Fisheries Management 11:468–471.

Diodati, P. J. 1996. Mortality of striped bass hooked and released in salt water. Transactions of the American Fisheries Society 125:300–307.

Lucy, J. A., and T. D. Holton. 1998. Release mortality in Virginia's recreational fishery for summer flounder, *Paralichthys dentatus*. Final contract report to the Virginia Marine Resource Commission. Virginia Marine Resource Report Number 97-8.

Malchoff, M. H. 1995. Effects of catch and release angling on important northeast marine fishes: mortality factors and applications to recreational fisheries. NA36FD102. Report of New York Sea Grant Extension Program to U.S. Department of Commerce, NOAA/NMFS, Gloucester, Massachusetts.

Malchoff, M. H. 1997. Short term hooking mortality of weakfish caught on single barbed hooks. North American Journal of Fisheries Management 17:477–481.

Waters, J. R., and G. R. Huntsman. 1986. Incorporating mortality from catch and release into yield-per-recruit analysis of minimum size limits. North American Journal of Fisheries Management 6:463–471.

Williams, E. H. 1995. Survival of fish captured by hook and released. Master's thesis. University of Rhode Island, Kingston, Rhode Island.

American Fisheries Society Symposium 30:110–113, 2002

EXTENDED ABSTRACT

Catch-and-Release Mortality Studies of Spotted Seatrout and Red Drum in Coastal Alabama

JIM DUFFY

Success of size-related fishery management measures, such as minimum length limits and slot length limits, can depend on the degree to which nonlegal individuals of the target species are able to survive hook and release events. Both spotted seatrout *Cynoscion nebulosus* and red drum *Sciaenops ocellatus* are designated as game fish in Alabama and can be taken in Alabama waters only by recreational fisheries using hook and line. Alabama regulates spotted seatrout fisheries, using a 10-fish daily bag and a minimum length limit of 355-mm (14 in) total length in all state waters. Anglers are allowed to harvest two undersized seatrout in their limit of 10, in a management effort to reduce waste (as a result of this study, the ADCNR/MRD removed the two-under provision on 1 January 2001). Red drum are regulated using a 3-fish daily bag and an exclusionary slot length limit of between 406 mm (16 in) and 660 mm (26 in). One of an angler's three red drum can exceed 660 mm (26 in) in total length.

The literature is inconclusive as to reasonable expectations for catch-and-release mortality in spotted seatrout and red drum, with estimates ranging up to 70% for spotted seatrout and up to 45% for red drum (Muoneke and Childress 1994). During 1994–1996, the Alabama Department of Conservation and Natural Resources, Marine Resources Division (ADCNR/MRD) quantified mortality associated with catch-and-release fishing for spotted seatrout and red drum. The ADCNR/MRD's primary objective was to determine catch-and-release mortality in undersized spotted seatrout (< 355 mm total length) and red drum (< 406 mm total length) associated with typical local angling methods for the two species. These studies were conducted in 0.1 ha culture ponds at the ADCNR/MRD's Claude Peteet Mariculture Center (CPMC) in Gulf Shores, Alabama. The CPMC supports 35 brackish-water research and pro-

Jim Duffy, Alabama Department of Conservation and Natural Resources, Marine Resources Division, Post Office Box 189, Dauphin Island, Alabama 36528, USA. Email: jduffy@gulftel.com

duction ponds and is situated on the Gulf Intracoastal Waterway (GIW) between Gulf Shores and Orange Beach. The CPMC acquires water for pond research activities from the GIW, and salinities typically range between 10 ppt and 20 ppt depending on area rainfall, though higher and lower values do occur during droughts or floods.

Repetitive catch-and-release mortality trials were conducted during early spring through late Fall, from 1994 through 1996. Undersized spotted seatrout and red drum were collected from local public waters and transferred to CPMC in boat-mounted livewells, stabilized in closed culture systems, then separated into three experimental groups for pond trials. Experimental fish were placed in three repository ponds, with a fishless pond on either side of each repository to receive either single or treble-hook caught fish. Seven complete trials, each consisting of three replicates for each hook type, were conducted on spotted seatrout in each of the first two years, and three trials were conducted on red drum in the final year.

Single #2 and treble #6 and #8 hooks were used with a variety of lures and live baits to catch experimental fish. Anglers ranged from expert to novice, and no special care was taken in handling or de-hooking captured fish. During the fishing phase of each trial, fish caught with single hooks were counted and released into one of the adjacent ponds, while treble-hooked fish were counted and released into the other. During each trial, fishing was conducted for up to two weeks, followed by a one-week delayed mortality period. Dead fish were counted and removed from receiving ponds as mortality occurred. All repository and receiving ponds were monitored closely throughout the trials to minimize fish removal by predatory birds and other wildlife. Single and treble-hook ponds were then drained, mortality was assessed by direct counts that were converted to percentages, and surviving fish were redistributed into repositories for another trial. During mortality trials, spotted seatrout were exposed to pond water temperatures between 21°C and 37°C, and red drum were exposed to pond water temperatures between 23°C and 38°C. Experimental fish were fed live prey from trawl samples taken periodically in area waters.

Analysis of variance (ANOVA) in a randomized complete block design was used for each annual experiment, with hook type as the only treatment. Data were blocked by trial to account for variability in pond water quality and water temperature. Percentage data were arcsin transformed to normalize data distributions prior to analysis.

During 1994, blocking had no effect on the model, and no difference in spotted seatrout mortality was detected between hook types at $\alpha = 0.05$ (Figure 1). Spotted seatrout mortality during 1994 averaged 16.3% for single hooks (246 capture events) and 14.1% for treble hooks (242 capture events). Observed mor-

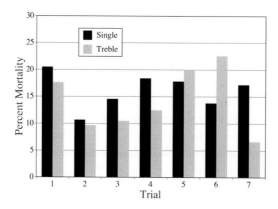

Figure 1. Catch-and-release mortality in spotted seatrout during studies comparing single and treble hooks conducted in 1994, Gulf Shores, Alabama.

tality in 1994 was so much lower than managers expected that the entire experiment was repeated in 1995. Again, no difference was detected between hook types at $\alpha = 0.05$ during 1995 (Figure 2), but blocking did improve the model, though only marginally. Spotted seatrout mortality during 1995 trials averaged 14.6% for single hooks (328 capture events) and 9.1% for treble hooks (329 capture events). Red drum mortality during 1996 trials did not differ between hook types at $\alpha = 0.05$, and averaged 2.4% for single hooks (41 capture events) and 9.9% for treble hooks (55 capture events). Almost all experimental red drum were lost during a weather-related dissolved oxygen depletion after the third trial in 1996, and the experiment was summarily discontinued.

Most mortality in caught-and-released spotted seatrout and red drum in these studies occurred during the first 24 hours following hooking events, and highest mortalities were observed when captures involved single hooks and live bait.

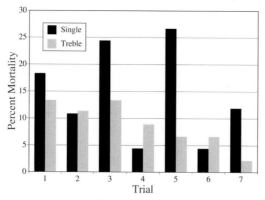

Figure 2. Catch-and-release mortality in spotted seatrout during studies comparing single and treble hooks conducted in 1995, Gulf Shores, Alabama.

Overall, however, mean catch-and-release mortalities were much lower than expected. All mortality during these trials was assumed to be the result of catch-and-release events, and because subject fish were held captive in shallow, warm water ponds with no cover or refuge, the results were taken by managers to represent worst-case scenarios. These results, obtained using locally-favored fishing techniques and tackle during the warmest months of the year, indicate that far fewer spotted seatrout and red drum succumb following catch-and-release events than is commonly believed and that the use of treble hooks doesn't necessarily induce excessive mortality in released fish, as some anglers believe. The ADCNR/MRD managers concluded from these studies that length-based regulation of Alabama's recreational fisheries for spotted seatrout and red drum is appropriate and that anglers could continue to use treble hooks without fear of disproportionately higher catch-and-release mortality.

Reference

Muoneke, M. I., and W. M. Childress. 1994. Hooking mortality: a review for recreational fisheries. Reviews in Fisheries Science 2(2):123–156.

American Fisheries Society Symposium 30:114–117, 2002

EXTENDED ABSTRACT

Short-Term Hook Release Mortality in Chesapeake Bay's Recreational Tautog Fishery

JON A. LUCY *and* MICHAEL D. ARENDT

Hook release mortality rates can be affected by various fishing practices including hook wound location, baited hooks versus lures, and fish handling stress, as well as environmental factors, i.e., water temperature and capture depth (Muoneke and Childress 1994). Release mortality is typically greater for fish with swim bladders taken from deeper water (Wilson and Burns 1996). Although hook release mortality rates of fish are variable depending upon the species in question, fishing practices, and fishing season (Muoneke and Childress 1994), fishery management plan (FMP) technical committees must often use discard mortality levels to estimate overall fishing mortality and update stock assessments without the benefit of research data.

In the mid-1980s, annual tautog *Tautoga onitis* landings declined throughout northeast and mid-Atlantic states, reaching record lows in 1993–1994. To reduce fishing mortality the Atlantic States Marine Fisheries Commission (ASMFC) developed a FMP for tautog in April 1996 (ASMFC 1996). Among its regulations states had to increase minimum catch sizes to 330 mm (13 inches) total length (TL) in 1997 and to 356 mm (14 in) TL in 1998. The tautog FMP assumed a recreational discard mortality of 25%.

In 1997 a study was initiated to estimate release mortality rates in Virginia's recreational tautog fishery (Lucy and Arendt 1999). The objective of the study was to quantify release mortality, particularly for sub-legal sized fish, at water temperature and depth ranges found in Chesapeake Bay. Fish were collected using recreational fishing gear (two-hook bottom rigs with fresh bait, i.e., clam

Jon A. Lucy, Sea Grant Marine Advisory Program, Virginia Institute of Marine Science, College of William and Mary, Post Office Box 1346, Gloucester Point, Virginia 23062, USA. Phone (804) 684-7166, Fax 804-684-7161, Email: lucy@vims.edu

Michael D. Arendt, Marine Resources Research Institute, South Carolina Marine Resources Division, Post Office Box 12559, Charleston, South Carolina 29422-2559, USA. Phone (843) 588-2209, Fax (843) 762-5110, Email: arendtm@mrd.dnr.state.sc.us

114

or hard crab) at various lower Bay fishing locations. Fish were captured by a mixed group of anglers and researchers aboard a charter fishing vessel during fall 1997 and 1998. Hooks varied, representing types and sizes typically used in the fishery (Eagle Claw 1/0–#3/0 Long-shank J-hooks and Mustad #2–3 blackfish hooks).

After being netted and having hooks removed, fish were measured, tagged using Virginia Game Fish Tagging Program (VGFTP) T-bar anchor tags (TBA2, Hallprint Ltd), and placed in an aerated, flow-through live well. Handling time and fish condition were recorded along with water depth, temperature, and hooking data (hook type, wound location, hook removal method, tissue damage, degree of bleeding), and swim bladder expansion effects (intestines protruding from vent or eyes bulging).

Fish were accumulated in the live well (3–10 fish, holding time less than two hours) before being placed in cubical, galvanized-wire cages (60 cm on a side with 13-mm mesh wire). Cages were lowered to be just above the bottom using single lines with floats. Suspended from the vessel's bow until the vessel prepared to change locations, cages were gently lowered to the bottom maintaining adequate separation distances from fishing structures to prevent cages hanging up during retrieval. To assess short-term release mortality, cage bottom time was targeted at 72–96 hours. Upon retrieving cages, numbers of dead fish were counted and surviving fish, typically recorded to be in good condition, were released with their tags in place.

During November–December 1997 and October–December 1998, 299 fish (235–521 mm TL) were caught and held in cages. Hooks lodged in fishes' lips or just inside the mouth accounted for 97% of fish caught with 1% deep hooked (leaders cut and hooks left in such fish during trials). Sub-legal size fish accounted for 16% of 1997 catches ($N = 29$), increasing to 39% ($N = 47$) in 1998. Shallow water trials accounted for 49% of captured fish and deeper water trials 51%. Forty-four percent were caught at warm water temperatures ($\geq 15.5C°$) and 56% at cool temperatures ($< 15.5°C$). Fish density per cage varied between three and eight fish in 1997 (mean = 5.2) and 5–10 fish in 1998 (mean = 7.2), with an overall mean of 6.0. Fish holding periods varied between 43 and 192 hours in 1997 and 65–144 hours in 1998, times outside the targeted range due to changing weather, boat availability, or difficulty in re-locating cages. Mean fish holding time (46 trials over two years) was 115 hours (4.8 days).

A two-sample t-test indicated mean fish length was similar between 1997 and 1998 ($N = 177$, mean TL = 376 mm; $N = 122$, mean TL = 366 mm, respectively). Only five fish died during the study (three in 1997, two in 1998), and descriptive statistics were used to calculate mean mortality). Chi-square (χ^2)

contingency tests indicated a significant difference in mortality between fish captured in deep (11–17 m) versus shallow (≤ 10 m) water (3.3% and 0%, respectively; $\chi^2 = 4.852$, df = 1, $p \leq 0.05$). Deep-water fish showed significantly greater instances of swim bladder expansion effects when landed (intestine protruding out vent, $\chi^2 = 30.169$, df = 1, $p \leq 0.05$; bulging eyes, $\chi^2 = 30.915$, df = 1, $p \leq 0.05$). No differences in mortality were demonstrated between warm versus cool water (two and three fish, respectively; $\chi^2 = 0.041$, df = 1, $p > 0.05$).

Longer than usual holding times occurred for three cages during 1997 (357 hours/15 days) and two cages in 1998 (264 hours/11 days) due to rough sea conditions. Of a total of 31 fish in these cages, one fish died (3.2%). Additional evidence of longer-term survival resulted from angler recaptures of some released test fish, i.e., 24 recaptures reported through the VGFTP from the general study area (19–737 days following release).

Because trial mortality estimates were not normally distributed, 95% confidence intervals around estimates were computed using confidence limits for percentages (Sokal and Rohlf 1969). Overall mortality for the two years was 1.7% (95% CI = 0.6-3.7%), similar to that found by Simpson (1999) in Connecticut (mortality = 2.7%; 95% CI = 0.8-4.3%). As a result of the two studies the ASMFC Tautog Technical Committee reduced the recreational fishery discard mortality rate used in stock assessment calculations in 2000 from 25% to 2.5% (G. White, ASMFC, personal communication). Low hook release mortality rates for the species in both northern and southern fishery areas support minimum size limits and bag limits being effective management tools for reducing fishing mortality in the hook and line fishery.

References

ASMFC (Atlantic States Marine Fisheries Commission). 1996. Fishery management plan for tautog, Report 25. ASMFC, Washington, D.C.

Lucy, J. A., and M. D. Arendt. 1999. Exploratory field evaluation of hook-release mortality in tautog (*Tautoga onitis*) in lower Chesapeake Bay. Virginia Institute of Marine Science, College of William and Mary, Virginia Marine Resource Report 99–10, Contract report (Project RF 97–17), Virginia Marine Resources Commission, Newport News, Virginia.

Muoneke, M. I., and W. M. Childress. 1994. Hooking mortality: a review for recreational fisheries. Reviews in Fisheries Science 2(2):123–156.

Simpson, D. 1999. A study of gear induced mortality in marine finfish, Job 4. Pages 121–125 *in* A study of marine recreational fisheries in Connecticut. Annual Report. Connecticut Department of Environmental Protection, Federal Aid to Sportfish Restoration Project F54R, Old Lyme, Connecticut (draft).

Sokal, R. R., and F. J. Rohlf. 1969. Biometry. Freeman, San Francisco, California.
Wilson, R. R., Jr., and K. M. Burns. 1996. Potential survival of released groupers caught deeper than 40 m based on shipboard and in-situ observations, and tag-recapture data. Bulletin of Marine Science 58(1):234–247.

Stress Effects Related to
Catch and Release

American Fisheries Society Symposium 30:121–134, 2002
© Copyright by the American Fisheries Society 2002

Strategies for Quantifying Sublethal Effects of Marine Catch-and-Release Angling: Insights from Novel Freshwater Applications

STEVEN J. COOKE

Department of Natural Resources and Environmental Sciences
University of Illinois
Center for Aquatic Ecology, Illinois Natural History Survey
607 East Peabody Drive
Champaign, Illinois 61820, USA

JASON F. SCHREER *and* KAREN M. DUNMALL

Department of Biology
University of Waterloo
200 University Avenue
Waterloo, Ontario N2L 3G1, Canada

DAVID P. PHILIPP

Department of Natural Resources and Environmental Sciences
University of Illinois
Center for Aquatic Ecology, Illinois Natural History Survey
607 East Peabody Drive
Champaign, Illinois 61820, USA

Abstract.—Traditional approaches for assessing the effects of catch-and-release angling have focused either on hooking injury, mortality associated with different handling and environmental conditions, or biochemical indicators of short-term stress response and recovery. These methodologies do not permit the collection of real-time data on the sub-lethal effects and recovery period associated with the angling event, nor do they provide information on long-term fitness impacts to angled individuals. The advent of hard-wired, archival, and telemetered technologies capable of collecting information on fish location, locomotory activity, cardiac function, and various environmental parameters provides researchers with powerful methodologies for monitoring the response of individual fish to different stressors. These technologies and approaches have been used primarily with freshwater fishes, but they may be applicable to marine environments. Compared with freshwater systems, there are unquestionably some additional challenges due to unique characteristics of the marine habitat (e.g., depth, vastness, salinity) and behaviors of marine fishes (e.g., migratory patterns). Irrespective of the challenges, fisheries scientists must begin to look beyond hooking mortality as an endpoint for assessing the success of a catch-and-release angling program. Studies need to be conducted that provide real-time information on sublethal physiological effects, disruptions in behavior, and long-term impacts on the fitness (lifetime reproductive success) of released fish. Despite the fact that managers are usually concerned with population level effects, additional individual-level comprehensive studies are required before we can attempt to understand if and how catch-and-release angling affects populations.

Introduction

Recreational anglers increasingly are participating in nonconsumptive fishing (i.e., catch-and-release angling or some form of selective harvest; Quinn 1996). One reason this change in angler behavior has arisen is in response to the overharvesting of fisheries. Today, a combination of voluntary (Quinn 1989) and mandated (Redmond 1986) catch-and-release programs exists (Barnhart and Roelofs 1977, 1989). Although most fisheries managers are concerned with population, community, and ecosystem level implications of catch-and-release angling, it is the effects of this practice on the individual organism that will culminate in changes at these higher levels of organization.

The possible consequences of catch-and-release angling range from no measurable impact to death. The majority of studies assessing the effects of catch-and-release angling have focused on two areas. The first is assessment of the degree of physical injury incurred by angled individuals coupled with the quantification of immediate or delayed mortality. The second is assessment of the short-term (hours or days) physiological or behavioral responses of individuals that do not die. Although research conducted in laboratories is helping us to understand why fish may die after severe exercise and handling (Wood et al. 1983), we still know relatively little about the physiology and behavior of free-swimming fish following release.

Fish respond to stress with a series of defense mechanisms that are energetically demanding (Barton and Iwama 1991). These defense mechanisms are difficult to identify, but certainly act to impair various physiological processes and likely cause altered behaviors (Heath 1990) that may make an organism susceptible to predation or induce hyperactivity, causing an unnecessary expenditure of energy (Black 1958). Broom and Johnson (1993) have postulated that stress also reduces individual fitness through a reduction in reproductive capability. Tests of that hypothesis, however, have not been forthcoming because measuring the fitness of an individual or groups of individuals over its/their lifetime is difficult as is identifying the stressor that has altered fitness. Many hooking mortality studies have documented high survival rates for fish that were angled and released (Muoneke and Childress 1994). Very few studies, however, have monitored the physiological disturbance associated with angling and handling and the subsequent recovery of free-swimming fish following release. Although high survival rates are fundamental to the goals of nonconsumptive fishing, an equally important goal is to minimize sublethal effects that may decrease fitness. For example, catch-and-release angling practices could disrupt reproductive activities, thereby impacting a population in several potential ways. Year-class strength could be decreased directly in response to a reduction in successful reproduction. Additionally, differential susceptibility of one sex or certain size classes of individuals could alter a population's reproductive characteristics by selectively disrupting the reproduction of those individuals. The opportunity for these impacts clearly is present, but the extent of their occurrence is unknown.

Herein, we review techniques that have been used successfully to obtain information on the sublethal effects of catch-and-release angling in freshwater fishes and assess their relevance and application to marine systems. We also highlight a series of novel and underutilized procedures for monitoring the disturbances associated with angling and discuss how these tools may help us to understand the recovery patterns and energetic costs associated with catch-and-release angling. In addition, we describe a set of desirable characteristics that we feel should be embodied in the "ideal" measure of the response of fish to angling. In particular, we emphasize the importance of measuring more than mortality and encourage scientists to consider sublethal effects, including the assessment of long-term impacts on fitness.

Assessing the Impacts of Catch-and-Release Angling

As the practice of catch-and-release angling has grown, so has the number of studies addressing the effects of that practice. Those studies range from being purely observational to being quite experimental in their approach. The following brief review of different methods for studying the impacts of catch-and-release angling highlights the basic principles behind those methods and provides some key supporting references.

Traditional Approaches

Hooking Injury and Mortality: Studies of physical injury and mortality related to angling are common (Muoneke and Childress 1994) and can be conducted by using mark–recapture techniques or by holding fish in artificial or natural environments, including cages (Matlock et al. 1993), pens (Schisler and Bergersen 1996), or on tethers (Loftus et al. 1988). Physical injury usually involves documenting the location and degree of tissue damage, which is typically a subjective classification (e.g., mild versus extreme). Hooking depth measurements adjusted proportionately to the length of the fish are also common (Dunmall et al. 2001). In one creative study, researchers examined the ocular lenses of fish held in live wells to determine rates of eye injury from handling (McLaughlin et al. 1997). Such unique approaches may be necessary to understand completely the scope of potential injuries that may be encountered during angling and subsequent handling.

Hooking mortality is usually defined as the fraction of fish that do not survive beyond a predetermined recovery period. There is, however, always the potential for the additional stress from holding the fish to bias hooking mortality estimates (Wright 1970). External marking programs have been used to assess hooking mortality (Jagielo 1999), particularly in marine environments; however, the biases associated with tagging mortality, tag loss, and poor tag recovery can confound results and conclusions (Candy et al. 1996).

Muscle and Blood Biochemistry: Biochemical studies can provide important information on the magnitude and duration of physiological disturbance associated with catch-and-release angling practices (Wydoski et al. 1976; Beggs et al. 1980; Gustaveson et al. 1991; Tufts et al. 1991). The high intensity anaerobic exercise experienced during exhaustive exercise accompanying angling (Wood et al. 1983) induces a variety of metabolic disturbances. These include glycogen depletion, alterations in the levels of adenosine triphosphate and phosphocreatine, and the accumulation of end products of anaerobic metabolism, such as lactate and H + protons (Driedzic and Hochachka 1978; Milligan and Wood 1986; Kieffer 2000). These physiological disturbances induce metabolic and respiratory blood acidoses that result in further ionic imbalance, as well as elevated cardiac output (Wood 1991). Hematological studies can be limited by the finite volume of blood that may be sampled without causing additional physiological disturbances. Furthermore, cannulation can result in a secondary stress response (e.g., Gamperal et al. 1994; Mazik et al. 1994). In addition, many experimental designs require that fish be sacrificed, resulting in the collection of samples from different individuals, thus reducing resolution and introducing additional sources of variation.

Studies have also assessed the physiological disturbance to white skeletal muscle (See Kieffer 2000 for review). White muscle is used extensively during the bouts of anaerobic burst swimming that accompany angling (Ferguson et al. 1993; Booth et al. 1995; Kieffer et al. 1995). Similar to hemato-

logical studies, these tissue analyses can provide information on the magnitude of physiological disturbance and the duration of recovery. White muscle acid–base and metabolite status (primarily muscle lactate, muscle pH, and metabolic protons) are often used as indicators of stress. A major drawback to most studies involving white muscle analyses is the level of invasiveness required; they almost always require terminal sampling.

Recent developments in nuclear magnetic resonance (NMR) imaging, including NMR spectroscopy (NMRS), permit the noninvasive and nondestructive measurement of the chemical compounds in intact tissues such as phosphorous compounds that fluctuate during exercise, indicating tissue energy status (Van Den Thillart and Van Waarde 1996). These techniques are particularly promising because they allow for the analysis of individual metabolic pathways. To date, studies using this technology have focused on purely physiological questions. This technology, however, could provide future insights into the physiological response of fish to catch-and-release angling stressors. In particular, NMRS may also provide new insights into the effects of air exposure on tissue-level metabolism and oxygen status.

Remote Approaches to the Observation of Behavior and Physiology

A common problem for many behavioral and physiological studies is collecting measurements on free-ranging organisms, including fish (Beamish 1978; Scherer 1992). That kind of information would be particularly useful for assessing the effects of catch-and-release angling. Advances in telemetry now permit the measurement of the behavior and physiology of free-swimming fishes, including activity, metabolic rate, body temperature, heart rate, etc., (Butler 1989), as well as a variety of environmental parameters, including external water or air temperature, light, depth, water conductivity, or some other indicator of habitat characteristics.

Recent advances in the miniaturization of telemetry devices has permitted the development of systems capable of relaying information on location, behavior, and physiology of many more species of fish without disrupting their behavior or physiology (Lucas et al. 1993; Winter 1996). This technology assumes that the transmitter or the attachment procedure does not affect the fish, an assumption that needs to be tested. As technology changes, we will undoubtedly be able to monitor more physiological and behavioral parameters remotely in free-swimming fish (Stasko and Pincock 1977; Baras 1991).

Locational Telemetry

Since 1957, conventional locational telemetry has been used to study the free-swimming behavior of numerous species (Baras 1991; Lucas and Baras 2000), but only in several recent accounts has this technology been applied to studies on catch-and-release angling. Locational telemetry involves attaching a radio or ultrasonic transmitter and then locating the fish using a manual tracking system or a fixed antenna or hydrophone array. The most common application of telemetry to catch-and-release angling has been to examine the postrelease behavior of fish displaced from where they were caught. This activity commonly occurs in competitive angling events (Ridgway and Shuter 1996; Stang et al. 1996). Usually, the objective of these studies is to assess the dispersal rates and homing tendencies of released fish to ensure that tournament release procedures do not create regions of locally high abundance. Several other telemetric studies have used the mobility of fish after release as an indication that they survived the catch-and-release angling event (Jolley and Irby 1979; Walker and Walker 1991; Bendock and Alexandersdottir 1993; Skomal and Chase 1997; Edwards 1998; Makinen et al. 2000; Whoriskey et al. 2000). In these studies, the postrelease behavior and survivorship was assessed for a period of up to several days or until the fish could no longer be located.

Environmental Telemetry

In some cases, temperature-sensitive transmitters have been used to assess behavior and mortality of postrelease fish (Bettoli and Osborne 1998). When fish exhibited negligible movement, and when water temperature data indicated consistently low temperatures indicative of resting on the bottom, the fish were determined to be dead (Bettoli and Osborne 1998). Other researchers have used pressure-sensitive depth tags to examine fish behavior and survival relative to thermal and oxygen stratification following hooking and release (Lee and Bergersen 1996). Perhaps the biggest limitation for all of these tech-

niques is the difficulty in obtaining information on control specimens. The effect of tagging usually cannot be separated from the effect of being hooked and released (Bettoli and Osborne 1998). As such, these studies become more observational than experimental. These studies can also become logistically difficult when dealing with species that are highly mobile; concentrated tracking efforts extending around the clock are often required to obtain sufficient data.

Activity Telemetry

Activity telemetry is used to assess the locomotory activity of fish on a finer scale than is possible with locational telemetry. Changes in activity levels of fish have recently been observed to be sensitive indicators of stress (Schreck 1990; Scherer 1992; Schreck et al. 1997). Oxygen consumption estimates, however, obtained from activity transmitters that have been calibrated in respirometers have only limited utility in studies of catch-and-release angling. Following release, many fish may remain motionless while the oxygen debt is repaid (Gaesser and Brooks 1984; Scarabello et al. 1991). Oxygen consumption estimates based upon activity signals would suggest that the metabolic rate is depressed, when, in fact, it is elevated. For this reason, Anderson et al. (1998) concluded that activity telemetry has limited utility for studies of catch-and-release angling. This technology, however, could be useful for monitoring catch-and-release impacts where locomotory activity displayed by fish is particularly relevant to the life history of a species (e.g., migrations, parental care, ram-obligate ventilators). To date, only one catch-and-release study has been conducted using this technology (Cooke et al. 2000).

Electromyograms (EMGs) are records of bioelectric potentials that are strongly correlated with the strength and duration of muscle contraction. Radio EMG transmitters are commercially available (Electromyogram, EMG, Lotek Engineering Inc., Newmarket, Ontario)[1] and are capable of detecting the fine-scale activity patterns of fish. Electrodes implanted in the axial swimming musculature detect muscle activity and emit signals when a predetermined threshold has been achieved (these are not "raw" electromyograms) (Kaseloo et al. 1992; Beddow and McKinley 1999). Cooke et al. (2000) used

---

1. Use of trade names does not imply endorsement by the agencies and organizations that we represent.

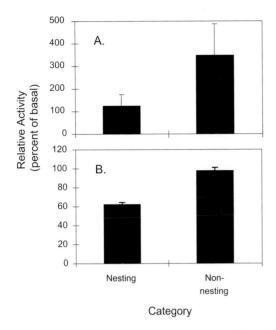

Figure 1. (A.) Locomotory activity of nesting ($N = 4$) and non-nesting ($N = 2$) male largemouth bass during 150 seconds of angling. The bars represent the mean (± 1 SE) locomotory activity during the angling period. (B.) Example of locomotory activity of nesting ($N = 4$) and non-nesting ($N = 2$) male largemouth bass following 150 seconds of angling. The bars represent the mean (± 1 SE) activity levels for the 24 hour period following angling. Data from Cooke et al. (2000).

EMG transmitters to assess the effects of catch-and-release angling on nest guarding male largemouth bass *Micropterus salmoides* during the parental care phase. These fish, implanted with transmitters, were held in experimental ponds prior to spawning. During angling nest guarding fish fought with lower intensity and when released they had impaired locomotory activity for up to 24 hours (Figure 1A, 1B). Although preliminary and limited to a short battery life, an acoustic transmitter that collects information on "raw" muscle EMG's also has been described recently (Dewar et al. 1999).

Early attempts to measure tail-beat frequency using radio telemetry (Ross et al. 1981; Johnstone et al. 1992) were apparently successful, but they have not become readily available in the commercial market and have not been applied to catch-and-release angling. The first attempt to correlate tail-beat frequency to ultrasonic telemetry signals was based on variations in continuous wave signals resulting from the undulations of body and tail (Doppler effect; Stasko and Horrall 1976). This approach has not been widely adopted. Two more recent devel-

opments, both of which are ultrasonic and thus applicable to marine environments, may be applicable to catch-and-release angling. The first is a tail-beat transmitter that emits a signal with every lateral tail-beat (Lowe et al. 1998). The second is a device that utilizes a pressure differential sensor capable of estimating energy output though the frequency and amplitude of tail-beats (Fred Voegli and Dale Webber, Vemco Inc., personal communication). These devices are less invasive than current EMG technologies.

Some researchers have attached speed-sensing transmitters to fish. Block et al. (1992) attached acoustic transmitters that relayed information on depth, water temperature and speed of blue marlin *Makaira nigricans*, as they were tracked for 25–120 hours. Speed was measured by a velocity meter equipped with a plastic propeller containing a magnet that activated a reed switch that was trailed from a semirigid stock attached to the transmitter. A paddle-wheel style acoustic activity transmitter was deployed by Sundström and Gruber (1998) on elasmobranchs. This device can be affixed quickly and calibrated in a respirometer, but occasionally the paddle wheel becomes stuck (this is a problem with all paddle wheels and propellers). In addition, speed-sensing devices may overestimate swimming speed and energy expenditure due to fish gliding and may also be influenced by water-current speed and direction (Brill et al. 1993).

Ventilatory Telemetry

Telemetry studies quantifying ventilatory/opercular rates have been sparse in the literature. Although this technology was developed more than 25 years ago, it has not become a well-used approach. The few studies that have been published do not investigate catch-and-release angling (Oswald 1978; Rogers and Weatherley 1983; Rogers et al. 1984).

Heart Rate Telemetry

Heart rate (HR) telemetry devices have taken several forms, all of which have electrodes placed in or adjacent to the pericardial cavity to detect electrical activity indicative of heartbeats. Heart rate telemetry has been used to assess the metabolic rate of free-swimming freshwater (Priede and Tytler 1977; Priede 1983; Armstrong et al. 1989; Lucas 1994) and marine fish (Priede and Tytler 1977; Scharold and Gruber 1991). Although success has varied (Thorarensen et al. 1996), at present, this may be one of the best ways to monitor postexercise physiological activity remotely, although it may not be suitable for all species (Anderson et al. 1998). Anderson et al. (1998) used prototype HR radio transmitters (Lotek Engineering) to monitor recovery of free-swimming Atlantic salmon *Salmo salar*. Following angling at various temperatures, HR only increased 15–30% above resting levels. The problem with using HR as an indicator of metabolic rate is that the majority of fish species increase cardiac output (CO) principally through an increase in stroke volume (SV) rather than HR (Farrell 1991; Farrell and Jones 1992; Thorarensen et al. 1996). For species that are frequency modulators (e.g., tuna, Brill and Bushnell 1991; Farrell 1991; smallmouth bass, *Micropterus dolomieu*, Schreer et al. 2001a), heart rate transmitters can provide reliable data, but for the majority of other species examined to date, (Farrell 1991), a more reliable correlate of oxygen consumption requires the measurement of CO, which is a function of both HR and SV (Thorarensen et al. 1996).

Cardiac Output

The measurement of CO addresses many of the shortcomings of activity transmitters and HR telemetry. Measuring locomotory muscle activity can be useful to determine if exposure to environmental factors modifies the activity level of the fish. Measuring that activity, however, will not allow detection of changes in metabolism associated with maintenance of homeostasis or recovery from oxygen debt following periods of increased activity. Heart function is influenced by variations in metabolism from all sources because oxygen consumption is a function of CO and the amount of oxygen that is extracted from the blood as it passes through tissues (EO_2). As mentioned above, HR may not always be a reliable correlate of oxygen consumption, and therefore, monitoring CO, which also yields HR and SV, is important.

Several techniques have been used to measure CO in fish, including indirect (Fick equation) and direct (cuff-type or cannulating electromagnetic or Doppler flow probes) methods (Farrell and Jones 1992). In our work, we use cuff-type ultrasonic Doppler flow probes that are inserted around the ventral aorta and hard-wired to a flowmeter (e.g., Cooke et al. 2001; Schreer et al. 2001a). The Doppler flow probe uses a crystal transducer to emit a pulsed sonic signal. Due to

Doppler shift, when the signal is reflected from a moving object in the blood (i.e., a red blood cell), a shift in the signal frequency is observed. This represents a velocity and is measured as a change in voltage. Peaks in voltage/velocity represent a heartbeat, and counting peaks per unit time yields HR. The mean voltage per unit time is an index of CO (absolute flow can be calculated in volume/time–1 via a postmortem calibration). Dividing CO by HR yields SV.

Although monitoring the CO of fish provides the most rigorous information regarding the metabolic response and recovery to angling, there are several limitations. First, there are currently no remote blood flow telemetry devices; all require a hard-wire for signal collection. As a result, all studies using CO must be conducted under confined laboratory or semiconstricted conditions. Several laboratories and companies are currently working on this problem, and it is expected that a telemetric version will be available in the near future. Second, CO and its components, HR and SV, provide only two of the three parameters necessary for calculating oxygen consumption, the third being EO_2. Changes in EO_2 may have a considerable effect on metabolic rate, especially in exercising fish. Two studies have assessed the cardiac disturbance associated with catch-and-release angling (Cooke et al. 2001; Schreer et al. 2001a). The first swam smallmouth bass in a respirometer at speeds that elicited burst responses similar to those observed during angling. Cardiac disturbance was influenced by both degree of exhaustion and water temperature, with time to recovery generally increasing with both parameters (Schreer et al. 2001a). In a second experiment, cardiac output was used to assess the effects of air exposure duration on recovery in rock bass *Ambloplites rupestris*. Long exposures (180 s) resulted in cardiac recovery periods lasting more than twice as long as short (30 s) exposures (Cooke et al. 2001). Examples of data generated from this approach are included as Figures 2 and 3, the effects of air exposure on sea-ranched Atlantic salmon and the effects of handling on Arctic char *Salvelinus alpinus*. Using this approach, it is possible to quantify the degree of cardiac disturbance and the duration required for cardiac parameters to normalize. Additional work is required to establish how different cardiac parameters correlate with levels of biochemical disturbance.

Long-Term Impacts

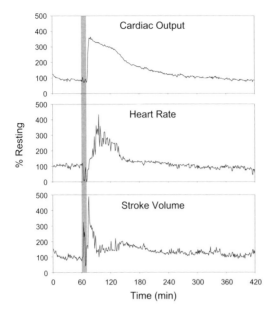

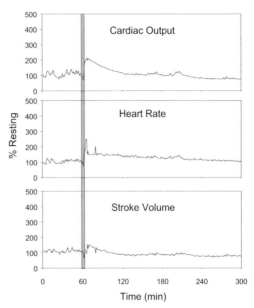

Figure 2. Example of cardiac response to 10 minute air exposure in a Norwegian sea-ranched Atlantic salmon (male, 1.320 kg, 605-mm total length) acclimated to fresh water at 5°C. Fish was removed from a 0.28 m² × 0.36 m round tank and exposed to air using a wetted sling. All values are percent resting with resting equal to 100%. The 10 minute air exposure (shaded area) ended when the fish was returned to the water.

Figure 3. Example of cardiac response to manual disturbance and physical handling in an Arctic char (male, 1.223 kg, 455-mm total length) acclimated to fresh water at 5°C. Chasing fish, which elicited burst swimming, occurred within a 0.28 m² × 0.36 m round tank for a duration of five minutes (shaded area). All values are percent resting with resting equal to 100%.

Reproductive Activity and Individual Fitness

There is a large suite of possible fitness related effects that may be manifested following catch-and-release angling (Table 1). Several studies have assessed the effects of chronic stress on hatchery fish and have concluded that it can result in smaller egg size, delayed ovulation, and reduced larval survival relative to control fish (Campbell et al. 1992,1994). Booth et al. (1995) found that late season catch-and-release angling had minimal effect on gamete viability of adult Atlantic salmon. In contrast, Pankhurst and Dedual (1993) documented changes in reproductive hormones resulting from catch-and-release angling, but suggested that it is unlikely that these changes would alter reproductive activity. Both studies did, however, propose that angling could disrupt other aspects of reproduction such as nest digging behavior, spawning intensity, or redd defense (Booth et al. 1995) and may have an inhibitory effect at earlier stages of sexual maturity (Pankhurst and Dedual 1993).

Direct assessments of the fitness impacts of catch-and-release angling, however, are difficult and rare, but represent an important component of the issue.

To date, the only conclusive link between the stress resulting from catch-and-release angling and failed reproduction of wild fish was found for centrarchids, in which the male provides sole parental care. In this circumstance, the angling of the male has obvious implications for white muscle disturbance (Kieffer et al. 1995). Locomotory impairments following catch-and-release events reduced the ability of the male to defend his brood successfully (Cooke et al. 2000). Furthermore, during the temporary removal

Table 1. Suite of possible fitness impacts resulting from catch-and-release angling.

Possible fitness impacts

- Smaller egg size
- Delayed ovulation
- Reduced gamete viability
- Reduced larval survival
- Reduced larval energy
- Changes in reproductive hormones
- Interruption of migration
- Reduced spawning intensity
- Reduced parental care
- Impaired competitive ability (mates, space)
- Inhibited sexual maturation
- Failed/foregone reproduction

of the male from the nest, predators may consume the developing offspring. Substantial brood predation often results in male abandonment and the subsequent destruction of the entire brood, leading to a reduction in the lifetime reproductive success of the male (Philipp et al. 1997). The centrarchid reproductive life history provides an ideal system for studying fitness impacts of angling, and forthcoming research from our laboratory will attempt to address this issue.

What is the Appropriate Approach?

To assess the pros and cons of catch-and-release angling, a critical first step involves determining the organizational level at which it is most appropriate to assess impacts. Most fisheries managers are concerned with population or community level impacts. Studies that assess the effects of stress at these organizational levels, however, usually do not provide information on how those stress effects are manifested by individuals (Maltby 1999). Molecular and cellular level studies provide insights into metabolic and biochemical disturbances from exercise, but this information has limited applicability at higher organizational levels. Maltby (1999) argues that there is no correct level to study stress. Instead, she advocates studies that integrate information from several levels (also see Adams 1990), which will provide more comprehensive insights into the effects of stress, the mechanistic bases, and their ecological and evolutionary consequences. Similar to ecotoxicologists, researchers examining the effects of catch-and-release angling on individuals face the challenge of ascribing ecological relevance to the putative resultant stresses. At the population level, one might ask, what does it matter if the behavior, physiology, or survival of an individual fish is impaired? There have been a few studies that have evaluated the impacts of catch-and-release angling at a variety of biological levels, including some at the level of the population (Heath 1990).

To understand the effects of catch-and-release angling on all relevant biological levels, a variety of methodologies must be employed. We propose a series of criteria that embody some of the most robust and desirable methodologies for measuring stress and recovery (Table 2). Studies that satisfy the requirements of an ideal monitoring technique will be the most useful in assessing how organisms respond to

different stressors; yet, it is clear that few current methodologies can satisfy many of these criteria.

Integrated approaches will provide the most comprehensive and robust information on the effects of catch-and-release angling. Extrapolating these findings to organismal fitness, bioenergetics models, and more widespread effects at the population level will provide the most complete picture as to the true impacts of catch-and-release angling. Such an interdisciplinary approach is very different from the way that these studies typically have been undertaken.

Prospectus for Marine and Freshwater Systems

Field Studies

Intrinsic to freshwater and marine environments are several characteristics that impose both technological and logistic constraints. Freshwater systems generally have fairly low conductivities, permitting the use of radio transmitters. Marine environments have high conductivities that rapidly attenuate short wavelength radio signals, thus requiring the use of ultrasonic transmitters. Attenuation rates can still be a limiting factor for some freshwater applications, such as monitoring fish residing at considerable depth, and consequently, the use of ultrasonic telemetry may be more appropriate than radio transmitters. Conducting telemetry studies in marine environments can be particularly difficult considering the vast area and great depths that fish may occupy. Some groups of fishes are localized and spend much of their lives associated with spatially-restricted habitats such as lagoons, but many species, including a large number of important recreational species (i.e., billfish), live in pelagic environments and can move great distances. Although it is inherently more difficult to obtain telemetric information in marine environments, some approaches and techniques used in freshwater environments may permit the collection of some relevant data on marine catch-and-release angling impacts. For example, it would be possible to capture certain species for telemetric implantation and release into enclosures. After an appropriate recovery period, catch-and-release angling experiments could be performed on those fish, allowing real-time monitoring of the energetic expenditure during the angling, as well as the duration of recovery needed following the event.

Table 2. Desirable characteristics for an "ideal" approach to the assessment of catch-and-release impacts.

Characteristic	Description
Objective and quantifiable	Central to any monitoring tool is the need to collect data that is objective and quantifiable. These types of data increase the ease of statistical analysis and remove the subjectivity that may bias results
High resolution – real time	Data can be collected on several different time scales. Tools that facilitate the real time monitoring of stress and recovery will be more likely to detect physiological disturbances. Studies that acquire data before, during, and after a perturbation will be the most useful in monitoring the physiological and behavioral status of the organism. Further, a nearly continuous data stream eliminates unknowns during times when fish were not being monitored and permits better trend through time detection.
Not terminal	Sampling methods that, themselves, do not result in the death of the organism, nor alter the behavior and physiology of the organism are important.
Free-swimming fish	Studies that focus on the in situ measurement of free-swimming fish during environmental perturbations will reflect the site-specific characteristics that are faced by the individual. These studies will also be able to detect how fish respond in their natural environment in the presence of the multitude of factors that are difficult to recreate in laboratory conditions (e.g., predation, habitat heterogeneity, etc.).
Adequate controls/ basal levels	Catch-and-release angling studies rarely have true controls or sham controls. Studies that compare fish that have been disturbed to those that have not been recently disturbed allows for greater justification in the attribution of findings to the perturbation being studied, and eliminates the problems associated with nuisance variance. Also, by monitoring individuals prior to disturbance, it will be possible to have complete records of basal levels, disturbance effects, and the subsequent recovery.
Recovery/sublethal effects	Monitoring techniques that provide information on the time required for different disturbances to normalize are required. Studies that are able to monitor recovery and detect sub-lethal effects are essential to understanding and quantifying the behavioral and physiological disturbances associated with catch-and-release angling that do not result in mortality.
Metabolic indicators/ energetics	Stressors and responses that can be quantified in an ecologically common currency (energy) will be useful for inferring the bioenergetic consequences of angling practices and will allow for more relevant comparisons between unrelated taxa.
Fitness	Experimental tests designed to determine the long-term impact of stressors on absolute fitness (lifetime reproductive success) or on fitness-related characters (e.g., fecundity, body condition, age at maturation) will be instrumental in developing a truly complete assessment of impacts of catch-and-release angling.

Marine telemetry studies of recreational fish often target larger-sized individuals than studies conducted in freshwater environments. Their size permits the attachment of devices that are also larger in size. It is often difficult to work with large fish, however, because they typically move through vast areas and do not do well in captivity. Some fishes, such as tunas, congregate in schools that can be followed by boat for days at a time. Devices that relay real-time information could be deployed on these fish, with data collected remotely from vessel-borne receiving systems. This approach has been used for locational data collection on a short-term basis (i.e., hours) for several marine species, such as tarpon *Megalops atlanticus* (Edwards 1998).

For those cases in which animals cannot be tracked directly, the use of archival or satellite-linked systems may be possible. These types of systems are commonly used on marine mammals and birds (e.g., Schreer and Kovacs 1997; Burns and Castellini 1998; Hooker and Baird 2001; Schreer et al. 2001b), but there are several key characteristics of these animals that make the use of these approaches more easily applicable than with fish. Many marine mammals and birds have strong site fidelity that increases the chances of recapturing study animals and consequently recovering archival recorders. Furthermore, the fact that all pinnipeds and marine birds have terrestrial phases further increases the chance of recovering equipment, as well as reducing logistical difficulties. Lastly, being air-breathers, all marine mammals and birds must periodically spend time at the surface to replenish oxygen reserves. This behavior enables antennas necessary for satellite transmissions to be above the water surface for at least a limited period of time, allowing for periodic data transmission to satellites. Fish have few of these characteristics, making the use of archival or satellite-linked systems much less feasible. One solution allowing the application of satellite technology to fish is the use of pop-up systems (e.g., Block et al. 1998). Satellite pop-up transmitters jettison when a corrosive release mechanism gives way. The transmitters rise to the surface of the water and transmit data to satellites. To date, these transmitters have focused on collecting water temperature data, permitting the determination of locations based upon ocean current temperatures. One of the few published studies using this technology (Lutcavage et al. 1999) angled the majority of the fish they monitored, although the results were not discussed in a catch-and-release framework.

Although there are currently no examples of the use of physiological telemetry in marine environments to assess the effects of catch-and-release angling, there are several examples of energetic and ecophysiological studies that provide direction for future angling studies. Sureau and Lagardère (1991) remotely monitored the heart rate and locomotory activity of sole *Solea solea* and sea bass *Dicentrarchus labrax*. Fish were released into a rectangular net pen (length 10 m, width 3 m) in a large seawater pond with direct connection to the ocean. Although these fish were only monitored for a short period of time, this type of controlled experiment coupling physiological and behavioral approaches could be used to study catch-and-release angling disturbance and recovery.

Net pens have been used for physiological telemetry studies, but such approaches have not yet been applied to catch-and-release angling impact assessments. In addition to net pens or large cages, experimental ponds or mariculture facilities operated by academic institutions, government agencies, or private organizations also provide opportunities to conduct physiological telemetry studies on the impacts of catch-and-release angling. In addition, the localized home range of some species could be exploited to collect information on free-ranging fish, if they reside in a spatially restricted area.

Devices that could be applied quickly to marine fish following capture could be used to collect information on free-swimming fish postrelease. Because those fish would have already been captured, it would be difficult to obtain baseline values and control for tagging effects. Since most of the physiological telemetry devices require anesthetization and surgery for attachment or implantation, such approaches are less feasible. Some devices, however, can be attached rapidly without anesthetization. In addition, by following an individual fish by boat, it would be possible to collect physiological data from acoustic physiological transmitters in a manner similar to tracking marine fish tagged with acoustic locational transmitters (e.g., Jolley and Irby 1979).

Laboratory Studies

Although we encourage collecting in situ data from free-swimming fish, it is important to note that controlled laboratory experiments can also provide important information. Reidy et al. (1995) compared the postexercise metabolic rates of Atlantic cod *Gadus morhua*, using several different exhaustion protocols including swimming challenges (i.e., u-crit, u-burst) and chasing tactics. Studies that include angling as an exhaustion method would provide the opportunity to assess which controlled exhaustion protocol most closely resembles that of angling fish in the wild. In some cases, minor changes in laboratory-based exercise protocols to increase their realism (e.g., through air exposure or other simulated handling practices) would increase validity. Large marine teleosts have also been exercised in respirometers (Graham et al. 1990; Dewar and Graham 1994), while, in some cases, also monitoring heart rate and stroke volume (Korsmeyer et al. 1997). These studies have some application to catch-and-release, although no study attempted to examine it directly. It should be noted, however, that wild free-swimming fish and wild fish held in captivity typically respond differently to stress. The difference in response can be highly variable, especially between species (Pickering et al. 1989).

The continued development and refinement of devices capable of remotely measuring biologically relevant parameters would continue to expand our ability to study the response of fish to angling and handling-induced stressors. One promising technique just now in development is the use of videographic recording devices that can be affixed to the organism. This technology already has been applied to marine mammal studies (Marshall 1998). As often is the case, fisheries applications of this technique will have to wait for the further miniaturization of electronic components, in particular, the constraints associated with power supply (battery size). Advances will also be required for free-swimming fish to accommodate devices attached in and around sensitive tissue for extended periods of time.

Conclusions

Fisheries managers should become more aware of the value of behavioral and physiological responses of fish in evaluating the effects of catch-and-release angling. Scientists must also attempt to codify more direct links between their findings and management implications (Loftus 1987). Ultimately, however, it is up to the fisheries scientist to provide managers with scientifically justifiable data that provide direction for the management of recreational fisheries. The imposition of regulations without suitable scientific backing will lead to poor levels of acceptance and compliance (American Fisheries Society 1995). With increasing ethical concerns over various aspects of angling (Balon 2000), quantifiable and objective measures of animal welfare are becoming more valuable. We also need to stop setting mortality as the end measure of the effects of catch-and-release angling. Information on sublethal effects will help managers to design and impose regulations designed to minimize the negative impacts of catch-and-release angling on fish, especially those that affect long-term fitness. Collecting this type of information will not be easy, but it will provide better evidence on the biological effects of catch-and-release angling. It may also be expensive; most of the approaches outlined in this paper require significant expenditure of capital. The question is whether we adopt a proactive approach by gathering appropriate data and enacting rational management decisions now, or take a reactive approach by waiting to deal with problems only as they arise. Those problems could range from collapses of fisheries to pressure from animal welfare constituencies to stop catch-and-release angling.

Many of the approaches outlined in this paper are applicable to the assessment of catch-and-release angling in both marine and freshwater systems. The challenge is to implement these approaches now. As fisheries managers, we need to realize that, although the population is the fundamental management unit of concern, we must begin by gaining an understanding of the effects that catch-and-release angling has on the individual. We need to focus on providing complete answers to difficult questions. There is no doubt that from the perspective of the individual fish, there is more to just surviving a catch-and-release angling event; we must consider these issues in a broader energetics and fitness framework.

Acknowledgments

Financial assistance for this publication was provided by the University of Waterloo, the Waterloo Biotelemetry Institute, the Natural Sciences and Engineering Research Council of Canada, the University of Illinois, and the Illinois Natural History Survey. SJC was further supported by a Julie Payette NSERC fellowship and a travel award to present this paper from the Graduate College, University of Illinois. We thank Fred Voegli of Vemco Inc. for providing us with information on forthcoming products. Gary Anderson, Rick Booth, and Toni Beddow were instrumental in the development of many of the ideas presented. We also thank Marty Golden and Jon Lucy for encouraging and facilitating our participation in this symposium. Earlier versions of this manuscript benefited from reviews by Scott McKinley, Mark Ridgway, Patricia Schulte, the Kaskaskia Field Station Discussion Group, and several anonymous reviewers.

References

Adams, S. M. 1990. Status and use of biological indicators for evaluating the effects of stress on fish. Pages 1–8 in S. M. Adams, editor. Biological indicators of stress in fish. American Fisheries Society, Symposium 8, Bethesda, Maryland.

American Fisheries Society. 1995. Special fishing regulations for managing freshwater sport fisheries: AFS draft position paper. Fisheries 20(1):6–8.

Anderson, W. G., R. Booth, T. A. Beddow, R. S. McKinley, B. Finstad, F. Økland, and D. Scruton. 1998. Remote monitoring of heart rate as a measure of recovery in angled Atlantic salmon, Salmo salar (L.). Hydrobiologia 371/372:233–240.

Armstrong, J. D., M. C. Lucas, I. G. Priede, and L. De Vera. 1989. An acoustic telemetry system for monitoring the heart rate of pike, Esox lucius L., and other fish in their natural environment. Journal of Experimental Biology 143:549–552.

Balon, E. K. 2000. Defending fishes against recreational fishing: an old problem to be solved in the new millennium. Environmental Biology of Fishes 57:1–8.

Baras, E. 1991. A bibliography on underwater telemetry. Canadian Report of Fisheries and Aquatic Sciences No. 1819.

Barnhart, R. A., and T. D. Roelofs. 1977. Catch-and-release fishing as a management tool. Humboldt State University, California Cooperative Fisheries Research Unit. Arcata, California.

Barnhart, R. A., and T. D. Roelofs. 1989. Catch-and-release fishing, a decade of experience. Humboldt State University, California Cooperative Fisheries Research Unit. Arcata, California.

Barton, B. A., and G. K. Iwama. 1991. Physiological changes in fish from stress in aquaculture with emphasis on the response and effects of corticosteroids. Annual Review of Fish Diseases 1:3–26.

Beamish, F. W. H. 1978. Swimming capacity. Pages 101–187 in W. S. Hoar and D. J. Randall, editors. Fish physiology. Volume VII, Locomotion. Academic Press, New York.

Beddow, T. A., and R. S. McKinley. 1999. Importance of electrode positioning in biotelemetry electromyographic studies of Atlantic salmon (*Salmo salar* L.) during forced swimming. Hydrobiologia 371/372:225–232.

Beggs, G. L., G. F. Holeton, and E. J. Crossman. 1980. Some physiological consequences of angling stress in muskellunge, *Esox masquinongy* Mitchell. Journal of Fish Biology 17:649–659.

Bendock, T., and M. Alexandersdottir. 1993. Hooking mortality of chinook salmon released in the Kenai River, Alaska. North American Journal of Fisheries Management 13:540–549.

Bettoli, P. W., and R. S. Osborne. 1998. Hooking mortality of striped bass following catch and release angling. North American Journal of Fisheries Management 18:609–615.

Black, E. C. 1958. Hyperactivity as a lethal factor in fish. Journal of the Fisheries Research Board of Canada 15:573–586.

Block, B. A., D. Booth, and F. G. Carey. 1992. Direct measurement of swimming speeds and depth of blue marlin. Journal of Experimental Biology 166:267–284.

Block, B. A., H. Dewar, C. Farwell, and E. D. Prince. 1998. A new satellite technology for tracking the movements of the Atlantic bluefin tuna. Proceedings of the National Academy of Science U.S.A. 95:9384–9389.

Booth, R. K., J. D. Kieffer, K. Davidson, A. T. Bielak, and B. L. Tufts. 1995. Effects of late-season catch and release angling on anaerobic metabolism, acid-base status, survival and gamete viability in wild Atlantic salmon (*Salmo salar*). Canadian Journal of Fisheries and Aquatic Sciences 52:283–290.

Brill, R. W., and P. G. Bushnell. 1991. Metabolic and cardiac scope of high energy demand teleosts, the tunas. Canadian Journal of Zoology 69:2002–2009.

Brill, R. W., D. B. Holts, R. K. C. Chang, S. Sullivan, H. Dewar, and F. G. Carey. 1993. Vertical and horizontal movements of striped marlin (*Tetrapturus audax*) near the Hawaiian Islands, determined by ultrasonic telemetry, with simultaneous measurement of oceanic currents. Marine Biology 117:567–574.

Broom, D. M., and K. G. Johnson. 1993. Stress and animal welfare. Chapman and Hall, London, England.

Burns, J. M., and M. A. Castellini. 1998. Dive data from satellite tags and time-depth recorders: a comparison in Weddell seal pups. Marine Mammal Science 14:750–764.

Butler, P. J. 1989. Telemetric recordings of physiological data from free-living animals. Pages 63–84 in P. J. Grubb and J. B. Whittaker, editors. Towards a more exact ecology. Blackwell Scientific Publications, Oxford, England.

Campbell, P. M., T. G. Pottinger, and J. P. Sumpter. 1992. Stress reduces the quality of gametes produced by rainbow trout. Biology of Reproduction 47:1140–1150.

Campbell, P. M., T. G. Pottinger, and J. P. Sumpter. 1994. Preliminary evidence that chronic confinement stress reduces the quality of gametes produced by brown and rainbow trout. Aquaculture 120:151–169.

Candy, J. R, E. W. Carter, T. P. Quinn, and B. E. Riddell. 1996. Adult Chinook salmon behavior and survival after catch and release from purse-seine vessels in Johnstone Strait, British Columbia. North American Journal of Fisheries Management 16:521–529.

Cooke, S. J., D. P. Philipp, K. M. Dunmall, and J. F. Schreer. 2001. The influence of terminal tackle on injury, handling time, and cardiac disturbance of rock bass. North American Journal of Fisheries Management 21:333–342.

Cooke, S. J., D. P. Philipp, J. F. Schreer, and R. S. McKinley. 2000. Locomotory impairment of nesting male largemouth bass following catch-and-release angling. North American Journal of Fisheries Management 20:968–977.

Dewar, H., M. Deffenbaugh, G. Thurmond, K. Lashkari, and B. A. Block. 1999. Development of an acoustic telemetry tag for monitoring electromyograms in free-swimming fish. Journal of Experimental Biology 202:2693–2699.

Dewar, H., and J. B. Graham. 1994. Studies of tropical tuna swimming performance in a large water tunnel. I. Energetics. Journal of Experimental Biology. 192:13–31.

Driedzic, W. R., and P. W. Hochachka. 1978. Metabolism in fish during exercise. Pages 503–543 in W. S. Hoar and D. J. Randall, editors. Fish physiology. Volume VII, Locomotion. Academic Press, New York.

Dunmall, K. M., S. J. Cooke, J. F. Schreer, and R. S. McKinley. 2001. The effect of scented lures on the hooking injury, and mortality of smallmouth bass caught by novice, and experienced anglers. North American Journal of Fisheries Management 21:242–248.

Edwards, R. E. 1998. Survival and movement patterns of released tarpon (*Megalops atlanticus*). Gulf of Mexico Science 16:1–7.

Farrell, A. P. 1991. From hagfish to tuna: a perspective on cardiac function in fish. Physiological Zoology 64:1137–1164.

Farrell, A. P., and D. R. Jones. 1992. The heart. Pages 1–88 in W. S. Hoar and D. R. Randall, editors. Fish physiology. Volume XIIa. Academic Press, New York.

Ferguson, R. A., J. D. Kieffer, and B. L. Tufts. 1993. The effects of body size on the acid-base and metabolite in the white muscle of rainbow trout before and after exhaustive exercise. Journal of Experimental Biology 180:195–207.

Gaesser, G. A., and G. A. Brooks. 1984. Metabolic bases of excess post-exercise oxygen consumption: a review. Medicine and Science in Sports and Exercise 16:29–43.

Gamperal, A. K., M. M. Vijayan, and R. G. Boutilier. 1994. Experimental control of stress hormone levels in fishes: techniques and applications. Reviews in Fish Biology and Fisheries 4:215–255.

Graham, J. B., H. Dewar, N. C. Lai, W. R. Lowell, and S. M. Arce. 1990. Aspects of shark swimming performance determined using a large water tunnel. Journal of Experimental Biology 151:175–192.

Gustaveson, A. W., R. S. Wydowski, and G. A. Wedemeyer. 1991. Physiological response of largemouth bass to angling stress. Transactions of the American Fisheries Society 120:629–636.

Heath, A. G. 1990. Summary and perspectives. Pages 183–191 *in* S. M. Adams, editor. Biological indicators of stress in fish. American Fisheries Society, Symposium 8, Bethesda, Maryland.

Hooker, S. K., and R. W. Baird. 2001. Diving, and ranging behaviour of odontocetes: a methodological review and critique. Mammal Review 31:81–105.

Jagielo, T. H. 1999. Movement, mortality, and size selectivity of sport- and trawl-caught lingcod off Washington. Transactions of the American Fisheries Society 128:31–48.

Johnstone, A. D. F., M. C. Lucas, P. Boylan, and T. J. Carter. 1992. Telemetry of tail beat frequency in Atlantic salmon (*Salmo salar*) during spawning. Pages 456–465 *in* I. M. Priede and S. W. Swift, editors. Wildlife telemetry-remote monitoring and tracking of animals. Ellis-Horwood, New York.

Jolley, J. W., Jr., and E. W. Irby, Jr. 1979. Survival of tagged and released Atlantic sailfish (*Istiophorus platypterus*: Istiophoridae). Bulletin of Marine Science 29:155–169.

Kaseloo, P. A., A. H. Weatherley, J. Lotimer, and M. D. Farina. 1992. A biotelemetry system recording fish activity. Journal of Fish Biology 40:165–179.

Kieffer, J. D. 2000. Limits to exhaustive exercise in fish. Comparative Biochemistry and Physiology. 126A:161–179.

Kieffer, J. D., M. R. Kubacki, F. J. S. Phelan, D. P. Philipp, and B. L. Tufts. 1995. Effects of catch-and-release angling on nesting male smallmouth bass. Transactions of the American Fisheries Society 124:70–76.

Korsmeyer, K. E., N. C. Lai, R. E. Shadwick, and J. B. Graham. 1997. Heart rate and stroke volume contributions to cardiac output in swimming yellowfin tuna: response to exercise and temperature. Journal of Experimental Biology 200:1975–1986.

Lee, W. C., and E. P. Bergersen. 1996. Influence of thermal and oxygen stratification on lake trout hooking mortality. North American Journal of Fisheries Management 16:175–181.

Loftus, A. J. 1987. Inadequate science transfer: an issue basic to effective fisheries management. Transactions of the American Fisheries Society 116:314–319.

Loftus, A. J., W. W. Taylor, and M. Keller. 1988. An evaluation of lake trout (*Salvelinus namaycush*) hooking mortality in the upper Great Lakes. Canadian Journal of Fisheries and Aquatic Sciences 45:1473–1479.

Lowe, C. G, K. N. Holland, and T. G. Wolcott. 1998. A new acoustic tailbeat transmitter for fishes. Fisheries Research 36:275–283.

Lucas, M. C. 1994. Heart rate as an indicator of metabolic rate and activity in adult Atlantic salmon, *Salmo salar*. Journal of Fish Biology 44:899–903.

Lucas, M. C., and E. Baras. 2000. Methods for studying spatial behaviour of freshwater fishes in the natural environment. Fish and Fisheries 1:283–316.

Lucas, M. C., A. D. F. Johnstone, and I. G. Priede. 1993. Use of physiological telemetry as a method of estimating metabolism of fish in the natural environment. Transactions of the American Fisheries Society 122:822–833.

Lutcavage, M. E., R. W. Brill, G. B. Skomal, B. C. Chase, and P. W. Howey. 1999. Results of pop-up satellite tagging of spawning size class fish in the Gulf of Maine: do North Atlantic bluefin tuna spawn in the mid-Atlantic? Canadian Journal of Fisheries, and Aquatic Sciences 56:173–177.

Makinen, T. S., E. Niemela, K. Moen, and R. Lindstrom. 2000.

Behaviour of gill-net and rod-captured Atlantic salmon (*Salmo salar* L.) during upstream migration and following radio tagging. Fisheries Research 45:117–127.

Maltby, L. 1999. Studying stress: the importance of organism-level responses. Ecological Applications 9:431–440.

Marshall, G. J. 1998. Crittercam: an animal-borne imaging and data logging system. Marine Technology Science Journal 32:11–17.

Matlock, G. C., L. W. McEachron, J. A. Dailey, P. A. Unger, and P. Chai. 1993. Short-term hooking mortalities of red drums and spotted seatrout caught on single-barb and treble hooks. North American Journal of Fisheries Management 13:186–189.

Mazik, P. M., S. M. Plakas, and G. R. Stehly. 1994. Effects of dorsal aorta cannulation on the stress response of channel catfish (*Ictalurus punctatus*). Fish Physiology and Biochemistry 12:439–444.

McLaughlin, S. A., J. M. Grizzle, and H. E. Whiteley. 1997. Ocular lesions in largemouth bass, *Micropterus salmoides*, subjected to the stresses of handling and containment. Veterinary and Comparative Ophthalmology 7:5–9.

Milligan, C. L., and C. M. Wood. 1986. Tissue intracellular acid-base status and the fate of lactate after exhaustive exercise in the rainbow trout. Journal of Experimental Biology 123:123–144.

Muoneke, M. I., and W. M. Childress. 1994. Hooking mortality: a review for recreational fisheries. Reviews in Fisheries Science 2:123–156.

Oswald, R. L. 1978. The use of telemetry to study light synchronization with feeding and gill ventilation rates in *Salmo trutta*. Journal of Fish Biology 13:729–739.

Pankhurst, N. W., and M. Dedual. 1993. Effects of capture and recovery on plasma levels of cortisol, lactate and gonadal steroids in a natural population of rainbow trout. Journal of Fish Biology 45:1013–1025.

Philipp, D. P., C. A. Toline, M. F. Kubacki, D. B. F. Philipp, and F. J. S. Phelan. 1997. The impact of catch-and-release angling on the reproductive success of smallmouth bass and largemouth bass. North American Journal of Fisheries Management 17:557–567.

Pickering, A. D., T. G. Pottinger, and J. F. Carragher. 1989. Differences in the sensitivity of brown trout, *Salmo trutta* L., and rainbow trout, *Salmo gairdneri* Richardson, to physiological doses of cortisol. Journal of Fish Biology 34:757–768.

Priede, I. G. 1983. Heart rate telemetry from fish in the natural environment. Comparative Biochemistry and Physiology 76A:515–524.

Priede, I. G., and P. Tytler. 1977. Heart rate as a measure of metabolic rate in teleost fishes: *Salmo gairdneri, Salmo trutta*, and *Gadus morhua*. Journal of Fish Biology 10:231–242.

Quinn, S. P. 1989. Recapture rates of voluntarily released largemouth bass. North American Journal of Fisheries Management 9:86–91.

Quinn, S. 1996. Trends in regulatory and voluntary catch-and-release fishing. Pages 152–162 *in* L. E. Miranda and D. R. DeVries, editors. Multidimensional approaches to reservoir fisheries management. American Fisheries Society, Symposium 16, Bethesda, Maryland.

Redmond, L. C. 1986. The history and development of warmwater fish harvest regulations. Pages 186–195 *in* G. E. Hall and

M. J. Van Den Avyle, editors. Reservoir fisheries management: strategies for the 80's. American Fisheries Society, Special Publication 3, Bethesda, Maryland.

Reidy, S. P., J. A. Nelson, Y. Tang, and S. R. Kerr. 1995. Postexercise metabolic rate in Atlantic cod and its dependence upon the method of exhaustion. Journal of Fish Biology 47:377–386.

Ridgway, M. S., and B. J. Shuter. 1996. Effects of displacement on the seasonal movements and home range characteristics of smallmouth bass in Lake Opeongo. North American Journal of Fisheries Management 16:371–377.

Rogers, S. C., D. W. Church, A. H. Weatherley, and D. G. Pincock. 1984. An automated ultrasonic telemetry system for the assessment of locomotor activity in free-ranging rainbow trout, *Salmo gairdneri*, Richardson. Journal of Fish Biology 25:697–710.

Rogers, S. C., and A. H. Weatherley. 1983. The use of opercular muscle electromyograms as an indicator of the metabolic costs of fish activity in rainbow trout, *Salmo gairdneri* Richardson, as determined by radiotelemetry. Journal of Fish Biology 23:535–547.

Ross, L. G., W. Watts, and A. H. Young. 1981. An ultrasonic biotelemetry system for the continuous monitoring of tailbeat rate from free-swimming fish. Journal of Fish Biology 18:479–490.

Scarabello, M., G. J. F. Heigenhauser, and C. M. Wood. 1991. The oxygen debt hypothesis in juvenile rainbow trout after exhaustive exercise. Respiration Physiology 84:245–259.

Scharold, J., and S. H. Gruber. 1991. Telemetered heart rate as a measure of metabolic rate in the lemon shark, *Negaprion brevirostris*. Copeia 1991:942–953.

Scherer, E. 1992. Behavioural responses as indicators of environmental alterations: approach, results, developments. Journal of Applied Ichthyology 8:122–131.

Schisler, G. J., and E. P. Bergersen. 1996. Postrelease hooking mortality of rainbow trout caught on scented artificial baits. North American Journal of Fisheries Management 16:570–578.

Schreck, C. B. 1990. Physiological, behavioral, and performance indicators of stress. Pages 29–37 in S. M. Adams, editor. Biological indicators of stress in fish. American Fisheries Society, Symposium 8, Bethesda, Maryland.

Schreck, C. B., B. L. Olla, and M. W. Davis. 1997. Behavioural response to stress. Pages 145–170 in G. K. Iwama, A. D. Pickering, J. P. Sumpter, and C. B. Schreck, editors. Fish stress and health in aquaculture. Society for Experimental Biology, Seminar Series 62. Cambridge University Press.

Schreer, J. F., S. J. Cooke, and R. S. McKinley. 2001a. Cardiac response to variable forced exercise at different temperatures - an angling simulation for smallmouth bass. Transactions of the American Fisheries Society 130:783–795.

Schreer, J. F., and K. M. Kovacs. 1997. Allometry of diving capacity in air-breathing vertebrates. Canadian Journal of Zoology 75:339–358.

Schreer, J. F., K. M. Kovacs, and R. J. O'Hara Hines. 2001b. Comparative diving patterns of pinnipeds and seabirds. Ecological Monographs 71:137–162.

Skomal, G. B., and B. C. Chase. 1997. Preliminary results on the physiological effects of catch and release on bluefin tuna (*Thunnus thynnus*) caught off Cape Hatteras, North Carolina.

Collective volume of scientific papers. International Commission for the Conservation of Atlantic Tunas 46:314–320.

Stang, D. L., D. M. Green, R. M. Klindt, T. L. Chiotti, and W. W. Miller. 1996. Black bass movements after release from fishing tournaments in four New York waters. Pages 163–171 in L. E. Miranda and D. R. DeVries, editors. Multidimensional approaches to reservoir fisheries management. American Fisheries, Symposium 16, Bethesda, Maryland.

Stasko, A. B., and R. M. Horrall. 1976. Method of counting tailbeats of free-swimming fish by ultrasonic telemetry techniques. Journal of the Fisheries Research Board of Canada 33:2596–2598.

Stasko, A. B., and D. G. Pincock. 1977. Review of underwater biotelemetry with emphasis on ultrasonic techniques. Journal of the Fisheries Research Board of Canada 34:1261–1285.

Sundström, L. F., and S. H. Gruber. 1998. Using speed-sensing transmitters to construct a bioenergetics model for subadult lemon sharks, *Negaprion brevirostris* (Poey), in the field. Hydrobiologia 371/372:241–247.

Sureau, D., and J. P. Lagardère. 1991. Coupling of heart rate and locomotor activity in sole, *Solea solea* (L.) and bass, *Dicentrachus labrax* (L.), in their natural environment by using ultrasonic telemetry. Journal of Fish Biology. 38:399–405.

Thorarensen, H., P. E. Gallaugher, and A. P. Farrell. 1996. The limitations of heart rate as a predictor of metabolic rate in fish. Journal of Fish Biology 49:226–236.

Tufts, B. L., Y. Tang, K. Tufts, and R. G. Boutilier. 1991. Exhaustive exercise in "wild" Atlantic salmon (*Salmo salar*): acid–base regulation and blood gas transport. Canadian Journal of Fisheries and Aquatic Sciences 48:868–874.

Van Den Thillart, G., and A. Van Waarde. 1996. Nuclear magnetic resonance spectroscopy of living systems: applications in comparative physiology. Physiological Reviews 76:799–837.

Walker, A. F., and A. M. Walker. 1991. The Little Gruinard Atlantic salmon (*Salmo salar* L.) catch and release tracking study. Pages 434–440 in I. G. Priede and S. M. Swift, editors. Wildlife telemetry-remote monitoring and tracking of animals. Ellis-Horwood, New York.

Whoriskey, F. G., S. Prusov, and S. Crabbe. 2000. Evaluation of the effects of catch-and-release angling on the Atlantic salmon (*Salmo salar*) of the Ponoi River, Kola Peninsula, Russian Federation. Ecology of Freshwater Fish 9:118–125.

Winter, J. 1996. Advances in underwater biotelemetry. Pages 555–590 in B. R. Murphy and D. W. Willis, editors. Fisheries techniques, 2nd edition. American Fisheries Society, Bethesda, Maryland.

Wood, C. M. 1991. Acid–base and ion balance, metabolism, and their interactions, after exhaustive exercise in fish. Journal of Experimental Biology 160:285–308.

Wood, C. M., J. D. Turner, and M. S. Graham. 1983. Why do fish die after severe exercise? Journal of Fish Biology 22:189–201.

Wright, S. 1970. A review of the subject of hooking mortalities in Pacific salmon (*Oncorhynchus*). Pacific Marine Fisheries Commission Annual Report 23:47–65.

Wydoski, R. S., G. A. Wedemeyer, and N. C. Nelson. 1976. Physiological response to hooking stress in hatchery and wild rainbow trout (*Salmo gairdneri*). Transactions of the American Fisheries Society 105:601–606.

American Fisheries Society Symposium 30:135-138, 2002
© Copyright by the American Fisheries Society 2002

EXTENDED ABSTRACT

The Physiological Effects of Angling on Post-Release Survivorship in Tunas, Sharks, and Marlin[1]

GREGORY B. SKOMAL *and* BRADFORD C. CHASE

Large numbers of tunas, sharks, and marlin are released annually by recreational and commercial rod-and-reel fishermen off the east coast of the United States. This is largely due to the federal imposition of quotas, minimum sizes, and bag limits on offshore anglers, coupled with a growing conservation ethic. Catch data collected in Massachusetts from 1991 to 1998 indicate that, on average, 96% of the blue sharks *Prionace glauca*, 75% of the school bluefin tuna *Thunnus thynnus*, 30% of the yellowfin tuna *Thunnus albacares*, and 99% of the white marlin *Tetrapturus albidus* were released annually by big game tournament participants. However, the extent to which angling affects post-release survivorship is unknown in these species. Increased angler-induced mortality will have important implications in release and quota management strategies.

Tunas, sharks, and billfish possess large amounts of anaerobic white muscle that reflects an ability of high work output in short bursts. Angling practices result in increased anaerobic activity, muscular fatigue, and time out of water. The physiological consequences of angling stress are poorly understood in large pelagic fishes. Available evidence supports the notion that high anaerobic muscular activity in fish causes extreme homeostatic disruptions that may impede normal physiological and behavioral function and, ultimately, reduce survivorship (Wood et al. 1983; Wood 1991; Milligan 1996). Since blood reflects changes in muscle biochemistry, these perturbations can be measured and quantified (Wells et al. 1986).

Gregory B. Skomal, Massachusetts Division of Marine Fisheries, Martha's Vineyard Marine Fisheries Station, Post Office Box 68, Vineyard Haven, Massachusetts 02568, USA. Email: gregory.skomal@state.ma.us

Bradford C. Chase, Massachusetts Division of Marine Fisheries, Annisquam River Marine Fisheries Station, 30 Emerson Avenue, Gloucester, Massachusetts 01930, USA. Email: brad.chase@state.ma.us

[1]*This is Massachusetts Division of Marine Fisheries Contribution No. 5.*

During the period 1993–1998, a two-tiered approach was used to quantify and evaluate the physiological effects of angling on post-release survivorship in large pelagic game fish. First, to quantify the physiological consequences of high anaerobic muscular exercise, blood was sampled from 312 fish comprising 12 species of tunas (230), sharks (77), and marlin (5), after exposure to rod-and-reel angling. Samples were also collected from electroshocked, free-swimming bluefin tuna (13), free-swimming blue sharks (2), and sharks caught on longline (61). Physical and environmental conditions related to each angling event were recorded and correlated to blood chemistry parameters. Secondly, to assess post-release behavior and survivorship relative to blood chemistry perturbations, blood-sampled tunas, sharks, and marlin were tagged with conventional tags and/or ultrasonic telemetry tags.

A preliminary analysis of blood chemistry data from 122 bluefin tuna, 64 yellowfin tuna, and 72 blue sharks was conducted relative to fight time; data from five white marlin were included for comparative purposes. Blood gases, pH, lactate, cortisol, and serum electrolyte, metabolite, and protein profiles show that these four species exhibited significant homeostatic perturbations as a consequence of extreme exhaustive exercise. Interspecific differences were found relative to the magnitude and nature of these disturbances; disruption was greatest in the tunas. The primary response to stress included a significant elevation of blood cortisol in bluefin tuna, yellowfin tuna, and white marlin. In the tunas, a significant increase occurred 10 minutes into the angling event. Although limited by sample size, cortisol levels measured in the white marlin were among the highest reported for any fish. Secondary effects included a significant drop in blood pH, elevations in blood lactate, and changes in serum electrolyte levels. These changes occurred after 5 minutes of exercise in the bluefin and yellowfin tunas, but took 20 minutes to develop in the blue shark (Table 1; Figure 1). Blood gas data indicate that this acidemia had both a metabolic and respiratory origin in the two tunas, but only metabolic in the blue shark.

Six blood-sampled fish that were tagged and released were subsequently recaptured: two bluefin tuna, one yellowfin tuna, and three blue sharks. Blood chemistry data from these fish indicated that the level of stress was commensurate with fight time. A total of 15 acoustic tracks were conducted on 7 bluefin tuna, 4 blue sharks, 2 yellowfin tuna, and 2 white marlin. These fish were exposed to prolonged angling bouts (mean = 46 minutes) and blood chemistry data were indicative of greater than average levels of stress. With the exception of one bluefin tuna, all tracked fish survived for the duration of the tracks, which ranged from 2 to 24 hours. All surviving fish exhibited distinct post-release recovery periods of two hours or less, characterized by limited vertical activity. It is

Table 1: Species-specific sample sizes for blood pH data in Figure 1.

Fight time Interval (min)	Bluefin tuna	Yellowfin tuna	Blue shark	White marlin
0	6	11[a]	1	
5	8	6	2	
10	18	24	5	
15	14	6	2	
20	11	4	2	
25	3	2	2	
30	4	1	4	
35	3	1	2	1
40	1			
45		1		1
50		1		1
55				1
60	1			
Total	69	46	20	4

[a] derived from Brill et al. 1992

hypothesized that physiological disturbances are corrected during this period. Moreover, fish may be vulnerable to predation at this time.

A single bluefin tuna angled for 42 minutes died immediately after release. This fish had a depressed blood pH and high blood lactate levels indicative of a severe acidemia. However, two surviving bluefin tuna exposed to longer angling bouts exhibited more extreme acid–base disruptions. The notable dif-

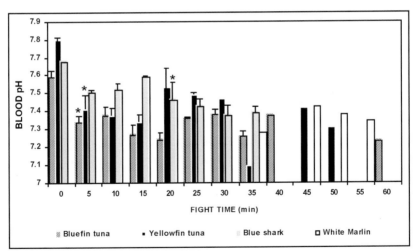

Figure 1. Changes in blood pH relative to fight time for bluefin tuna, yellowfin tuna, blue sharks, and white marlin; mean + SEM. * indicates significant change (analysis of variance (ANOVA), $p < 0.05$).

ference between these fish was that the single mortality was not resuscitated at the side of the vessel before release. It is hypothesized that the five to seven minutes of resuscitation given to the latter two fish allowed for carbon dioxide offloading and oxygen delivery. In the single mortality, it is possible that muscular fatigue associated with the angling bout precluded obligatory ram ventilation after release, leading to respiratory failure.

The results of this study support the hypothesis that pelagic game fish are capable of recovery when handled properly and not subjected to extensive physical trauma. In addition, when the duration of the angling bouts was minimized, the magnitude of the acidemia was reduced, thereby potentially reducing the vulnerability of fish to predation during the recovery period. Moreover, resuscitation of tunas and marlin after angling bouts in excess of 15 minutes may enhance survivorship.

References

Brill, R. B., P. G. Bushnell, D. R. Jones, and M. Shimizu. 1992. Effects of acute temperature change, *in vivo* and *in vitro*, on acid-base status of blood from yellowfin tuna (*Thunnus albacares*). Canadian Journal of Zoology 70:654–662.

Milligan, C. L. 1996. Metabolic recovery from exhaustive exercise in rainbow trout. Comparative Biochemistry and Physiology 113A(1):51–60.

Wells, R. M. G., R. H. McIntyre, A. K. Morgan, and P. S. Davie. 1986. Physiological stress responses in big game fish after capture: observations on plasma chemistry and blood factors. Comparative Biochemistry and Physiology 84A(3):565–571.

Wood, C. M. 1991. Acid-base and ion balance, metabolism, and their interactions after exhaustive exercise in fish. Journal of Experimental Biology 160:285–308.

Wood, C. M., J. D. Turner, and M. S. Graham. 1983. Why do fish die after severe exercise? Journal of Fish Biology 22(2):189–201.

American Fisheries Society Symposium 30:139–143, 2002

EXTENDED ABSTRACT

Effects of Catch and Release on Physiological Responses and Acute Mortality of Striped Bass

JULIE A. THOMPSON, STEVEN G. HUGHES,
ERIC B. MAY, *and* REGINAL M. HARRELL

The Atlantic striped bass *Morone saxatilis* fishery is important economically, both commercially and recreationally. More than 6.39 million kg were caught recreationally (including fish released alive) during 1999, from Maine to North Carolina. Commercially, more than 3,000,000 kg of striped bass worth nearly US$11 million dollars were caught (National Marine Fisheries Service, Fisheries Statistics and Economics Division, personal communication). To maintain the productivity of a popular commercial and recreational fishery, managers in many states utilize restrictive harvest regulations as a means to limit the pressure on limited fishery resources (Graff 1989). However, for this strategy to be effective, the targeted species must survive the trauma of catch and release. Fish caught by commercial or recreational methods often struggle to complete exhaustion. This can result in severe physiological disturbances, and a significant percentage may die (Black 1958).

The primary objective of this study was to determine the effect of angling time on striped bass by monitoring short-term survival and changes in blood gases and acid–base balance. A secondary objective was to determine if seasonal temperatures had any effect on the survival and physiological status of the fish.

Julie A. Thompson, United States Fish and Wildlife Service, 177 Admiral Cochrane Drive, Annapolis, Maryland 21401, USA. Email: julie_thompson@fws.gov.

Steven G. Hughes, Maryland Cooperative Fish and Wildlife Research Unit, University of Maryland Eastern Shore, Princess Anne, Maryland 21853, USA. Email: shughes@mail.umes.gov.

Eric B. May, University of Maryland Eastern Shore Department of Natural Sciences, Princess Anne, Maryland 21853, USA. Email: ebmay@mail.umes.gov.

Reginal M. Harrell, Maryland Cooperative Extension Service, Post Office Box 169, Queenstown, Maryland 21658, USA

Wild striped bass (36–76 cm TL) were held for 21–24 days in 4.57 m² by 3.05 m deep net-pens on the Tred Avon River, a tributary of the Chesapeake Bay. For the study, fish were caught by hook and line at 8°C in winter and 26°C in summer with a medium action spinning rod fitted with a single-barbed hook (1/0 Eagle Claw 95) baited with cut *Clupea harengus*. Angling time ranged in increments of one to five minutes before removal from the water when the fish were unhooked, bled, tagged in the dorsal musculature with a serially num-bered T-bar tag (Floy Tag 95, Seattle, Washington), and measured for weight and length. Control fish were lifted from the water immediately (0–30 s) after they were hooked and divided into three groups consisting of fish that were: bled and tagged; tagged but not bled; and not tagged or bled. This was done to determine if there was an effect of tagging and/or bleeding on acute mortality. Fish that were hooked in vital organs or that were bleeding were removed from the study in order to evaluate stress-induced mortality. Fish were then placed in another net-pen and monitored for mortality for 72 hours. We analyzed blood pH, HCO_3-, pCO_2, TCO_2, pO_2, and O_2 saturation immediately upon landing the fish, using an IRMA 95 Blood Gas Analyzer (Diametrics Medical Inc., 2658 Patton Road, St. Paul, Minnesota). Lactate (La⁻) was measured only on the fish caught at 8°C, using a YSI 95 Lactate Meter (Yellow Springs, Ohio). An Analy-sis of Variance (ANOVA) for unbalanced study design was used to determine differences in blood parameter values between playing times (PROC GLM). Differences between multiple treatment means were analyzed by a least-square means test. Effects of angling time and temperature and possible interactions between the two on the various blood parameters were also tested.

There was a significant effect ($P < 0.05$) of angling time on all the blood parameters at summer and winter temperatures, with the exception of oxygen values (Table 1). As angling time increased, there were significant decreases in pH, HCO_3-, and TCO_2 and significant increases in pCO_2 and for fish held at 8°C, La⁻. Higher summer temperatures resulted in significantly lower ($P<0.05$) blood pH, HCO_3-, TCO_2, pO_2, and O_2 saturation values, while fish caught in the winter had significantly higher pCO_2 levels. Striped bass suffered a meta-bolic and respiratory acidosis as a consequence of hooking and angling, which were more pronounced as angling time increased. There was also a more severe acid–base disturbance in fish caught at 26°C. Largemouth bass *Micropterus salmoides* (Gustaveson et al. 1991) and striped bass (Tomasso et al. 1996) sub-jected to angling for up to five minutes had more pronounced physiological effects in warmer water.

Temperatures and angling time also affected mortality of striped bass, which increased up to three minutes at 26°C (Figure 1). There was no mortality at any of the angling times at 8°C. Our mortality results, however, were higher than

Table 1. Effect of playing time and temperature on blood parameters (mean ± S.E.M.) of striped bass. Letters denote significant ($P \leq 0.05$) differences between treatment means within a season. Asterisks denote significant ($P \leq 0.05$) differences between seasonal treatment means for a playing time. Mean length and weight of fish caught at 26°C was 567.5 ± 8.1mm and 1739.7 ± 70.5g (S.E.M.) and at 8°C was 510 ± 12.6mm and 1551.9 ± 158.5g (S.E.M.).

Angling Time (minutes)	N	Temperature (°C)	pH	HCO_3^- (mM)	TCO_2 (mM)	pCO_2 (mmHg)	pO_2 (mmHg)	O_2 saturation (%)	La- (mmol/L)
0	11	26	$7.56 \pm 0.07^*_a$	$5.67 \pm 0.37^*_a$	$5.88 \pm 0.54^*_a$	$6.54 \pm 0.76^*_a$	$56.64 \pm 11.91^*$	70.77 ± 9.20	—
1	10	26	$7.46 \pm 0.05^*_a$	$6.37 \pm 0.41^*_{ab}$	$6.65 \pm 0.41^*_{ab}$	$9.26 \pm 0.99^*_{abc}$	$32.3 \pm 4.32^*$	$48.96 \pm 8.94^*$	—
2	11	26	$7.34 \pm 0.02^*_b$	$5.05 \pm 0.29^*_a$	$5.35 \pm 0.32^*_b$	$9.70 \pm 0.85^*_{bc}$	50.27 ± 10.74	56.3 ± 10.42	—
3	11	26	$7.22 \pm 0.04^*_{bc}$	$4.64 \pm 0.35^*_{bc}$	$5.00 \pm 0.37^*_{bc}$	$11.87 \pm 1.25^*_c$	55.09 ± 11.62	$55.52 \pm 10.84^*$	—
4	11	26	$7.26 \pm 0.07^*_{bc}$	$3.97 \pm 0.44^*_d$	$4.25 \pm 0.43^*_d$	$9.15 \pm 1.07^*_c$	$42.45 \pm 8.08^*$	$50.51 \pm 10.33^*$	—
5	11	26	$7.17 \pm 0.05^*_c$	$3.54 \pm 0.44^*_d$	$3.84 \pm 0.45^*_d$	$9.64 \pm 1.06^*_c$	$59.73 \pm 10.24^*$	$60.72 \pm 10.65^*$	—
0	10	8	$7.79 \pm 0.02_a$	$9.74 \pm 0.41_a$	$9.94 \pm 0.41_a$	$21.52 \pm 1.16_a$	82.26 ± 9.13	91.7 ± 3.21	$1.48 \pm 0.25_a$
1	5	8	$7.71 \pm 0.04_{ab}$	$9.44 \pm 0.53_a$	$9.67 \pm 0.53_a$	$24.6 \pm 1.5_{ab}$	87.76 ± 0.56	82.4 ± 8.72	$1.51 \pm 0.33_a$
2	5	8	$7.55 \pm 0.03_b$	$8.90 \pm 0.16_{ab}$	$9.22 \pm 0.15_a$	$33.32 \pm 1.65_c$	41.72 ± 2.96	62.18 ± 5.13	$2.19 \pm 0.26_{ab}$
3	5	8	$7.60 \pm 0.02_b$	$8.32 \pm 0.45_b$	$8.59 \pm 0.45_b$	$28.02 \pm 1.13_a$	88.74 ± 12.65	92.8 ± 1.77	$2.18 \pm 0.16_{ab}$
4	5	8	$7.56 \pm 0.02_b$	$8.99 \pm 0.43_{ab}$	$9.30 \pm 0.44_a$	$32.82 \pm 1.5_b$	88.41 ± 14.69	90.02 ± 4.53	$2.97 \pm 0.34_b$
5	5	8	$7.60 \pm 0.04_b$	$8.61 \pm 0.56_{ab}$	$8.88 \pm 0.55_{ab}$	$28.42 \pm 0.82_a$	97.6 ± 17.45	93.16 ± 2.34	$4.12 \pm 0.38_c$

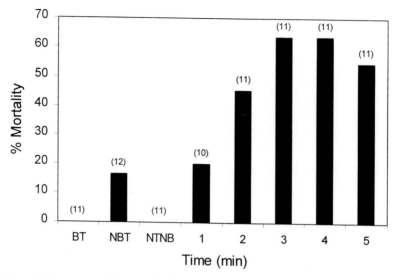

Figure 1. Percent mortality of striped bass caught on hook and line at 26°C and angled for 0–5 minutes. Control groups are: BT = Bled and tagged; NBT = No bleed but tagged; and NTNB = No bleed, no tag. Sample sizes are indicated in the parenthesis.

other studies conducted on striped bass, perhaps due to longer handling times and air exposure. The vulnerability of striped bass to handling stress, especially at warmer temperatures, is well documented (Harrell 1988), and Ferguson and Tufts (1992) found a much greater extracellular acidosis in rainbow trout *Oncorhynchus mykiss* that were exercised and then exposed to air than in fish just exercised. We tested the effects of tagging and bleeding on striped bass mortality and found a slight tagging effect (16.67%). Another cause of higher mortality in our study, however, was probably due to fighting the fish to exhaustion, as indicated by the significant changes in pH, blood gas values, and increases in mortality as fish were angled for longer periods. Capture by hook and line induces a biochemical response, and muscular energy is expended, which produces acid metabolites. With severe stress from prolonged exercise, some of these anaerobic metabolites are discharged into the blood and disturb blood chemistry and hematological parameters associated with respiratory gas transport.

Management implications from this study are two-fold, regulatory and educational. Results of this study provide us with a reasonable basis upon which we can inform anglers about their responsibilities. If anglers are to play a role in minimizing the impact of catch and release on striped bass, then this study would argue for education programs that stress the speed of capture and release, especially in summer months, thereby reducing respiratory and metabolic acidosis. In those cases where catch-and-release programs are being designed around striped bass, there may be periods when it should be curtailed (e.g., summer months, which this study suggests is a more stressful period).

Acknowledgments

Financial support for this research was provided by U.S. Fish and Wildlife Service-Reverted Dingell Johnson Fund program.

References

Black, E. C. 1958. Hyperactivity as a lethal factor in fish. Journal of the Fisheries Research Board of Canada 15:573–586.

Ferguson, R. A., and B. L. Tufts. 1992. Physiological effects of brief air exposure in exhaustively exercised rainbow trout (*Oncorhynchus mykiss*): implications for "catch and release fisheries." Canadian Journal of Fisheries and Aquatic Sciences 49:1157–1162.

Graff, D. R. 1989. Catch-and-release: where it's hot and where it's not. Pages 5–15 *in* R. A. Barnhart and T. D. Roelefs, editors. Catch-and-release fishing–a decade of experience. Humboldt State University, California Cooperative Fisheries Unit, Arcata, California.

Gustaveson, W. A., R. S. Wydoski, and G. A. Wedenmeyer. 1991. Physiological response of largemouth bass to angling stress. Transactions of the American Fisheries Society 20:629–636.

Harrell, R. M. 1988. Catch and release mortality of striped bass with artificial lures and baits. Proceedings of the 41st Annual Conference Southeastern Association of Fish and Wildlife Agencies 41(1987):70–75.

Tomasso, A. O., J. J. Isely, and J. R. Tomasso. 1996. Physiological responses and mortality of striped bass angled in freshwater. Transactions of the American Fisheries Society 125:321–325.

American Fisheries Society Symposium 30:144–147, 2002
© Copyright by the American Fisheries Society 2002

EXTENDED ABSTRACT

A Bioenergetic Evaluation of the Chronic-Stress Hypothesis: Can Catch-and-Release Fishing Constrain Striped Bass Growth?

JASON D. STOCKWELL[1], PAUL J. DIODATI,
and MICHAEL P. ARMSTRONG[2]

Although many studies have examined the effect of stress (i.e., catch-and-release fishing or exhaustive swimming) on fish, most have addressed either physiological disturbances or posthooking mortality. To our knowledge, only three studies have tested for indirect or sub-lethal effects of catch-and-release fishing: Kieffer et al. (1995) demonstrated that smallmouth bass *Micropterus dolomieu* offspring suffered considerable predation when adult males were angled from their nest sites and subsequently released; Clapp and Clark (1989) found that hooked-and-released smallmouth bass grew less than unhooked fish; and Diodati and Richards (1996) found that hooked-and-released striped bass *Morone saxatilis* had decreased condition factor compared with unhooked fish. For catch-and-release management strategies to succeed, hooking mortality should be minimal, and sub-lethal effects should not become magnified at the population level. Sub-lethal effects can include slower growth rates, decreased fecundity, or any type of resultant behavior that decreases fitness.

Age-9 through age-12 striped bass caught in the Massachusetts' commercial fishery have decreased in both mass at age and length at age, since the early 1980s (Stockwell and Diodati, unpublished data). When compared with stock

Jason D. Stockwell, Massachusetts Division of Marine Fisheries, Annisquam River Marine Fisheries Field Station, 30 Emerson Avenue, Gloucester, Massachusetts 01930, USA. Email: jds@jax.org

[1]*Present address: The Jackson Laboratory, 600 Main Street, Bar Harbor, Maine 04609, USA.*

Paul J. Diodati, Massachusetts Division of Marine Fisheries, 251 Causeway Street, Suite 400, Boston, Massachusetts 02114, USA. Email: paul.diodati@state.ma.us

Michael P. Armstrong, Massachusetts Division of Marine Fisheries, Annisquam River Marine Fisheries Field Station, 30 Emerson Avenue, Gloucester, Massachusetts 01930, USA.

[2]*Corresponding author: Email:michael.armstrong@state.ma.us*

Massachusetts Division of Marine Fisheries Contribution No. 2

abundance estimates, these data appear to indicate density-dependent growth (Stockwell and Diodati, unpublished data). However, other factors may contribute to the observed decreases, including stress from catch-and-release fishing.

The Massachusetts' recreational fishery was estimated to have caught and released more than 7 million striped bass in 1998, out of more than 15 million striped bass caught and released coastwide (National Marine Fisheries Service, Fisheries Statistics and Economics Division, personal communication). Total stock abundance of age-1+ striped bass coastwide was estimated at 35.8 million fish in 1998 (ASMFC 2000). The proportion of the coastwide population that resides in Massachusetts waters during the fishing season (May–October) is not known, but seven million fish probably represent a large proportion of the locally-available striped bass. Coupled with the potential for hook-and-release fishing to reduce striped bass growth (Diodati and Richards 1996), these observations suggest that the chronic-stress hypothesis is plausible. If catch-and-release fishing does pose a serious health risk to striped bass stocks, then understanding the potential scope of its effect is necessary to better identify appropriate management strategies that account for this phenomenon.

We evaluated the potential effects of catch-and-release fishing on seasonal growth estimates of striped bass, using the bioenergetics model for striped bass developed by Hartman and Brandt (1995). All simulations were run using Fish Bioenergetics 3.0 (Hanson et al. 1997). We ran baseline simulations from 15 May to 15 October for a 1,600-g fish (about 550-mm total length), given a food-limited (growth = 12.5% of body mass) and a food-unlimited (growth = 50% of body mass) environment. We then ran simulations, where the fish was caught and released one to three times, with a one to three day period of lost feeding opportunities after each hooking event.

Our results indicate that under food-limited conditions, a striped bass can have a 13–30% decrease in seasonal growth when caught and released two or more times with at least two days of no feeding following each hooking event (Figure 1). When food-unlimited conditions existed, three catch-and-release events with three days of no feeding resulted in only a 14% decrease in growth. These results are likely conservative, as we did not include energetic costs of the actual fight or its duration, or mechanical injury to body parts (e.g., jaw and eyes). We did not find any substantial differences in decreased growth when timing of catch-and-release events was varied. However, seasonal changes in predator diet or energy densities of predator and prey, coupled with seasonal water temperature fluctuations, could drastically change this result. Timing of hook-and-release events may be a critical issue, if striped bass rely on a specific time period for a majority of their seasonal growth (e.g., late season abundance of juvenile prey fishes).

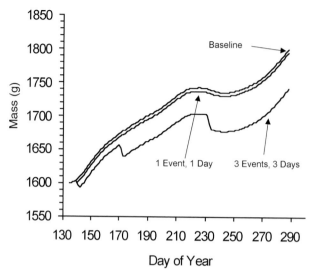

Figure 1. Growth trajectories of a 1,600-g striped bass growing 12.5% of its body weight, with no hook-and-release event (Baseline); one catch-and-release event with a one-day, no-feeding effect (1 event, 1 day); and three catch-and-release events with a three day, no-feeding effect (3 events, 3 days). Simulations were run from 15 May to 15 October.

Our simple modeling exercise indicates that catch-and-release fishing can have serious sub-lethal consequences on individual fish when food is limited. Combined with the magnitude of the catch-and-release fishery in Massachusetts and the observed declines in size at age, our modeling suggests catch-and-release fishing may be a significant contributor to declines in the overall health of striped bass stocks along the Atlantic Coast.

References

ASMFC (Atlantic States Marine Fisheries Commission). 2000. Status of the Atlantic striped bass. 1999. ASMFC, Striped Bass Technical Committee Report, Washington, D.C.

Clapp, D. F., and R. D. Clark, Jr. 1989. Hooking mortality of smallmouth bass caught on live minnows and artificial spinners. North American Journal of Fisheries Management 9:81–85.

Diodati, P. J., and R. A. Richards. 1996. Mortality of striped bass hooked and released in salt water. Transactions of the American Fisheries Society 125:300–307.

Hanson, P. C., T. B. Johnson, D. E. Schindler, and J. F. Kitchell. 1997. Fish Bioenergetics 3.0. University of Wisconsin, Sea Grant Institute, Madison, Wisconsin.

Hartman, K. J., and S. B. Brandt. 1995. Comparative energetics and the development of bioenergetics models for sympatric estuarine piscivores. Canadian Journal of Fisheries and Aquatic Sciences 52:1647–1666.

Kieffer, J. D., M. R. Kubacki, F. J. S. Phelan, D. P. Philipp, and B. L. Tufts. 1995. Effects of catch-and-release angling on nesting male smallmouth bass. Transactions of the American Fisheries Society 124:70–76.

American Fisheries Society Symposium 30:148–151, 2002
© Copyright by the American Fisheries Society 2002

EXTENDED ABSTRACT

Survival of Reef Fish after Rapid Depressurization: Field and Laboratory Studies

KAREN M. BURNS *and* VICTOR RESTREPO

Undersized catch is a serious problem in reef fish fisheries. Current U.S. state and federal management plans enforce minimum size regulations for species in the grouper/snapper complex, but, to be effective, a high rate of postrelease survival must occur over all depths fished. Survival rates are known to vary by depth of capture, among other factors (Gitschlag and Renaud 1994). Rapid depressurization of physoclistic (closed swim bladder) fish caught at depth can be harmful, even lethal, to fish. Reef fish brought rapidly to the surface from any appreciable depth, experience rapid expansion of swim bladder gases leading to ruptured swim bladders, bloating, protrusion of internal organs and eyes, and emboli. Although Wilson and Burns (1996) proved that red grouper *Epinephelus morio* and scamp *Mycteroperca phenax* can potentially survive in high enough percentages to justify a minimum size rule, if fish are rapidly returned to habitat depth, severe abdominal bloating and stomach protrusion hinders the fish's ability to return to depth on its own following release. Without an easy shipboard method of aiding the descent of these bloated, undersized fish, they become easy prey for sea birds and predatory fishes.

A shipboard reef fish venting study funded by Florida Sea Grant was conducted to determine the efficacy of venting in enhancing the survival of undersized catch in reef fish fishery and to test the hypothesis that venting enhances survival in some species but not others. Study objectives were accomplished by integrating an appropriate experimental design into the existing and long-term tag/recapture study, in progress at Mote Marine Laboratory, Sarasota, Florida (Schirripa et al. 1993). Tag returns were used as a measure of

Karen M. Burns, Center for Fisheries Enhancement, Mote Marine Laboratory, 1600 Ken Thompson Parkway, Sarasota, Florida 34236, USA. Email: kburns@mote.org

Victor Restrepo, Ph.D., International Commission for the Conservation of Atlantic Tunas, c/o Corazón de Maria 8, Sixth Floor, 28002 Madrid, Spain. Email: victor.restrepo@iccat.es

survival. Since the start of the program, 8,623 fish, 5,578 red grouper, 2,705 gag *Mycteroperca microlepis*, and 340 red snapper *Lutjanus campechanus* were caught by fishers on headboats, charter boats, and recreational vessels, tagged with dart tags, and released off both coasts of Florida. Half the fish were to be vented, the other half not vented. Unfortunately, participants did not vent equal numbers of fish by depth category. A total of 915 fish, 605 red grouper, 274 gag, and 36 red snapper, were recaptured. Recaptures were divided into discreet depth categories: 0–12.2, 12.5–21.3, 21.6–30.5, 30.8–61, and 61+ meters (0–40, 41–70, 71–100, 101–200, and 200+ feet, respectively). More vented than not vented red grouper and gag were recaptured in 21.3 m (70 ft) and deeper (Figure 1A and B). This was not the case for red snapper, where more non-vented than vented fish were recaptured at all depths (Figure 1C).

Two models were developed for red grouper and gag, representing alternative treatments of data to analyze short-term and long-term recaptures using methods developed by Hoenig et al. (1990) and Porch (1998; insufficient data were available for red snapper). Model 1 was developed to analyze short-term recaptures (within 1 month of tagging) to determine if immediate survival after tagging was affected by venting and depth of capture. Model 2 was developed to analyze effects of time, depth, and venting on long-term (1 year or longer) fish survival. Results of the application of model 1 to red grouper and gag are consistent with the hypothesis that venting improves the immediate survival of these species when caught in waters greater than 21.3 m (70 ft). Results from the application of Model 2 suggest that, over the long-term, other factors such as year, depth of capture, or location may be more important to fish survival than venting.

A laboratory depressurization study, funded by the Central Offshore Anglers, was conducted to help interpret tag return results. Red grouper and red snapper were captured at depths less than 27.4 m in the Gulf of Mexico and South Atlantic and brought to the laboratory for study. Potential survival of captive fish, with clinical signs of damage due to rapid depressurization, was evaluated. Potential survival was defined as the ability of a fish to recuperate from the original trauma related to capture and release and survive in good condition for at least a short duration. All experimental fish, not sacrificed for determining physiological damage and healing survived. Depressurization in the laboratory was simulated using hyperbaric chambers. Both red grouper and red snapper swim bladders ruptured at 21.3 m (70 ft), which corresponded to the depth at which they ruptured during capture. The rupture wounds in red grouper, which have a relatively large swim bladder to total body size ratio, extended from one third to almost half the length of the swim bladder; the wounds in red snapper were substantially smaller. Despite the difference in wound size, the swim bladders

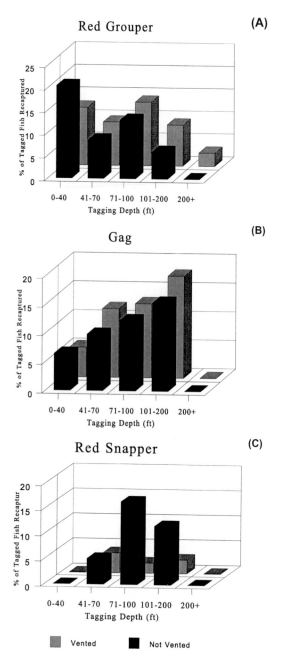

Figure 1. Comparison of tag returns of vented and nonvented reef fish at 0–12.19 m, 12.5–21.33 m, 21.64–30.48 m, 30.78–60.96 m, and 60.96 m+.

in both species healed sufficiently so as to be functional, in less than or equal to four days.

Both tag returns and the laboratory results support the hypothesis that venting can be a useful practice for some bottom dwelling fish with large swim bladders, providing a slight edge for survival. Venting, however, has no effect on emboli and appears not to be beneficial for all species (e.g., red snapper which are much more susceptible to hook mortality than red grouper or gag). Therefore, red snapper recaptures reflect both depth and hook mortality.

A study by Collins et al. (1999) found that black sea bass *Centropristis striata* (benthic dweller similar to the red grouper and gag in both anatomy, physiology, and habitat) benefitted from venting. The vermilion snapper *Rhomboplites aurorubens*, which, based on its anatomy and physiology, should also benefit from venting, did not benefit as much as the black sea bass (Collins et al. 1999). The vermilion snapper is not a benthic species, instead inhabiting the water column over reefs. Although venting would allow this species to overcome surface buoyancy, the fish would be unable to maintain position in the water column until the swim bladder healed, subjecting it to benthic predators. Consequently, a wide variety of factors including anatomy and physiology, hook mortality, and habitat should be considered when analyzing data from venting studies.

References

Collins, M. R., J. C. McGovern, G. R. Sedberry, H. Scott Meister, and R. Pardieck. 1999. Swim bladder deflation in the black sea bass and vermilion snapper: potential for increasing postrelease survival. North American Journal of Fisheries Management 19:828–832.

Gitschlag, G. R., and M. L. Renaud. 1994. Field experiments on survival rates of caged and released red snapper. North American Journal of Fisheries Management 14:131–136.

Hoenig, J. M., P. Pepin, and W. D. Lawing. 1990. Estimating relative survival rate for two groups of larval fishes from field data: do older larvae survive better than young? Fishery Bulletin 88:485–491.

Porch, C. E. 1998. Estimating Atlantic bluefin tuna mortality from the release and recapture dates of recovered tags. International Commission for the Conservation of Atlantic Tunas, Collected Volume of Scientific Papers, SCRS/98/65, Miami, Florida.

Schirripa, M. J., K. Burns, and J. A. Bohnsack. 1993. Reef fish release survival based on tag and recovery data. National Marine Fisheries Service Southeast Fisheries Science Center, Miami Laboratory, Contribution No. MIA 92/93.

Wilson, R. R., and K. M. Burns. 1996. Potential survival of released groupers caught deeper than 40m based on shipboard and in situ observations and tag-recapture data. Bulletin of Marine Science 58:234–247.

Conventional and Ultrasonic
Tagging Studies

American Fisheries Society Symposium 30:155–171, 2002

In-Water Conventional Tagging Techniques Developed by the Cooperative Tagging Center for Large, Highly Migratory Species

Eric D. Prince,[1] Mauricio Ortiz, Arietta Venizelos, *and* David S. Rosenthal

U.S. Department of Commerce
National Oceanic and Atmospheric Administration
National Marine Fisheries Service
75 Virginia Beach Drive
Miami, Florida 33149, USA

Abstract.—The Cooperative Tagging Center (CTC) of the National Marine Fisheries Service's Southeast Fisheries Science Center operates one of the largest and oldest fish tagging programs of its type in the world. Since 1954, more than 35,000 recreational and commercial fishing constituents have voluntarily participated in the CTC, and this has resulted in tagging more than 245,000 fish of 123 species. Although some tagging activities have been conducted by scientists, most of the tag release and recovery activities were achieved by recreational and commercial fishery constituents. Five large highly migratory species have historically represented the Program's primary target species, including Atlantic bluefin tuna *Thunnus thynnus*, blue marlin *Makaira nigricans*, white marlin *Tetrapturus albidus*, sailfish *Istiophorus platypterus*, and broadbill swordfish *Xiphias gladius*. Tagging equipment and procedures for catching, tagging, and resuscitation of species too large to be brought aboard fishing vessels have evolved and improved considerably over the years. This paper presents a review of the development of the most efficient tagging, handling, and dehooking techniques used on a variety of large, highly migratory species in the CTC. In addition, the results of a comparative tag retention study on billfish are presented, comparing stainless steel dart tags used for nearly 30 years with a hydroscopic nylon double-barb dart tag, recently developed in conjunction with The Billfish Foundation. Recommendations are made on the best techniques, procedures, and equipment for in-water tagging of large, highly migratory species.

Introduction

It is difficult to pinpoint the origin of catch-and-release fishing practices for large, highly migratory species in the Atlantic Ocean. An argument can be made that at least one major development in the evolution of these practices for Atlantic pelagics in the U.S. recreational fishery coincided with the initiation of the Cooperative Tagging Center (CTC), pioneered by Frank J. Mather III of Woods Hole Oceanographic Institution (WHOI) in 1954 (Scott et al. 1990). The CTC, known prior to 1995 as the Cooperative Game Fish Tagging Program (CGFTP), has always been a joint research effort by scientists and recreational and commercial fishing constituents. The program was designed to provide basic information on the movements and biology of highly migratory species in the Atlantic Ocean, Gulf of Mexico, and Caribbean Sea, through direct participation of the public in scientific research. Atlantic bluefin tuna *Thunnus thyn-* nus was the primary target species when the program first started, but after a few years the program expanded to include blue marlin *Makaira nigricans*, white marlin *Tetrapturus albidus*, sailfish *Istiophorus platypterus*, and broadbill swordfish *Xiphias gladius*. Some of the other scombrids currently included in the program are yellowfin tuna *Thunnus albacares*, albacore tuna *T. alalunga*, bigeye tuna *T. obesus*, and blackfin tuna *T. atlanticus*. In 1973, the CGFTP became a cooperative effort between WHOI and the National Marine Fisheries Service (NMFS). With the retirement of Dr. Mather in 1980, the NMFS Southeast Fisheries Science Center (SEFSC) assumed sole responsibility for operation of the program.

Justification for the CTC tagging program has been, from its inception, based on the need for biological data on large, highly migratory species. Tagging meaningful numbers of large oceanic pelagic species without constituent participation, particu-

[1]Email: eric_prince@noaa.gov

larly the rare event Istiophorids (Prince and Brown 1991), would be difficult if not impossible to accomplish at a reasonable cost. In addition to gaining important biological information, the CTC has resulted in a virtual windfall of positive public relations, as well as the unanticipated development and subsequent popularity of catch-and-release fishing practices (Pepperell 1990). As a result of the initial success of the CTC, the concept of constituent-based marine tagging programs has been widely embraced, as reflected by the development of similar programs in Australia (Pepperell 1990), New Zealand (Murray 1990), and South Africa (van der Elst 1990), as well as programs on large Atlantic sharks (Kohler et al. 1998) and on Pacific Istiophoridae (Squire 1974; Holts and Prescott 2000).

From 1954 to 1999, more than 35,000 recreational and commercial fishermen have participated in the CTC and tagged more than 245,000 fish representing 123 species (Table 1; Scott et al. 1990; Ortiz et al. 1999). At present, about 10,000 persons are listed as active participants in the CTC. Program participants reside not only in the USA, but also in Canada, Mexico, South America, West Africa, Brazil, and numerous Caribbean island nations. Historical recapture rates since 1954 (Table 1) range from almost 12% for Atlantic bluefin tuna to less than 1% for blue marlin. Data generated by the program are widely used by a variety of state and federal fisheries agencies, as well as international fisheries organizations. For example, since the International Commission for the Conservation of Atlantic Tunas (ICCAT) started conducting stock assessments of highly migratory species in the mid-1970s, the commission has relied heavily upon the CTC database as a primary source of information concerning movement patterns, defining management units, and in estimating growth and other life history parameters of these species (Miyake 1990; Jones and Prince 1998).

Many of the CTC target species are too large to be brought on board for tagging. Therefore, one of the major challenges during the early stages of the program was developing in-water tagging techniques that could be used easily, safely, and effectively by volunteer fishermen and scientists. Over the past four decades, the techniques have evolved and improvements made to reduce the hazards of tagging the larger tunas and billfishes (Scott et al. 1990; Ortiz et al. 1999).

This paper reviews the development of efficient tag and release methods in the CTC for large, highly migratory species. The techniques described for in-water tagging reflect the development of improved fish-handling procedures used at boatside, as well as describing tagging equipment and methods for catching, tagging, dehooking, and resuscitation. In addition, results are presented on the performance of individual taggers and from a study conducted on billfish that compared tag retention of a stainless steel dart tag with that of a hydroscopic nylon double-barb dart tag. The overall objective of this paper is to provide an overview, guidance, and recommendations on the best equipment, techniques, and procedures for a successful constituent-based program for in-water tagging of large, highly migratory species.

Table 1. Release and recapture statistics for the major target species of the Cooperative Tagging Center, 1954–1999. The category "all species" is composed of 123 different species, including major and minor target species (Istiophoridae, Xiphiidae, Scombridae), as well as many inshore non-target species that have been opportunistically tagged over the years by Program participants (Scott et al. 1990).

| Species | Number of fish | | |
	Releases	Recaptures	Percent recaptured
Blue marlin	23,528	205	0.87
White marlin	31,277	577	1.84
Sailfish	65,065	1,182	1.82
Swordfish	9,983	348	3.49
Bluefin tuna	39,357	4,609	11.71
All species	247,658	10,979	4.43

History of Tag Development

From 1954 to 1981, a stainless steel dart tag designed by Mather (1960, 1963) and manufactured by Floy Tag Manufacturing Company[2] was used almost exclusively by the CTC to tag large, highly migratory species (McFarlane et al. 1990; Figure 1, top). This dart tag (FH 69 series) used a brass sleeve crimped on the end of the monofilament shaft to hold the yellow vinyl tubing (containing the legend) in place. The anchor portion of the tag consisted of a stainless steel barb that was inserted into the dorsal musculature of the fish. The legend contained the word "reward," as well as a unique tag number and the return address of the NMFS Miami laboratory (Scott et al. 1990). This tag was modified in 1981, as a result of field observations that noted that many of these tags, especially from recaptured bluefin tuna, were returned with the tubing and its imprinted legend missing (i.e., only the monofilament shaft was projected from the dorsal musculature). It was found that the brass sleeve often corroded completely, allowing the tubing to slip off and be lost. To prevent this known source of shedding, the original design was modified by Floy Tag Company (FH 69S), using a plastic heat shrink sleeve that was slipped over the doubled end of the monofilament to retain the identification tubing. In 1981, the original FH 69 series dart tag was replaced in the CTC by the FH 69S series dart tag (Figure 1, bottom).

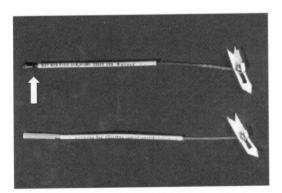

Figure 1. Original stainless steel dart tag (FH 69) with brass crimp (see arrow) securing the legend, used in the Cooperative Tagging Center from 1954 to 1981 (top). Modification of original stainless steel dart (FH 69S), using shrink tubing over doubled monofilament to secure the legend (bottom).

Yamashita and Waldron (1958) modified Mather's dart tag design by using a nylon anchor while tagging skipjack tuna *Katsuwonus pelamis*. They reported significantly higher returns compared with stainless steel dart tags. Hydroscopic nylon dart tags in three different sizes (18, 10, and 6.5 mm in diameter) were first developed by the CTC on an experimental basis and used briefly on bluefin tuna in the middle to late 1970s (Scott et al. 1990). These tags were later miniaturized for use in smaller king mackerel *Scomberomourus cavalla* and red drum *Sciaenops ocellatus* in the 1980s (Fable 1990; Gutherz et al. 1990). Gutherz et al. (1990) first reported encouraging results using a nylon anchor dart tag prototype (E series tag) on red drum at the Fish-Marking Techniques Symposium (Parker et al. 1990) in September 1989. They found that fish tissue (connective tissue and muscle) encapsulated and adhered to the nylon anchor head within a minimum of at least 166 d after placement. In fact, Gutherz et al. (1990) reported that tags so encapsulated were almost impossible to take out by hand and had to be cut out of the fish with a knife.

The findings of Gutherz et al. (1990) motivated The Billfish Foundation (TBF) and the NMFS to jointly develop a larger nylon anchor for a tag that could be used on billfish and other large, highly migratory species. A formal agreement between these two agencies to develop the hydroscopic (porous) nylon tag was finalized in late 1990. This agreement also included provisions to increase cooperation between these agencies in running the constituent-based tagging programs. For example, TBF agreed to provide NMFS with electronic copies of the release and recovery database on a regular and timely basis (Peel et al. 1998).

During the initial tag development phase, the design of the two nylon barbs of the anchor was modified to expand outward into the adjacent musculature with backward pressure. This feature resulted in their designation as "intramuscular tags." The anchors of the tags were made in an injection mold with hydroscopic nylon, similar to surgical grade nylon. The intent was to eventually develop an anchoring mechanism that could: be placed easily and properly by fishers using in-water tagging techniques on large, highly migratory species; increase

2. The mention of commercial products or entities does not imply endorsement by the National Marine Fisheries Service or the authors.

the biological compatibility of the tags to encourage the adherence of tissue to the nylon anchor to minimize long term shedding; and increase the short-term retention of the tag, even when accidentally placed in muscle tissue, using an intramuscular anchoring system. Since tag placement on a live fish using in-water tagging techniques is inherently imprecise, the use of intramuscular tags was considered an improvement over the stainless steel dart tag that worked best when carefully placed and anchored between dorsal spine pterygiophores. The stainless steel material used to make the anchor was also relatively soft, pliable, and easily bent when pulling this tag out of the fish. Conversely, the barbs of the nylon anchor were virtually impossible to bend. In addition, hydroscopic nylon is a relatively inert material compared with stainless steel. This feature was thought to be an advantage in reducing the instances of tissue inflammation and necrosis, which were often observed near the stainless steel tag wound site in recaptured fish. Necrotic and inflamed tissue surrounding the anchoring site was thought to contribute to tag shedding.

The Billfish Foundation started distributing an 8-mm diameter hydroscopic nylon anchor dart tag to tagging program participants in late 1990 (Peel et al. 1998). Parallel to the field application of the larger nylon dart tags used on billfish by TBF, a joint double-tagging study on billfish, comparing the tag retention of stainless steel dart tags (hereafter referred to as steel tags or Tag A, Figure 2, top) and the TBF nylon anchor tags (hereafter referred to as nylon tags or Tag B, Figure 2, bottom) was initiated by TBF and NMFS in 1990. By 1995, the CTC adopted the TBF design as the primary tag issued to participants based on three lines of evidence: results testing a miniaturized version of the TBF design on red drum and red snapper held in captivity were very encouraging and indicated superior retention qualities of the double-barb nylon anchor (Jones, in press); the TBF tag recovery rates for billfishes the first four to five years of using the nylon tag were comparable to, or better than, those of the CTC using the steel tag (Peel et al. 1998); and preliminary results of a comparative tagging study, comparing the tag retention of the nylon tag with the steel tag used on billfish (Figure 3) indicated better tag performance and retention qualities of the nylon tag relative to the steel tag (Jones et al. 1996).

Figure 2. Stainless steel dart tag, Tag A (top) and hydroscopic nylon double-barb dart tag, Tag B (bottom) used in the double-tagging study to evaluate retention of the two tag types on billfishes (1990–1999).

Tag Recoveries

The primary source of information for the CTC has always been the recovery of tagged fish. For many years, however, promotion of the recovery aspect was a secondary consideration (Scott et al. 1990). As a part of recent efforts to improve the quality and quantity of tag recovery data, tagging kits (Figure 4), which have been issued to CTC participants since the program's inception, are continually modified. Currently these kits include: a zip-lock plastic container for storage of tagging materials; the most recent issue of the NMFS tagging newsletter which summarizes current tagging results and procedures; a CTC brochure explaining the program tagging procedures; a tag release flag; tag release cards with tags; a fish tag issue "report card" (i.e. inventory card); a stainless steel applicator; if requested, a tagging pole; and most recently, a fluorescent orange recapture (recovery) card. This last item was added because experience with tag recoveries indicated that the majority of the fishing public did not remember the information needed to report a recapture. Fluorescent orange was chosen as the color for the card, allowing it to be located easily when needed. Also, to facilitate reporting, the legend on the dart tag was modified to include a toll-free phone number and the CTC address.

As part of this overall effort to improve tag recovery rates, outreach efforts promoting the use of recovery cards and other tag recovery activities have been made in the domestic and international media through the CTC tagging newsletter and the ICCAT Tag Recovery Network (Block et al. 2001). Recovery cards, now printed in English and Spanish, have been made available to recreational and commercial fishing constituents at important fishing sites both in the United States and abroad.

To provide an incentive to report a tag recovery, a small monetary reward (US$5) used to be awarded. After 1981, this policy was changed and currently a hat, embroidered with the emblems of the program, is sent to participants reporting recoveries. In addition, ICCAT supports a $500 annual lottery drawing for constituents reporting tag recoveries for the major pelagic species.

Tagging Research

Comparative Tag Retention Study

A comparative double-tagging study was conducted to determine which of two tag types had the best retention qualities when applied by fishery constituents using an in-water approach on large billfish. The null hypothesis to be tested was that retention of the steel tag (tag A, FH 69S or R series) and the nylon tag (tag B, BF or HM series) was equal (Figure 2). The only difference in design between the two tags was the anchoring mechanism—stainless steel versus hydroscopic nylon. The length and diameters of the streamer portions of the tags, as well as the length of tag applicators that determine depth of anchor penetration, were the same. We recommended that one tag be placed on each side of the billfish.

Comparative Tagging Methods: Double-tagging procedures were developed to minimize factors that might have a differential effect on tag retention. Only experienced commercial and recreational fishery constituents who had previously participated in TBF and CTC billfish tagging programs were allowed to participate in this study (Ortiz et al. 1999). This was done to reduce individual tagger variation and to standardize (to the extent possible) tagging techniques. We opted to use experienced fishery constituents for tagging, instead of scientists or trained technicians, because the new tag was developed for

use in the constituent-based CTC and TBF tagging programs (Dugger 1992[3]). In addition, using scientists and trained technicians for tagging was beyond the financial feasibility of this project. We recommended that one tag be placed on each side of the billfish, whenever possible, to avoid physical contact between tags. Tagging on both sides also increased tag visibility and the potential for recoveries. However, tagging on both sides of the fish usually involved longer handling times, and this was not always possible under field conditions. When tagging on the same side of billfish could not be avoided, we recommended that the two tags be inserted far enough apart that the tags could not touch each other (Figure 3).

Tagging kits for the double-tagging study were assembled by NMFS and distributed by TBF. Each tag release card in the kit had steel and nylon tags attached. The alphanumeric tag numbers were printed on each tag release card prior to distribution. The numeric serial numbers for both tag types were matched for each pair of tags, but the steel tag used an R prefix, and the nylon tag used a BF or HM prefix in front of the serial number of the tag legend. Each tag type required a different stainless steel applicator, and several applicators of each type were also supplied to participants. The color of the legend for the steel tags (Tag A) was yellow, while the legend of the nylon tag (Tag B) was orange. Specific instructions for participating in the tagging study were communicated to participants by written instructions, telephone calls, popular media[2], and the CTC newsletter (Jones et al. 1995).

Figure 3. A hydroscopic nylon double-barb dart tag (left) and a stainless steel dart tag (right) used to double tag billfish, such as this blue marlin, to assess the relative retention of the two tag types.

3. Dugger, A. 1992. The Billfish Foundation. Sport Fishing Magazine. 1992. February:47–51. World Publications, Inc., Winter Park, Florida

Statistical Analysis: Data from the double-tagging study were compiled and analyzed at the CTC. A relative tag retention rate (RRR) was calculated as the total number of steel tag returns (defined as fish recaptures with both steel and nylon tags plus fish recaptures with only steel tags) over the total number of nylon tag returns (defined as fish recaptures with both nylon and steel tags plus fish recaptures with only nylon tags). A 2×2 contingency table of tag type (steel and nylon) and tag fate (return or loss) was used to test the null hypothesis that the retention of steel tags was equal to the retention of nylon tags (Snedecor and Cochran 1967). The corresponding chi-square statistic was estimated as

$$X^2 = \sum ij[(f_{ij} - F_{ij})^2 / F_{ij}]$$

for $i = 1, 2$ (Tag Type) and $j = 1, 2$ (Tag result; 1 Return, 2 Lost)

where:

f_{ij} = observed number of tag recaptures for steel and nylon tags

F_i = expected - number of tag recaptures for steel and nylon tags

This analysis assumed that there was no difference in tag retention rates among fish species and that immediate shedding after the tagging procedure (Type I tag shedding) was similar for both tag types. It also assumed that there was a sufficient time between release and recapture events, such that the differences in tag retention were mainly due to each tag type's retention qualities.

Individual Tagging Performance

Throughout the years of the program, many of the improvements in tagging equipment, fish handling procedures, and methods of dehooking and resuscitation were developed by captains who were major participants in the CTC (Jones et al. 1995). As a quantitative measure of how these improvements could affect tagging performance, we evaluated tag recapture rates of fish tagged by some of the top individual CTC participants as a proxy for tagger performance. Tags used in this particular fishery were from the CTC as well as from The Billfish Foundation. Individual tag recapture rates were then computed for the top captains in order to provide insight into tagger performance.

Results and Discussion

Comparative Tag Retention Study

A total of 3,038 marlin, sailfish, and swordfish, were double-tagged with the steel (R series) and nylon tags (BF/HM series) from 1990 to 1999 (Table 2). Of these, 1,069 were blue marlin, 947 were sailfish, 590 were swordfish, and 432 were white marlin. More than 50% of the total number of double-tagged billfish were tagged by only seven individuals. During the ten-year duration of the project, 2.8% or 86 billfish (including swordfish) were recaptured; 41 had both tags present; 11 had only steel tags present; and 34 had only nylon tags present (Table 2). The relative tag retention rate (RRR) for each species was 85.7% for blue marlin, 64.7% for white marlin, 57.7% for sailfish, 72.7% for swordfish, and 69.3% for all species combined. Therefore, the improved retention of the nylon tags compared with steel tags for these categories ranged from 14.3% (blue marlin) to 42.3% (sailfish). Assuming all other factors influencing tag retention remained constant between species, steel tags were retained 69.3% as well as nylon tags for all species combined. The chi-square statistic using a 2 × 2 contingency table for all billfish species combined was highly significant (X^2 = 15.92, $P = 0.0001$, with 1 df), and the null hypothesis was rejected.

Better tag retention of the nylon tag is also supported by a recent report that indicates improvements in the tag recapture rates for each species of billfish in the Billfish Foundation and CTC tagging programs over the last decade (Jones and Prince 1998; Prince et al. 2000). This is highlighted by the recapture rates for Atlantic white marlin in the TBF tagging program, which has achieved recapture rates greater than 2% for the first time since the program started in 1990. No other constituent-based tagging program targeting Istiophoridae throughout the world's oceans have reported recapture rates this high (Murray 1990; Pepperell 1990; Scott et al. 1990; Holts and Prescott 2000; Ortiz et al., in press).

Individual Tagging Performance

A total of 6,421 bluefin tuna were tagged and released off Hatteras, North Carolina, from 1994 to 1999 (Table 3). The biggest single release year for this fishery was 1996, when a total of 2,827 bluefin

Table 2. Comparative tagging study for blue marlin, white marlin, sailfish and swordfish in the North Atlantic using steel tags (FH69S or R series) and nylon tags (BF or HM series). The relative retention rate (RRR) is calculated as the numbers of steel tags retained over numbers of nylon tags retained (see text).

| Species | Number of fish | | Number of tags returned | | | Relative retention rate (%) |
	Double tagged	Recaptured	Both	Steel	Nylon	
Blue marlin	1,069	26	13	5	8	85.7
White marlin	432	18	10	1	7	64.7
Sailfish	947	29	12	3	14	57.7
Swordfish	590	13	6	2	5	72.7
Total	3,038	86	41	11	34	69.3

Table 3. Tag releases and recaptures of bluefin tuna by the Hatteras, North Carolina, recreational fishing fleet, 1994–1999. Tagging agencies include the Cooperative Tagging Center (CTC) and the Billfish Foundation (TBF).

| Year | Number released | | | Number recaptured | | |
	NMFS[a]	TBF[b]	Total	NMFS	TBF	Total
1994	37	9	46			
1995	671	123	794	11	3	14
1996	1,688	1,139	2,827	52	20	72
1997	1,830	599	2,429	89	50	139
1998	187	14	201	22	8	30
1999	124	– c	124	10	– c	10
Total	4,537	1,884	6,421	184	81	265

a. Tagging agency, CTC, NMFS
b. Tagging agency, TBF
c. No data

tuna were tagged and released from this location using both the CTC and TBF tags. The historical bluefin tuna tag recapture rate in the CTC from 1954 to 1999 was about 12% (Table 1), with the majority of these returns being made within the first six years after release. Although 265 bluefin tuna recaptures of the Hatteras releases have been reported through 1999, this represents a recovery rate of only 4.1%. However, these results are expected to improve as the time at liberty for many of these releases increases and allows for additional recoveries. This analysis evaluated the top captains who participated in the Cape Hatteras bluefin tuna fishery (releasing > 400 fish) from 1994 to 1999.

The most substantive contribution to the tag and release effort during this period was made by the seven captains of the Hatteras, North Carolina, fishing fleet who accounted for 67% of the total number of releases and a similar percentage of recoveries (Figure 5). The tag recapture percentage for fish released by six of the seven captains was close to or exceeded the 4.1% average from 1994 to 1999 (Fig-

ure 6), and the top recapture percentage for an individual captain was 5.7% (Figure 6). One of the outcomes of this intensive effort was the development of innovative tagging equipment and procedures that

Figure 4. Many of the components of the Cooperative Tagging Center kits remained the same since the program started in 1954. However, incentives for return of tag recaptures changed after 1981 from monetary rewards to embroidered hats. In addition, fluorescent orange tag recapture cards were added to the kits in 1992.

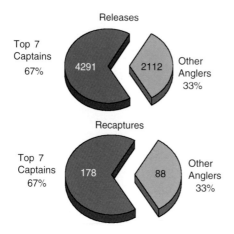

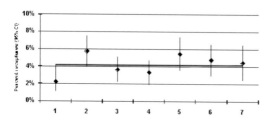

Figure 5. Bluefin tuna tag releases (top) off Hatteras, North Carolina, 1994–1999. Tag recaptures of Hatteras-released bluefin tuna (bottom), 1994–1999.

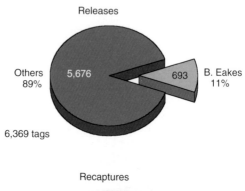

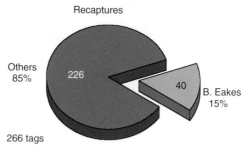

6,369 tags

266 tags

Figure 7. Captain Bob Eakes released 11% of the total number of tagged bluefin tuna off Hatteras, North Carolina. 1994–1999 (top). Fifteen percent of the Hatteras bluefin tuna released by Captain Eakes off Hatteras, North Carolina, were subsequently recaptured (bottom).

Figure 6. Tagging performance of the top seven captains (releasing > 400 fish) participating in the recreational fishery for bluefin tuna off Hatteras, North Carolina, 1994–1999. The solid horizontal line represents the overall recapture percent for all bluefin tuna released off Hatteras, North Carolina, from 1994 to 1999.

were subsequently adopted by the CTC (Jones et al. 1995; Ortiz et al. 1999). For example, tagging innovations certainly contributed to the performance of one of the top captains[4] in the Hatteras fleet, who accounted for 11% of the total number of tag released bluefin tuna (1994–1999), while the recaptures for this captain represented 15% of the total number of recaptures resulting from Hatteras released bluefin tuna (Figure 7). These tagging procedures included: use of circle hooks in combination with dead natural bait to minimize hook injuries (Figure 8); use of a dual applicator tagging pole with parallel and perpendicular applicators for greater accuracy in tag

Figure 8. Circle hooks are used in combination with dead natural bait and heavy chumming (i.e., chunk fishing) by the Hatteras fishing fleet targeting bluefin tuna.

4. Captain Bob Eakes was one of the top tagging participants in the Hatteras fleet. He had the highest bluefin tuna tag recapture percentage of any participant in this fishery (5.7%; Figure 6) and accounted for 11% of all tag released Hatteras bluefin (Figure 7), while about 15% of the recaptures from Hatteras releases were originally tagged by Captain Eakes (Figure 7). These included five transAtlantic recoveries. Captain Eakes developed numerous tagging innovations and procedures while participating in the Hatteras bluefin tuna fishery, and many of these procedures were eventually adopted by most of the Hatteras fleet, as well as the CTC.

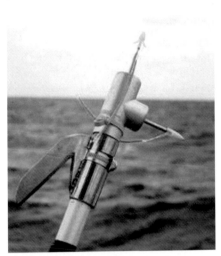

Figure 9. Dual applicator tagging pole, with a perpendicular as well as parallel applicator, used to improve the accuracy of tag placement into giant bluefin tuna caught off Hatteras, North Carolina (see text).

Figure 10. Use of the perpendicular applicator (see white arrow) to tag bluefin tuna when they turn sideways to the boat improves the precision of tag placement.

placement (Figures 9 and 10); use of a dehooking tool to remove circle hooks (Figure 11) to minimize post release trauma; and use of resuscitation techniques (Figure 12) prior to releasing fish in order to

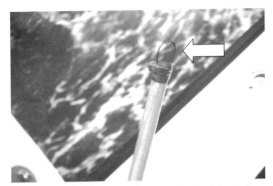

Figure 11. Dehooking device for removing circle hooks from bluefin tuna. The wire loop (see white arrow) is put under the point of the circle hook lodged in the jaw hinge and the hook is pulled through the hook wound; the hook is then cut from the leader, which is pulled back through the wound to release the fish.

improve the short-term condition of the tagged fish.

Tagging Procedures

It is inherently more difficult to tag a large, active fish in the water than it is to tag a smaller fish that can be controlled aboard a boat where precise placement of the tag can be accomplished. For this reason, development of in-water techniques that can be used easily, safely, and effectively by volunteer recreational and commercial constituents targeting large, highly migratory species has been a challenge. Nevertheless, tagging equipment and procedures for catching, tagging, dehooking, and resuscitation have improved over the past 46 years of the CTC.

Fishing Techniques

The general types of fishing techniques used by participants in the CTC for tagging large, pelagic species include: (1) rod and reel trolling with artificial baits; (2) rod and reel trolling with natural live or dead baits; (3) rod and reel still fishing with natural live or dead baits; (4) longline fishing with natural dead or live baits; (5) and purse-seine fishing. Consistent with the theme of promoting the live release of fish tagged in the CTC, we strongly recommend the use of circle hooks as terminal gear (a hook where the point is at a 90-degree angle to the hook shaft), whenever possible. Use of circle hooks is particularly appropriate whenever live or dead bait fishing techniques are used, as with fishing techniques 2, 3, and 4 (above). This recommendation is supported by the most recent research on the use of circle hooks for recreational fishing for billfish and tuna, which indicates this terminal gear promotes the

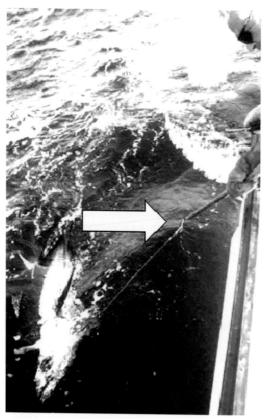

Figure 12. Resuscitation techniques for bluefin tuna caught on circle hooks. A dehooking device (see Figure 11) or a small gaff is used to pull the hook (white arrow) through the hook wound and hold the fish in place during resuscitation. After resuscitation is finished, the hook is cut and the leader is pulled back through the hook wound to release the fish.

live release of these species by minimizing deep hooking, foul hooking, and bleeding (Prince et al; Skomal et al, both this volume). One caveat that needs to be recognized with the use of circle hooks is that any offset of the point of the circle hook greater than about four to six degrees can result in deep hooking rates comparable to "J" hooks (Prince et al., this volume). In addition, reports by Berkeley and Edwards (1997) and Falterman and Graves (this volume) indicate that billfish and tuna caught on circle hooks during longline fishing also have markedly less physical damage associated hook trauma using this terminal gear, in contrast with straight shank or "J" hooks.

Fish Handling

Handling large, highly migratory species at boat-side is one of the most difficult parts of the tagging

process; therefore, the decision to tag or not should be left to the discretion of the captain. For very large tuna and billfish, two deckhands are normally used, one to control the fish using the leader and the other to tag (Figure 13). One of the primary considerations is whether the fish is "played down" to a point where it is subdued near the boat. As a rule of thumb, tagging green fish (i.e., fish that are very active or wild when brought near the boat) is not recommended and can be very dangerous to the crew and the fish itself, as well as risking damage to the boat. The more active the fish, the more difficult it is to place the tag in the correct target location (Figure 14). Very experienced crews do attempt to tag fish that are not completely subdued, and the decision to proceed should always be made by experienced captains familiar with their crew's abilities to tag properly. The entire tagging process, including fish handling, becomes increasingly more difficult in rough seas, and this should also be considered when deciding to tag. One of the recent innovations that can improve billfish handling at boat-side is the use of a tool called a snooter (Figure 15). This tool is composed of a plastic polyvinyl chloride (PVC) pipe with a rope running inside that leads to a multistrand stainless steel wire loop. The loop is placed over the upper bill of the billfish, pulled tight, and the fish is secured by tying off the rope on a cleat of the boat. The snooter allows the fish to be secured while submerged in the water during the tagging process, eliminating the need for a crew member to hold the bill of the fish, which can be very dangerous.

Figure 13. Two crew members tagging a large blue marlin— one handles the leader and brings the fish alongside the boat and the other inserts the tag.

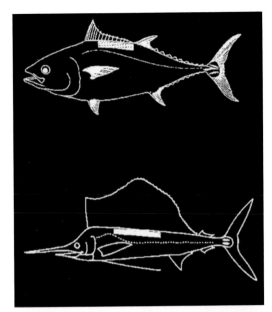

Figure 14. Target area (rectangles) for tagging tuna (top) and billfish (bottom) recommended by the Cooperative Tagging Center. Tags should be placed above the lateral line, away from the head and other vital organs, along the dorsal musculature.

Figure 15. A "snooter" used to control a billfish at boatside during the tagging process. The snooter is made of a PVC pipe and has a rope running through it connected to a wire loop. When pulled tight, the upper bill (see white arrow) is secured and the snooter rope is tied to a cleat.

Tagging Procedure and Equipment

The results of the comparative tagging study indicate that, when applied by fishery constituents, the nylon tag facilitates better retention compared with the steel tag (Table 2). Therefore, we recommend the use of the nylon tag for constituent-based tagging programs that apply in-water tagging techniques targeting large, highly-migratory species. The biological compatibility of the hydroscopic nylon material and the unique design of the double barbs, which promote intramuscular anchoring, likely contributed to the improved rates of retention observed in the double-tagging study. This is particularly true in situations where in-water tagging is dictated by the large size of the fish and often results in imprecise tag placement, as compared with in-boat tagging where precise tag placement is easily accomplished.

One of the most important factors in tagging large, highly migratory species involves proper tag placement in the desired target area (Figure 14). For both billfish and tuna, the tag should be placed in the dorsal musculature, above the lateral line and away from the head, gills plates, eyes, and other vital organs. This tag position will promote rapid healing of the tag wound and minimize the chance for serious injury. The target area advertised in the early part of the CTC was closer to the head than the current target area. However, over time, we have found that a target area starting just posterior to the gill plates was risky due to possible movement of the fish, which sometimes resulted in tags being lodged inappropriately (Figure 16). The preferred way for inserting the tag into the fish is to take a downward or dorsal tag placement approach over the

Figure 16. Poorly placed tags, such as this one in the cranium (white arrow), are likely to account for a large proportion of tag shedding.

fish's back (Figure 13). The tag should be placed as close to the dorsal spines as possible. Tags should be placed away from the head at a distance equal to at least one half the length of the pectoral fins. We recognize that dorsal tag placement over the back of the fish cannot always be accomplished because many fish, particularly tuna, turn sideways when brought alongside the boat (Figure 10). This also happens periodically with billfish. The dual-applicator tagging pole (Figure 9) promotes improved tag placement in these situations, due to the added flexibility of being able to insert the tag with a hammering motion using the perpendicular applicator (Figure 10). By equipping the tagging pole with dual applicator pins (parallel and perpendicular), the tagger has the flexibility to make last minute adjustments in the way the tag is placed in the fish, depending on the position of the fish at boat-side.

The dorsal tag placement approach avoids the dense concentration of highly vascularized red muscle tissue adjacent to the lateral line. This area should be avoided in order to minimize hemorrhaging and promote healing of the tag wound. In most species of billfish and tuna, there is little, if any, red muscle tissue along the back next to the dorsal spines. *Poor tag placement can kill fish*, particularly if vital organs are damaged (Figure 17). Sublethal effects of poor tag placement can result in less than optimum tagging results, which contribute, at best, to tag shedding or infection (Figures 16 and 18), or, at worst, to mortality (Figures 17). As a general rule of thumb, it is better to slow down the tagging process and wait for the fish to be subdued at boat-side to ensure proper placement of the tag in the target area.

When inserting the tag, the depth of tag placement is determined by the length of the stainless steel applicator that extends beyond the tagging pole. After 1997, the stainless steel applicator issued by the CTC was increased from two to three inches for both the TBF and CTC tagging programs to allow for deeper tag placement. We *strongly* encourage the use of this longer applicator, even in the smallest sailfish, which are still large enough to accommodate a 3-in deep placement of the tag.

Measuring Fish Length

Prior to release, if possible, we recommend measuring the length of the fish (Figure 19). One approach used by CTC participants is to use a fiberglass tape

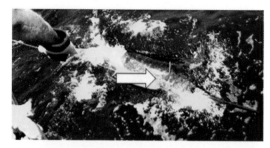

Figure 17. Poor placement of tags, such as this one near the edge of the operculum in a white marlin, can result in mortality, particularly if vital organs are damaged. Note the bleeding from the tag wound (see white arrow).

Figure 18. Serious infections that do not result in mortality can result from poor tag placement. This fish was recovered after several months and the wound was caused by the placement of the tag below the lateral line, in the vicinity of the caudal portion of the peritoneal cavity.

Figure 19. Measures of length can usually be obtained with a fiberglass tape, as illustrated here with a blue marlin.

to measure lower jaw fork length for billfish or fork length for tuna. The fish must be calm at boat-side as, even under these circumstances, getting an accurate measurement is difficult. Some participants have developed customized measuring tapes or ropes with a clip at one end to go over the leader. When the clip is placed over the leader it rests at the jaw hinge. A tennis ball is often fixed to the other end and trails along the fish's back towards the tail. Several markings are usually made on the tape to correspond to the maximum length standards for each species of Atlantic billfish or tuna. This method does not always result in an exact measure of length and usually necessitates some extrapolation to compensate for the length lost by starting the measurement at the jaw hinge, instead of at the tip of the lower jaw. However, this approach is usually better than guessing.

Dehooking

For the first 40 years of the CTC, most participants were advised not to remove the hook from the fish. Instead, the instructions suggested that priority should be given to keeping the tagging event short and cutting the leader as close as possible to the fish. The Hatteras fishery for bluefin tuna provided an opportunity to observe and examine about 100 tag recaptures, particularly wounds that resulted from hooks left in fish. Observations of these returns indicated that removing hooks is preferable, if circumstances permit, since approximately 25% of the hooks remained in the fish more than a year after release, and hook wounds and related infections were commonplace. In addition to the dehooking tool developed for circle hooks (Figure 11), other commercially available dehookers (Figure 20) developed for "J" hooks have been reported to be effective by CTC participants and the manufacturers and should be used whenever possible.

Resuscitation

Resuscitation is normally considered only when a

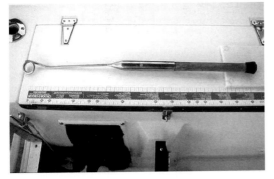

Figure 20. Commercially available de-hookers are very effective in removing "J" hooks from large highly migratory species.

fish is too weak from the fight to swim away from alongside the boat under its own power. Failure to resuscitate a weak fish can result in mortality from exhaustion or predation by sharks. The techniques for resuscitation of tuna and billfish differ somewhat because billfish have an extended upper bill, which serves as a "handle" during resuscitation, while tuna do not. The resuscitation techniques for bluefin tuna are recommended for tuna caught on circle hooks (Figure 12). If tuna are caught on "J" hooks, resuscitation may require the crew to simply keep the hook(s) in place until the fish regains strength. There are several different approaches for resuscitation of billfish. Some captains have their crew lean over the gunnel and hold onto the upper bill with the head of the fish submerged, while towing the fish slowly at two to three knots until they observe the fish has regained strength. This approach is very difficult to apply during rough sea conditions and can be quite dangerous. A preferred approach for resuscitation of billfish is to use a heavy fishing outfit (130-lb gear) with 1,000-lb test nylon cord as the terminal leader. The cord is tied to the upper bill with a slip knot, and the fish is towed ahead slowly at two to three knots (about 40–50 yards or 36–46 m) behind the boat until the angle of the line decreases from about 160 degrees to 45 degrees (Figure 21). As the fish regains strength and is able to maintain its body position in the water column, the angle of the line will decrease. When the fish has regained its strength, the fish is led back close to the boat, the slipknot is pulled, and the fish is released. This approach to resuscitation provides the crew with a more objective basis for deciding when the fish is ready to be released and is much safer than having a crew member lean over the gunnel and hold the upper bill with the head submerged. Use of a snooter is another option for resuscitation of billfish that avoids the problem of having a crew member hold the upper bill during resuscitation (Figure 15).

Tag Release Card

An essential element to the success of any tagging program is that participants conscientiously fill out tag release cards promptly after the tagging event. When participants do not take the time to properly complete and return the release cards, release data will be unavailable. This problem compromises the recapture data and negatively impacts the program.

Figure 21. One way of resuscitating billfish is by tying 1,000 pound nylon cord to the upper bill with a slip knot (see white arrows, top) and then towing the fish slowly (2–3 knots) until the angle of the line decreases from about 160 degrees (middle red triangle) to about 45 degrees (bottom red triangle), which indicates the fish has recovered (see text).

When fishing is good, there is often not enough time to completely fill out the release cards immediately after the fish is tagged and released. In this situation, we suggest that, at a minimum, the date, species, estimated size, and location be filled out immediately. These critical components of the release card are highlighted in bold print on the card (Figure 22), while the remaining information can be completed at a later time.

A major problem associated with missing release cards arises when a participant who was issued tags with specific identification numbers, gives these tags to someone else. This practice should be avoided as it hinders the program's ability to match tags to individuals. To make the tagging program work, it is necessary to properly fill out the tag release card (Figure 22) and return it to the CTC as soon as possible, preferably within a week of release, since many tagged fish are recaptured during their first month at-large. We also encourage participants to keep an independent log or file of personal tagging activities to ensure CTC records reflect each tagging participant's records.

Reporting Recaptures

The primary source of information for the CTC has always been the recovery of tagged fish. However, throughout the history of the CTC, the program has been known among participants and the press as a "tag and release" activity. Unfortunately, this reference has had the effect of reducing the focus on activities relative to recovery of tagged fish. Starting in the late 1980s, a number of steps were taken to highlight the critical program activity of reporting recaptured fish. Increasing the recapture rate for Istiophoridae (less than 2%; Table 1) is particularly important because of the relatively low recapture rates for this species group, not only in the CTC, but also world-wide (Miyake 1990; Murray 1990; Pepperell 1990; van der Elst 1990).

Since recapturing a tagged fish is a rare event, all fish brought alongside the boat should be examined on *both* sides to see if a tag is present. It is not always easy to recognize a tagged fish, since marine growth often covers the legend, and as the fish grows, the length of the legend extending outside the fish is reduced over time (Figure 23). The CTC database has many instances where fishers have tagged a fish and released it, only to notice another tag on the other

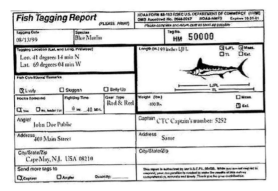

Figure 22. Current tag release card issued to participants in the Cooperative Tagging Center.

Figure 23. This tag-recaptured blue marlin had been at large for more than seven years. The tag legend is difficult to see (see white arrow) because it is covered by green algae and the growth of the fish has reduced the length of the legend extending outside the fish.

side of the fish as it swam away. Recaptured fish should be reported to the CTC or a local fisheries conservation agency as soon as possible.

Recommendations

Tag Release Activities

Conditions and opportunities for using in-water tagging techniques can vary depending on numerous factors, including weather, species, and circumstances involving individual fish. The following general recommendations should be considered when using in-water tagging techniques on large, highly migratory species:

(1) Use circle hooks whenever possible when using dead or live bait, as this terminal gear minimizes deep hooking, foul hooking, and bleeding. Circle hooks reduce the physical trauma related to hook damage and promote the live release of tagged fish. Use of circle hooks on lures is not recommended at this time, due to incomplete information;

(2) Only attempt to tag fish that are calm or subdued at boat-side. If the fish is still active, slow down the tagging activity and wait until the fish is subdued before attempting to insert the tag in the target area. Speed tagging lends itself to inaccurate tag placement, increases the potential of injuring the fish as well as the crew, or can cause damage to the vessel. For these reasons, we discourage speed tagging;

(3) When possible, use a snooter on billfish, as this tool increases the control over the fish and reduces the injury hazards to the crew;

(4) Attempt to measure the length of the fish when circumstances permit, as measured size is always better than estimated size;

(5) Use a dual applicator tagging stick to increase the flexibility of the angle of tag entry and promote accurate tag placement. This is particularly important when tagging tuna and billfish that often turn sideways when they are brought alongside the boat;

(6) Use appropriate hydroscopic nylon double-barb dart tags, as these tags have significantly higher retention rates compared with stainless steel dart tags, when applied by recreational and commercial constituents using in-water tagging techniques on large, highly migratory species;

(7) Remove hooks whenever possible. Use of a dehooker can facilitate quick and easy de-hooking;

(8) Resuscitate all fish that show an inability to maintain their body position in the water due to exhaustion from the fight. Resuscitation methods can differ between tuna and billfish. A snooter can be helpful in resuscitating billfish; and

(9) Fill out fish tagging report cards immediately and mail them back to the appropriate tagging agency as soon as possible.

Tag Recapture Activities

The following recommendations for tag recovery should be adopted by all fishers, even those that do not participate in the tagging portion of the program:

(1) Examine the dorsal musculature on both sides of each fish caught to see if a tag is present;

(2) If the fish is going to be taken legally, cut the old tag off. Measure and record the length and weight of the fish. If the fish is to be released, lean over the side of the boat, cut the old tag off and re-tag the fish so it can be re-released. In this case, try to measure the length of the fish before release. Tags that look old can indicate that the fish has been at-large for a long time, and long-term recaptures are particularly valuable;

(3) Record the recovery information, including species, latitude and longitude of the recapture site, date, method of fishing, and size of fish on the CTC fluorescent orange tag recapture card; and

(4) Report tag recovery information to the appropriate fisheries agency as soon as possible. Contact information is printed on the tags. You can get additional Atlantic tagging information for large pelagic species from the following web-sites: Southeast Fisheries Science Center [http://www.sefsc.noaa.gov/], Atlantic States Marine Fisheries Commission [http://fwie.fw.vt.edu/tagging], The Billfish Foundation [http://www.billfishfoundation.org], and the International Commission for the Conservation of Atlantic Tunas [http:// www.iccat.es].

References

Berkeley, S. A., and R. E. Edwards. 1997. Factors affecting billfish capture and survival in longline fisheries: potential application for reducing by catch mortality. International Commission for the Conservation of Atlantic Tunas, Madrid, Spain. Collective volume. Scientific Papers XLVIII(1): 255–262.

Block, B. A., H. Dewar, S. B. Blackwell, T. D. Williams, E. D. Prince, C. J. Farwell, A. Bostany, S. L. Teo, A. Seitz, A. Walli, and D. Fudge. 2001. Migratory movements, depth preferences, and thermal biology of Atlantic bluefin tuna. Science 293:1310–1314.

Fable, W. A. 1990. Summary of king mackerel tagging in the southeastern USA: mark-recapture techniques and factors influencing tag returns. Pages 161–167 *in* N. C. Parker, A. E. Giorgi, R. C. Heidinger, D. B. Jester, Jr., E. D. Prince, and G. A. Winans, editors. Fish-marking techniques. American Fisheries Society, Symposium 7, Bethesda, Maryland

Gutherz, E. J., B. A. Rohr, and R. V. Minton. 1990. Use of hydroscopic molded nylon dart and internal anchor tags on red drum. Pages 152–160 *in* N. C. Parker, A. E. Giorgi, R. C. Heidinger, D. B. Jester, Jr., E. D. Prince, and G. A. Winans, edi-

tors. Fish-marking techniques. American Fisheries Society, Symposium 7, Bethesda, Maryland.

Holts, D. B., and D. W. Prescott. 2000. 2000 Billfish newsletter. National Oceanic and Atmospheric Administration, National Marine Fisheries Service, Southwest Fisheries Science Center, La Jolla, California.

Jones, C. D. In press. Performance, uncertainties, and management implications of dart tags on red snapper (*Lutjanus campechanus*) and red drum (*Sciaenops ocellatus*). A dissertation submitted in partial fulfillment of the requirements for the degree of Doctor of Philosophy, Rosentstiel School of Marine, and Atmospheric Science, University of Miami, Miami, Florida.

Jones, C. D., M. T. Judge, M. A. Ortiz, D. S. Rosenthal, and E. D. Prince. 1995. Cooperative tagging center annual newsletter: 1993. National Oceanic and Atmospheric Administration Technical Memorandum, NMFS-SEFSC-423, Miami, Florida.

Jones, C. D., and E. D. Prince. 1998. The cooperative tagging center mark-release database for Istiophoridae (1954-1995) with an analysis of the West Atlantic ICCAT billfish tagging program. International Commission for the Conservation of Atlantic Tunas, Madrid, Spain. Collective Volume Scientific Papers XLVII:311–322.

Jones, C. D., D. S. Rosenthal, T. L. Jackson, M. T. Judge, and E. D. Prince. 1996. Cooperative tagging center annual newsletter: 1996. National Oceanic and Atmospheric Administration Technical Memorandum, NMFS-SEFSC-391, Miami, Florida.

Kohler, N. E., J. G. Casey, and P. A. Turner. 1998. NMFS cooperative shark tagging program, 1962-93: an atlas of shark tag and recapture data. Marine Fisheries Review 60(2):1–87.

Mather, F. J., III. 1960. Recaptures of tuna, marlin, and sailfish tagged in the western North Atlantic. Copeia 1960:149–151.

Mather, F. J., III. 1963. Tags and tagging techniques for large pelagic fishes. International Commission for the Northwest Atlantic Fisheries Special Publication 4:288–293.

McFarlane, G. A., R. S. Wydoski, and E. D. Prince. 1990. External tags and marks. Pages 9–29 *in* N. C. Parker, A. E. Giorgi, R. C. Heidinger, D. B. Jester, Jr., E. D. Prince, and G. A. Winans, editors. Fish-marking techniques. American Fisheries Society, Symposium 7, Bethesda, Maryland.

Miyake, P. M. 1990. History of the ICCAT tagging program, 1971–1986. Pages 746–764 *in* N. C. Parker, A. E. Giorgi, R. C. Heidinger, D. B. Jester, Jr., E. D. Prince, and G. A. Winans, editors. Fish-marking techniques. American Fisheries Society, Symposium 7, Bethesda, Maryland.

Murray, T. 1990. Fish-marking techniques in New Zealand. International Commission for the Conservation of Atlantic Tunas, Madrid, Spain. Collective Volume Scientific Papers XLVII:311–322.

Ortiz, M., E. D. Prince, J. E. Serafy, D. B. Holts, K. B. Davy, J. G. Pepperell, M. B. Lowry, and J. C. Holdsworth. In press. An analysis of the major constituent based billfish tagging programs in the world oceans. Proceedings of the 3rd International Billfish Symposium, Cairns, Australia, 19–23 August 2001.

Ortiz, M., D. S. Rosenthal, A. Venizelos, M. I. Farber, and E. D. Prince. 1999. Cooperative tagging center annual newsletter: 1998. National Oceanic and Atmospheric Administration

Technical Memorandum, NMFS-SEFSC-423, Miami, Florida.

Parker, N. C., A. E. Giorgi, R. C. Heidinger, D. B. Jester, Jr., E. D. Prince, and G. A. Winans, editors. 1990. Fish-Marking Techniques. American Fisheries Society, Symposium 7, Bethesda, Maryland.

Peel, E. M., J. Rice, M. Ortiz, and C. D. Jones. 1998. A summary of The Billfish Foundation's tagging program (1990–1996). International Commission for the Conservation of Atlantic Tunas, Madrid, Spain. Collective Volume Scientific Papers, XLVII:323–335.

Pepperell, J. G. 1990. Australian Cooperative Game-Fish Tagging Program, 1971–1987. Pages 765–774 in N. C. Parker, A. E. Giorgi, R. C. Heidinger, D. B. Jester, Jr., E. D. Prince, and G. A. Winans, editors. Fish-marking techniques. American Fisheries Society, Symposium 7, Bethesda, Maryland.

Prince, E. D., and B. Brown. 1991. Coordination of the ICCAT enhanced research program for billfish. Pages 13–18 in D. Guthrie, J. M. Hoenig, M. Holliday, C. M. Jones, M. J. Mills, S. A. Moberly, K. H. Pollock, and D. R. Talhelm, editors. Creel and angler surveys in fisheries management. American Fisheries Society, Symposium 12, Bethesda, Maryland.

Prince, E. D., M. A. Ortiz, D. Rosenthal, A. Venizelos, and K. B. Davy. 2000. An update of the tag release and recapture files for Atlantic Istiophoridae. Proceedings of the Fourth ICCAT Billfish Workshop. International Commission for the Conservation of Atlantic Tunas, Madrid, Spain, Collective Volume of Scientific Papers 53.

Scott, E. L., E. D. Prince, and C. D. Goodyear. 1990. History of the cooperative game fish tagging program in the Atlantic Ocean, Gulf of Mexico, and Caribbean Sea, 1954–1987. Pages 841–853 in N. C. Parker, A. E. Giorgi, R. C. Heidinger, D. B. Jester, Jr., E. D. Prince, and G. A. Winans, editors. Fish-marking techniques. American Fisheries Society, Symposium 7, Bethesda, Maryland.

Snedecor, G. W., and W. G. Cochran. 1967. Statistical methods. The Iowa State University Press, Ames, Iowa.

Squire, J. L. Jr. 1974. Migration patterns of Istiophoridae in the Pacific Ocean as determined by cooperative tagging programs. Pages 226–237 in R. S. Shomura and F. Williams, editors. Proceedings of the International Billfish Symposium, Kailua-Kona, Hawaii, 9–12 August 1972, part 2. Review and contributed papers. NOAA Technical Report, NMFS SSRF-675.

van der Elst, R. P. 1990. Marine fish tagging in South Africa. Pages 854–862 in N. C. Parker, A. E. Giorgi, R. C. Heidinger, D. B. Jester, Jr., E. D. Prince, and G. A. Winans, editors. Fish-marking techniques. American Fisheries Society, Symposium 7, Bethesda, Maryland.

Yamashita, D., and K. Waldron. 1958. An all-plastic dart-type fish tag. California Fish and Game 44:311–317.

American Fisheries Society Symposium 30:172–179, 2002
© Copyright by the American Fisheries Society 2002

Factors Affecting Robust Estimates of the Catch-and-Release Mortality Using Pop-Off Tag Technology

C. Phillip Goodyear

415 Ridgewood Road
Key Biscayne, Florida 33149, USA
Email: phil_goodyear@msn.com

Abstract.—Most billfish caught by recreational and U.S. longline fishermen are returned to the sea and, because of their overfished status, the United States has urged that all live billfish taken in Atlantic longline fisheries be released. Knowledge of the proportion of these fish that die due to the catch-and-release process, is important both for stock assessment, and to know the potential benefit of releasing fish taken as bycatch in commercial fisheries. Existing information indicates that the magnitude of this mortality is low, but comes from a limited number of studies using small numbers of ultrasonic tags. Recent technology that uses tags that release from the fish after a preprogrammed time, and then transmit data to satellites, offers the potential for developing better estimates of release mortality. This paper uses simulation techniques to examine factors leading to robust estimates of release mortality. Most sources of error in tagging experiments will lead to upward bias in the estimates. These include tag failure, tagging induced mortality, natural mortality, and tag shedding. Given the importance of the estimate to future billfish management, initial studies should focus on proving the technology. Tag failures produce ambiguous results and should be minimized, to the extent possible, or eliminated from the analysis where appropriate. Under perfect conditions (no tag failure, no tag induced mortality, and no tag shedding), individual experiments should apply a minimum of about 100 tags. The length of time from tagging until the tag releases from the fish should only be long enough for the catch-and-release mortality to be fully expressed. Because each fishing mode is likely to have a different release mortality rate, each experiment only estimates the release mortality rate for the species, gear, and fishing method employed in the fishery studied. The number of tags required to estimate the total number of deaths of released fish, of all species, could be in the tens of thousands. However, a well-researched experimental design might reduce the required number of tags significantly.

Introduction

U.S. fisheries currently return to the sea nearly all Atlantic billfish (sailfish and marlins) that are caught. Almost all those caught in rod and reel fisheries, and about half of those caught in U.S. longline fisheries (which cannot legally land billfish) are alive at the time of release. It is likely that some of the released fish die as a result of the experience, and in the case of the rod-and-reel fishery, release mortality may represent the largest fraction of deaths attributable to this mode of fishing. Data available to characterize the magnitude of the release mortality rate are generally sparse and often anecdotal in nature, leading to great uncertainty in the actual numbers of billfish deaths. This situation fosters conflict between the recreational and commercial sectors of the fishing industry. These undocumented deaths also compromise the adequacy of the time series of catch

estimates upon which stock assessments for the several species rely. If these losses are an important part of the total removals, they should be included in stock assessments (Mesnil 1996).

Large, highly-migratory pelagic species, such as billfish, are difficult to observe directly and cannot be constrained within artificial structures like smaller species, where such methods have proven useful (e.g., Gitschlag and Renaud 1994; Render and Wilson 1994). Most studies of postrelease billfish mortality have used acoustic tags to characterize postrelease behavior. For example, Edwards et al. (1989) monitored the movements of seven blue marlin *Makaira nigricans* equipped with sonic transmitters for a period of less than 24 hours. All seven specimens survived and showed substantial movement. In another study, Jolley and Irby (1979) applied eight acoustic tags to assess immediate mortality of tagged and released Atlantic sailfish *Istiophorus platypterus*. All sailfish were caught by rod and reel, tagged externally with ultrasonic transmitters, and tracked for periods of about three hours to just over a day. Seven sailfish survived. One that had sustained a severe eye injury during the catch, tag, and release experience bled profusely and was attacked and killed by a shark 6.5 hours after release. Holts and Bedford (1990) applied sonic tags to eleven striped marlin *Tetrapturus audax* off the U.S. California coast and followed them for up to two days. None of the fish died during the experiment. More recently, Pepperell and Davis (1999) use sonic tags to study the postrelease behavior of eight black marlin *M. indica* tagged off the Great Barrier Reef, Australia. One fish was killed by a shark, and two of the tags were apparently shed soon after release, a factor that had been observed in at least two other studies with billfish (Yuen et al. 1974; Block et al. 1992).

Pepperell and Davis (1999) summarized the available data from eight experiments with four billfish species that used acoustic tags. The number of tags applied ranged from 5 to 12 among the various studies. Most fish were tracked for a period of less than one day. Tag shedding was observed in three of the eight studies and accounted for 25% of the tags in one study. Postrelease mortality estimates ranged from 0–50% and, where the cause was known, death was attributed to sharks.

Recent developments in tagging technology have demonstrated the efficacy of single-point, pop-off satellite tags to study the movements of pelagic fish (Block et al. 1998). These tags are attached externally to the fish, and are released at a preprogrammed time by using a corrosive linkage. The tags record temperature information while attached to the fish and, upon release, float to the surface and transmit their data to Argos satellites. Trends in the temperature data provide information about the movement of the fish through the water column and, consequently, can be used to determine if the fish is alive, and the location of the tag indicates distance traveled. This technology has the advantage over sonic tags in that there is no requirement to follow each fish with sonic tracking equipment. As a consequence, many more fish may be tagged during an experiment.

The current study uses computer simulation to examine the robustness of release-mortality estimates that might be derived by using pop-off tag technology for billfish.

Methods

The basic data that would be available from a release-mortality experiment that uses pop-off satellite tags will be the total number of fish tagged (N), the number of fish deemed alive at the time the tags released from the fish (A), the number of fish deemed to have died before the tags released (D), and the number of tags that did not report. The release mortality probability (R) can then be estimated as

$$R = \frac{D}{N} \tag{1}$$

or,

$$R = 1 - \frac{A}{N}. \tag{2}$$

These two equations will be the same if there are no tag failures, or if all tag failures (tags not reporting data to the satellite) are assumed to be a result of catch-and-release mortality. If there is any additional probability of mortality caused by the stress of the tagging experience itself (T), then R, estimated from the preceding equations, will overestimate the true value of the release mortality fraction. To adjust for this, R would be more appropriately calculated as

$$R = 1 - \frac{A(1-T)}{N}. \tag{3}$$

It is unclear how the additional mortality from the tagging experience might be separated from the mortality from the catch-and-release experience by using data derived from a satellite tagging experiment using pop-off technology. As a consequence, this study employs equation (1) to estimate the release mortality fraction.

The behavior of the distribution of the estimates of release mortality (R), with respect to its actual value, the number of tags applied (N), the tagging mortality fraction (T), the probability that tags are shed before the programmed pop-off day, tag failure, and natural mortality were examined by using simulation techniques. Distributions of the estimates were derived from the outcomes of 1,000 simulated experiments for a particular combination of assumptions about tag-induced mortality, natural mortality, tag shedding, tag failure, and the release mortality probability. Each simulated tag was followed hourly from tagging to simulated pop off. The probability that the tag would be associated with an event (mortality or shedding) was compared with a random number drawn from a uniform distribution each hour. If the probability exceeded the random number, the tag was placed in one of the observation bins for the simulated event, and the simulation for the next tag was begun. There were three observation bins: tag failures that reported no data, tags that remained on live fish to the end of the experiment and reported normally, and tags that reported but lacked the data trends that would indicate the fish was alive at the end of the experiment. Simulated mortalities and shed tags were placed in this latter bin. Tag failures could be assumed to be mortalities or be excluded from the analysis. Mortalities resulting from catch and release and tagging were assumed to occur at a constant instantaneous rate from tagging to the end of the period required for the mortality to be fully expressed (days to full expression, a deterministic variable in the analysis). Shedding was assumed to occur at a constant instantaneous rate from tagging to the programmed pop-off day, a deterministic variable in the analysis.

Simulated experiments were conducted for release mortality rates of 5%, 10%, 25%, 50%, and 75% with 10–1,000 tags and no other sources of error (other mortality, tag failure, or shedding) to examine the effect of sample size on the probability distribution of the release mortality estimates. Additional simulations were conducted to examine the impact on release mortality estimates of tag failures, tag shedding, tagging mortality, natural mortality, and the relation between the time for the release mortality to be fully expressed and the programmed pop-off day. All variables were assumed to be independent.

Results

The distributions of 1,000 estimates of the release mortality fraction with an underlying true value of 0.10 is shown in Figure 1 for 1,000 tags per trial experiment, and in Figure 2 for 25 tags per trial experiment. No other complicating factors, such as natural mortality, tagging induced mortality, tag shedding, or tag failure were involved in the analyses presented in these two figures. In both cases, the means of the estimates corresponded to the underlying true mean. In the case of 1,000-tag trials, the median was also at the true value. In contrast, inspection of Figure 2 reveals no estimate that corre-

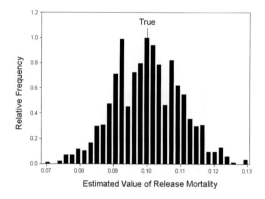

Figure 1. Frequency distribution of the estimated values of release mortality from 1,000 trial experiments, each with 1,000 tags and without other complicating factors and a true value of 0.10.

sponded to the true value. This is the result of the lack of precision caused by the small number of tags involved in each experiment. The true value of 0.10 cannot be estimated from an experiment involving application of 25 tags because the observations are integer values, and no integer divided by 25 gives 0.10. The problem with the precision of the estimates becomes increasingly severe as the number of tags applied in an experiment declines. This problem and the general nature of ratios combine to make most of the estimate distributions depart from normality.

The effect of the number of tags applied in an experiment on accuracy and precision of the estimates was examined by plotting the 90% confidence interval (the 5th and 95th percentiles) of the simulated distribution of estimates for several levels of the underlying release mortality rate (Figures 3–7). No other complicating factors are considered in the analyses depicted in these figures. In each, the true value is indicated by the middle, horizontal, dashed line. The upper and lower, dashed, horizontal lines indicate a region that is ± 25% of the actual value of the release mortality. The point where these lines intersect the lines depicting the 90% confidence interval indicates the number of tags required to have a 90% probability that an estimate arising from an experiment will be within 25% of the true value, if no tags fail and there is no tag shedding, no tagging induced mortality, and no natural mortality during the experiment.

It would appear that a thousand or so tags would be required to achieve a 90% probability that the estimate will be within 25% of the true release mortal-

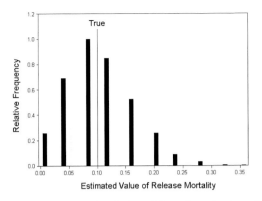

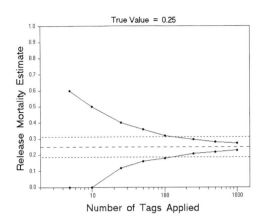

Figure 2. Frequency distribution of the estimated values of release mortality from 1,000 trial experiments, each with 25 tags, without other complicating factors and a true value of 0.10.

Figure 5. Effect of number of tags on the 90% confidence interval for estimates of release mortality for an underlying true value of 0.25.

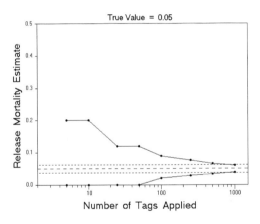

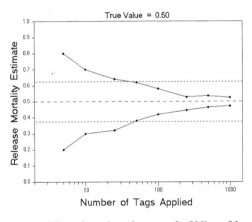

Figure 3. Effect of number of tags on the 90% confidence interval for estimates of release mortality for an underlying true value of 0.05.

Figure 6. Effect of number of tags on the 90% confidence interval for estimates of release mortality for an underlying true value of 0.50.

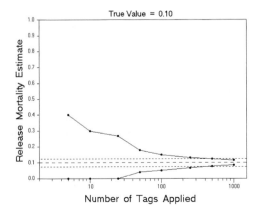

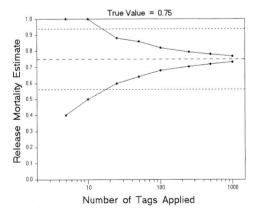

Figure 4. Effect of number of tags on the 90% confidence interval for estimates of release mortality for an underlying true value of 0.10.

Figure 7. Effect of number of tags on the 90% confidence interval for estimates of release mortality for an underlying true value of 0.75.

ity fraction, if it is about 0.05 or below (Figure 3). The same level of precision would require between 250 and 500 tags for the underlying true release mortality rate of 0.10, and somewhat more than 100 tags at a true release mortality of 0.25 (Figures 4 and 5). At a true release mortality rate of 0.50, about 50 tags would be required to achieve this level of precision (Figure 6). The requisite number drops to about 20 for a release mortality of 0.75 (Figure 7).

An alternate perspective on precision is given by the number of tags required to have a 90% probability that an estimate arising from an experiment will be within five percentage points of the true value (as opposed to within 5% of the true value). By using this criterion, about 80 tags would be needed for a true release mortality of 0.05, 100 for a release mortality of 0.1, 200 for a release mortality of 0.25, 200 for a release mortality of 0.50, and about 250 tags for a release mortality of 0.75. Again, these sample sizes are for the ideal conditions of no tags failure, no tag shedding, no tagging-induced mortality, and no natural mortality during the experiment.

The influence of tag failures on the estimates of release mortality depends in part on how the data are treated (Figure 8). If it is assumed that tags that failed to report represent mortalities, then tag failures will be added to the numerator of equation 1, and the release mortality fraction will be overestimated, as shown in Figure 8. If the actual level of release mortality is low, then the bias caused by assuming tag failures represent fish deaths can lead to substantial overestimates of the release mortality rate. However, the bias can be completely removed if the tags that failed to report are simply eliminated from the analysis (Figure 8).

The duration of the experiment, in terms of days to tag pop off, is also an important consideration. The longer the tag is deployed, the more likely it is to be shed or to malfunction or for the fish to succumb to natural mortality. The implications of the selection of alternative days to pop off in the face of natural mortality, only ($M = 0.3$), are shown in Figures 9 and 10, assuming five days are required for the catch-and-release mortality to be fully expressed and that the experiments involved 25 or 100 tags, respectively. Median estimates for both levels of tagging were below the true value of 0.1, when the duration of the experiment was shorter than the time required for the catch-and-release mortality to be

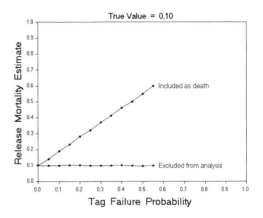

Figure 8. Effect of including tag failures as deaths on the estimates of release mortality.

fully expressed. Median estimates were at, or very close to, the true values when the pop-off day coincided with the time required for the mortality to be fully expressed, but were higher than the true value if the duration of the experiment exceeded the required interval. Inspection of these two figures also reveals an upward trend in the mortality estimates with increasing days to pop off. This is simply the result of the cumulative effect of natural mortality. For the case of experiments using 25 tags and pop off 120 days after tagging, the upper 90% confidence interval is nearly four times higher than the true value.

The computer program developed to implement this study (available from the author) allows for consideration of a very large number of parameter combinations for different possible conditions. Most of the variables that may affect the outcome of the type of experiment considered here would tend to bias the estimates of release mortality upward. An example is given in Figure 11, based on the distribution of estimates for a true release mortality of 0.10 with a 5% tag failure considered as mortality, a tag shedding probability of 5%, a tagging mortality 0.5%, and exposure to natural mortality ($M = 0.15$) for ten days. Five days were required for the catch-and-release mortality to be fully expressed. The value of the true release mortality was not contained in the cumulative frequency distribution of the estimates.

Discussion

The reason to study the percentage of released billfish that die as a result of the catch-and-release expe-

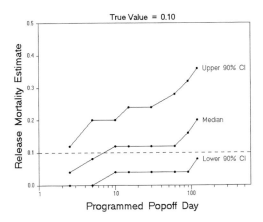

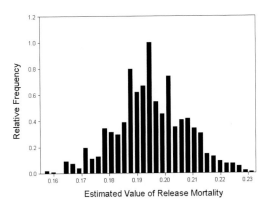

Figure 9. Effect of duration of experiment on the estimate of release mortality for experiments with 25 tags, given a natural mortality of 0.3, where the full expression of the mortality occurred within five days. CL = confidence limit.

Figure 11. Cumulative effect of 5% tag failure, 0.5% tagging mortality, 5% tag shedding, and natural mortality on the distribution of estimates of release mortality for an underlying true rate of 0.10.

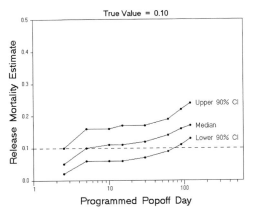

Figure 10. Effect of duration of experiment on the estimate of release mortality for experiments with 100 tags, given a natural mortality of 0.3, where the full expression of the mortality occurred within five days.

rience is to improve the estimates of total removals that will subsequently be reflected in more accurate assessments of the status of the stocks. The results of this study indicate that individual experiments involving fewer than 100 tags have a rather high probability of producing estimates of release mortality that deviate from the true value by more than five percentage points, and by 25% or more of the true value. Obviously, the degree of tolerance for error in the estimate of release mortality depends upon its actual magnitude. If the actual value is zero, and the result of an experiment estimates that one fish in a total catch of 1,000 fish will die, the percentage error is infinite but is of little consequence. On the other hand, if the result of an experiment pro-

vides an estimate of release mortality that, when applied, produces estimates of the number of deaths attributable to a fishery that are substantially in error, both the assessment process and management could be negatively impacted.

It is unclear how the additional mortality from the tagging experience might be separated from the mortality from the catch-and-release experience using data derived from a satellite tagging experiment. Some other experimental design might be utilized for this purpose. However, if the additional mortality attributable to the tagging experience is not estimated then the study result will be ambiguous, unless the total number of postrelease deaths is very close to zero. Unless this is the case, estimates of release mortality rates derived by using this approach will tend to be higher than the true values.

There has been a tendency to ascribe the failures of tags to report to postrelease mortality (tags trapped beneath the carcass of a dead fish, etc.). However, the technology is still quite new, and failures of mechanical or electronic components may also cause a tag not to report. Inclusion of tag failures with those fish considered to have died as a result of the catch-and-release experience will bias the release mortality estimates upwards if the tags fail to report for any reason other than having been attached to a fish that died. This problem will be of particular concern if significant numbers of tags fail to report in an experiment and may contribute significant uncertainty to estimates.

Similar concerns surround the issue of tag shedding. Four of the fifty-seven acoustic tags placed on billfish in the literature summarized by Pepperell et al. (1999) were believed to have fallen off the fish. Any pop-off tags that suffer a similar fate will lack data trends that indicate they are attached to live animals when they report. Absent other information, these tags will most likely be attributed to dead fish. Consequently, tag shedding will also bias estimates of the release mortality rates upwards. Tag shedding, tag failure, and the cumulative impact of natural mortality are all likely to increase with longer intervals between tag application and pop off. All three factors act to bias the release mortality estimates upward. As a consequence, it is important that the duration of experiments to estimate release mortality rates by using pop-off tags be no longer than required for the vast majority of the mortality to be fully expressed. Tag failures produce ambiguous results and should be minimized to the extent possible or eliminated from the analysis where appropriate. These issues will be important decisions in the development of an experimental design for any such study.

It is also noteworthy that the tag requirements for the 90% confidence intervals evaluated in this study are based on the assumption that each tagged fish in the study has the same probability of dying as a result of the catch-and-release experience. In reality, the probability of a fish dying as result of being caught and released can be expected to vary by species, size of the fish, type of gear (e.g., line class for recreational fishermen; and length, set time, set depth for long lines), type of hook (J versus circle, small versus large), type of bait (artificial versus natural; live or dead), skill level of the fishermen or captains involved, and perhaps important environmental variables such as water temperature. A study designed to estimate the average release mortality fraction would either have to include these different modes randomly, so that the result would be representative of the fishery as a whole, or must stratify the study to cover each significant mode of fishing for each species. In this latter case, the average release mortality fraction would be derived from the individual mode estimates weighted by the proportions of the total catch they represent. The latter approach is more realistic but requires identification of all important modes for each species and detailed knowledge of the proportions of total released catch

for each mode as a part of the development of the experimental design.

Although the required number of tags may be significantly reduced by a well thought out experimental design, it is easy to conceive that such an experiment could require the application of tens of thousands of tags. Given that most of the uncontrolled sources of variation will tend to bias the estimates upward, it seems apparent that an important first step should involve the verification of the technology, particularly with respect to tag failures, tag shedding, and assuring that the tagging process itself does not add to the mortality arising from the catch-and-release experience.

Acknowledgments

I thank E. Prince and J. Graves for helpful discussions about the technology and the manuscript. I also thank J. Boreman, S. Christensen, and one anonymous reviewer for their helpful suggestions. This study was supported by The Billfish Foundation. The computer program used to conduct the analyses reported herein can be obtained from the author.

References

Block, B. A., D. T. Booth, and F. G. Carey. 1992. Depth and temperature of the blue marlin *Makaira nigricans* observed by acoustic telemetry. Marine Biology 114:175–183.

Block, B. A., H. Dewar, T. Williams, C. Farwell, and E. D. Prince. 1998. A new satellite technology for tracking the movements of Atlantic bluefin tuna. Proceedings of the National Academy of Science, USA 95:9384–9389.

Edwards, R. E., A. P. McAllister, and B. D. Fortune. 1989. Billfish mortality and survivability. Technical Report Number 8, South Atlantic Fishery Management Council Contribution Number13. Mote Marine Laboratory, Sarasota, Florida.

Gitschlag, G. R., and M. L. Renaud. 1994. Field experiments on survival rates of released red snapper. North American Journal of Fisheries Management 14:131–136.

Holts, D., and D. Bedford. 1990. Activity patterns of striped marlin in the south California Bight. Pages 81–93 *in* R. H. Stroud, editor. Planning the future of billfishes: research and management in the 90s and beyond. Proceedings of the International Billfish Symposium, Kailua-Kona, Hawaii, 9–12 August 1972. Part 2. Contributed Papers: Marine Recreational Fisheries 13.

Jolley, J. W., Jr., and E. W. Irby, Jr. 1979. Survival of tagged and released Atlantic sailfish *Istiophorus platypterus* Istiophoridae determined with acoustical telemetry. Bulletin of Marine Science 29(2):155–169.

Mesnil, B. 1996. When discards survive: accounting for survival of discards in fisheries assessments. Aquatic Living Resources 9:209–215.

Pepperell, J. G., and T. L. O. Davis. 1999. Post-release behaviour of black marlin caught by sport fishermen off the Great Barrier Reef with sportfishing gear. Marine Biology 135(2):369–380.

Render J. H., and C. A. Wilson. 1994. Hook-and-line mortality of caught and released red snapper around oil and gas platform structural habitat. Bulletin of Marine Science 55:1106–1111.

Yuen, H. S. H., A. E. Dizon, and J. H. Uchiyama. 1974. Notes on the tracking of the Pacific blue marlin, *Makaira nigricans*. In R. S. Shomura and R. Williams, editors. Proceedings of the International Billfish Symposium, Kailua-Kona, Hawaii, 9-12 August 1972. Part 2. Review and Contributed Papers: NOAA Technical Report NMFS SSRF-675:2.

American Fisheries Society Symposium 30:180–183, 2002

EXTENDED ABSTRACT

Survival of Juvenile Northern Bluefin Tuna Following Catch and Release, using Ultrasonic Telemetry

RICHARD BRILL, MOLLY LUTCAVAGE,
GREG METZGER, PETER BUSHNELL,
MICHAEL ARENDT, *and* JON LUCY

Current population assessments for northern bluefin tuna *Thunnus thynnus* are based primarily on catch-per-unit effort data from fisheries targeting both adults and juveniles, but remain highly controversial. As a result, aerial surveys have been used for population assessments of adults (Lutcavage et al. 1997), and similar fishery-independent measures of juvenile abundance are considered a priority. Juvenile northern bluefin tuna (formally defined as age-classes 1–5 years, body mass 6–60 kg) appear in the surface waters off the east coast of the United States (from North Carolina to Rhode Island) in June and July (Mather et al. 1995) and present an opportunity for population assessments using aerial surveys. Design of the surveys and interpretation of the data can be significantly improved, however, by an a priori understanding the distribution and behavior of these highly mobile fish in relation to oceanographic conditions (Newlands and Lutcavage 2001). We, therefore, undertook a study of the horizontal and vertical movements of juvenile bluefin tuna using ultrasonic depth-sensitive

Richard Brill, Pelagic Fisheries Research Program, University of Hawaii at Manoa, Honolulu, Hawaii, USA. Email: rbrill@honlab.nmfs.hawaii.edu.

Molly Lutcavage, Edgerton Research Laboratory, New England Aquarium, Central Wharf, Boston, Massachusetts 02110, USA. Email: mlutcavg@neaq.org.

Greg Metzger, Department of Biology, Southampton College, Long Island University, 239 Montauk Highway, Southampton, New York 11968, USA.

Peter Bushnell, Department of Biological Science, Indiana University South Bend, 1700 Mishawaka Avenue, South Bend, Indiana 46634–7111, USA.

Michael Arendt and Jon Lucy, Virginia Sea Grant College Program, Marine Advisory Services, Virginia Institute of Marine Science, Gloucester Point, Virginia 23062, USA. Email: lucy@vims.edu.

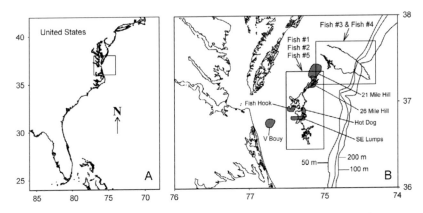

Figure 1. (A) Map of the east coast of the United States. The rectangle shows the area enlarged in panel B. **(B)** Movements of five juvenile bluefin tuna *Thunnus thynnus*. The limit of the continental shelf is shown by the 50 m, 100 m, and 200 m isobath lines. The topographic features considered by local fishermen to aggregate juvenile bluefin tuna are shown by the shaded areas, and names are taken from local fishing charts.

transmitters. Because fish behaviors were monitored continuously for up to 48 hours, we were also able to assess survival following catch and release.

Juvenile bluefin tuna (74–106 cm fork length) were captured using standard recreational trolling gear from the western Atlantic Ocean, near Virginia's eastern shore. Fish were reeled to the surface and brought aboard the tracking vessel using a plastic sling. Once boated, the hook was removed and straight-line fork length measured. A depth-sensitive ultrasonic transmitter (model V32, Vemco, Ltd.) was attached below the second dorsal fin, using two plastic cable ties passed through the dorsal musculature, and the fish was released within about five minutes. Bearing to the tagged fish was determined using a directional hydrophone (model V10 or V11, Vemco, Ltd.) and an ultrasonic receiver (model VR60, Vemco, Ltd.). Fish depth was decoded by the receiver and recorded directly by an attached laptop computer. Geographic location of the tracking vessel was recorded every minute using a second lap top computer connected to a Global Positioning System receiver.

Fish swam 152–289 km within 30–48 hours following release (average speed ≈ 5 km/h). Their courses repeatedly crossed over themselves, so that the distances between start and end points of the tracks were only 8–53 km (Figure 1A, B). Four of the five fish spent the entire time they were followed over the continental shelf in relatively shallow water (generally < 40 m deep; Figure 2). All fish made use of the entire water column, in spite of relatively steep vertical thermal gradients (≈ 24°C at the surface and ≈ 12C°at 40 m depth), but spent the majority of their time (≈ 90%) above 15 m (> 22°C). Although we have no

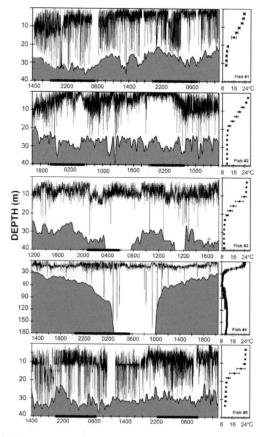

Figure 2. Vertical movements of five juvenile bluefin tuna. Bottom topography is shown by the shaded area, and the heavy horizontal solid bars indicate nighttime. Shown to the right of each vertical movement plot is the temperature (mean ± SEM)—depth data recorded during each track using a Sippican expendable bathythermograph (XBT) system.

direct confirmation, we suspect the frequent vertical movements reflect feeding behaviors for capturing sand lance *Ammodytes* spp., which occur throughout the water column during daylight, can be abundant in the areas where we tracked the fish, and are common prey of juvenile bluefin tuna in this area (Mason 1976; Eggleston and Bochenek 1989).

Based on the cumulative distances traveled and the extensive vertical mobility displayed following release, we surmise that all five fish survived long-term. It should be noted, however, that two additional tuna showed some bleeding from around the mouth and gills while aboard the tracking vessel, due to hook wounds. One was judged too badly injured to be released, and the other was tagged and released but died within two hours. Our observations suggest that juvenile bluefin tuna released from recreational trolling gear survive when hook wounds are not severe and handling time is minimal.

Acknowledgments

This project was funded by a grant from the National Marine Fisheries Service to the Edgerton Research Laboratory, New England Aquarium. RWB's participation was funded through Cooperative Agreements NA37RJ0199 and NA67RJ0154 from the National Oceanic and Atmospheric Administration with the Joint Institute for Marine and Atmospheric Research, University of Hawaii. We gratefully acknowledge Mark Luckenbeck and the staff and students of the Virginia Institute of Marine Science's Eastern Shore Laboratory for their gracious hospitality and extraordinary efforts to make this project a success. The views expressed herein are those of the authors and do not necessarily reflect the views of the National Oceanic and Atmospheric Administration (NOAA) or any of its subagencies. Reference to trade names does not imply endorsement by the National Marine Fisheries Service, NOAA, or the U.S. Department of Commerce.

References

Eggleston, D. B., and E. A. Bochenek. 1989. Stomach contents and parasite infestation of school bluefin tuna *Thunnus thynnus* collected from the Middle Atlantic Bight, Virginia. Fishery Bulletin 88:389–395.

Lutcavage, M., S. Kraus, and W. Hoggard. 1997. Aerial assessment of giant bluefin tuna in the Bahama Banks-Straits of Florida, 1995. Fishery Bulletin 95:300–310.

Mason, J. M. 1976. Food of small, northwestern Atlantic bluefin tuna, *Thunnus thynnus* (L) as ascertained through stomach content analysis. Master's thesis. University of Rhode Island, Kingston, Rhode Island.

Mather, F. J., J. M. Mason, and A. C. Jones. 1995. Historical document: life history and fisheries of Atlantic bluefin tuna. NOAA Technical Memorandum, NMFS-SEFSC-370, Miami, Florida.

Newlands, N., and M. Lutcavage. 2001. From individuals to local populations densities: movements of North Atlantic bluefin tuna (*Thunnus thynnus*) in the Gulf of Maine/northwest Atlantic. Pages 421–443 *in* J. Sibert and J. Nielsen, editors. Electronic tagging and tracking of marine fishes. Kluwer Academic Publishers, Dordrect, The Netherlands.

American Fisheries Society Symposium 30:184–188, 2002

EXTENDED ABSTRACT

Intermediate-Term (6 month) Survival of Adult Tautog Following Catch and Release, Determined by Ultrasonic Telemetry

MICHAEL D. ARENDT *and* JON A. LUCY

Adult tautog *Tautoga onitis* (400–514 mm total length [TL]) were internally tagged with ultrasonic transmitters in order to study seasonal occurrence, site utilization, and daily activity patterns at natural and manmade study sites within areas of known tautog habitat in the lower Chesapeake Bay near Cape Charles, Virginia (Arendt et al. 2001a, 2001b). In addition to these data, catch-and-release survival data were also gathered and are presented in this paper.

Tautog were opportunistically collected using standard two-hook bottom rigs, tagged with ultrasonic transmitters, and released at sites where collected within two hours of capture. Two groups of fish were released: the first (fall group) from 9 November to 8 December 1998 ($n = 19$) and the second (spring group) from 21 April to 9 June 1999 ($n = 14$). The ultrasonic transmitters (V-16–1H-256, Vemco, Ltd.) were surgically implanted into the visceral cavity between the pelvic fins and anus, just dorsal to the ventral midline in 27 male and 6 female tautog. All fish were subdued to level-four anesthesia, using MS-222 (325 mg/L) prior to surgery. Incision closure was made using surgical sutures, staples, and acrylic adhesive glue. Antibiotics (0.5 mL) were administered intramuscularly near the base of the caudal peduncle. All surgical procedures and materials were sterile and aseptic, and procedures were approved by the Research on Animal Subjects Committee at the College of William and Mary. Anesthesia, surgery, and revival of tagged tautog lasted approximately 20 minutes. Tautog were released within 15 minutes, after recovery from surgery.

Michael D. Arendt, Marine Resources Research Institute, Marine Resources Division, South Carolina Department of Natural Resources, 217 Fort Johnson Road, Charleston, South Carolina 29422–2559, USA. Email: arendtm@mrd.dnr.state.sc.us.

Jon A. Lucy, Sea Grant Marine Advisory Program, Virginia Institute of Marine Science, 1208 Greate Road, Gloucester Point, Virginia 23062, USA. Email: lucy@vims.edu.

Table 1. Survival status of ultrasonically tagged adult tautog (*n* = 33, 400–514 mm TL) in lower Chesapeake Bay. See text for detailed description of survival assuredness scenarios.

Scenario	n	Observation period	Days of VR1 data	Days detected
1	9	Nov 1998 – Nov 1999	59–157	115–212
2	9	Nov 1998 – Jun 1999	159–187	
3	3	Dec 1998 – Apr 1999	69, 100, 129	
4	3	Jun 1999 – Nov 1999	59, 105, 105	126, 138, 138
5	3	Nov 1998 – Nov 1999	11, 161, 166	
6	6	Dec 1998 – Nov 1999		9, 34–64, 175

Two transmitter versions were used. Random repeat-code (RCODE) transmitters emitted signals randomly between 45 and 75 seconds. Two submerged automated acoustic receivers (VR1, Vemco, Ltd.) were moored at each of four study sites, providing 24 hour coverage at sites between November 1998 and October 1999. Receivers recorded the identification number of the fish and the date and time that the fish was detected. Fixed-rate signal versions (FCODE) of the transmitter emitted signals every 6–12 seconds and enabled physical positions of tagged fish to be determined. Positional 'fixes' were obtained using a surface receiver (VR60, Vemco, Ltd.) and a directional hydrophone (V10, Vemco, Ltd.).

Twenty-seven tautog (22 males, 5 females) were tagged and released with RCODE transmitters and six tautog (5 males, 1 female) with FCODE transmitters. Postrelease recovery periods were determined for RCODE tautog, based on irregular detection patterns recorded by VR1 receivers prior to the onset of a regular, diurnal detection pattern (Arendt and Lucy 2000). Postrelease recovery (mean ± std. dev.) was 3.5 ± 1.5 days (range, 1.5–7.4 d) for 15 RCODE tautog in fall 1998 and 2.0 ± 1.9 days (range, 1–6.8 d) for 11 RCODE tautog in spring 1999 (Arendt 1999). Survival times were conservatively determined for six scenarios that progressed from recaptured fish to periodic detection of tagged fish without continuous VR1 receiver data (Table 1). Postrelease survival was documented for 9–187 days and 11–212 days for fall and spring-released tautog, respectively.

Nine tautog were recaptured 115–212 days after release (scenario 1). Two tautog released in fall 1998 were recaptured 2.2–10.2 km away from release sites by commercial fishing gears (crab pot, gill net) in spring 1999. Seven tautog released in spring 1999, including one FCODE tautog for which no VR1 data were collected, were recaptured at release sites by recreational fishers in fall 1999. Necropsy examination of eight tautog recaptured revealed good incision closure, encapsulation of transmitters in intestinal mesentery, and no evidence of internal tissue trauma or organ dysfunction. One tautog recaptured in a crab pot in spring 1999 appeared malnourished, and no food items were found in the stomach; however, this tautog may have been trapped in the crab pot for as long as three days. All tautog recaptured in fall 1999 by recreational fishers put up strong fights, were fat, and their stomachs contained a variety of food items including crabs, bryozoans, and blue mussel. VR1 receivers recorded diel activity (Figure 1), and thus survival, for these seven tautog 59–157 days prior to their recapture.

The VR1 receiver data, collected for the duration of transmitter battery life for tautog released in fall 1998 (scenario 2), recorded diel activity, and thus survival, of nine tautog for 157–187 days after release. Three additional RCODE tautog released in fall 1998 were only detected 69, 100, and 129 days following release (scenario 3). It was unclear if these fish moved away from release sites and did not return, if transmitters failed, or if fish were involuntarily removed from release sites and not reported. Receiver data were not collected for the duration of transmitter battery life for tautog released in spring 1999 (scenario 4). Receiver data, and thus survival, were recorded for three tautog released in spring 1999 for 59, 105, and 105 days after release; however, these three tautog were also detected at release sites using the VR60 receiver 126, 138, and 138 days after release, respectively. Two tautog released in fall 1998, and one tautog released in spring 1999, moved away and returned to release sites or were detected away from release sites 11, 161, and 166 days after release (scenario 5).

Minimal activity data were collected for six tautog, although there was no reason to suspect that these fish did not survive (scenario 6). Five FCODE tautog were detected at release sites over a period of 9–64 days following release, and one RCODE tautog was detected at the release site or at another site 2.2 km south of the release site over a period of 175 days. Positional 'fixes' were periodically obtained for three FCODE tautog released in fall 1998 for up to 9–21 days following release. Although the majority of these 'fixes' were obtained during the postrelease recovery period, these 'fixes' document some movement, and thus survival, for these three tautog.

Postrelease survival was documented for 9–187 days for 19 tautog released in fall 1998 and for 11–212 days for 14 tautog released in spring 1999. Survival times were conservatively determined using a scale of assuredness that progressed from recaptured fish to periodic detection of tagged fish without continuous VR1 receiver data. High survival rates for tautog tagged and released with ultrasonic transmitters corroborate high short-term survival (98%; $n = 294$ of 299 surviving) for tautog caught at the same sites and retained in wire cages on the seafloor for 2–15 days prior to release (Lucy and Arendt 1999). Long-term survival (19–737 d) of tautog at these specific sites is also documented for

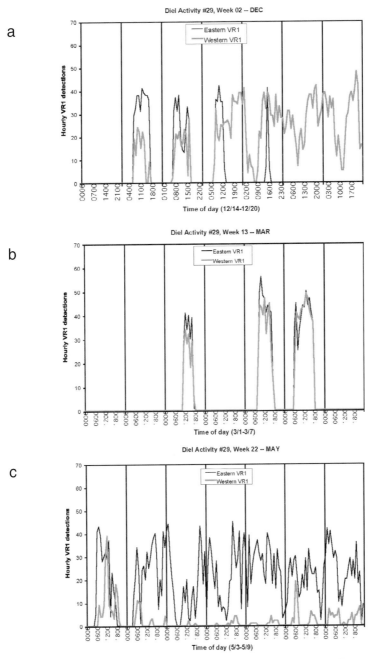

Figure 1. Weekly VR1 receiver detection records for a single recaptured tautog (at-large 7 December 1998–19 May 1999) in fall (a), winter (b), and spring (c). Diel detection patterns were used to infer activity, and thus survival, of tautog at sites monitored by receivers.

24 tautog (8% recapture rate) recaptured after being released from wire cages, including one tautog recaptured after 19 days, tagged and released with an ultrasonic transmitter, monitored by VR1 receivers, and recaptured again 164 days later. Short and long-term survival (0–1,214 d) is also documented for 708 tautog (14.8% recapture rate) tagged, released, and recaptured at various sites in the lower Chesapeake Bay and adjacent coastal Virginia waters through the Virginia Game Fish Tagging Program (VGFTP) between 1995 and 1999 (Lucy et al. 2000). Tag-recapture data for the VGFTP also include one tautog tagged, released, and recaptured at the same site where released after 34 days and, then, tagged and released with an ultrasonic transmitter as part of this study. This tautog was subsequently monitored at this same site for 67 days, then detected again during visits to this site over a 58-day period, after removal of VR1 receivers from this site.

References

Arendt, M. D. 1999. Seasonal residence, movement, and activity patterns of adult tautog, *Tautoga onitis*, in lower Chesapeake Bay. M.S. Thesis, School of Marine Science, College of William and Mary/VIMS, Gloucester Point, Virginia.

Arendt, M. D., and J. A. Lucy. 2000. Recovery period, and survival of ultrasonically tagged adult tautog in the Lower Chesapeake Bay using automated receivers. Pages 117–125 *in* J. H. Eiler, D. J. Alcorn, and M. R. Neuman, editors. Biotelemetry 15: proceeding of the 15th International Symposium on Biotelemetry. Juneau, Alaska, USA. International Society on Biotelemetry, Wageningen, The Netherlands.

Arendt, M. D., J. A. Lucy, and D. A. Evans. 2001a. Diel and seasonal activity patterns of adult tautog, Ta*utoga onitis*, in lower Chesapeake Bay, inferred from ultrasonic telemetry. Environmental Biology of Fishes 62:379–391.

Arendt, M. D., J. A. Lucy, and T. A. Munroe. 2001b. Seasonal occurrence and site utilization patterns of adult tautog, *Tautoga onitis* (Labridae) at manmade and natural structures in lower Chesapeake Bay. Fishery Bulletin 99:519–527.

Lucy, J. A., and M. D. Arendt. 1999. Exploratory field evaluation of hook-release mortality in tautog (*Tautoga onitis*) in Lower Chesapeake Bay, Virginia. Virginia Marine Resource Report 99-10, VSG 99-14, Gloucester Point, Virginia.

Lucy, J. A., M. D. Arendt, and C. M. Bain, III. 2000. Virginia game fish tagging program. 1999. Annual report. Virginia Marine Resource Report No. 2000-04, VSG-00-07. Gloucester Point, Virginia.

American Fisheries Society Symposium 30:189–194, 2002

EXTENDED ABSTRACT

A Pneumatic Cradle for Handling and Tagging of Wahoo and other Large Pelagic Fishes

ANSON NASH, JOHN WHITING, *and*
BRIAN E. LUCKHURST[1]

The Bermuda Division of Fisheries commenced a study in 1995 of the fishery biology of various pelagic species taken around the island by both commercial and recreational anglers. The most important of these pelagic species is the wahoo *Acanthocybium solandri*, which has had the highest landings of any species in the commercial fishery since the mid-1980s. These landings have shown a generally increasing trend over time and peaked in 1997 at 105 mt (Luckhurst and Trott 2000).

The research program on wahoo involves basic fishery biological sampling, including size (fork length), weight, sex, stage of gonadal development, and tissue sampling for genetics analysis. In addition, the sagittal otoliths (earbones) are extracted for use in an age and growth analysis. An initial examination of the sagittal otoliths has revealed a complex microstructure with few clear marks that can be used for aging purposes (Luckhurst et al. 1997).

Wahoo are generally considered to be a highly migratory species, but there is very little data available to assess movement patterns, due to the paucity of wahoo tagging that has been conducted in the region. One aspect of this research program is a scientific tagging study to examine the possibility that Bermuda may have a resident population of wahoo and/or that wahoo exhibit migratory behavior in the tropical western Atlantic, which includes the Bermuda seamount. In order to handle specimens safely at sea, we designed and built a cradle for the handling and tagging of wahoo, as an essential component of this research program. The challenge was to produce a design that would allow the safe and

Anson Nash, John Whiting, and Brian E. Luckhurst, Bermuda Division of Fisheries, Post Office Box CR 52, Crawl CR BX, Bermuda

[1]*Corresponding author: bluckhurst@bdagov.bm*

efficient handling of a species that is known for its formidable set of teeth, while allowing researchers to measure, tag, and sample.

Wahoo are captured by trolling with live bait or with an artificial lure using rod and reel. Fish are fought to the vessel as quickly as possible, so as not to exhaust the fish before tagging and release. A captured specimen (Figure 1) is guided into the tagging cradle using a 3-m long fiberglass tube, with a slit in the tube for the fishing line, deployed over the stern of the vessel (Figure 2), through which the specimen is pulled once the fish is fought to the vessel. This prevents the fish from being injured while being brought aboard. The cradle design incorporates a new innovation that allows researchers to handle specimens with a greater degree of control through the use of an adjustable air bladder built into the cradle. Specimens can be positioned directly in the cradle when they are pulled out of the tube and constrained by the inflation of the air bladder, which allows for more efficient handling of specimens for accurate tag placement, injection, and measurement.

The cradle consists of a 1.2-m length of 30-cm diameter polyvinyl chloride (PVC) water pipe attached to an aluminum base frame provided with handles (Figure 3). The top half of the pipe is divided into three hinged sections that are secured to the bottom half of the pipe with Velcro straps. The cradle is lined with 2.5-cm thick insulation foam covered with a smooth, white PVC material (Herculite). The air bladder is fitted between the bottom half of the pipe, and the foam and is provided with a through-hull, quick-release fitting, which accepts a hose attached to a bellows-type foot pump used to inflate the bladder. Air pressure is maintained with the foot pump in the 35–60 millibar range and is monitored using the low-pressure dial gauge (Figure 3). There is an adjustable plate, which rotates into place to allow the positioning of the head for the measurement of fork length. A hose connected to the wash-down pump on the research vessel is placed into the mouth to ensure that the gills remain moist during tagging. The selected section of the cradle (usually the middle section) can be opened to allow for tagging (Figure 4) and oxytetracycline (OTC) injection. Tagged fish are injected to produce a mark on the otoliths, which can be viewed under ultraviolet light with a microscope. These marks can be used in validating estimates of age when the fish is recaptured and the otolith is examined. When sampling is completed, the nose plate is rotated away and the hook is removed. The hose fitting for the foot pump is disconnected, which allows the air bladder to deflate. The cradle is then carried to the gunnel of the vessel, and the specimen is released head first into the sea, using the cradle as a chute. This procedure from bringing the fish on board to releasing it normally took less than two minutes.

Figure 1. Captured wahoo being guided into the fiberglass tube.

Figure 2. Fiberglass tube deployed over the stern of the research vessel to pull the wahoo directly into the tagging cradle on deck.

To date, we have successfully tagged and released 15 wahoo. The initial validation of this tagging system was demonstrated when the first tagged wahoo was recaptured after 10 months at liberty. This specimen was originally tagged and released (weighing 5 kg) off the northeast point of the Bermuda reef platform and was recaptured (weighing 15 kg) on Challenger Bank, to the southwest of the island. This represents very rapid growth in this specimen and provides some of the first documentary evidence of the growth rate of wahoo. The minimum distance moved by this specimen was approximately 64 km, but it is unknown whether the specimen remained in Bermuda waters during its time at liberty.

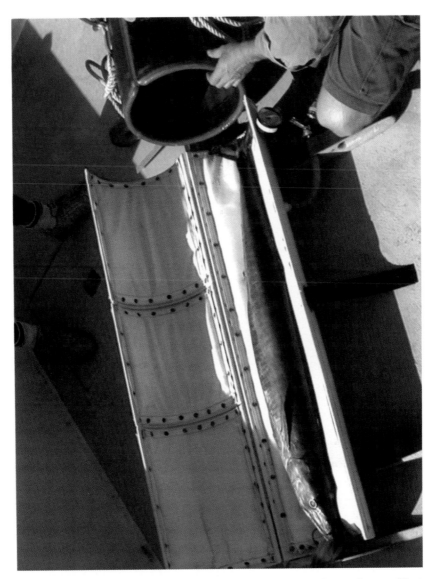

Figure 3. Pneumatic tagging cradle with hinged top sections, hose for attachment of foot pump to inflate the air bladder, and pressure gauge.

We have also tested the cradle by tagging small (5–6 kg) yellowfin tuna *Thunnus albacares* and blackfin tuna *T. atlanticus*. This tagging program will continue over the next several years, and we hope that the use of this tagging system will help to increase survivorship of tagged specimens and allow us to learn more about the growth and movements of these important pelagic species.

Figure 4. Wahoo being tagged with center section of tagging cradle open.

References

Luckhurst, B. E., J. M. Dean, M. Reichert, M. Cameron, S. Manuel, and T. Trott. 1997. Use of microstructure analysis of the sagittal otoliths to estimate age of the wahoo *Acanthocybium solandri* from Bermuda. Proceedings of the Gulf and Caribbean Fisheries Institute 49:64–70.

Luckhurst, B. E., and T. Trott. 2000. Bermuda's commercial line fishery for Wahoo and Dolphinfish. 1987-97: landings, seasonality and catch per unit effort trends. Proceedings of the Gulf and Caribbean Fisheries Institute 51:404–413.

American Fisheries Society Symposium 30:195–198, 2002

EXTENDED ABSTRACT

Virginia Game Fish Tagging Program: Trained Anglers Making a Contribution to Fisheries Research, Management, and Conservation

JON A. LUCY, CLAUDE M. BAIN III,
and MICHAEL D. ARENDT

Initiated in 1995, the Virginia Game Fish Tagging Program (VGFTP) is a cooperative project of the Virginia Marine Resources Commission and the Virginia Institute of Marine Science (VIMS) funded primarily from Virginia's saltwater recreational fishing license revenues. The program has three objectives: to provide a quality tagging program involving trained anglers in developing a database which enhances understanding and management of fish species important to the state's marine recreational fisheries; to educate anglers about what can be learned from tagging programs as well as programs' limitations; and to update or collect previously unavailable tagging data on selected finfish in Virginia's coastal waters.

To keep the program manageable, participation is currently limited to less than 200 anglers. Participants must attend one of four training workshops held annually before receiving any tagging equipment and must renew their registration each year to remain active. If anglers either lose interest in tagging or cease fishing regularly, the annual registration requirement provides a simple mechanism for anglers to leave the program, making way for new participants.

Jon A. Lucy, Sea Grant Marine Advisory Program, Virginia Institute of Marine Science, Gloucester Point, Virginia 23062, USA. Phone (804) 684-7166, Fax (804) 684-7161, Email: lucy@vims.edu

Claude M. Bain, III, Virginia Saltwater Fishing Tournament, Virginia Marine Resources Commission, 968 Oriole Drive South, Virginia Beach, Virginia 23451, USA. Phone (757) 491-5160, Fax (757) 491-5172, email: mrcswt@visi.net

Michael D. Arendt, Marine Resources Research Institute, South Carolina Marine Resources Division, Post Office Box 12559 Charleston, South Carolina 29422-2559, USA. Phone (843) 406-4066, Fax (843) 762-5110, Email: arendtm@mrd.dnr.state.sc.us

Workshops highlight fish recaptures during the past year and recent uses of the database by researchers and fishery managers. Instructing participants on proper fish handling and tagging techniques, coordinators discuss the rationale for specific practices and provide detailed handouts on proper tag placement, maintenance of tagging equipment (tagging guns and T-bar tags), and recording/reporting tagged fish data. Experienced taggers, many of whom attend the workshops, share information on any tagging and data problems encountered in the field, helping to resolve such issues efficiently.

New participants practice inserting tags in fresh, dead fish before receiving tagging equipment. Working in small groups, sometimes with experienced taggers, new participants find the hands-on sessions produce a level of confidence important to their progressing toward effective tagging under fishing conditions. Overseeing the sessions helps coordinators maintain consistency in tagging practices, a constant concern for angler-assisted tagging programs (Loftus et al. 2000).

The T-bar tag (Hallprint, Ltd.), having a 1 mm (0.04 inch) diameter anchor section, and the small size of the tagging needle (19 mm [0.75 inches] long, 2 mm [0.08 inches] diameter) minimize fish tagging trauma. Fish under 254 mm (10 inches) total length (TL) typically are not tagged. Concerning tag retention rates (using 7–14 day flow-through tank studies), the T-bar tag has out performed single barb, nylon dart tags in tautog *Tautoga onitis* and weakfish *Cynoscion regalis* while demonstrating 100% retention in spotted seatrout *Cynoscion nebulosus*.

As of 1999, the VGFTP targeted eight species (Table 1). A major strength of the program is its flexibility to take advantage of sudden increases in abundance of species for which little or no tagging data exist in area waters (Lucy and Davy 2000), i.e., weakfish in 1996, black sea bass *Centropristis striata* and red drum *Sciaenops ocellatus* in 1997. Fish recapture rates have ranged from 8 to 16% for all but weakfish and spotted seatrout (Table 1). Exhibiting only a 1% recapture rate, weakfish was dropped from the program in 2000. Spotted seatrout, of special interest to anglers, remains in the program. Recaptures are reported by telephone, the majority being from anglers but also from commercial fishers. Persons reporting recaptured fish receive a thank you letter (detailing the fish's length, tagging location and date) along with a cap or VGFTP decal as a reward for reporting the fish.

Special conservation certificates are annually awarded participants tagging at least 25 fish per year, with the proportion of such anglers increasing from 25% in 1997–1998, to 33% during 1999 (Lucy et al. 2000). Plaques are also awarded annually to anglers tagging the most fish for each program species. To reinforce quality tagging, participants having 10 or more of their tagged fish recaptured during a given year also receive special recognition.

Table 1. Tagging effort and recapture results for the VGFTP, 1995–1999.

Species	Number tagged	Number recaptured	Recapture Rate
Black drum *Pogonias cromis*	642	57	9%
Black sea bass *Centropristis striata*	5,345	867	16%
Cobia *Rachycentron canadum*	363	45	12%
Weakfish (Gray Trout) *Cynoscion regalis*	8,979	64	1%
Red drum *Sciaenops ocellatus*	2,222	278	12%
Spadefish *Chaetodipterus faber*	1,592	129	8%
Spotted seatrout *Cynoscion nebulosus*	2,470	74	3%
Tautog *Tautoga onitis*	4,764	708	15%

Program data are proving useful to fishery researchers and managers as indicated by the following examples. Data were used in developing the Tautog Fishery Management Plan (ASMFC 1996), especially regarding size distribution of fish released in the southern area fishery. Virginia tautog recaptures documented fish 279–457 mm (11–18 in) TL which had largely remained on various sites inside Chesapeake Bay throughout the year, possibly even over multiple years, unlike seasonal inshore-offshore movements demonstrated for larger fish (> 305 mm [12 inches] TL) in New York and Rhode Island waters (Olla et al. 1974). Tag return data also supported estimates of lower fishing mortality in the Virginia fishery compared to areas north of New Jersey (White et al. 1997).

Single and multiple recapture events for tautog, black sea bass, red drum, Atlantic spadefish *Chaetodipterus faber*, and cobia *Rachycentron canadum* suggest strong seasonal, and even year-to-year affinity for Chesapeake Bay and adjacent coastal sites. Cobia recaptures of 96–132 cm (38–52 in) TL fish, known to spawn during summer in Chesapeake Bay, indicate such fish, while ranging in winter as far south as Florida, likely return regularly to the Bay over periods of at least one to four years. Multiple recaptures of the referenced species also indicate a high tolerance for hook-and-line capture and release practices and, thereby, the likelihood of low release mortalities for the species in Virginia's fisheries.

Late summer-fall migration of drum and trout species from Virginia waters has been consistently demonstrated, with fish moving along North Carolina beaches towards Oregon Inlet and into Pamlico Sound, as well as south of Cape Hatteras. Red drum and black drum *Pogonias cromis* (254–406 mm [10–16 in] TL), tagged in lower Chesapeake Bay and within Virginia Beach's Rudee Inlet (ocean inlet south of the Bay mouth), occasionally exhibit rapid southward movement. Recaptures of such fish from Kitty Hawk/Nags Head and Oregon Inlet

(North Carolina) beaches have occurred within 1, 5, 7, and 16 days following release.

The program continues to enhance and expand understanding of the dynamics of Virginia's coastal fisheries using trained anglers in a cost-effective way to collect new data that would likely otherwise not be obtainable. Benefits accrue both to anglers and the fisheries on which they depend (Lucy and Davy 2000).

References

ASMFC (Atlantic States Marine Fisheries Commission). 1996. Fishery management plan for tautog, Report 25. ASMFC, Washington, D.C.

Loftus, A. J., J. Waldon. V. Fay, K. Davy, and J. Lucy. 2000. Overview of angler-based tagging programs, and management issues. Fisheries 25(4):8–13.

Lucy, J. A., M. D. Arendt, and C. M. Bain, III. 2000. Virginia game fish tagging program annual report. 1999. Virginia Institute of Marine Science, College of William and Mary. Virginia Marine Resource Report Number 2000-04.

Lucy, J. A., and K. B. Davy. 2000. Benefits of angler-assisted tag, and release programs. Fisheries 25(4):18–22.

Olla, B. L., A. J. Bejda, and A. D. Martin. 1974. Daily activity, movements, feeding, and seasonal occurrence in the tautog, *Tautoga onitis*. Fishery Bulletin 72 (1):27–35.

White, G. G., J. E. Kirkely, and J. A. Lucy. 1997. Quantitative assessment of fishing mortality for tautog (*Tautog onitis*) in Virginia. Preliminary report to Virginia Marine Resources Commission, Newport News, Virginia. Department of Fisheries Science and Marine Advisory Program, Virginia Institute of Marine Science, College of William and Mary.

Angler Attitudes and Behavior

American Fisheries Society Symposium 30:201–204, 2002

EXTENDED ABSTRACT

The Discourse about Catch and Release in Recreational Fishing in Europe: Implications for North America

ØYSTEIN AAS, CAROL E. THAILING,
and ROBERT B. DITTON

The term "catch-and-release fishing," defined as angling where all fish caught are released, has various meanings for anglers, conservationists, managers, scientists, and politicians. This paper presents and discusses alternative perspectives of catch and release in Europe. The discourse on catch and release in Europe is multifaceted with evidence of much contentiousness between anglers, biologists, and fishery managers. Instead of studying the extent and character of catch-and-release fishing in Europe (a Europe-wide angler survey would be required to achieve this), we have sought perspectives from nongovernmental organizations and governmental agencies.

Content analysis, as described by Weber (1990), was used to identify the underlying meanings attributed to catch-and-release fishing, as reported and discussed throughout Europe. The sample text for analysis was drawn from available literature using general current periodicals. The population sampled was not restricted to any particular group of journals but included both social and natural science resources. This was further extended by including European contacts identified by either their personal involvement in or listing on the American Fisheries Society (AFS) Committee on the Human Dimensions of Recreational Fisheries, the European Inland Fisheries Advisory Commission (EIFAC), and the Food and Agriculture Organization of the United Nations (FAO). The first

Øystein Aas, Norwegian Institute for Nature Research, Fakkelgarden, N-2624 Lillehammer, Norway. Email: Oystein.Aas@nina.no

Carol E. Thailing, Fermata, Inc., Post Office Box 5485, Austin, Texas 78763-5485, USA. Email: carolt@io.com

Robert B. Ditton, Department of Wildlife and Fisheries Sciences, Texas A&M University, College Station, Texas 77843-2258, USA. Email: rditton@unix.tamu.edu

organization was chosen to highlight social scientists, while the latter two were used to sample fisheries managers and scientists in the European community. Due to time, language, resource, and funding constraints, this effort relied heavily on literature, including translations available in English from European countries where our sources were located: Finland, Norway, Scotland, Germany, Belgium, the Czech Republic, Northern Ireland, England, and Wales. To maintain a unified perspective of the text, entire documents were analyzed instead of isolated sections. Text was analyzed to determine which key terminology was present and how that terminology was being used throughout the text (Weber 1990). Values were not attributed based solely on word frequency counts because of the various contexts in which words such as "recreational," "fishing," and "angling" were presented, as well as the multiple interpretations of these words (Weber 1990). Synonyms, words similar in meaning or representing similar ideas, were grouped categorically.

The results demonstrate that the European discourse concerning catch and release is characterized by complex and multifaceted arguments, in which most themes of concern are used both to support and oppose this practice. For some in Europe, catch and release is an unethical and reprehensible fishing practice. For others, catch-and-release fishing is both an ethical and a sustainable approach to resource management. There are groups both pro and con catch and release in most countries studied. In some countries, the practice of catch and release gains increasing support, primarily in northern countries with coldwater game fisheries (i.e., the British Isles, Norway, and Sweden). In other areas, the best example being parts of Germany, catch and release of fish above minimum size is prohibited (Berg and Rösch 1998).

Content analysis revealed notable systematic regional differences (Table 1). In east-central mainland Europe, the focus seems to be on the formal regulations related to fishing and the treatment of the catch. This is not unexpected, based on the strong bureaucratic and regulation traditions in former Eastern Europe countries. In England, Northern Ireland, and Scotland, the greatest focus is on the conservation and management aspects related to catch and release (i.e., the conservation effect and eventual mortality problems). Subsistence aspects seem to be strongest in northern countries like Norway and Finland, with a more rural culture. Another difference that emerged was that between representatives for authorities on one side and angler organizations on the other. Authorities were generally more skeptical of catch and release, compared with angler organizations. International organizations or bodies (i.e., NASCO) were often neutral to catch and release, underlining the voluntary aspect and the need to take into account different national cultures and traditions, in combination with varying biological needs and effects of catch and release (NASCO undated).

Table 1. Six most prominent themes related to catch and release perceptions found in the European literature.

Rank	Finland	Norway	Scotland	England and Wales
1	Welfare	Recreation	Conservation	Conservation
2	Mortality	Subsistence	Regulatory	Management
3	Management	Welfare	Management	Regulatory
4	Regulatory	Mortality	Resource	Mortality
5	Resource	Ethics	Sport/Game	Resource
6	Conservation	Management	Mortality	License

Rank	Northern Ireland	Belgium	Czech Republic	Germany
1	Mortality	Recreation	Regulations	Welfare
2	Recreation	Resource	License	Regulatory
3	Conservation	Management	Keeping	License
4	Resource	Conservation	Recreation	Skills/Training
5	Management	License	Sport/Game	Mortality
6	Regulatory	Regulatory	Conservation	Recreation

The different perspectives of catch and release in the European countries studied may be attributable to cultural differences in the conduct and meaning of recreational fishing in these countries (Aas and Kaltenborn 1995). In countries (e.g., Norway and Finland) where fishing is mainly about harvesting fish, catch and release, and its challenge, sport, and adventure benefits are viewed by some groups as antithetical. Other groups often view these perspectives as complementary and want to combine the opportunity to harvest fish with catch and release, in certain situations. In other countries (e.g., Scotland, Belgium, the Czech Republic), where fishing is about harvest as well as the challenge and sport involved in hooking and landing fish, catch and release is more likely to be seen as an appropriate solution for anglers to lessen their impacts on fish populations. Another possible explanation for the observed differences is the generally strong involvement from the veterinary profession in this discussion in several countries (Berg and Rösch 1998; Norwegian Advisory Board on Animal Welfare Issues 1998). Animal welfare issues seem to be a more prominent theme among veterinarians, compared with fish biologists.

The growth of common rules and regulations within the European Union (EU) in many areas, including veterinary issues and animal welfare, raises the question of whether the union will establish regulations regarding catch and release that are obligatory for member countries. With a closer analysis of the

EU countries in this study, very different views on the issue among EU countries become apparent. In addition, the intergovernmental North Atlantic Salmon Conservation Organization (NASCO), with a strong EU representation, has a pragmatic and conservation-oriented view on catch and release (NASCO undated). This suggests that an EU decision prohibiting catch and release in general is not probable. The above-presented views might also characterize common attitudes of recreational fishing participants in the United States today. Some in the United States, perhaps the majority, think fishing is about capturing fish for extrinsic purposes, whereas the remainder know how to catch fish but choose to take a conservative approach with regard to fishery resources, while at the same time emphasizing the intrinsic benefits of fishing. The difference is that, in Europe, some governments are legitimizing traditional approaches that emphasize catch and kill only and rejecting alternate approaches that emphasize the "fishing experience" and a conservative approach to harvesting to promote resource sustainability.

Further analysis of European literature, as well as additional European contacts, are needed to more completely understand the perceptions of catch-and-release fishing in Europe and how attitudes towards catch and release change over time. Such knowledge is needed to guide management decisions, which most likely must reflect diverse and differing attitudes towards catch and release among various angler segments, in the near future.

References

Aas, Ø., and B. P. Kaltenborn. 1995. Consumptive orientation of anglers in Engerdal, Norway. Environmental Management 19:751–761.

Berg, R., and R. Rösch. 1998. Animal welfare and angling in Baden-Württemberg, Germany. Pages 88–92 in P. Hickley and H. Tompkins, editors. Recreational fisheries. Social, economic and management Aspects. Fishing News Books/Blackwell Scientific Publications Scientific/Food and Agricultural Organization of the United Nations/European Inland Fisheries Advisory Committee.

NASCO (North Atlantic Salmon Conservation Organization). Undated. Guidelines on catch and release. Brochure published by NASCO (An intergovernmental commission consisting of the USA, Canada, Denmark (on behalf of Faroe Islands, and Greenland), the European Union, Iceland, Norway, and Russia). NASCO headquarter, Edinburgh, United Kingdom.

Norwegian Advisory Board on Animal Welfare Issues. 1998. Consideration: angling –catch-and-release practice. Unpublished report. Oslo, Norway.

Weber, R. 1990. Basic content analysis: 2nd edition. The Sage University Papers Series, volume 49. Sage Publications, Inc., California.

American Fisheries Society Symposium 30:205–207, 2002

EXTENDED ABSTRACT

Understanding Catch-and-Release Behavior among U.S. Atlantic Bluefin Tuna Anglers

STEPHEN G. SUTTON *and* ROBERT B. DITTON

With the increased popularity of catch-and-release angling, there is a growing need to better understand the social, psychological, and demographic characteristics of anglers who chose to participate in this type of fishing. In this paper, we investigate the relationship between catch-and-release participation by bluefin tuna anglers and two sub-dimensions of specialization hypothesized to explain catch-and-release behavior among marine anglers: commitment to angling, and consumptive orientation. We also investigate the relationship between catch-and-release behavior and a number of demographic variables (gender, age, income, and years of education) and situational variables (angling party size, hours fished, number of tuna caught, and whether another species of tuna was retained) thought to influence an angler's decision to practice catch and release. Data are from a survey of Atlantic bluefin tuna *Thunnus thynnus* anglers fishing off the coast of Hatteras, North Carolina, in 1997 (Ditton et al. 1998). Catch-and-release behavior was measured by a dichotomous variable that indicated whether a bluefin tuna had been retained by the angler's fishing party on the day it was sampled.

Buchanan (1985) defined commitment as "the pledging or binding of an individual to behavioral acts" and identified at least two components that influence the degree to which an individual becomes bound to an activity. The first, persistence of goal-directed behavior over time, implies a willingness to devote time and effort to the activity and will likely result in decreased interest in and opportunity for participation in other recreational activities. An index of persistence of fishing behavior over time was created by combining four variables that measure previous fishing experience and avidity: total number of years fishing, total number of years fishing for bluefin tuna, total number of days fished during the previous 12 months, and total number of days fished in salt water

Stephen G. Sutton and Robert B. Ditton, Department of Wildlife and Fisheries Sciences, Texas A&M University, 2258 Texas A&M University, College Station, Texas 77843–2258, USA

during the previous 12 months. The second component of commitment, affective attachment, reflects the importance of the activity to the individual's self-concept. A high affective attachment to fishing provides a motivation to continue participating in fishing in the future. A measure of affective attachment was created by combining four variables that reflect the importance of fishing to the individual: importance of fishing related to other outdoor activities, number of fishing-related magazine subscriptions, number of fishing-related organization memberships, and self-perceived level of fishing ability. A positive relationship between the two components of commitment and catch-and-release behavior is hypothesized.

Consumptive orientation is defined as the degree to which an angler values the catch-related outcomes of the angling experience. Graefe (1980) suggests that consumptive orientation consists of at least four dimensions representing number of fish caught, importance of catching something, keeping fish, and the challenge/trophy aspects of fishing. Consumptive orientation was measured by asking anglers to rate their level of agreement with 16 statements related to various catch-related aspects of fishing. Related items were grouped and summed to create separate indices for each dimension. Anglers who place low importance on dimensions of consumptive orientation should be more likely to practice catch and release because fishing satisfaction for these anglers is not highly dependent on catching and/or keeping fish.

Results of a logistic regression analysis to test the effects of the independent variables on catch-and-release behavior are presented in Table 1. For the commitment to fishing variables, the probability of releasing all bluefin tuna was positively related to affective attachment but was not significantly related to the extent to which fishing behavior persists over time. For the consumptive orientation variables, the probability of releasing all tuna was negatively related

Table 1. Results of the logistic regression analysis to test the effects of the commitment, consumptive orientation, situational, and demographic variables on catch-and-release behavior. Only those variables found to be significant were included in the final model.

Parameter	Estimate	P-value	Odds ratio
Intercept	-0.135	0.851	
Affective attachment	0.121	0.007	1.29
Importance of keeping fish	-0.109	0.036	0.89
Number of tuna caught	-0.039	0.005	0.96
Fishing party size	-0.273	0.001	0.76
Gender	1.254	0.021	3.50

Number of observations = 398 (release = 97; retain = 301)
Model chi-square = 38.3
Model p-value < 0.0001
Percent concordance = 69.5%

to the importance attached to keeping fish, but was not related to the impor-tance attached to the number of fish caught, catching something, or the trophy/challenge aspects of fishing. For the demographic variables, the proba-bility of releasing all tuna was greater for female anglers than for male anglers, but was not related to anglers' age, level of income, or education level. For the situational variables, the probability of releasing all tuna was negatively related to fishing party size and number of tuna caught, but was unrelated to hours fished or whether another species of tuna had been retained by the group that day.

Study results suggest that anglers for whom fishing is an integral part of their lifestyle are motivated to practice catch and release as a conservation measure to ensure that fishing opportunities will be available in the future. Previous fish-ing experience appears to be important in determining catch-and-release behavior only to the extent that continued participation in fishing provides an opportunity for the angler to develop an affective attachment to the activity. The results also suggest that, although some anglers may place low importance on the number of fish caught, catching something, or the trophy/challenge aspects of fishing, this does not necessarily mean that the fishing activity of these "low consumptive" anglers will have a lower impact on the resource than those anglers classified as "high consumptive"; some tuna anglers placed low impor-tance on one or more of these catch-related aspects of fishing but still chose to retain a bluefin tuna. The effects of the situational variables (fishing party size and number of tuna caught) probably represent anglers' attempts to maximize trip satisfaction in light of observed attributes of the fishing trip; whether releas-ing or retaining a tuna results in greater overall trip satisfaction depends in part on how anglers evaluate these and other attributes of the fishing trip.

Results provide some initial insights into the factors that influence anglers' decisions to retain or release caught fish. Future research should build on the theoretical approach taken here as well as on other human dimensions research to construct a well-grounded understanding of catch-and-release behavior.

References

Buchanan, T. 1985. Commitment and leisure behavior: a theoretical perspective. Leisure Sciences 7:401–420.

Ditton, R. B., B. L. Bohnsack, and J. R. Stoll. 1998. A social and economic study of the win-ter recreational Atlantic bluefin tuna fishery in Hatteras, North Carolina. Report prepared for the American Sportfishing Association, Alexandria, Virginia.

Graefe, A. R. 1980. The relationship between level of participation and selected aspects of specialization in recreational fishing. Doctoral dissertation. Texas A&M University, College Station, Texas.

American Fisheries Society Symposium 30:208–211, 2002

EXTENDED ABSTRACT

To Keep or Release:
Understanding Differences in Angler Behavior

ANTHONY J. FEDLER

The use of catch-and-release-related management tools has generated controversy and conflict among marine recreational anglers, yet little research has been undertaken to understand the basis of these differing views. Most information on the acceptability of catch-and-release regulations has been obtained from public-hearing testimony and written public comments by activist anglers and angling organizations. Little is known about the catch-and-release orientation of anglers beyond a handful of studies that have principally focused on freshwater anglers. Marine anglers may differ from freshwater anglers both in terms of the proportion of the angling population which practices catch and release and support for catch-and-release regulations. Furthermore, some anglers release fish that are below or above legal limits, but harvest legal fish and consider this catch-and-release fishing. This paper uses results from several studies of marine recreational anglers to bring some understanding to these differing views of catch-and-release angling.

Data from three surveys of marine anglers, the 1996 National Survey of Fishing, Hunting and Wildlife Associated Recreation (USFWS 1997), a statewide survey of marine and freshwater anglers in Maryland (Fedler 1989), and a survey of marine anglers in Florida (Fedler et al. 2000) were used to: identify the number of anglers that have an affinity for catch-and-release fishing; compare release-oriented anglers and harvest-oriented anglers across an array of motivational, fishing site selection, and management variables; and characterize how implementing catch-and-release regulations for specific species would impact marine anglers.

The 1996 National Survey of Fishing, Hunting and Wildlife Associated Recreation (National Survey) asked anglers if they participated in catch-and-release fishing during 1996 (USFWS 1997). No definition of catch-and-release

Anthony J. Fedler, Human Dimensions Consulting, 9707 SW 55th Road, Gainesville, Florida 32608–4336, USA. Email: tfedler@gru.net

fishing was given. Within this context, 57% of anglers fishing exclusively in freshwater, 66% fishing in both freshwater and salt water, and 41% fishing solely in salt water reported they engaged in catch-and-release fishing. Among anglers fishing in salt water, as the number of days fishing increased, so did the propensity to report catch-and-release fishing. Among marine anglers fishing 10 or fewer days, 37% reported catch-and-release fishing. About 40% of anglers fishing 11–30 days and 59% fishing over 30 days annually reported catch-and-release fishing.

Data from a survey of saltwater anglers in Maryland (Fedler 1989) were used to develop an attitudinal scale to classify marine anglers on a harvest-release continuum. Responses to five statements concerning harvesting and releasing fish were summed to create a harvest-release scale (scale alpha = 0.86) score for each angler. Scale scores were used to classify anglers into three groups: harvest-oriented (43%), harvest-and-release-oriented (33%), and release-oriented (24%). This distribution of marine anglers across the three groups was reversed from freshwater anglers: harvest-oriented (21%), harvest and release-oriented (32%), and release-oriented (47%).

Saltwater anglers in the three harvest-release groups were compared across 19 motivational and 16 management-related statements, with 12 statements found to be significantly different (Table 1). Only 2 of the 19 general motivation statements were rated significantly different across the three groups. The motivations "to obtain fish for eating" and "to catch my limit" were each rated differently across the three groups. This adds further validity to the release-oriented scale used to classify anglers. Harvest-oriented anglers rated both of these statements much higher than the combination group or the release-oriented group. The finding that the three groups rated other general motivations like fishing for relaxation, sport, peace and solitude, and escaping other people likewise suggests that they are very similar in their noncatch-related attitudes.

Differences in reasons for selecting the location of the most recent fishing trip were catch-related (Table 1). Harvest-oriented anglers rated catching the type of fish, catching a limit, and good fishing more importantly than the other two groups. All three groups rated reasons such as convenience, closeness to home, large fish, and doing something with family and friends alike.

Release-oriented anglers also showed stronger support for many fishery management alternatives (Table 1). Of the 16 management alternatives rated in the survey by Fedler (1989), harvest-oriented and release-oriented anglers differed on 7 that affected the number and size of fish caught, when and how fish could be caught, and where they could be caught. Anglers did not differ on management alternatives focusing on habitat or access improvement, minimum size limits, spawning season closures, and gear restrictions. This analysis further

Table 1. Differences among harvest- and release-oriented marine anglers across general motivation, reasons for choosing last fishing trip location, and management regulation variables.

	Mean Score[3]				
	Harvest oriented	Harvest & release	Release oriented	F	P
General motivations[1]					
To obtain fish for eating	4.17a	3.33b	1.58c	66.97	< 0.001
To catch my limit of fish	2.39a	1.82b	1.34c	11.83	< 0.001
Reasons for choosing fishing trip location[2]					
It has the types of fish I like to catch	4.79a	4.49b	3.77c	9.20	< 0.001
I can usually catch my limit	2.91a	2.35b	1.79b	6.27	0.002
It usually has good fishing	4.64a	4.31b	3.83b	7.82	0.001
Management alternative support[1]					
Releasing fish above a certain size length	3.23a	3.55ab	3.88b	6.21	0.002
Releasing fish within a certain length range but keeping the fish above or below this range	2.70a	3.09b	3.32b	6.35	0.002
Being able to keep only a certain number of fish you catch per day	3.58a	3.81a	4.41b	12.63	< 0.001
Not being able to fish in certain restricted areas	3.21a	3.39a	3.78b	5.12	0.006
Prohibiting certain types of baits	2.66a	2.95a	3.31b	7.21	0.001
Not being able to retain certain fish species caught in certain areas	3.03a	3.36b	3.85c	10.78	< 0.001
Placing a harvest moratorium on certain fish species which have low populations	4.06a	4.24ab	4.40b	3.49	0.032

[1]Response format ranged from (1) strongly disagree to (5) strongly agree.
[2]Response format ranged from (1) not at all important to (6) extremely important.
[3]Means with different suffix letters are significantly different at $p < 0.05$.

confirms that the basic difference between harvest-oriented and release-oriented anglers lies in their consumptive orientation.

Fedler et al. (2000) developed an interactive decision support system, based upon strategic choice modeling protocols, to model angler responses to potential management actions for king mackerel *Scomberomorus cavalla*, red snapper *Lutjanus campechanus*, and grouper *Mycteroperca* spp. By setting the bag limit to zero in the model, anglers would be forced to fish for the three species under catch-and-release-only conditions. The responses of anglers to implementation of catch-and-release regulations for the three species showed that anglers would reduce the number of trips made for king mackerel by 54%, red snapper by 63%, and grouper by 63%. In most cases, anglers would reallocate their trips to other species. However, 10% of the king mackerel, 14% of the red snapper, and 28% of the grouper trips would be reallocated to a nonfishing activity. In other words, when faced with catch-and-release regulations for these three species, many anglers would not go fishing. About one-third or more of the anglers would continue catch-and-release fishing for the three species.

Beyond the descriptive characteristics of anglers, this paper suggests that further examination of the catch-and-release behavior of marine anglers is needed. Does releasing fish caught after a bag limit is attained constitute catch-and-release fishing? Does releasing legal-sized fish with the hope of catching a larger fish to take home constitute catch-and-release fishing? Many anglers believe so. Other anglers believe catch-and-release angling means not harvesting any fish or releasing nontarget species. Defining what is meant by catch-and-release fishing is still an important endeavor after more than two decades of use as a management tool. A more fundamental question to be investigated is "under what conditions do marine anglers practice catch and release?" Is it personal philosophy, species-related, situation-related, or a combination of these and other factors that influence an individual angler to practice catch-and-release angling? Clearly, an angler's attitude towards harvesting or releasing fish plays an important role. But after 20 years or more of catch-and-release research, we still have many questions to answer in order to understand angler catch-and-release behavior and use it more effectively as a management tool.

References

Fedler, A. J. 1989. The demand for warmwater and Chesapeake Bay angling in Maryland. Report submitted to the Maryland Department of Natural Resources, Tidewater Administration, Annapolis, Maryland.

Fedler, A. J., S. M. Holland, and W. Haider. 2000. Modeling the effects of fisheries regulations and trip attributes on angler behavior. Report submitted to the National Marine Fisheries Service, Southwest Regional Office, St. Petersburg, Florida. MARFIN Grant Number NA87FF0428.

USFWS (U.S. Fish and Wildlife Service). 1997. 1996 National Survey of Fishing, Hunting, and Wildlife-Associated Recreation. U.S. Department of the Interior, Washington, D.C

American Fisheries Society Symposium 30:212–214, 2002

EXTENDED ABSTRACT

National Marine Fisheries Service's Recreational Fisheries Database: Applications in Catch-and-Release Behavior and Angler Profiling

BRAD GENTNER

The Fisheries Statistics and Economics division of the National Marine Fisheries Service (NMFS) conducts the Marine Recreational Fishery Statistic Survey (MRFSS). The MRFSS is conducted in every region (Northeast, Southeast, and Pacific Coast) of the U.S. covering every coastal state except Texas, Alaska, and Hawaii. This survey is designed to take a random sample of fishing trips to gather catch, effort, participation, demographic, and socioeconomic data. The MRFSS consists of two independent, but complementary surveys conducted every year in every region in six two-month waves, all across the United States. The first part consists of an intercept survey conducted at fishing access sites and is designed as a random sample of recreational trips. This sample is stratified by year, sub-region, state, wave, mode, fishing area, catch type, and species, and over 125,000 interviews were conducted in 1998. During the intercept interview, biological data are collected by measuring and weighing available catch. Disposition of catch not retained is also solicited to characterize release behavior. The second part of the survey involves a random digit dial survey of all coastal counties. This phase is used to develop the overall recreational angling participation level, both catch and effort, for coastal counties. From this survey, angler catch and effort can be estimated. This data set provides a consistent, standardized time series that stretches back to 1979.

In order to characterize the economic value and the economic impact of recreational angling, a series of economic add-on surveys were developed. Valuation surveys contain all the data necessary to estimate travel cost and random utility models. Some of the surveys also contain contingent valuation questions. Economic impact surveys collect detailed trip-level and yearly expenditures on

Brad Gentner, National Marine Fisheries Service F/ST1, 1315 East West Highway, Silver Spring, Maryland 20910, USA. Email: brad.gentner@noaa.gov.

recreational marine angling. Region of purchase is also collected. While these surveys collect data used to analyze valuation and expenditure models, they also collect socioeconomic and demographic data useful for angler profiling. Portions of these economic surveys are added on to the intercept survey. These intercepted anglers are then asked to participate in a telephone follow-up interview to gather more in depth economic information. Some of these questions are also added on to the random digit dial survey to increase the richness of economic data sets. Valuation surveys conducted included Northeast 1994, Southeast 1997, and Pacific Coast 1998. Expenditure surveys conducted included Northeast 1998, Southeast 1999, and Pacific Coast 2000. All of the data collected in these various economic add-on surveys has been analyzed and the results of these analyses are available on our publications web site (*www.st.nmfs.gov/st1/econ/pubs.html*). NMFS continues to explore new ground with its economic add-on surveys. In 2000, a conjoint mail survey was administered to anglers in the Northeast to explore the trade-offs anglers make in the face of changing summer flounder, *Paralichthys dentatus*, regulations. This effort will be expanded to the Southeast and Pacific Coast regions once the Northeast pilot has been evaluated.

Beyond these uses, the combined MRFSS base surveys and the socioeconomic add-on surveys can be used to explore catch and release behavior and angler socioeconomic profiling. For example, data from the Northeast region economic add-on survey was used to profile catch and release behavior for striped bass, *Morone saxatilis*. Striped bass total catch has steadily increased until 1998, when catch drastically fell. During this time the number of fish released fluctuated slightly and in 1998, 93.3% of striped bass caught were released. These database queries were conducted using the MRFSS web page. Using only the data from those anglers targeting striped bass, during 1998 in the Northeast region ($n = 5,789$), one can examine how much catch for an average trip was released, and whether those releases were voluntary or motivated by either size or bag regulations. In 1998, 89% of all striped bass caught were released because they could not legally be retained due to size or bag restrictions. On the other hand, 4% of all fish caught were released voluntarily. While this information is not currently available in the MRFSS web queries, this information is collected as part of the base MRFSS. The MRFSS data sets are publicly available on their web site at *www.st.nmfs.gov/st1/recreational/ data.html*.

Currently, this type of data is also available for the Southeast region, including the Gulf States, and the Pacific Region. In addition to these catch profiles, socioeconomic and demographic profiles have been developed for all states participating in the survey and those are available as PDF files from *www.st.nmfs.gov/st1/econ/rec_econ.html*. Household income distribution, employment status, preferences for regulations, and some general facts are presented for each state. The Marine Recreation Fisheries Statistics website, *www.st.nmfs.gov/st1/recreational/index.html*, contains more in depth information regarding the MRFSS survey and allows the user to query the MRFSS data sets. It is hoped that this brief introduction to the MRFSS data and its capabilities will allow researchers to better utilize this data resource. For more information please visit the web pages listed above.

Management Issues

American Fisheries Society Symposium 30:217–229, 2002

Negative Implications of Large Minimum Size Regulations on Future Mean Size at Age: An Evaluation Using Simulated Striped Bass Data

C. Phillip Goodyear

415 Ridgewood Road
Key Biscayne, Florida 33149, USA
Email: phil_goodyear@msn.com

Abstract.—One component of the management regimen employed to rebuild the Atlantic coastal migratory stock of striped bass *Morone saxatilis* was the imposition of large size limits to reduce fishing mortality to zero, on the 1982 and subsequent year-classes, until 95% of the females had an opportunity to reproduce at least once. Such size limits introduce size-selective mortality that favors the survival of slower-growing members of the population and may select for slower growth in succeeding generations. Size-at-age data from the Hudson River population were used to examine the effect of alternative size limits on the length distributions of survivors by age using simulation. The results indicate that minimum sizes currently in use can cause profound changes in the size composition of the spawning stock. The mean asymptotic length of unfertilized eggs under equilibrium conditions was estimated as an index of the extent to which these changes may influence future growth. With the current best estimates of growth parameters and fecundity at size, this index was reduced by only about 3%. However, because of the size-selective mortality in the existing fishery and uncertainty arising from sampling difficulties, growth is probably poorly characterized by the existing data. Sensitivity analyses revealed that some reasonable combinations of growth and minimum sizes can induce changes in the mean asymptotic length of unfertilized eggs by more than 10%, which would be about 30% in terms of asymptotic mean weight. The extent to which this selective force might be expressed in succeeding generations is uncertain. However, reliance on minimum sizes to constrain catch has the potential to cause profound changes in growth and probably should not be adopted for long-term management of striped bass until this problem is better understood.

Introduction

The Atlantic coastal migratory stocks of striped bass *Morone saxatilis*, supported by spawning grounds in the Chesapeake Bay, declined precipitously during the 1970s as a consequence of excessive fishing mortality (Field 1997). This event spurred research and management intervention beginning in the early 1980s to rebuild the resource. Management authority rested with the Atlantic States Marine Fisheries Commission (ASMFC) through its Interstate Fisheries Management Plan for Striped Bass, which was first adopted in 1981. State compliance with the provisions of the plan became mandatory in 1984 with the promulgation of the Atlantic Striped Bass Conservation Act (PL 98–613). The plan was amended in 1984 and again in 1985 to provide for increased conservation of the resource. The 1985 amendment called for state regulations to reduce fishing mortality on the 1982 year-class females and all subsequent

year classes of Chesapeake Bay stocks to zero until 95% of the females of these year classes had an opportunity to reproduce at least once (ASMFC 1985). The amendment suggested establishment of increasingly large minimum size limits as one approach to achieve this objective. This strategy was adopted for the coastal waters (as opposed to bays), and the minimum sizes were increased on an almost annual basis to 91 cm (36 in) total length (TL) by 1989. The coastal-water size limits were lowered in many states with the recovery of the stocks since 1990, and in 1996 they varied from 71 to 86 cm (28–34 in).

The striped bass population of the Hudson River did not experience the same decline in abundance as the Chesapeake stock, during the 1970s and 1980s (Field 1997). However, their postspawning distribution along the Atlantic coast is basically the same area occupied by coastal migrants from the Chesapeake during the summer and fall months (Dorazio et al.1994; Waldman et al. 1990, 1997). Consequently, the relatively large minimum size limits imposed to conserve and rebuild the Chesapeake stocks of striped bass also applied to the Hudson River population as well.

Minimum sizes can contribute to size-selective fishing mortality, and large minimum sizes can significantly enhance the relative survival of slower-growing members of a population (Parma and Deriso 1990; Goodyear 1996). To the extent that growth is a heritable trait, this process may select for slow growth in succeeding generations (Parma and Deriso 1990). This problem has been raised as a possible issue with respect to the decline in weight at age in other species (Wohlfarth 1986, McAllister et al. 1992; Krohn and Kerr 1997).

This paper utilizes simulation techniques to evaluate the potential influence of alternative size limits on the distributions of size at age for the Hudson River striped bass spawning stock and develops a measure of the potential magnitude of the selective force.

Methods

The model used to examine the potential effects of alternative size limits on the size composition of the striped bass spawning population is an elaboration of the model described by Goodyear (1989). In this model, growth is characterized by dividing the population into an arbitrary number of phenotypic morphs representing portions of the population that differ in growth attributes, and each morph is modeled separately. Given the sexual dimorphism in growth observed in striped bass (Mansueti 1961), each sex is modeled separately. Population characteristics are then evaluated by summing over the morphs and sexes. This approach to characterizing growth is an "assignment-at-birth" (Kirkpatrick 1984), in which the growth of each individual follows a distinct pattern that is completely determined at some initial (prerecruit) stage.

The model uses a seasonal time scale, which is monthly for this analysis. I adopted the value of natural mortality used in the most recent stock assessment of $M = 0.15$ (ASMFC 1997). This level of natural mortality implies a long life span, so the model considered 50 discreet ages to minimize effects of truncating the age distribution. The number of survivors of sex S and morph M at age A and season P (N_{SAMP}) is

$$N_{SAMP} = R_{SAM} \exp(-\mu_{SAMP}),$$

where R_{SAM} is the initial recruitment of age A of sex S represented by morph M, and μ_{SAMP} is the cumulative total mortality suffered by morph M of sex S from recruitment to season P at age A, or

$$\mu_{SAMP} = \sum_{I=0}^{A-1} \sum_{J=1}^{\Omega} (M_J + F_{IJM})$$
$$+ \sum_{J=1}^{P-1} (M_J + F_{AJM}),$$

where Ω is the number of seasons within a year and is set to 12, for analyses conducted for this report. The seasonal natural mortality (M_J) used in the present evaluation was 1/12 the annual assumed rate. The F_{ijm} is the instantaneous fishing mortality for morph M during season J when it was age I. For the analyses conducted here, the relative susceptibility of striped bass to fishing was assumed constant over age except for the effect of minimum size on retention of captured fish. The instantaneous rate of fishing mortality, F, for striped bass above the minimum size was varied to examine the effect of the magnitude of fishing on the relative survival of the different morphs to the spawning ages. For ages and seasons when the morph is below the minimum size, the fishing mortality is reduced to dF, where d is the fraction of the discarded catch that dies. Note that if a size limit were sufficiently high that some morphs never reach it during their lifetime, and the discard mortality, d, is less than 100%, then there would be no age where the fishing mortality averaged over all morphs would equal F. The value of d was set to 0.07, based on the recreational hooking mortality rate assumed in the most recent stock assessment (ASMFC 1997).

The mean asymptotic length of a fish that develops from a fertilized egg would probably be a reasonable approximation of the selective pressure induced by minimum sizes, if growth is completely heritable. In this situation, growth would be completely determined by the genetic contributions from both parents. Unfortunately, data to characterize the reproductive importance of males by size or age are unavailable. Consequently, the ratio of the mean asymptotic length of the unfertilized eggs, λ, was evaluated with and without size limits, as a first order approximation of the potential magnitude of the selective force of size limits. This measure is the average asymptotic length of the fish arising from the eggs produced by the females during a spawning year, if the genetic contribution from males is ignored. It was estimated for the stable age distribution, assuming constant recruitment as

$$\lambda = \left(\sum_{A=1}^{\Delta} \sum_{M=1}^{O} L\infty_M E_{AM} N_{AM} \right) \bigg/ \left(\sum_{A=1}^{\Delta} \sum_{M=1}^{O} E_{AM} N_{AM} \right),$$

where Δ is the number of ages in the unfished population, O is the number of discreet morphs considered, $L\infty_M$ = asymptotic size of female morph M, E_{AM} = mean fecundity of morph M females at age A, and. N_{AM} = number of age A survivors of female morph M at the beginning of the spawning season. The fecundity of females at the time of spawning was evaluated from their length, using the polynomial equation of Goodyear (1984) derived from fecundity and maturity data presented by Lewis and Bonner (1966) and Mansueti (1961).

Size-at-age data for Hudson River striped bass were obtained from the New York Department of Environmental Conservation (NYDEC; K. Hattala and K. McKown, personal communications). Additional samples from coastal waters were obtained from the National Marine Fisheries Service (NMFS; Gary Shepherd, Northeast Fisheries Science Center, personal communication). The latter data were a compilation of samples collected by many investigators, using a variety of gears in inshore and coastal waters from North Carolina to Maine that had been used in the most recent stock assessment for this species (ASMFC 1997). The former data were used to describe mean total length at age. L_t by sex for Hudson River striped bass using the von Bertalanffy growth equation

$$L_t = L\infty \left(1 - e^{-k(t-t_0)} \right),$$

where $L\infty$ is mean asymptotic total length, k is the Brody growth coefficient, and t_0 is the hypothetical age at which the fish would have zero length, if it had always grown in the manner described by the equation (Ricker 1975). These data were also used

to characterize the distribution of lengths about the mean and to examine the distributions of size at age available to the coastal fisheries.

Data from the recreational fishery were obtained from the NMFS Marine Recreational Fisheries Statistics Survey (MRFSS). These data included estimates of striped bass catch and release by year and the size composition of the recreational harvest each year. These data provided information about the proportion of the striped bass recreational catch that was being released.

Results

The size-at-age data available from the Hudson River sampling consisted of collections by gill net, haul seine, and electrofishing. Inspection of these data, stratified by gear type, revealed the expected selectivity bias in length frequencies at age in samples collected with gill nets. The electrofishing samples were generally upstream from the spawning grounds and were not confined to the spawning season. Consequently, these samples were eliminated from further consideration, and only the haul seine data from the NYDEC spawning stock survey were employed to estimate growth. The length frequencies and sample size for the selected data are given in Figures 1 and 2.

Inspection of the length frequencies of males and females by age confirmed the sexual dimorphism in growth previously reported for striped bass (Mansueti 1961). Consequently, separate growth equations were developed for each sex, by fitting von Bertalanffy growth equations to the mean observed lengths and ages of each age-class well-represented in the samples for each sex (Figures 3 and 4). For both sexes there were few observations of length at age for young fish, undoubtedly due to the difficulty of identifying the sex of immature individuals. Also, there were very few fish older than about 15 years of age in the samples, probably because of lowered abundance resulting from longer exposure to natural and fishing mortality. Consequently, the fitted relationships do not include data from the full range of ages in the stock.

Additional age-length data from the consolidated stock-assessment NMFS data file were available to characterize size at age but did not provide information on sex. Since the sexual dimorphism in size at age increases with age, the lengths at age for the

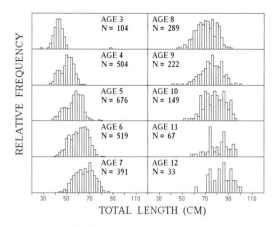

Figure 1. Length frequencies of male Hudson River striped bass from NYDEC spawning stock surveys.

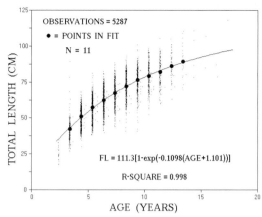

Figure 3. Scattergram of male Hudson River striped bass from NYDEC spawning stock surveys and fitted von Bertalanffy growth equation.

youngest fish in these samples might reasonably represent the size of young striped bass of both sexes at early ages. Samples that had been collected with gear other than gill nets from New York northward were extracted from the available data file and stratified by age. Since the emigration of striped bass from the Chesapeake Bay generally doesn't occur in significant numbers before the spring of their second calendar year of life (Merriman 1941; Dorazio et al. 1994), most individuals in their first or second calendar year of life in this area should be from the Hudson River.

The data were inspected to identify clusters of measurements where there were sufficient numbers of observations of lengths at age, within time intervals sufficiently short that growth within the inter-

val was not an important consideration. The resulting best set of length-frequency information is presented in Figure 5 for ages 1–12. The mean size at age for each sex was interpolated from age 0 to the youngest ages included in the von Bertalanffy fit by drawing a smooth curve through the observed mean size during January at age 1 and the predicted length at the age of the youngest age-class included in the fit (Figures 3 and 4). Otherwise, mean size at age used in this analysis was the predicted value from the appropriate von Bertalanffy equation (Table 1), and within-year growth was assumed constant.

The shape of the distribution of size at age was evaluated to determine the appropriate distribution for the simulation model. Inspection of the length

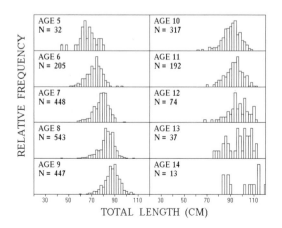

Figure 2. Length frequencies of female Hudson River striped bass from NYDEC spawning stock surveys.

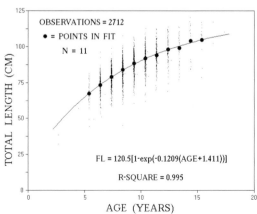

Figure 4. Scattergram of female Hudson River striped bass from NYDEC spawning stock surveys and fitted von Bertalanffy growth equation.

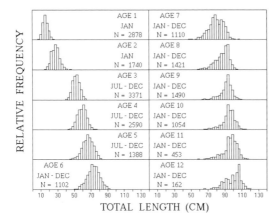

Figure 5. Length frequencies of selected samples of striped bass from coastal waters by age.

frequencies in Figures 1 and 2 does not provide firm guidance on the shape of the underlying distribution of size at age, especially since size-selective fishing may have altered the distributions in the older age classes. These data were further stratified to month (May and June) and age and the distributions tested for normality using Chi Square goodness-of-fit test. For the male samples, 6 of the resulting 17 month-age strata with 25 or more observations failed the test of normality. However, there was an apparent effect of month and age, as none of the 7 June-age samples failed the test of normality, and the 6 of 10 May-age samples that failed the test of normality were the youngest ages with sufficient sample sizes

Table 1. Mean total lengths at age for male and female striped bass used in this study as predicted from the von Bertalanffy growth equation (Ricker 1975).

Age	Length (cm) Male	Length (cm) Female	Age	Length (cm) Male	Length (cm) Female
1	16.2	16.2	16	94.2	105.8
2	28.1	32.5	17	96.0	107.4
3	38.3	45.6	18	97.6	108.9
4	46.2	56.7	19	99.0	110.2
5	54.3	64.9	20	100.3	111.4
6	60.2	71.3	21	101.4	112.4
7	65.5	76.9	22	102.4	113.3
8	70.3	81.8	23	103.4	114.2
9	74.5	86.2	24	104.2	114.9
10	78.4	90.1	25	104.9	115.5
11	81.8	93.6	30	107.6	117.8
12	84.8	96.6	35	109.1	119.0
13	87.6	99.4	40	110.0	119.6
14	90.1	101.8	45	110.6	120.0
15	92.3	103.9	50	110.8	120.2

to conduct the test. It is possible that this result is an artifact of the effect of sample size on the power of the test. However, it also may be an outcome of non-randomness associated with relative maturation of individuals by size within age, since mature individuals would be more likely identified to sex and be present in the sampling areas.

The same type of examination of the female length-frequency data revealed that 4 of the 12 age-month strata failed the test of normality. Consequently, it is not evident that a normal distribution is completely appropriate for describing the variation of length at age for the unfished condition of striped bass. The propensity for samples to fail the test for normality might be the result of the underlying true distribution of size at age not being normal. Or, it might be the result of sampling, spatial distributions of striped bass by length, size-selective mortality, or some other vagary. However, data from the youngest age-group of males in Figure 1 and the January samples of age 1 for sexes combined do not show a strong skew that would suggest the normal distribution is inappropriate for this analysis. Consequently, the prefishing distribution of size at age was assumed to be normal for the purpose of this study.

Given the selection of a normal distribution to characterize the distribution about the mean size at age, the coefficient of variation (CV) is useful for specifying the cumulative frequency distribution of lengths at age. Consequently, I estimated the CV for each age used to fit the von Bertalanffy equation by sex (Figure 6). The average CV was 0.12 for males and 0.085 for females. For each sex, I regressed the CV on age, to determine if it changed with age. The CV declined slightly with age for the males, but the trend was not significant. For females, the CV initially declined with age but increased with the older fish, such that the slope of the relation was positive. However, as with the males, the regression was not significant. Consequently, I assumed that the CV was constant with age and that it was equal to the mean of the observed values (0.12 for males and 0.085 for females).

The length distribution for each sex in the model population was divided into 101 equal length intervals with a cumulative range of ± 3 standard deviations from the mean. Initial recruitment to each morph was based on the proportion of the cumula-

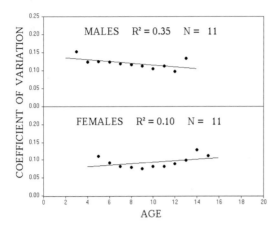

Figure 6. Coefficient of variation (CV) of size at age for male and female striped bass and associated regressions.

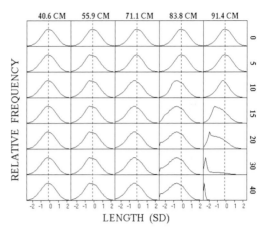

Figure 8. Change in survivorship by growth morph and age for female striped bass at several different size limits.

tive normal distribution within the length range represented by morph. All analyses were performed for the stable age distribution and assumed recruitment, and all other factors were constant.

Calculations of the relative change in size distributions of survivors at age were made using these estimates of the growth parameters and a level of fishing mortality equal to the most recent estimate for fully recruited striped bass in the coastal fishery of $F = 0.31$ (ASMFC 1997). Analyses considered no minimum size and minimum sizes of 40.6, 55.9, 71.1, 83.8, and 91.4-cm total length (TL). The distributions of survivors by morph at age were plotted for each sex (Figures 7 and 8). At the 40.6 cm minimum size limit, there was an almost imperceptible shift of the distribution to the left with increasing age for both sexes. At the 55.9-cm minimum size,

the effect was more discernible and was slightly more pronounced for females. At minimum sizes of 71.1 cm and larger, the effect of the size limit on the relative survival of faster versus slower-growing morphs was very pronounced for males (Figure 7). A similar trend is seen for females but beginning at a slightly higher minimum size (Figure 8).

The length-frequency distributions for males, females, and sexes combined, that arise from the analyses with minimum sizes set to 71.1 cm and 91.4 cm, are presented in Figures 9–14. In each of these figures, the smooth curve is the result of the analysis with fishing mortality, but no size limit is imposed, and all other conditions are the same. For the smaller of these two size limits, the effects on the distribution of male survivors is more dramatic than that of the females through age 12 (Figures 9

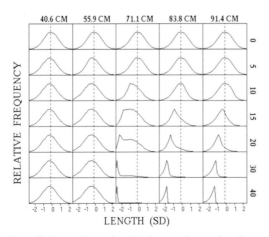

Figure 7. Change in survivorship by growth morph and age for male striped bass at several different size limits.

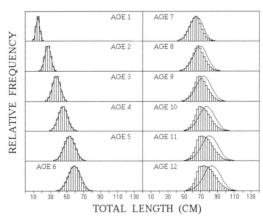

Figure 9. Simulated length frequencies of male striped bass with (bars) and without (smooth curve) a 71.1 cm minimum size at $F = 0.31$.

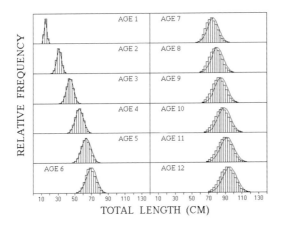

Figure 10. Simulated length frequencies of female striped bass with (bars) and without (smooth curve) a 71.1 cm minimum size at $F = 0.31$.

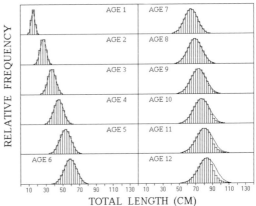

Figure 12. Simulated length frequencies of male striped bass, with (bars) and without (smooth curve) a 91.4 cm minimum size at $F = 0.31$.

and 10). With the larger size limit, the effect is more pronounced for females (Figures 12 and 13).

The length-frequency distributions for sexes combined are noticeably skewed with a left-hand tail, even for the analyses that assume no minimum size (Figures 11 and 14). Among other considerations, this finding suggests that the observation of right-handed truncation of length-frequency distributions from unsexed samples (as in many of the length frequencies in Figure 5) is not necessarily evidence for reduced survival of faster-growing individuals. It may, rather, only reflect the mixing of the two distributions, arising from the sexual dimorphism of growth.

However, the additional effect of the size-selective mortality imposed by the minimum size causes the distributions to become even more skewed. In the case of the 71.1-cm size limit, the distribution of lengths is shifted to the left and appears increasingly truncated on the left, with age (Figure 11). In contrast, with the larger 91.4-cm size limit, the combined length frequencies appear truncated on the other side and become progressively more so with age (Figure 14).

The decline in the mean asymptotic length of unfertilized eggs, for the minimum sizes evaluated here, for the current best estimate of fishing mortality in the stock ($F = 0.31$), increased from less than 1% to about 3%, as the minimum size increased from 40.6 cm to 91.4 cm.

These estimates, of course, are conditioned on the accuracy of the growth parameters used in the analy-

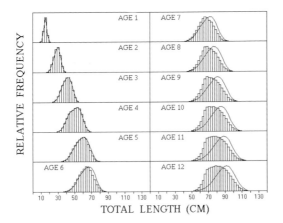

Figure 11. Simulated length frequencies of striped bass, sexes combined, with (bars) and without (smooth curve) a 71.1 cm minimum size at $F = 0.31$.

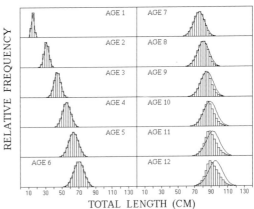

Figure 13. Simulated length frequencies of female striped bass with (bars) and without (smooth curve) a 91.4 cm minimum size at $F = 0.31$

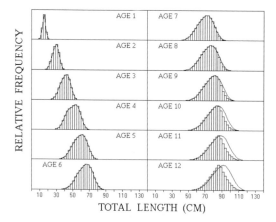

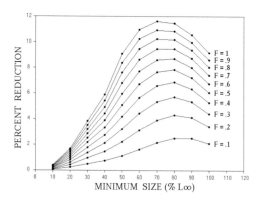

Figure 14. Simulated length frequencies of striped bass, sexes combined, with (bars) and without (smooth curve) a 91.4 cm minimum size at $F = 0.31$

Figure 15. Percent reduction in mean asymptotic length of unfertilized eggs, as a function of minimum size and fishing mortality.

ses. To study the problem more thoroughly, I evaluated the percent reduction in mean asymptotic length of unfertilized eggs as a function of fishing mortality, CV of size at age, the value of k in the von Bertalanffy equation, and minimum size. Since the parameters, $L\infty$ and k of the von Bertalanffy equation cannot vary independently and pass through a common age and length (except at the intercept), the value of $L\infty$ for each value of k was adjusted so that the resulting equation passed through the observed mean length at age 10. As a consequence, the minimum sizes were set as a percentage of $L\infty$. Analyses were performed with no minimum size and for minimum sizes of 10–100% of $L\infty$ in 10% intervals; values of k ranged from 0.05 to 0.25 in increments of 0.05; and the instantaneous fishing mortality rate was varied from 0.1 to 1.0 in increments of 0.1.

The percentage reduction in the mean asymptotic length of unfertilized eggs increased with increasing fishing mortality rates, and with increasing minimum sizes to some intermediate minimum size and then declined as the minimum size approached $L\infty$. The results for constant CV of 0.15 and von Bertalanffy k of 0.15 show that the maximum percentage reduction in mean asymptotic length of unfertilized eggs increased from about 2% to nearly 12% as fishing mortality increased from 0.1 to 1.0 (Figure 15). Also, the minimum size at which the bias was maximized decreased with increasing fishing mortality from about 90% of $L\infty$ at $F = 0.1$ to 70% of $L\infty$ at $F = 1.0$ (Figure 15).

A similar analysis, holding fishing mortality constant at $F = 0.5$ and the von Bertalanffy k constant at

0.15, while varying the CV of size at age from 0.05 to 0.25 over minimum sizes from 10 to 100% of $L\infty$, is presented in Figure 16. The percentage reduction in mean asymptotic length of eggs increased with increasing CV for all minimum sizes considered. As with increasing fishing mortality, the effect of increasing the size limit for each CV examined was an initial increase in the bias, followed by a decline at the largest size limits considered. The maximum bias observed was about 14%, at a minimum size of 80% of $L\infty$ for CV = 0.25. The minimum size at which the bias was maximized decreased with increasing CV from about 90% of $L\infty$ at CV = 0.05 to 70% of $L\infty$ at CV = 0.25 (Figure 16).

Analyses that varied the von Bertalanffy k and minimum size, while holding the CV constant at 0.15 and fishing mortality constant at $F = 0.5$, are presented in Figure 17. These results also show that the percentage reduction in the mean asymptotic length of unfertilized eggs initially increases with increasing minimum size, but then declines after some intermediate minimum size is reached. In contrast to the other parameters, the absolute magnitude of the maximum bias was only marginally changed by the value of the von Bertalanffy k, over the range evaluated. However, the size limit at which the bias was maximized increased with increasing k from about 40% of $L\infty$ for $k = 0.05$ to 90% of $L\infty$ for $k = 0.25$ (Figure 17).

The likelihood that the fishery is actually causing such selection is related to the fraction of the catch that is being released because of the size limits. Observations of the sizes of striped bass encountered during the intercept portion of MRFSS, from

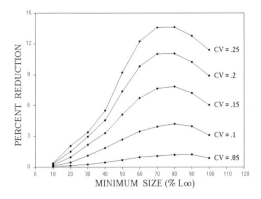

Figure 16. Percent reduction in mean asymptotic length of unfertilized eggs, as a function of minimum size and CV of length at age.

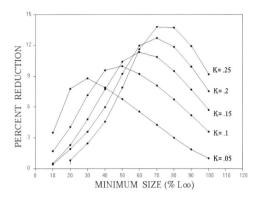

Figure 17. Percent reduction in mean asymptotic length of unfertilized eggs, as a function of minimum size and the value of the von Bertalanffy parameter _k_.

1981 to 1996 from New York northward, were sorted into three groups. The first group consisted of observations that had been made in locations and seasons where the minimum size had been less than 71 cm, the second included observations where the minimum size was 71 cm, and the last included observations where the minimum size was at least 91 cm. The length frequencies of these observations of the recreational landings for these three groupings show a rather dramatic effect of the regulations on the size composition of the recreational harvest (Figure 18).

In addition to harvest, MRFSS also estimates the numbers of striped bass that are discarded by anglers each year. This data indicates that, for this same area, the discard rate increased from about 50% to almost 98% in 1989, as a result of the increased size limits (Figure 19). A discard rate of 50% means that one out of every two fish caught is released. At 98%, 49 of every 50 fish caught are released. While many of the releases may be due to factors other than the minimum size, it seems clear that the minimum sizes that have been employed in striped bass management have imposed size selective mortality that would enhance survival of slower-growing individuals over their faster-growing siblings.

Discussion

The potential effects of size limits in the range of 40.6 cm TL (16 in) to 91.4 cm TL (36 in) on survivor-length frequencies at age are depicted in Figures 7 and 8. At the 40.6-cm size limit, all of the morphs grew to sizes larger than the minimum size fairly early in their life. Consequently, the duration

of differential fishing mortality across morphs within a cohort was relatively short, and the size bias in survivorship is not large. At the larger minimum sizes for both sexes, recruitment of a year-class to the fishery occurs over an extended period, and the slower-growing members of the cohort suffer much less exposure to the full impact of fishing mortality than the faster-growing members. In the case of males, the bias begins to diminish with size limits greater than 71.1 cm. This is simply the result of the higher size limit increasing the proportion of the length distribution protected from the fishery. Further increases in the size limit would continue to fill in the distribution until the size limit exceeded the size of any fish in the population. At this point, the size bias would disappear, but so would all harvesting. Intermediate size limits tend to maximize the selection for slow growth among survivors.

The unit developed here as an index of the magnitude of the potential selective force, the percent change in the mean length of unfertilized eggs (λ), has both positive and negative attributes. On the positive side, it accounts for the entire reproductive history of individuals who may have contributed significantly to reproduction before being exposed to the increased risk of harvesting as they grow into legal sizes. On the other hand, it assumes that the asymptotic size is completely controlled by heritable processes. Also, the contribution of males is neglected completely by this measure, as it is currently defined, and it does not attempt to capture any multigenerational feedback.

Males were only excluded from the analysis

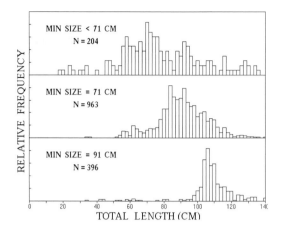

Figure 18. Length frequencies of striped bass sampled from the recreational harvest from New York through Maine for three size-limit regimes.

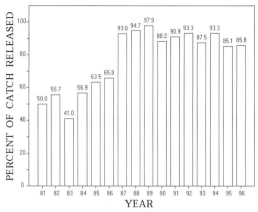

Figure 19. Percent of the recreational catch of striped bass from New York through Maine that were released during the years 1981–1996, estimated by MRFSS.

because data was unavailable that would characterize the reproductive importance of males by size or age. The analyses could be significantly enhanced with such data. As a consequence, λ serves only as a first-order approximation of the importance of the potential selection that might result from the size-selective mortality associated with minimum sizes.

With the current best estimates of the growth parameters, fecundity at size and fishing mortality, λ was reduced by only about 3% at the minimum size of 91.4-cm TL (36 in), which was widely adopted as a management tool in 1989. This same measure was about 2% for a minimum size of 71.1-cm TL (28 in), which was widely adopted for management in 1995. These results would appear to suggest the possibility that the potential selective force is of minimal concern. However, since weight is typically a cubed function of length, the level of change in mean asymptotic weight could be on the order of 4–10%, if these results accurately characterize the processes involved. In part, the accuracy of these estimates depends upon the adequacy of the striped bass growth model.

The potential effects of size limits greater than 55.9-cm TL (22 in) on survivor length frequencies is clearly illustrated by the results shown in Figures 7–14. Actual size limits for striped bass in the coastal waters of New Jersey northward have been 61-cm TL (24 in) or greater since 1985. It seems unlikely that size-at-age data collected from a population subjected to such size limits would reflect the average growth of individuals in a population that would

exist in the absence of fishing. Consequently, analyses of such data could never be expected to accurately recover the growth parameters of the original population (Goodyear 1995; Martinez-Garmendia 1997).

This observation implies that the von Bertalanffy parameter estimates, derived from the Hudson River striped bass spawning stock sampling data, are likely biased with respect to the growth of average recruits to the population. In particular, the mean asymptotic maximum length, $L\infty$, is most likely biased downward for both sexes. Similarly, the size-selective mortality imposed by a size limit would likely cause an upward bias in the growth coefficient, k, of the von Bertalanffy equation (Martinez-Garmendia 1997). And, if faster-growing fish mature earlier than their slower-growing siblings, then k might also be inflated because the slower-growing (and immature) fish would be relatively less abundant in the samples from the spawning stock upon which the growth model was based. These same factors would tend to bias the estimates of the CV of length at age downward, because parts of the (unfished) distributions would be underrepresented in the samples. In addition to these considerations, the paucity of observations of older fish in the stock makes the estimates of $L\infty$ uncertain at best (Vaughan and Kanciruk 1982).

The results of the sensitivity analyses of the percent reduction in the mean asymptotic length of unfertilized eggs, λ, indicate certain combinations of parameters could lead to changes of about 20%, which implies potential reductions in asymptotic weights of about 50%. However, the parameter combinations that produced the highest λ values were at fishing mortality rates of $F = 1.0$ and a CV of size at age of 0.25. This value for the CV is unlikely to be valid for striped bass; however, the upper limit of the potential magnitude of F is less certain.

Recall that F in this analysis applies to fully-recruited growth morphs that are above the minimum size. Where size limits are sufficiently high that some morphs never attain the minimum size during their lifespan, there will be no age in the population where the fishing mortality for the age will be as high as the fishing mortality rate on those individuals that exceed the minimum size. As a consequence, the fishing mortality rates estimated by age for stock assessment purposes tend to be less than the fishing mortality rate on the fully-recruited individuals of each age. The actual potential magnitude of the fishing mortality on fully-recruited individuals in the stock has not been estimated but could be considerably higher than the current best estimate of $F = 0.31$ from the most recent assessment (ASMFC 1997).

The results of the sensitivity analysis for parameter ranges that may be reasonably considered, given knowledge about the uncertainty in growth and mortality rates, suggest that values of λ in excess of 10% are well within the realm of possibility. This would imply potential reductions in asymptotic weights of up to about 30%. Inclusion of males in the analysis (i.e., estimating λ as a percent reduction in the mean asymptotic length of *fertilized* eggs) would probably reduce these values because of the earlier age at maturity for males. However, since all of the growth parameters are different for the two sexes, the actual outcome of including the males in the calculation is not clear.

Recent fecundity data for the Hudson River or any other stock of striped bass were unavailable. The fecundity-at-size equation used in this analysis was developed for an earlier study (Goodyear 1984). It was based on data on fecundity by size collected from the Roanoke River, from 1958 to 1963 (Lewis and Bonner 1966), and maturity-at-age data collected from size-selective fishing gears in Maryland, in the late 1950s (Mansueti 1961). Since the Maryland samples were taken near spawning areas, the proportion of mature fish in these samples was likely upwardly biased. If so, then the maturity schedule

drawn from Mansueti's work probably overestimates the percent mature for young females. If so, then the estimates of λ, herein, are biased downward.

The level of mortality associated with fish caught and released because of the minimum size is an important factor for the type of analyses considered herein. Higher mortality rates of fish discarded because of minimum sizes tend to reduce the selection for slow growth among survivors. The present analyses assume a discard mortality of 7%, based on the value used for the recreational fishery in the most recent stock assessment (ASMFC 1997). The discard mortalities estimated for the commercial gears ranged from 5% to 47%, depending on gear type. However, the ratio of commercial to recreational discards averaged only 0.15 for the last five years in the assessment (1992–1996). Also, the predominant harvesting method in the area of greatest abundance of Hudson River striped bass (New Jersey northward) is hook and line. Consequently, while the overall discard mortality for the Hudson River stock is uncertain, it is probably not much different than that for the recreational component of the fishery.

The importance of the selection for slow growth among survivors in the spawning stock depends upon the degree to which growth is heritable. Interspecific differences in asymptotic sizes suggest that some aspect of growth must be heritable. Although realized growth depends on available resources, there is strong evidence that growth is a heritable trait. Most of the direct evidence is from studies of domesticated stocks. Kinghorn (1983) and Gjedrem (1983) compiled the results of genetic studies of heritabilities of body-weights for many stocks involving five fish species. Mean heritability varied by species from 0.04 to 0.49. Gjedrem (1975) predicted a gain in mean weight of 3.5–7% per year for selective breeding of rainbow trout *Oncorhynchus mykiss*, based on heritabilities of 0.1–0.2. This compared favorably with experimental findings of a 30.1% net genetic gain in mean weight of rainbow trout in 8 years of selective breeding (Kincaid et al. 1977). Other studies have also shown that size and age at maturation are heritable (McKenzie et al. 1983; Gall et al. 1988; Tipping 1991; Reznick et al. 1997; Svensson 1997).

Several studies of fished wild stocks have noted changes in growth with exploitation that may have had a genetic basis (Wohlfarth et al. 1975; Ricker 1981; Wohlfarth 1986; Nelson and Soule 1987; Nuhfer and Alexander 1994; Krohn and Kerr 1997). These observations provide only circumstantial evidence because each case is confounded by possible alternative explanations. However, it is unlikely that even rather considerable changes in growth in important exploited populations could be unambiguously attributed to an underlying genetic cause using retrospective analyses of observed downward trends in growth. Such data will probably require well designed and executed large-scale fishing experiments, as proposed by McAllister et al. (1992) for pink salmon *O. gorbusha*. Even then, it could be argued that the conclusions derived might be only applicable to the particular species or even the stock that was the subject of the experiment.

The large size limits that were established as a protective measure to increase survival of the 1982 year-class of striped bass from the Chesapeake Bay were put in place to constrain the striped bass harvest and not to optimize yield per recruit or some other aspect of the fishery. In the short term, these measures performed well and increased survival and spawning stock biomass that led to stock recovery. However, adoption of large size limits to constrain total harvesting levels may induce important selection for slow growth in both the Hudson River population and those of the more southern spawning grounds, as well. The problem is not yet well understood, and the appropriate information to judge the significance of the potential for long-term impairment of the productivity of the stock will be difficult and possibly impossible to obtain.

This analysis was based on data for Hudson River striped bass, but there is little reason to believe that other species would not be similarly affected, to a greater or lesser degree. The results of the current study argue against using minimum sizes as a principal mode of constraining total catches, at least until the problem is better understood. So long as such size limits remain a management measure of choice, research should continue on this topic. Important areas for future research include determination of the actual distributions of sizes at age across ages for both sexes in the absence of size-selective fishing mortality; a better characterization of the relationships among fecundity and size and age; the relative value of sperm with size and age of

the males to the fertilization of ova; and further investigations into the heritability of growth in striped bass and other species.

Acknowledgments

I thank Kathy Hattala, NYDEC, who provided data on the size and age composition of the Hudson River striped bass spawning stock, and Kim McKown, NYDEC, who provided additional age-length data from the Hudson River and western Long Island Sound. I also thank Patty Phares, NMFS, for providing the MRFSS striped bass statistics, and Gary Shepherd, NMFS, for a compilation of size-at-age data for Atlantic coastal striped bass. The research contained in this report has been financed through a research grant from the Hudson River Foundation for Science and Environmental Research, Inc. The views expressed herein do not necessarily reflect the belief or opinions of the Foundation, which assumes no responsibility for liability for the contents or use of the information herein.

References

ASMFC (Atlantic States Marine Fisheries Commission). 1985. Interstate fisheries management plan for the striped bass of the Atlantic coast from Maine to North Carolina: amendment 3. ASMFC, Washington, D.C.

ASMFC (Atlantic States Marine Fisheries Commission). 1997. Stock assessment of Atlantic striped bass. 26th stock assessment workshop stock assessment review committee. ASMFC, Washington, D.C.

Dorazio, R. M., K. A. Hattala, C. M. McCollough, and J. E. Skjeveland. 1994. Tag recovery estimates of migration of striped bass from spawning areas of the Chesapeake Bay. Transactions of the American Fisheries Society 123:950–963.

Field, J. D. 1997. Atlantic striped bass management: where did we go right? Fisheries 22 (7):6–8.

Gall, G. A. E., J. Baltodano, and N. Huang. 1988. Heritability of age at spawning for rainbow trout. Aquaculture 68:93–102.

Gjedrem, T. 1975. Possibilities for genetic gain in salmonids. Aquaculture 6:23–29.

Gjedrem, T. 1983. Genetic variation in quantitative traits and selective breeding in fish and shellfish. Aquaculture 33:51–72.

Goodyear, C. P. 1984. Analysis of potential yield per recruit for striped bass produced in Chesapeake Bay. North American Journal of Fisheries Management 4:488–496.

Goodyear, C. P. 1989. LSIM-a length-based fish population simulation model. NOAA (National Oceanic and Atmospheric Administration) Technical Memorandum NMFS (National Marine Fisheries Service)-SEFC-219. Miami, Florida.

Goodyear, C. P. 1995. Mean size at age: an evaluation of sampling strategies using simulated red grouper data. Transactions of the American Fisheries Society 124:746–755.

Goodyear, C. P. 1996. Minimum sizes for red grouper: consequences of considering variable size at age. North American Journal of Fisheries Management 16:505–511.

Kincaid, H. L., W. R. Bridges, and B. von Limbach. 1977. Three generations of selection for growth rate in fall-spawning rainbow trout. Transactions of the American Fisheries Society 106:621–628.

Kinghorn, B. P. 1983. A review of quantitative genetics in fish breeding. Aquaculture 31:283–304.

Kirkpatrick, M. 1984. Demographic models based on size, not age, for organisms with indeterminate growth. Ecology 65:1874–1884.

Krohn, M. M., and S. R. Kerr. 1997. Declining weight at age in northern cod and the potential importance of the early years and size-selective fishing mortality. NAFO Scientific Council Studies 29:43–50.

Lewis, R. M., and R. R. Bonner, Jr. 1966. Fecundity of the striped bass, Roccus saxatilis (Walbaum). Transactions of the American Fisheries Society 95:328–331.

Mansueti, R. J. 1961. Age, growth, and movements of the striped bass, Roccus saxatilis, taken in size selective fishing gear in Maryland. Chesapeake Science 2:9–36.

Martinez-Garmendia, J. 1997. Effects of length-at-age data on growth and management benchmark F0.1 estimates in the face of size-selective mortality. Fisheries Research 32:233–247.

McAllister, M. K., R. M. Peterman, and D. M. Gillis. 1992. Statistical evaluation of a large-scale fishing experiment designed to test for a genetic effect of size-selective fishing on British Columbia pink salmon (Oncorhynchus gorbusha). Canadian Journal of Fisheries and Aquatic Sciences 49:1294–1304.

McKenzie, W. D., D. Crews, K. D. Kallman, D. Policansky, and J. Sohn. 1983. Age, weight and the genetics of sexual maturation in the platyfish, Xiphophorus maculatus. Copeia 183:770–774.

Merriman, D. 1941. Studies on the striped bass (Roccus saxatilis) of the Atlantic coast. U.S. Fish and Wildlife Service. Fishery Bulletin 50:1–77.

Nelson, K., and M. Soule. 1987. Genetical conservation of exploited fishes. Pages 345–368 in N. Ryman and F. Utter, editors. Population genetics and fishery management. Washington Sea Grant, University of Washington Press, Seattle, Washington.

Nuhfer, A. J., and G. R. Alexander. 1994. Growth, survival and vulnerability to angling of three wild brook trout strains exposed to different levels of angler exploitation. North American Journal of Fisheries Management 14:423–434.

Parma, A. M., and R. B. Deriso. 1990. Dynamics of age and size composition in a population subject to size-selective mortality: effects of phenotypic variability in growth. Canadian Journal of Fisheries and Aquatic Sciences 47:274–289.

Reznick, D. N., F. H. Shaw, F. H. Rodd, and R. G. Shaw. 1997. Evaluation of the rate of evolution in natural populations of guppies (Poecilia reticulata). Science 275:1934–1937.

Ricker, W. E. 1975. Computation and interpretation of biological statistics of fish populations. Fisheries Research Board of Canada Bulletin 191.

Ricker, W. E. 1981. Changes in the average size and average age of Pacific salmon. Canadian Journal of Fisheries and Aquatic Sciences 38:1636–1656.

Svensson, E. 1997. The speed of life-history evolution. Tree 12(10): 380–381.

Tipping, J. M. 1991. Heritability of age at maturity in steelhead. North American Journal of Fisheries Management 11:105–108.

Vaughan, D. S., and P. Kanciruk. 1982. An empirical comparison of estimation procedures for the von Bertalanffy growth equation. Journal du Conseil International pour l'Exploration de la Mer 40:211–219.

Waldman, J. R., D. J. Dunning, Q. E. Ross, and M. T. Mattson. 1990. Range dynamics of Hudson River striped bass along the Atlantic coast. Transactions of the American Fisheries Society 119:902–919.

Waldman, J. R., R. A. Richards, W. B. Shill, I. Wirgin, and M. C. Fabrizio. 1997. An empirical comparison of stock identification techniques applied to striped bass. Transactions of the American Fisheries Society 126:369–385.

Wohlfarth, G. 1986. Decline in natural fisheries - a genetic analysis and suggestion for recovery. Canadian Journal of Fisheries and Aquatic Sciences 43:1298–1306.

Wohlfarth, G., R. Moav, and G. Hulata. 1975. Genetic differences in the Chinese and European races of the common carp. 2. Multicharacter variation - a response to the diverse methods of fish cultivation in Europe and China. Heredity 34:341–350.

American Fisheries Society Symposium 30:230–233, 2002

EXTENDED ABSTRACT

The Role of Catch-and-Release Mortality Estimates in the Assessment of Marine Fish Populations

GARY R. SHEPHERD[1] *and* MARK TERCEIRO[2]

Catch-and-release fishing has become an increasingly common management tool in marine recreational fisheries. Reduced bag limits, restrictive size limits, and an increasing conservation awareness among fishermen all contribute to the growing number of marine fish subjected to catch and release. Effort by recreational anglers along the Atlantic coast of the United States has averaged 37.8 million trips per year over the past two decades. In some fisheries, recreational discard losses may equal or exceed landings. The conservation benefit of catch-and-release fishing is a function of the hooking mortality associated with the practice. The potential impact of excessive hooking mortality may significantly affect fisheries resources and needs to be considered in stock assessments.

A principal model used in fish stock assessments is virtual population analysis (VPA). The model uses the number of removals in a cohort over time to estimate the population size that would have been necessary to produce that level of catch. For instance, if fishing removed one million fish from a cohort over a number of years, in addition to losses due to natural mortality, one could conclude that the starting stock size for that cohort had to be greater than one million fish. Total annual catch used in the model is divided into age groups and includes recreational and commercial landings as well as recreational and commercial discard losses. Striped bass *Morone saxatilis* and summer flounder *Paralichthys dentatus* were used to illustrate the importance of catch-and-release data in assessment results and the implication of incorrectly identifying species in hooking mortality rates. The total number of striped bass and summer flounder released in recreational fisheries exceeded both recreational

Gary R. Shepherd and Mark Terceiro, Northeast Fisheries Science Center, National Marine Fisheries Service, 166 Water Street, Woods Hole, Massachusetts 02543, USA

[1]*Email: gary.shepherd@noaa.gov*
[2]*Email: mark.terceiro@noaa.gov*

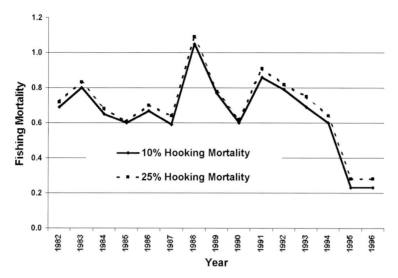

Figure 1. VPA estimates of age-1 summer flounder fishing mortality, with hooking mortality levels of 10 and 25%.

and commercial landings. Therefore, the assessment results could vary significantly depending on the number of releases killed by hooking mortality.

Discard estimates were derived by applying release mortality rates (8% for striped bass and 10% for summer flounder) to the total number of releases. Mortality rates were determined in studies using fish hooked and released under varying conditions then held in captivity (Diodati and Richards 1996; Lucy and Holton 1998; Malchoff and Lucy 1998; Gearhart 1999). Total number and size of releases were determined by the Marine Recreational Fisheries Statistical Survey (MRFSS) and data collected by volunteer anglers.

The impact of changing the release mortality rate assumption on the estimates of population fishing mortality rates (F) and numbers depends on both the size of the change and the proportion of the total catch accounted for by the affected catch. The recreational fishery discards of summer flounder accounted for 14.2% of the age-0 catch and 15.5% of the age-1 total catch during 1982–1996, under a 25% release mortality rate assumption. Under the current 10% release mortality assumption, recreational fishery discards accounted for 6.8% of the age-0 and 7.2% of the age-1 total catch estimated for 1982–1996. The average estimate of age-1 fishing mortality from 1982 to 1996 decreased 5.8%, with a change from 25% to 10% hooking mortality (Figure 1). The change in F was greatest in the terminal year with a 17.6% decrease. The second effect was on the VPA estimates of population numbers at age, which also decreased

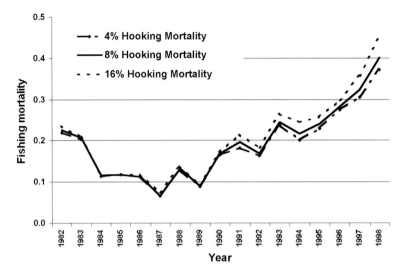

Figure 2. VPA estimates of age 4–13 striped bass fishing mortality, with hooking mortality levels of 4, 8, and 16%.

with the new release mortality assumption, by an average of about 4% for both age 0 and 1.

The sensitivity of striped bass fishing mortality rates and stock size estimates to various hooking mortality rates were more modest than summer flounder, due to differences in catch levels and age classes affected by hooking mortality. Doubling the hooking mortality rate to 16% increased the 1982–1998 estimate of fully recruited F by 2.5%. Reducing the hooking mortality rate by half to 4% decreased full F by 1.5% (Figure 2). The impact on stock size was similar; doubling hooking mortality resulted in a 10.9% increase in estimated stock size, while reducing hooking mortality by half reduced stock size estimates by 5.3%. The effect of changes was greatest in the terminal year, although stock size estimates varied less than 10% and F estimates by 12.5% with a doubling of hooking mortality rates.

The direction of changes in the VPA stock size estimates relative to changes in hooking mortality rates are not intuitive. An increase in release mortality resulted in a modest increase in the estimates of stock size and, to a lesser degree, fishing mortality. The direction of change in stock sizes and F estimates result from the underlying premise of the VPA. If more fish were removed from the population, then mortality increases. However, there also had to be more fish in the initial population estimate. In many VPA models, the trends in stock size are calibrated or tuned using relative abundance indices from fishery independent surveys, which reflect the changes in population abundance resulting from removals by the fishery and natural mortality. In the final step of VPA calculations, the population numbers are scaled to absolute numbers by the size of the catch. Therefore, if the catch number increases, estimates of starting population size also increase.

Although changes in hooking mortality rates resulted in relatively small changes in the results, improvements in recreational discard data are still warranted. It is well documented for many species that discard mortality varies according to terminal tackle, handling time, water temperature, and salinity. With better information about fishing practices among areas and seasons, in addition to better biological samples (lengths, weights, etc.) of released fish, analysts will be able to reduce uncertainty about hooking mortality estimates incorporated into stock assessment models.

References

Diodati, P. J., and R. A. Richards. 1996. Mortality of striped bass hooked and released in salt water. Transactions of the American Fisheries Society 125(2):300–307.

Gearhart, J. 1999. Short-term hooking mortality of summer flounder in North Carolina. Semi-annual report for North Carolina Division of Marine Fisheries, Atlantic Coastal Fisheries Conservation Management Act Project 2-ACA-003. Morehead City, North Carolina.

Lucy, J. A., and T. D. Holton. 1998. Release mortality in Virginia's recreational fishery of summer flounder, *Paralichthys dentatus*. Virginia Marine Resource Report # 97-8. Newport News, Virginia.

Malchoff, M. H., and J. Lucy. 1998. Short-term hooking mortality of summer flounder in New York and Virginia. Interim report for Cornell University/Department of Environmental Conservation Project MOU 000024, Riverhead, New York.

American Fisheries Society Symposium 30:234–236, 2002

EXTENDED ABSTRACT

Preliminary Analysis of No-Take Reserves on World Records at Cape Canaveral, Florida

JAMES A. BOHNSACK

Introduction

Two aquatic areas, covering approximately 22% (40 km^2) of the Merritt Island Wildlife Refuge (MIWR), were closed to fishing beginning in 1962 for security of the Kennedy Space Center at Cape Canaveral, Florida. This action created the first estuarine, largest and oldest no-take reserves in North America. Areas surrounding the no-fishing areas are important for recreational fishing, including catch-and-release sport fishing (Cocking 1999).

Johnson et al. (1999) compared fish populations in three no-fishing areas with three adjacent fished areas at Cape Canaveral between 1986 and 1990. They documented significantly higher average fish biodiversity and catch per unit effort (CPUE) for several economically important species in no-fishing zones than in surrounding fished areas in the Mosquito Lagoon, South Banana River, and Indian River Lagoon. Fishes captured from no-take areas also tended to be larger and older than those from fished areas, and many were in breeding condition. Tagging showed that some fishes moved from protected areas to surrounding fished areas. Johnson et al. (1999) did not, however, investigate impacts of the no-take reserves on nearby fisheries.

Using available published International Game fish Association (IGFA) world records from 1955 through 1997 (e.g., IGFA 1997), two hypotheses were tested: the first, that the number of world records around Cape Canaveral was no different than those from other areas around Florida (spatial hypothesis) and the second, that the proportion of recreational world records near MIWR has not changed since areas were closed to fishing (temporal hypothesis).

IGFA world record listings were examined for the four game fish species that Johnson et al. (1999) had documented in the no-take reserves: common snook *Centropomus undecimalis*, spotted seatrout *Cynoscion nebulosus*, black

James A. Bohnsack, Southeast Fisheries Science Center, National Oceanic and Atmospheric Administration, 75 Virginia Beach Drive, Miami, Florida 33149, USA. Email: jim.bohnsack@noaa.gov

drum *Pogonias cromis* and red drum *Sciaenops ocellatus*. World records are landed according to IGFA rules and are determined based on fish weight and line strength categories for spinning and fly rods (IGFA 1997). The spatial hypothesis was tested by dividing the coastline of Florida into 50-km (30-mi) segments centered on Cape Canaveral and tallying the total number of IGFA world records reported from each coastal segment for each species. The time hypothesis was tested by comparing the percentage of IGFA world records landed within 50 km on either side of Cape Canaveral over time. Percentage of world records was used as a parameter because the number of official IGFA categories was expanded in 1982.

Spatial Hypothesis Test

A total of 41 of 121 IGFA world records from Florida were reported for the four species within 50 km of Cape Canaveral, more than any other area in Florida. These records included 20 of 31 for red drum from Florida, 6 of 19 for black drum, 13 of 32 for spotted sea trout, but only 2 of 39 for common snook. The distribution of records for spotted seatrout, black drum, and red drum was highly concentrated in the proximity of Cape Canerval, followed by smaller concentrations in Everglades National Park at the southern tip of Florida. Few common snook records were reported near MIWR, partly because MIWR was located at the extreme northern range for common snook. Also, Johnson et al. (1999) reported that, unlike the other three species, common snook were not year-round residents of MIWR.

Temporal Hypothesis Test

The percentage of IGFA world records from within 50 km of Cape Canaveral increased following closing portions of MIWR to fishing in 1962. The first records were reported in the 1970s, a decade after closure, and then increased in the 1980s and 1990s. In the 1990s, the majority of all world records came from around Cape Canaveral for red drum, black drum, and spotted seatrout. Snook records were highly concentrated at the southern end of the Indian River Lagoon.

To support the prediction that no-take zones benefit surrounding recreational fisheries, it was necessary to demonstrate that areas surrounding the no-take zones had a higher than expected proportion of world records compared with other Florida coastal areas and that the proportional number of world records increased following the creation of the no-take zones. Results from this study support both predictions. The Cape Canaveral region had a higher number of IGFA world record fishes than any other similar-sized area in Florida. The spatial test was not sufficient, however, to demonstrate that no-take reserves helped support surrounding fisheries, since the area could have been especially productive independent of no-take zones. Conclusive evidence, however, was provided by the temporal changes, since world record fishes only began to be landed approximately a decade after these areas were closed to fishing.

World record-sized fish require the production of a sufficient number of recruits to overcome various sources of natural and fishing mortality, so that some individuals can live long enough to achieve large size. Also, some time was necessary for populations to recover in the no-take areas in terms of recruitment, increased abundance, and growth. Eventually, dispersal of fish from reserves helped supply fish to surrounding areas. The widespread adoption and growth of catch-and-release fishing in surrounding areas also reduced fishing mortality (Cocking 1999) and benefited the recreational fishery. Over the study period, numerous conservation regulations were applied to these species throughout Florida, including bag limits, minimum-size and slot-size limits, and closed seasons, as well as net bans and prohibitions on commercial fishing in some areas. However, the fact is that the greatest number and the most recent records came from areas in proximity to MIWR.

In conclusion, the spatial and temporal distribution of IGFA world records indicate that the no-fishing zones at Merritt Island Wildlife Refuge have benefited recreational fisheries for at least three important resident game fish species. As one of the largest and oldest no-take zones in North America, MIWR has one of the most well documented examples of no-take reserves benefiting nearby surrounding fisheries. No-take reserves combined with a strong catch-and-release ethic help ensure healthy recreational fisheries.

Acknowledgments

I thank Jon Lucy for his encouragement to submit this poster despite my not being able to attend the conference.

References

Cocking, S. 1999. A trip worth the trouble. Miami Herald (March 8):C18.

IGFA (International Game Fish Association). 1997. World Record Game Fishes. IGFA, Pompano Beach, Florida.

Johnson, D. R., N. A. Funicelli, and J. A. Bohnsack. 1999. Effectiveness of an existing estuarine no-take fish sanctuary within the Kennedy Space Center, Florida. North American Journal of Fisheries Management 19:436–453.

American Fisheries Society Symposium 30:237–239, 2002

EXTENDED ABSTRACT

Importance of Release Habitat for Survival of Stocked Barramundi in Northern Australia

D. JOHN RUSSELL[1] *and* MICHAEL A. RIMMER[2]

Barramundi *Lates calcarifer* is a large, euryhaline, catadromous centropomid found throughout much of the Indo-West Pacific, including northern Australia where it is highly sought after as a sport, recreational, and commercial species. It also supports a growing aquaculture industry, and it was the successful development of technology for the large-scale production of this species that prompted interest in stock enhancement. There is evidence that the recreational and commercial fisheries are in decline (Rimmer and Russell 1998), and stock enhancement is perceived as one of a number of management tools that could be used to address this issue. Stock enhancement programs in Queensland coastal rivers have been under way since the early 1990s. Additionally, new put-and-take recreational fisheries for barramundi have been created in freshwater impoundments using hatchery-reared barramundi.

Since 1992, the Queensland Department of Primary Industries (DPI) has released more than 120,000 hatchery-reared juvenile barramundi as small as 30 mm total length (TL) into the Johnstone River in northeastern Australia, as part of an experimental stock-enhancement program. Stocked fish take between three to four years before they are recruited into the fishery but now make up about 19% and 13% of the recreational and commercial catches, respectively (Russell and Rimmer 1997; Rimmer and Russell 1998). The study also provided useful information on barramundi movements. Most (62%) stocked fish, particularly juveniles, were recaptured within 3 km of their release location, and 37% made intra-riverine movements of between 3 and 37 km. Five fish made inter-riverine or coastal movements (Russell and Rimmer 1997; Rimmer and Russell 1998).

D. John Russell and Michael A. Rimmer, Northern Fisheries Center, Post Office Box 5396, Cairns, Queensland 4870, Australia

[1]*Email: russellj@dpi.gld.gov.au*
[2]*Email: rimmerm@dpi.gld.gov.au*

One of the primary objectives of the DPI research program was to determine optimal release strategies, particularly the importance of release habitat. To this end, experimental stockings were undertaken between 1992/1993 and 1994/1995, where about 17,000 hatchery-reared fish between 30 mm and 60 mm TL were released into each of three different habitats. To differentiate them from naturally-recruited fish and to allow subsequent determination of stocking sites, the fish were all marked with coded wire tags implanted into a cheek muscle. The different release habitats were an upper tidal location on the North Johnstone River at the upper limit of tidal influence, which was characterized by extensive macrophyte beds, predominantly *Vallisneria* spp; a mangrove-lined tidal creek in the lower estuary; and a freshwater riverine site with deep pools linked by shallow riffles.

The monitoring program relied heavily on tag returns from recreational anglers and commercial fishers. As there was no way of flagging the presence of the tags to fishers, it was necessary to develop a program to monitor recreational and commercial catches. Recreational anglers were asked to assist by delivering all the heads or carcasses of barramundi they caught to central depots where they were periodically scanned for the presence of tags. All anglers were subsequently notified of the results by mail. As an incentive to supply samples, all participating anglers were entered into an annual lottery and given feedback through regular newsletters and newspaper articles. Commercial catches were monitored for the presence of tags through regular visits to fish processors. The DPI research staff also undertook quarterly fishery independent monitoring at two locations using a boat-mounted electrofisher. Recapture rates between each of the three release habitats were compared using a generalized linear model with a logit link and binomial error distribution.

To date, 209 fish released as part of the experimental stocking between 1992/1993 and 1994/1995 have been recaptured. Because catches made near release sites might be biased by stocked fish remaining resident, only fish recaptured at a distance of at least 3 km away ($N = 120$) were included in the analyses. The number of recaptures per 1,000 stocked fish from the upper tidal site was significantly greater than the recapture rates from both the estuarine ($P = 0.009$) and the freshwater sites ($P = 0.004$; Figure 1). It is postulated that this is because the thick weed beds at the upper tidal site provided plentiful cover for the juvenile fish, as well an abundant source of food, including small crustaceans and fishes.

Release habitat type appears to be an important factor in increasing the survival of stocked barramundi. The more than two-fold improvement in recapture rates associated with stocking fish in the weed beds at the upper tidal site indicates that considerable effort should be made to select suitable sites for release

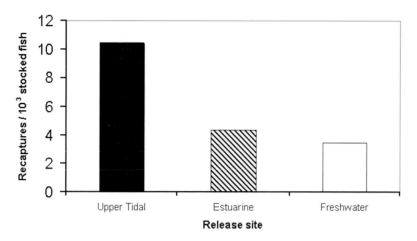

Figure 1. Recaptures of barramundi stocked into three types of release habitat.

of juvenile barramundi. Coded wire tags provided a means of marking juveniles both to discriminate stocked fish and to obtain biological information that was pertinent to the management of the fishery. A combination of positive feedback, well-directed publicity, and incentives enabled the collection of valuable catch data from recreational and commercial fishers despite difficulties and challenges associated with not having a visible fish tag.

Acknowledgments

We thank Joanne De Faveri who provided valuable advice on the statistical analyses and Andrew McDougall, Sarah Kistle, Adam Fletcher, and Graham Vallance for technical assistance. This work was funded by the Queensland Government's Private Pleasure Vessel Levy fund.

References

Rimmer, M. A., and D. J. Russell. 1998. Survival of stocked barramundi, *Lates calcarifer*, in a coastal river system in far northern Queensland, Australia. Bulletin of Marine Science 62(2):325–336.

Russell, D. J., and M. A. Rimmer. 1997. Assessment of stock enhancement of barramundi, *Lates calcarifer* (Bloch) in a coastal river system in far north Queensland, Australia. Pages 498–503 *in* D. A. Hancock, D. C. Smith and J. P. Beumer, editors. Developing and sustaining world fisheries resources –the state of science and management. Proceedings of 2nd World Fisheries Congress, 28 July–2 August, 1996, Brisbane, Queensland, Australia.

Index